ANNUAL EDITIONS

United States History
Volume 1—Colonial Through Reconstruction
Twenty-Second Edition

EDITOR

Robert James Maddox (Emeritus)
Pennsylvania State University
University Park

Robert James Maddox, distinguished historian and professor emeritus of American history at Pennsylvania State University, received a BS from Fairleigh Dickinson University in 1957, an MS from the University of Wisconsin in 1958, and a PhD from Rutgers in 1964. He has written, reviewed, and lectured extensively, and is widely respected for his interpretations of presidential character and policy.

The McGraw·Hill Companies

Mc Graw Hill) Connect Learn Succeed™

ANNUAL EDITIONS: UNITED STATES HISTORY, VOLUME 1, TWENTY-SECOND EDITION

Published by McGraw-Hill, a business unit of The McGraw-Hill Companies, Inc., 1221 Avenue of the Americas, New York, NY 10020. Copyright © 2013 by The McGraw-Hill Companies, Inc. All rights reserved. Printed in the United States of America. Previous edition(s) © 2012, 2011, 2010, and 2009. No part of this publication may be reproduced or distributed in any form or by any means, or stored in a database or retrieval system, without the prior written consent of The McGraw-Hill Companies, Inc., including, but not limited to, in any network or other electronic storage or transmission, or broadcast for distance learning.

Some ancillaries, including electronic and print components, may not be available to customers outside the United States.

This book is printed on acid-free paper.

Annual Editions® is a registered trademark of The McGraw-Hill Companies, Inc.

Annual Editions is published by the **Contemporary Learning Series** group within the McGraw-Hill Higher Education division.

1 2 3 4 5 6 7 8 9 0 QDB/QDB 1 0 9 8 7 6 5 4 3 2

ISBN: 978-0-07-805114-2
MHID: 0-07-805114-2
ISSN: 0733-3560 (print)
ISSN: Pending (online)

Managing Editor: *Larry Loeppke*
Senior Developmental Editor: *Jill Meloy*
Permissions Supervisor: *Lenny J. Behnke*
Marketing Specialist: *Alice Link*
Project Manager: *Connie Oertel*
Design Coordinator: *Margarite Reynolds*
Cover Designer: *Studio Montage, St. Louis, Missouri*
Buyer: *Susan K. Culbertson*
Media Project Manager: *Sridevi Palani*

Compositor: Laserwords Private Limited
Cover Image Credits: © Comstock/PunchStock (inset); © BananaStock/PunchStock (background)

www.mhhe.com

Editors/Academic Advisory Board

Members of the Academic Advisory Board are instrumental in the final selection of articles for each edition of ANNUAL EDITIONS. Their review of articles for content, level, and appropriateness provides critical direction to the editors and staff. We think that you will find their careful consideration well reflected in this volume.

ANNUAL EDITIONS: United States History, Volume 1
22nd Edition

EDITOR

Robert James Maddox (Emeritus)
Pennsylvania State University
University Park

ACADEMIC ADVISORY BOARD MEMBERS

Preface

In publishing ANNUAL EDITIONS we recognize the enormous role played by the magazines, newspapers, and journals of the public press in providing current, first-rate educational information in a broad spectrum of interest areas. Many of these articles are appropriate for students, researchers, and professionals seeking accurate, current material to help bridge the gap between principles and theories and the real world. These articles, however, become more useful for study when those of lasting value are carefully collected, organized, indexed, and reproduced in a low-cost format, which provides easy and permanent access when the material is needed. That is the role played by ANNUAL EDITIONS.

The writing of history has changed dramatically since the first edition of this anthology. A look at the table of contents will show that individuals and groups previously ignored or downplayed are now being given much fuller attention. The westward expansion of this nation, for instance, usually was depicted as a triumphant migration that overcame great obstacles to "settle" the frontier. But what whites considered a process of civilization was to Native Americans a disastrous invasion of their lands. Some tribes were demoralized by the destruction of buffalo herds upon which their cultures and sustenance rested. Most finally were herded onto reservations where they became little more than wards of the federal government. Attempts to tell the story from their standpoint, as in the article "How the West Was Lost," enrich our understanding of the past.

A similar process has taken place with regard to the treatment of women, blacks, and others who were marginalized in conventional histories. Earlier accounts, when they treated such groups at all, tended to focus attention on notable leaders rather than the rank and file members. This was understandable as source material about prominent figures was more readily available. The development of history "from the bottom up" has produced a great deal of writing about the lives of ordinary people as exemplified by several essays in this volume. The tendency toward inclusion has to be applauded.

Another recent development in writing about the past has been an emphasis on viewing issues within broader contexts than those which were obtained in one or another colony or in the United States as a whole during its early national period. One essay included in this edition, for example, analyzes the American Civil War and its aftermath as it played out on the "world stage." Events that previously were treated in isolation are now presented within the framework of how they influenced or were influenced by other people and other nations. "Transnational history," as it has been called, can provide insights previously lacking in conventional histories.

There has been a downside. A deplorable tendency in recent historical writing has been the practice of enlisting the past to promote specific agendas, however admirable those agendas might be. "Objective" history is impossible to attain, of course, because each of us carries intellectual baggage that pushes us toward one interpretation rather than another. But efforts to create a "usable past" often have resulted in gross distortions of the historical record.

It is tempting for both authors and readers to analyze and judge the past from the standpoint of present-day knowledge and assumptions. How easy it is to criticize people born in the eighteenth century, for instance, on the grounds that the ideas they held and the practices they followed have since become discredited. Who could believe in witchcraft? Who could defend slavery? Who could see "the natural order of things" in the relegation of women and other groups to second-class citizenship? The fact is that many intelligent and reasonable people in earlier times held just such beliefs. Treating our predecessors with contempt because they did not hold the beliefs that many of us now take for granted can be comforting because it assures us of our own intellectual and moral superiority. One should keep in mind, however, many of today's "truths" will seem equally wrong-headed to people looking back at us hundreds of years from now, assuming we do not destroy the planet before then.

Annual Editions: United States History, Volume I is designed for non-specialized survey courses. We have attempted to present a fair sampling of articles that incorporate newer approaches to the study of history as well as more traditional ones. The sources from which these essays have been taken for the most part are intended for the general reader: they require no particular expertise to understand them and they avoid the dreadful jargon that permeates so much of modern academic writing.

This volume contains a number of features designed to aid students, researchers, and professionals. These include a *topic guide* for locating articles on specific subjects; the *table of contents abstracts* that summarize each essay, with key concepts in bold italics; and a comprehensive *index*. Articles are organized into four units, each preceded by an overview that provides a background for informed reading of the articles, emphasizes critical issues, and presents questions involving *learning outcomes* and *critical thinking and reflections*.

Every revision of *Annual Editions: United States History, Volume I* replaces about fifty percent of the previous articles with new ones. We try to update and improve the quality of the sections, and we would like to consider alternatives that we may have missed. If you find an article that you think merits inclusion in the next edition, please send it to us (or at least send us the citation, so that the editor can track it down for consideration). We welcome your comments about the readings in this volume. Your suggestions will be carefully considered and greatly appreciated.

Robert James Maddox

Robert James Maddox
Editor

The Annual Editions Series

VOLUMES AVAILABLE

Adolescent Psychology

Aging

American Foreign Policy

American Government

Anthropology

Archaeology

Assessment and Evaluation

Business Ethics

Child Growth and Development

Comparative Politics

Criminal Justice

Developing World

Drugs, Society, and Behavior

Dying, Death, and Bereavement

Early Childhood Education

Economics

Educating Children with Exceptionalities

Education

Educational Psychology

Entrepreneurship

Environment

The Family

Gender

Geography

Global Issues

Health

Homeland Security

Human Development

Human Resources

Human Sexualities

International Business

Management

Marketing

Mass Media

Microbiology

Multicultural Education

Nursing

Nutrition

Physical Anthropology

Psychology

Race and Ethnic Relations

Social Problems

Sociology

State and Local Government

Sustainability

Technologies, Social Media, and Society

United States History, Volume 1

United States History, Volume 2

Urban Society

Violence and Terrorism

Western Civilization, Volume 1

World History, Volume 1

World History, Volume 2

World Politics

Contents

UNIT 1
The New Land

The concepts in bold italics are developed in the article. For further expansion, please refer to the Topic Guide.

UNIT 2
Revolutionary America

The concepts in bold italics are developed in the article. For further expansion, please refer to the Topic Guide.

UNIT 3
National Consolidation and Expansion

The concepts in bold italics are developed in the article. For further expansion, please refer to the Topic Guide.

The concepts in bold italics are developed in the article. For further expansion, please refer to the Topic Guide.

UNIT 4
The Civil War and Reconstruction

The concepts in bold italics are developed in the article. For further expansion, please refer to the Topic Guide.

The concepts in bold italics are developed in the article. For further expansion, please refer to the Topic Guide.

Correlation Guide

The *Annual Editions* series provides students with convenient, inexpensive access to current, carefully selected articles from the public press. **Annual Editions: United States History, Volume 1: Colonial Through Reconstruction, 22/e** is an easy-to-use reader that presents articles on important topics such as *America's First Immigrants, the Revolution, the Civil War, Reconstruction* and many more. For more information on *Annual Editions* and other *McGraw-Hill Contemporary Learning Series* titles, visit www.mhhe.com/cls.

This convenient guide matches the units in **Annual Editions: United States History, Volume 1, 22/e** with the corresponding chapters in three of our best-selling McGraw-Hill History textbooks by Davidson et al., Davidson et al., and Brinkley.

Annual Editions: United States History, Volume 1, 22/e	United States: A Narrative History, Volume 1: To 1877, 6/e by Davidson et al.	Experience History, Volume 1: To 1877, 7/e by Davidson et al.	American History: Connecting with the Past, Volume 1, 14/e by Brinkley
Unit 1: The New Land	**Chapter 1:** The First Civilizations of North America **Chapter 2:** Old Worlds, New Worlds (1400–1600) **Chapter 3:** Colonization and Conflict in the South (1600–1750) **Chapter 4:** Colonization and Conflict in the North (1600–1700) **Chapter 5:** The Mosaic of Eighteenth-Century America (1689–1771)	**Chapter 1:** The First Civilizations of North America **Chapter 2:** Old Worlds, New Worlds, 1400–1600 **Chapter 3:** Colonization and Conflict in the South, 1600–1750 **Chapter 4:** Colonization and Conflict in the North, 1600–1700 **Chapter 5:** The Mosaic of Eighteenth-Century America, 1689–1768	**Chapter 1:** The Collision of Cultures **Chapter 2:** Transplantations and Borderlands **Chapter 3:** Society and Culture in Provincial America **Chapter 4:** The Empire in Transition
Unit 2: Revolutionary America	**Chapter 6:** Toward the War for American Independence (1754–1776) **Chapter 7:** The American People and the American Revolution (1775–1783) **Chapter 8:** Crisis and Constitution (1776–1789)	**Chapter 6:** Toward the War for American Independence, 1754–1776 **Chapter 7:** The American People: The American Revolution, 1775–1783 **Chapter 8:** Crisis and Constitution, 1776–1789	**Chapter 5:** The American Revolution **Chapter 6:** The Constitution and the New Republic **Chapter 7:** The Jeffersonian Era
Unit 3: National Consolidation and Expansion	**Chapter 8:** Crisis and Constitution (1776–1789) **Chapter 9:** The Early Republic (1789–1824) **Chapter 10:** The Opening of America (1815–1850) **Chapter 11:** The Rise of Democracy (1824–1840) **Chapter 12:** The Fires of Perfection (1820–1850) **Chapter 14:** Western Expansion and the Rise of the Slavery Issue (1820–1850)	**Chapter 8:** Crisis and Constitution, 1776–1789 **Chapter 9:** The Early Republic, 1789–1824 **Chapter 10:** The Opening of America, 1815–1850 **Chapter 11:** The Rise of Democracy, 1824–1840 **Chapter 12:** The Fires of Perfection, 1820–1850 **Chapter 14:** Western Expansion and the Rise of the Slavery Issue, 1820–1850	**Chapter 8:** Varieties of American Nationalism **Chapter 9:** Jacksonian America **Chapter 10:** America's Economic Revolution **Chapter 11:** Cotton, Slavery, and the Old South **Chapter 12:** Antebellum Culture and Reform **Chapter 13:** The Impending Crisis
Unit 4: The Civil War and Reconstruction	**Chapter 13:** The Old South (1820–1860) **Chapter 14:** Western Expansion and the Rise of the Slavery Issue (1820–1850) **Chapter 15:** The Union Broken (1850–1861) **Chapter 16:** Total War and the Republic (1861–1865) **Chapter 17:** Reconstructing the Union (1865–1877)	**Chapter 13:** The Old South, 1820–1860 **Chapter 14:** Western Expansion and the Rise of Slavery, 1820–1850 **Chapter 15:** The Union Broken, 1850–1861 **Chapter 16:** Total War and the Republic, 1861–1865 **Chapter 17:** Reconstructing the Union, 1865–1877	**Chapter 11:** Cotton, Slavery, and the Old South **Chapter 14:** The Civil War **Chapter 15:** Reconstruction and the New South

Topic Guide

This topic guide suggests how the selections in this book relate to the subjects covered in your course. You may want to use the topics listed on these pages to search the Web more easily.

On the following pages a number of websites have been gathered specifically for this book. They are arranged to reflect the units of this Annual Editions reader. You can link to these sites by going to www.mhhe.com/cls

All the articles that relate to each topic are listed below the bold-faced term.

Internet References

The following Internet sites have been selected to support the articles found in this reader. These sites were available at the time of publication. However, because websites often change their structure and content, the information listed may no longer be available. We invite you to visit www.mhhe.com/cls for easy access to these sites.

Annual Editions: United States History, Volume 1

General Sources

American Historical Association (AHA)
www.historians.org

This site is an excellent source for data on just about any topic in American history. All affiliated societies and publications are noted, and AHA and its links provide material related to myriad fields of history.

American Studies Web
www.georgetown.edu

Links to a wealth of Internet resources for research in American studies, from agriculture and rural development, to government, to race and ethnicity, are provided on this eclectic site.

Harvard's John F. Kennedy School of Government
www.ksg.harvard.edu

Starting from this home page, click on a huge variety of links to information about American history, politics, and government, including material related to debates of enduring issues.

History Net
www.thehistorynet.com

Supported by the National Historical Society, this site provides information on a wide range of topics. The articles are of excellent quality, and the site has book reviews and even special interviews. It is also frequently updated.

Library of Congress
www.loc.gov

Examine this website to learn about the extensive resource tools, library services/resources, exhibitions, and databases available through the Library of Congress in many different subfields of government studies.

Smithsonian Institution
http://www.si.edu

This site provides access to the enormous resources of the Smithsonian, which holds some 140 million artifacts and specimens for "the increase and diffusion of knowledge." Learn about American social, cultural, economic, and political history from a variety of viewpoints here.

UNIT 1: The New Land

Early America
http://earlyamerica.com/earlyamerica/index.html

Explore the "amazing world of early America" through early media data at this site. Topics include Pages of the Past, Lives of Early Americans, Notable Women of Early America, Milestone Events, and many more.

1492: An Ongoing Voyage/Library of Congress
http://lcweb.loc.gov/exhibits/1492

Displays examining the causes and effects of Columbus's voyages to the Americas can be accessed on this website. "An Ongoing Voyage" explores the rich mixture of societies coexisting in five areas of this hemisphere before European arrival. It then surveys the polyglot Mediterranean world at a dynamic turning point in its development.

The Mayflower Web Page
www.mayflowerhistory.com

The Mayflower Web Page represents thousands of hours of research, organization, and typing; it grows daily. Visitors include everyone from kindergarten students to history professors, from beginning genealogists to some of the most noted genealogists in the nation. The site is a merger of two fields: genealogy and history.

UNIT 2: Revolutionary America

The Early America Review
www.earlyamerica.com/review

Explore the website of *The Early America Review,* an electronic journal of fact and opinion on the people, issues, and events of eighteenth-century America. The quarterly is of excellent quality.

House of Representatives
www.house.gov

This home page of the House of Representatives will lead to information about current and past House members and agendas, the legislative process, and so on.

National Center for Policy Analysis
www.public-policy.org/web.public-policy.org/index.php

Through this site, click onto links to read discussions of an array of topics that are of major interest in the study of American history, from regulatory policy and privatization to economy and income.

Supreme Court/Legal Information Institute
http://supct.law.cornell.edu/supct/index.html

Open this site for current and historical information about the Supreme Court. The archive contains a collection of nearly 600 of the most historical decisions of the Court.

U.S. Senate
www.senate.gov

The U.S. Senate home page will lead to information about current and past Senate members and agendas, legislative activities, committees, and so on.

The White House
www.whitehouse.gov

Visit the home page of the White House for direct access to information about commonly requested federal services, the White House Briefing Room, and all of the presidents and vice presidents. The "Virtual Library" provides an opportunity to search White House documents, listen to speeches, and view photos.

The World of Benjamin Franklin
www.fi.edu/franklin

Presented by the Franklin Institute Science Museum, "Benjamin Franklin: Glimpses of the Man" is an excellent multimedia site that lends insight into Revolutionary America.

Internet References

UNIT 3: National Consolidation and Expansion

Consortium for Political and Social Research
www.icpsr.umich.edu

At this site, the Interuniversity Consortium for Political and Social Research offers materials in various categories of historical, social, economic, and demographic data. Presented is a statistical overview of the United States beginning in the late eighteenth century.

Department of State
www.state.gov

View this site for an understanding into the workings of what has become a major U.S. executive branch department. Links explain what the Department does, what services it provides, what it says about U.S. interests around the world, and much more information.

Mystic Seaport
http://amistad.mysticseaport.org

The complex Amistad case is explored in a clear and informative manner on this online educational site. It places the event in the context of the issues of the 1830s and 1840s.

Social Influence Website
www.workingpsychology.com/intro.html

The nature of persuasion, compliance, and propaganda is the focus of this website, with many practical examples and applications. Students of such topics as the roles of public opinion and media influence in policy making should find these discussions of interest.

University of Virginia Library
www.lib.virginia.edu/exhibits/lewis_clark

Created by the University of Virginia Library, this site examines the famous Lewis and Clark exploration of the trans-Mississippi west.

Women in America
http://xroads.virginia.edu/~HYPER/DETOC/FEM

Providing the views of women travelers from the British Isles, France, and Germany on the lives of American women, this valuable site covers the years between 1820 and 1842 and is informative, stimulating, and highly original.

Women of the West
www.wowmuseum.org

The home page of the Women of the West Museum offers several interesting links that include stories, poems, educational resources, and exhibits.

UNIT 4: The Civil War and Reconstruction

The American Civil War
http://sunsite.utk.edu/civil-war/warweb.html

This site provides a wide-ranging list of data on the Civil War. Some examples of the data that are available are army life, the British connection, diaries/letters/memos, maps, movies, museums, music, people, photographs, and poetry.

Anacostia Museum/Smithsonian Institution
www.si.edu/archives/historic/anacost.htm

This is the home page of the Center for African American History and Culture of the Smithsonian Institution, which is expected to become a major repository of information. Explore its many avenues.

Abraham Lincoln Online
www.netins.net/showcase/creative/lincoln.html

This is a well-organized, high-quality site that will lead to substantial material about Abraham Lincoln and his era. Discussions among Lincoln scholars can be accessed in the Mailbag section.

Gilder Lehrman Institute of American History
www.digitalhistory.uh.edu/index.cfm?

Click on the links to various articles presented through this website to read outstanding, first-hand accounts of slavery in America through the period of Reconstruction.

Secession Era Editorials Project
http://history.furman.edu/~benson/docs/dsmenu.htm

Newspaper editorials of the 1800s regarding events leading up to secession are presented on this Furman University site. When complete, this distinctive project will offer additional features that include mapping, statistical tools, and text analysis.

UNIT 1

The New Land

Unit Selections

1. **America's First Immigrants,** Evan Hadingham
2. **1491,** Charles C. Mann
3. **Massacre in Florida,** Andrés Reséndez
4. **Jamestown Hangs in the Balance,** James Horn
5. **A Pox on the New World,** Charles C. Mann
6. **Champlain among the Mohawk, 1609: A Soldier-Humanist Fights a War for Peace in North America,** David Hackett Fischer
7. **New Amsterdam Becomes New York,** Russell Shorto
8. **Taken by Indians,** Kevin Sweeney
9. **Blessed and Bedeviled,** Helen Mondloch
10. **Pontiac's War,** Alan Taylor

Learning Outcomes

After reading this Unit, you will be able to:

- Discuss the methods archaeologists and others have used to help determine the dates when early cultures existed as well as the level of technology they achieved, and also the reasons for their decline.

- Analyze the various methods Native American tribes used to cope with the onslaught of European armies and settlers. Were there practical alternatives they ignored, or were they doomed by overwhelming numbers and firepower?

- Cite and discuss specific examples of how what we call "American" history in the early colonial period was determined by European rivalries acted out on a world stage.

- Critically analyze the conditions and beliefs that existed at the time of the Salem Witch trials. How did they coalesce to produce what can be described as "mass hysteria"?

Student Website

www.mhhe.com/cls

Internet References

Early America
   http://earlyamerica.com/earlyamerica/index.html
1492: An Ongoing Voyage/Library of Congress
   http://lcweb.loc.gov/exhibits/1492
The Mayflower Web Page
   www.mayflowerhistory.com

Europeans had been fascinated with the "New World" long before they were able to mount expeditions to actually go there. Artists and writers imagined all sorts of exotic plants and animals, and depicted human inhabitants as ranging from the most brutal savages to races of highly advanced peoples. These latter were reputed to have constructed cities of great splendor, where fabulous treasures of precious metals and jewels lay for the taking. The "age of exploration" had to await the sufficient accumulation of capital to finance expeditions and the advanced technology to make them feasible. Motives were mixed in undertaking such ventures: the desire to explore the unknown, national rivalries, the quest for routes to the Far East, converting the heathens to Christianity, and pure greed were among them. Spain and Portugal led the way, followed by France and England.

The "new world," of course, was new only to Europeans. The inhabitants had lived here for a long time without even knowing (let alone caring) that Europe existed. Estimates are that there were from 80 to 100 million people living in the Western Hemisphere at the time the explorations began. In the region that became the United States there were no powerful empires such as those developed by the Aztecs in Mexico or the Incas in Peru. There were, however, fairly sophisticated settlements such as the small town of Cahokia, located near present-day St. Louis, Missouri. European incursions proved catastrophic for peoples at whatever stage of civilization. Not only did some of the explorers treat indigenous peoples with great brutality, they brought with them a variety of deadly diseases against which natives had no defenses. The expansion of Europe, therefore, came at the expense of millions of unfortunates in the new world.

For years the conventional wisdom was that what we call "Native Americans" emigrated here from Asia across the Bering land bridge to Alaska. The article "America's First Immigrants" shows that this view has been challenged by archaeologists who have found settlements dating from at least 1,000 years before this migration is supposed to have occurred. In "1491" the author discusses population estimates and what is known about their societies, and suggests that they had a far larger impact on the environment than previously suspected. "A Pox on the New World" discusses the devastating impact communicable diseases had on Native Americans. Successive diseases also swept through European settlements as well as those of the Indians.

Developments in history often have an air of inevitability about them. At times, however, matters of chance or actions that have unanticipated consequences play an important role. Several articles in this unit explore what might be called the "what ifs" of history. "Massacre in Florida" discusses how a relatively small military encounter in 1565 between the Spanish and the French had a great impact on the future of European settlements. "Jamestown Hangs in the Balance" shows how close Jamestown came to being abandoned. "Champlain among the Mohawk, 1609" describes how this French "Soldier-Humanist" tried to establish a French sphere of interest based on peaceful cohabitation with the native population. Had he succeeded, the history of what became the United States would have been very different. "New Amsterdam Becomes New York" tells how easily

© Library of Congress Prints and Photographs Division (LC-USZ62-57620)

the English acquired this Dutch settlement, and in the process inherited the traditions of tolerance, free trade, and a multiethnic population.

White settler Mary Rowlandson was captured by Indians during a raid on her small town in Massachusetts. "Taken by Indians" describes the courage and ingenuity she displayed during her ordeal. A book she wrote years later became the first, and one of the most powerful, examples of what has been called the "captivity narrative," which became very popular in American literature and imagination.

The idea that witches existed was commonly held in New England during the seventeeth century, as it was elsewhere. The Salem Witch Trials have received great attention from historians, novelists, and playwrights. "Blessed and Bedeviled" analyzes the causes of this phenomenon, and suggests that under certain circumstances something very much like it could occur in modern society.

The last essay in this unit, "Pontiac's War," tells how the execution of an Indian slave women aroused a huge furor among a number of tribes, because they resented the notion that they were subject to British law. Led by Ottawa Chief Pontiac, these tribes formed a coalition that seized British forts around the Great Lakes and in the Ohio Valley. Realizing that retaliation would touch off a costly and protracted war, the British hastened to placate the Indians by treating them as allies rather than as enemies. One of the results of this new policy was that many of these same tribes remained loyal to the British when the Americans launched their own rebellion.

America's First Immigrants

You were probably taught that the hemisphere's first people came from Siberia across a long-gone land bridge. Now a sea route looks increasingly likely, from Asia or even Europe.

EVAN HADINGHAM

About four miles from the tiny cattle town of Florence, Texas, a narrow dirt road winds across parched limestone, through juniper, prickly pear and stunted oaks, and drops down to a creek. A lush parkland of shade trees offers welcome relief from the 100-degree heat of summer. Running beside the creek for almost half a mile is a swath of chipped, gray stone flakes and soil blackened by cooking fires—thousands of years of cooking fires. This blackened earth, covering 40 acres and almost six feet thick in places, marks a settlement dating back as far as the last ice age 13,000 years ago, when mammoths, giant sloths and saber-toothed cats roamed the North American wilderness.

Since archaeologists began working here systematically seven years ago, they have amassed an astonishing collection of early prehistoric artifacts—nearly half a million so far. Among these are large, stone spearheads skillfully flaked on both sides to give an elegant, leaf-shaped appearance. These projectiles, found by archaeologists throughout North America and as far south as Costa Rica, are known as Clovis points, and their makers, who lived roughly 12,500 to 13,500 years ago, are known as Clovis people, after the town in New Mexico near where the first such point was identified some seven decades ago.

A visit to the Gault site—named after the family who owned the land when the site was first investigated in 1929—along the cottonwood- and walnut-shaded creek in central Texas raises two monumental questions. The first, of course, is, Who were these people? The emerging answer is that they were not simple-minded big-game hunters as they have often been depicted. Rather, they led a less nomadic and more sophisticated life than previously believed.

The second question—Where did they come from?—lies at the center of one of archaeology's most contentious debates. The standard view holds that Clovis people were the first to enter the Americas, migrating from Siberia 13,500 years ago by a now-submerged land bridge across the Bering Strait. This view has been challenged recently by a wide range of discoveries, including an astonishingly well-preserved site in South America predating the supposed migration by at least 1,000 years.

Researchers delving into the origins question have sought to make sense of archaeological finds far and wide, from Canada, California and Chile; from Siberia; and even, most controversially, from France and Spain. The possibility that the first people in the Americas came from Europe is the boldest proposal among a host of new ideas. According to University of Texas at Austin archaeologist Michael Collins, the chief excavator of the Gault site, "you couldn't have a more exciting time to be involved in the whole issue of the peopling of the Americas. You can't write a paper on it and get it published before it's out of date. Surprising new finds keep rocking the boat and launching fresh waves of debate."

In 1932, an American archaeologist identified distinctive spearheads associated with mammoth skeletons near Clovis, New Mexico. The discovery supported an emerging realization that humans lived with now-extinct ice age creatures in North America.

For prehistoric people, one of the chief attractions of the Gault site was a knobby outcrop of a creamy white rock called chert, which conceals a fine, gray, glasslike interior. If struck expertly with a stone or antler tool, the rock fractures in predictable ways, yielding a Clovis point. In the end, each spearhead has distinctive grooves, or "flutes," at the base of each face and was fastened to a wooden shaft with sinew and resin.

Ancient pollen and soil clues tell archaeologists that the climate in Clovis-era Texas was cooler, drier and more tolerable than today's summertime cauldron. Vast herds of mammoths, bison, horses and antelope ranged on the grasslands southeast of Gault, and deer and turkeys inhabited the plateau to the west. Along the creek, based on bones found at the site, Clovis hunters also preyed on frogs, birds, turtles and other small animals.

This abundance of food, coupled with the exceptional quality of the chert, drew people to Gault in large numbers. Unlike the majority of Clovis sites, which are mostly the remains of temporary camps, Gault appears to have been inhabited over long periods and thus contradicts the standard view that Clovis people were always highly mobile, nomadic hunters. Michael Collins says that of the vast quantity of artifacts found at the site, many are tool fragments, left behind by people who'd stuck around long enough to not only break their tools but also to salvage and rework them. The researchers also unearthed a seven by seven foot square of gravel—perhaps the floor of a house—and a possible well, both signs of more than a fleeting presence.

Another clue was concealed on a 13,000-year-old Clovis blade about the size of a dinner knife. Under a magnifying lens, the blade's edge is glossy, rounded and smooth. Marilyn Shoberg, a stone tool analyst on the Gault team who has experimented with replicas, says the blade's polish probably came from cutting grass. This grass could have been used for basketry, bedding, or thatching to make roofs for huts.

Among the most unusual and tantalizing finds at the Gault site are a hundred or so fragments of limestone covered with lightly scratched patterns. Some resemble nets or basketry, while a few could be simple outlines of plants or animals. Although only a dozen can be securely dated to Clovis times, these enigmatic rocks are among the very few surviving artworks from ice age America.

"What this site tells us is that Clovis folks were not specialized mammoth hunters constantly wandering over the landscape," says Collins. "They exploited a variety of animals, they had tools for gathering plants and working wood, stone and hide, and they stayed through the useful life of those tools. All these things are contrary to what you'd expect if they were highly nomadic, dedicated big-game hunters." Yet this unexpected complexity sheds only a feeble glimmer on the more contentious issue of where the Clovis people came from and how they got here.

In the old scenario, still popular in classrooms and picture books, fur-clad hunters in the waning moments of the last ice age, when so much seawater was locked up in the polar ice caps that the sea level was as much as 300 feet lower than today, ventured across a land bridge from Siberia to Alaska. Then, pursuing big game, the hunters trekked south through present-day Canada. They passed down a narrow, 1,000-mile-long treeless corridor bounded by the towering walls of retreating ice sheets until they reached the Great Plains, which teemed with prey. The human population exploded, and the hunters soon drove into extinction some 35 genera of big animals (see box on page 6). All of these were supposedly dispatched by the Clovis point, a Stone Age weapon of mass destruction.

Digging at the Gault site in central Texas, according to project director Michael Collins, has almost doubled the number of Clovis artifacts excavated in North America. Researchers there have also uncovered evidence of ice age art.

For more than half a century, this plausible, "big-game" theory carried with it an appealing, heroic image. As James Adovasio of Mercyhurst College puts it in his book *The First Americans,* it was as if the ice sheets had parted "like the Red Sea for some Clovis Moses to lead his intrepid band of spear-toting, mammoth-slaying wayfarers to the south." But recent discoveries are indicating that almost everything about the theory could be wrong. For one thing, the latest studies show that the ice-free corridor didn't exist until around 12,000 years ago—too late to have served as the route for the very first people to come to America.

Clovis people buried caches of tools. Some stashed points were crafted from exotic stone; others seem too big and thin to have functioned as weapons. One cache was found with a child's bones, suggesting that burying tools could be a ritual act.

Perhaps the strongest ammunition against the old scenario comes from Monte Verde, an archaeological site on a remote terrace, which is today some 40 miles from the Pacific in southern Chile. Here, about 14,500 years ago, a hunting-and-gathering band lived year-round beside a creek in a long, oval hide tent, partitioned with logs. Archaeologist Tom Dillehay of Vanderbilt University began probing Monte Verde in 1977, unearthing the surface of the ancient encampment, complete with wood, plants and even remains of food, all preserved under a layer of waterlogged peat. Dillehay recovered three human footprints, two chunks of uneaten mastodon meat and possibly even traces of herbal medicine (indicated by nonfood plants still used by healers in the Andes). The dating of these extraordinary finds, at least 1,000 years before the earliest Clovis sites in North America, aroused skepticism for two decades until, in 1997, a group of leading archaeologists inspected the site and vindicated Dillehay's meticulous work.

No such triumph has emerged for any of the dozen or so sites in North America claimed to predate Clovis. But among the most intriguing is a rock overhang in Pennsylvania called Meadowcroft, where a 30-year campaign of excavation suggests that hunters may have reached the Northeast 3,000 or 4,000 years before the Clovis era.

Saber-toothed cats prowled North America for millions of years. For some reason, they died out about 13,000 years ago.

Meanwhile, genetics studies are pointing even more strongly to an early entry into the continent. By analyzing the mitochondrial DNA of living Native Americans, Douglas Wallace, a geneticist at the University of California at Irvine, and his colleagues have identified five distinct lineages that stretch back like family trees. Mitochondria are the cells' energy factories. Their DNA changes very little from one generation to the next, altered only by tiny variations that creep in at a steady and predictable rate. By counting the number of these variations in related lineages, Wallace's team can estimate their ages. When the team applied this technique to the DNA of Native Americans, they reached the stunning conclusion that there were at least four separate waves of prehistoric migration into the Americas, the earliest well over 20,000 years ago.

If the first Americans did arrive well before the oldest known Clovis settlements, how did they get here? The most radical theory for the peopling of the New World argues that Stone Age mariners journeyed from Europe around the southern fringes of the great ice sheets in the North Atlantic. Many archaeologists greet this idea with head-shaking scorn, but the proposition is getting harder to dismiss outright.

Dennis Stanford, a Clovis expert at the Smithsonian Institution's Department of Anthropology who delights in prodding his colleagues with unconventional thinking, was a longtime supporter of the land bridge scenario. Then, with the end of the cold war came the chance to visit archaeological sites and museums in Siberia—museums that should have been filled with tools that were predecessors of the Clovis point. "The result was a big disappointment," says Stanford. "What we found was nothing like we expected, and I was surprised that the technologies were so different." Instead of a single leaf-shaped Clovis spearhead, ice age Siberian hunters made projectiles that were bristling with rows of tiny razor-like blades embedded in wooden shafts. To Stanford, that meant no Siberian hunters armed with Clovis technology had walked to the Americas.

Meanwhile, Bruce Bradley, a prehistoric stone tool specialist at Britain's University of Exeter, had noticed a strong resemblance between Clovis points and weapons from ice age Europe. But the idea that the two cultures might be directly connected was heretical. "It certainly wasn't part of the scientific process at that point," Bradley says. "There was no possibility, forget it, don't even think about it." Bradley eventually pursued it to the storerooms of the Musée National de Préhistoire in Les Eyzies-de-Tayac in southwest France, where he pored through boxes of local prehistoric stone tools and waste flakes. "I was absolutely flabbergasted," he recalls. "If somebody had brought out a box of this stuff in the United States and set it down in front of me, I'd have said, 'Man, where did you get all that great Clovis stuff?'" But the material was the work of a culture called the Solutrean that thrived in southwest France and northern Spain during the coldest spell of the ice age, from around 24,000 to 19,000 years ago.

Thousands of years before their successors created the masterworks of Lascaux and Altamira, Solutrean-age artists began painting vivid murals in the depths of caves such as Cougnac and Cosquer. They made delicate, eyed sewing needles out of bone, enabling them to stitch tightfitting skin garments to repel the cold. They devised the *atlatl,* or spear thrower, a hooked bone or wood handle that extends the reach of the hunter's arm to multiply throwing power. But their most distinctive creation was a stone spearhead shaped like a laurel leaf.

Apart from the absence of a fluted base, the Solutrean laurel leaf strongly resembles the Clovis point and was made using the same, highly skillful flaking technique. Both Clovis and Solutrean stone crafters practiced controlled overshot flaking, which involved trimming one edge by striking a flake off the opposite side, a virtuoso feat of handiwork rarely seen in other prehistoric cultures. To Bradley, "there had to be some sort of historic connection" between the Solutrean and Clovis peoples.

Dennis Stanford and Bruce Bradley say that similarities between Clovis and Solutrean finds are overwhelming.

Critics of the theory point to a yawning gap between the two peoples: roughly 5,000 years divide the end of Solutrean culture and the emergence of Clovis. But Stanford and Bradley say that recent claims of pre-Clovis sites in the southeastern United States may bridge the time gap. In the mid-1990s at Cactus Hill, the remains of an ancient sand dune overlooking the Nottoway River on Virginia's coastal plain, project director Joseph McAvoy dug down a few inches beneath a Clovis layer and uncovered simple stone blades and projectile points associated with a hearth, radiocarbon dated to some 17,000 to 19,000 years ago. This startlingly early date has drawn skeptical fire, but the site's age was recently confirmed by an independent dating technique. Stanford and Bradley suggest that the early people at Cactus Hill were Clovis forerunners who had not yet developed the full-blown Clovis style. They are convinced that many more sites like Cactus Hill will turn up on the East Coast. But the burning question is, Did these ice age Virginians invent the Clovis point all by themselves, or were they descendants of Solutreans who brought the point with them from Europe?

Many archaeologists ridicule the notion that people made an arduous, 3,000-mile journey during the bleakest period of the ice age, when the Atlantic would have been much colder and stormier than today. Stanford believes that traditional Inuit technology suggests otherwise; he has witnessed traditional seagoing skills among Inupiat communities in Barrow, Alaska. Inupiat hunters still build large skin-covered canoes, or *umiaks,* which enable them to catch seals, walrus and other sea

Hunted to Extinction?

At the end of the last ice age, 35 genera of big animals, or "megafauna," went extinct in the Americas, including mammoths, mastodons, giant ground sloths, giant beavers, horses, short-faced bears and saber-toothed cats. Archaeologists have argued for decades that the arrival of hunters wielding Clovis spear points at around the same time was no coincidence. Clovis hunters pursued big game—their signature stone points are found with the bones of mammoths and mastodons at 14 kill sites in North America. Experiments carried out with replica spears thrust into the corpses of circus elephants indicate that the Clovis point could have penetrated a mammoth's hide. And computer simulations suggest that large, slow-breeding animals could have easily been wiped out by hunting as the human population expanded.

But humans might not be entirely to blame. The rapidly cycling climate at the end of the ice age may have changed the distribution of plants that the big herbivores grazed on, leading to a population crash among meat-eating predators too. New research on DNA fragments recovered from ice age bison bones suggests that some species were suffering a slow decline in diversity—probably caused by dwindling populations—long before any Clovis hunters showed up. Indigenous horses are now thought to have died out in Alaska about 500 years before the Clovis era. For mammoths and other beasts who did meet their demise during the Clovis times, many experts believe that a combination of factors—climate change plus pressure from human hunters—drove them into oblivion.

Amid all the debate, one point is clear: the Clovis hunter wasn't as macho as people once thought. Bones at the Gault site in central Texas reveal that the hunters there were feeding on less daunting prey—frogs, birds, turtles and antelope—as well as mammoth, mastodon and bison. As the late, renowned archaeologist Richard (Scotty) MacNeish is said to have remarked, "Each Clovis generation probably killed one mammoth, then spent the rest of their lives talking about it."

and medium-sized game with a similar, limited range of raw materials—stone, bone, ivory, antler, wood and sinew. They're going to come up with similar solutions."

More tellingly, in Straus' view, is that he can find little evidence of seafaring technology in the Solutrean sites he has dug in northern Spain. Although rising sea levels have drowned sites on the ice age coastline, Straus has investigated surviving inland cave sites no more than a couple of hours' walk from the beach. "There's no evidence of deep-sea fishing," says Straus, "no evidence of marine mammal hunting, and consequently no evidence, even indirect, for their possession of seaworthy boats."

And David Meltzer, an archaeologist at Southern Methodist University and a critic of the European-origins idea, is struck more by the differences between the Solutrean and Clovis cultures than their similarities—particularly the near-absence of art and personal ornaments from Clovis. Still, he says, the controversy is good for the field. "In the process of either killing or curing" the theory, "we will have learned a whole lot more about the archaeological record, and we'll all come out smarter than we went in."

Besides crossing the land bridge from Asia and traveling to ice age America from Europe by boat, a third possible entryway is a sea route down the west coast. Using maritime skills later perfected by the Inuit, prehistoric south Asians might have spread gradually around the northern rim of the Pacific in small skin-covered boats. They skirt the southern edge of the Bering land bridge and paddle down the coast of Alaska, dodging calving glaciers and icebergs as they pursue seals and other marine mammals. They keep going all the way to the beaches of Central and South America. They arrive at Monte Verde, inland from the Chilean coast, some 14,500 years ago. Each new generation claims fresh hunting grounds a few miles beyond the last, and in a matter of centuries these first immigrants have populated the entire west coast of the Americas. Soon the hunters start moving inland and, in the north, their descendants become the Clovis people.

Clovis people may well have reached North America via sea route. Seals and other marine prey may have sustained them until they found New World hunting grounds.

Many archaeologists now accept the west coast theory as a likely solution to the origin of the earliest Americans. On Prince of Wales Island in southeastern Alaska, inside the aptly named On Your Knees Cave, University of South Dakota paleontologist Timothy Heaton and University of Colorado at Boulder archaeologist E. James Dixon recovered an accumulation of animal bones from the last ice age. When mile-high ice sheets still straddled the interior of the continent 17,000 years ago, ringed seals, foxes and seabirds made their home on the island. "Humans could easily have survived there," Heaton says.

The ultimate evidence for the western sea route would be the discovery of pre-Clovis human remains on the coast. No

mammals that abound along the frozen edges of the pack ice. When twilight arrives or storms threaten, the hunters pull their boats up on the ice and camp beneath them. Ronald Brower of the Inupiat Heritage Center in Barrow says, "There's nothing that would have prevented . . . people from crossing the Atlantic into the Americas 19,000 years ago. It would be a perfectly normal situation from my perspective."

A different critique of the out-of-Europe theory dismisses the resemblance between Solutrean and Clovis points. Many archaeologists suggest that similarities between Clovis and Solutrean artifacts are coincidental, the result of what they call convergence. "These were people faced with similar problems," says Solutrean expert Lawrence Straus of the University of New Mexico. "And the problems involved hunting large-

such luck. Dixon and Heaton have found human jaw fragments and other remains in the On Your Knees Cave, but those date to about 11,000 years ago—too recent to establish the theory. And what may be the oldest-known human remains in North America—leg bones found on Santa Rosa Island, off the California coast—are from 13,000 years ago, the heart of the Clovis era. Still, those remains hint that by then people were plying the waters along the Pacific Coast.

If the trail of the very earliest Americans remains elusive, so, too, does the origin of the Clovis point. "Although the technology needed to produce a Clovis point was found among other cultures during the ice age," says Ken Tankersley of Northern Kentucky University, "the actual point itself is unique to the Americas, suggesting that it was invented here in the New World." If so, the spearhead would be the first great American invention—the Stone Age equivalent of the Swiss Army Knife, a trademark tool that would be widely imitated. The demand for the weapon and the high-quality stone it required probably encouraged Clovis people to begin long-distance trading and social exchanges. The spearhead may also have delivered a new level of hunting proficiency and this, in turn, would have fueled a population spurt, giving Clovis people their lasting presence in the archaeological record.

Sheltering from the broiling heat under the cottonwoods at Gault, Michael Collins told me of his conviction that the Clovis people who flocked to the shady creek were not pioneers but had profited from a long line of forebears. "Clovis represents the end product of centuries, if not millennia, of learning how to live in North American environments," he said. "The Clovis culture is too widespread, is found in too many environments, and has too much evidence for diverse activities to be the leavings of people just coming into the country." Collins reminded me that his team has investigated less than 10 percent of the enormous site. And archaeologists have barely scratched the surface of a handful of other Gault-size, Clovis-era sites—Williamsburg, in Virginia, for instance, or Shoop, in Pennsylvania. "One thing you can be sure," he said, beaming, "there'll be great new discoveries just around the corner."

Critical Thinking

1. Discuss some of the ways earliest settlers in the New World tried to control their environment rather than just live off the land.

2. Who were the Clovis people? What discoveries have demolished the myth that they were exclusively nomadic hunters of big game?

EVAN HADINGHAM is the senior science editor of the PBS series NOVA and the author of books on prehistory.

1491

Before it became the New World, the Western Hemisphere was vastly more populous and sophisticated than has been thought—an altogether more salubrious place to live at the time than, say, Europe. New evidence of both the extent of the population and its agricultural advancement leads to a remarkable conjecture: the Amazon rain forest may be largely a human artifact.

CHARLES C. MANN

The plane took off in weather that was surprisingly cool for north-central Bolivia and flew east, toward the Brazilian border. In a few minutes the roads and houses disappeared, and the only evidence of human settlement was the cattle scattered over the savannah like jimmies on ice cream. Then they, too, disappeared. By that time the archaeologists had their cameras out and were clicking away in delight.

Below us was the Beni, a Bolivian province about the size of Illinois and Indiana put together, and nearly as flat. For almost half the year rain and snowmelt from the mountains to the south and west cover the land with an irregular, slowly moving skin of water that eventually ends up in the province's northern rivers, which are sub-subtributaries of the Amazon. The rest of the year the water dries up and the bright-green vastness turns into something that resembles a desert. This peculiar, remote, watery plain was what had drawn the researchers' attention, and not just because it was one of the few places on earth inhabited by people who might never have seen Westerners with cameras.

Clark Erickson and William Balée, the archaeologists, sat up front. Erickson is based at the University of Pennsylvania; he works in concert with a Bolivian archaeologist, whose seat in the plane I usurped that day. Balée is at Tulane University, in New Orleans. He is actually an anthropologist, but as native peoples have vanished, the distinction between anthropologists and archaeologists has blurred. The two men differ in build, temperament, and scholarly proclivity, but they pressed their faces to the windows with identical enthusiasm.

Indians were here in greater numbers than previously thought, and they imposed their will on the landscape. Columbus set foot in a hemisphere thoroughly dominated by humankind.

Dappled across the grasslands below was an archipelago of forest islands, many of them startlingly round and hundreds of acres across. Each island rose ten or thirty or sixty feet above the floodplain, allowing trees to grow that would otherwise never survive the water. The forests were linked by raised berms, as straight as a rifle shot and up to three miles long. It is Erickson's belief that this entire landscape—30,000 square miles of forest mounds surrounded by raised fields and linked by causeways—was constructed by a complex, populous society more than 2,000 years ago. Balée, newer to the Beni, leaned toward this view but was not yet ready to commit himself.

Erickson and Balée belong to a cohort of scholars that has radically challenged conventional notions of what the Western Hemisphere was like before Columbus. When I went to high school, in the 1970s, I was taught that Indians came to the Americas across the Bering Strait about 12,000 years ago, that they lived for the most part in small, isolated groups, and that they had so little impact on their environment that even after millennia of habitation it remained mostly wilderness. My son picked up the same ideas at his schools. One way to summarize the views of people like Erickson and Balée would be to say that in their opinion this picture of Indian life is wrong in almost every aspect. Indians were here far longer than previously thought, these researchers believe, and in much greater numbers. And they were so successful at imposing their will on the landscape that in 1492 Columbus set foot in a hemisphere thoroughly dominated by humankind.

Given the charged relations between white societies and native peoples, inquiry into Indian culture and history is inevitably contentious. But the recent scholarship is especially controversial. To begin with, some researchers—many but not all from an older generation—deride the new theories as fantasies arising from an almost willful misinterpretation of data and a perverse kind of political correctness. "I have seen no evidence that large numbers of people ever lived in the Beni," says Betty

J. Meggers, of the Smithsonian Institution. "Claiming otherwise is just wishful thinking." Similar criticisms apply to many of the new scholarly claims about Indians, according to Dean R. Snow, an anthropologist at Pennsylvania State University. The problem is that "you can make the meager evidence from the ethnohistorical record tell you anything you want," he says. "It's really easy to kid yourself."

More important are the implications of the new theories for today's ecological battles. Much of the environmental movements is animated, consciously or not, by what William Denevan, a geographer at the University of Wisconsin, calls, polemically, "the pristine myth"—the belief that the Americas in 1491 were an almost unmarked, even Edenic land, "untrammeled by man," in the words of the Wilderness Act of 1964, one of the nation's first and most important environmental laws. As the University of Wisconsin historian William Cronon has written, restoring this long-ago, putatively natural state is, in the view of environmentalists, a task that society is morally bound to undertake. Yet if the new view is correct and the work of humankind was pervasive, where does that leave efforts to restore nature?

The Beni is a case in point. In addition to building up the Beni mounds for houses and gardens, Erickson says, the Indians trapped fish in the seasonally flooded grassland. Indeed, he says, they fashioned dense zigzagging networks of earthen fish weirs between the causeways. To keep the habitat clear of unwanted trees and undergrowth, they regularly set huge areas on fire. Over the centuries the burning created an intricate ecosystem of fire-adapted plant species dependent on native pyrophilia. The current inhabitants of the Beni still burn, although now it is to maintain the savannah for cattle. When we flew over the areas, the dry season had just begun, but mile-long lines of flame were already on the march. In the charred areas behind the fires were the blackened spikes of trees—many of them one assumes, of the varieties that activists fight to save in other parts of Amazonia.

After we landed, I asked Balée, Should we let people keep burning the Beni? Or should we let the trees invade and create a verdant tropical forest in the grasslands, even if one had not existed here for millennia?

Balée laughed. "You're trying to trap me, aren't you?" he said.

Like a Club between the Eyes

According to family lore, my great-grandmother's great-grandmother's great-grandfather was the first white person hanged in America. His name was John Billington. He came on the *Mayflower,* which anchored off the coast of Massachusetts on November 9, 1620. Billington was not a Puritan; within six months of arrival he also became the first white person in America to be tried for complaining about the police. "He is a knave," William Bradford, the colony's governor, wrote to Billington, "and so will live and die." What one historian called Billington's "troublesome career" ended in 1630, when he was hanged for murder. My family has always said that he was framed—but we *would* say that, wouldn't we?

A few years ago it occurred to me that my ancestor and everyone else in the colony had voluntarily enlisted in a venture that brought them to New England without food or shelter six weeks before winter. Half the 102 people on the *Mayflower* made it through to spring, which to me was amazing. How, I wondered, did they survive?

In his history of Plymouth Colony, Bradford provided the answer: by robbing Indian houses and graves. The *Mayflower* first hove to at Cape Cod. An armed company staggered out. Eventually it found a recently deserted Indian settlement. The newcomers—hungry, cold, sick—dug up graves and ransacked houses, looking for underground stashes of corn. "And sure it was God's good providence that we found this corn," Bradford wrote, "for else we know not how we should have done." (He felt uneasy about the thievery, though.) When the colonists came to Plymouth, a month later, they set up shop in another deserted Indian village. All through the coastal forest the Indians had "died on heapes, as they lay in their houses," the English trader Thomas Morton noted. "And the bones and skulls upon the several places of their habitations made such a spectacle" that to Morton the Massachusetts woods seemed to be "a new found Golgotha"—the hill of executions in Roman Jerusalem.

To the Pilgrims' astonishment, one of the corpses they exhumed on Cape Cod had blond hair. A French ship had been wrecked there several years earlier. The Patuxet Indians imprisoned a few survivors. One of them supposedly learned enough of the local language to inform his captors that God would destroy them for their misdeeds. The Patuxet scoffed at the threat. But the Europeans carried a disease, and they bequeathed it to their jailers. The epidemic (probably of viral hepatitis, according to a study by Arthur E. Spiess, an archaeologist at the Maine Historic Preservation Commission, and Bruce D. Spiess, the director of clinical research at the Medical College of Virginia) took years to exhaust itself and may have killed 90 percent of the people in coastal New England. It made huge differences to American history. "The good hand of God favored our beginnings," Bradford mused, by "sweeping away great multitudes of the natives . . . that he might make room for us."

By the time my ancestor set sail on the *Mayflower,* Europeans had been visiting New England for more than a hundred years. English, French, Italian, Spanish, and Portuguese mariners regularly plied the coastline, trading what they could, occasionally kidnapping the inhabitants for slaves. New England, the Europeans saw, was thickly settled and well defended. In 1605 and 1606 Samuel de Champlain visited Cape Cod, hoping to establish a French base. He abandoned the idea. Too many people already lived there. A year later Sir Ferdinando Gorges—British despite his name—tried to establish an English community in southern Maine. It had more founders than Plymouth and seems to have been better organized. Confronted by numerous well-armed local Indians, the settlers abandoned the project within months. The Indians at Plymouth would surely have been an equal obstacle to my ancestor and his ramshackle expedition had disease not intervened.

Faced with such stories, historians have long wondered how many people lived in the Americas at the time of contact. "Debated since Columbus attempted a partial census on Hispaniola in 1496," William Denevan has written, this "remains one of the great inquiries of history." (In 1976 Denevan assembled and edited an entire book on the subject, *The Native Population of the Americas in 1492*.) The first scholarly estimate of the indigenous population was made in 1910 by James Mooney, a distinguished ethnographer at the Smithsonian Institution. Combing through old documents, he concluded that in 1491 North America had 1.15 million inhabitants. Mooney's glittering reputation ensured that most subsequent researchers accepted his figure uncritically.

That changed in 1966, when Henry F. Dobyns published "Estimating Aboriginal American Population: An Appraisal of Techniques With a New Hemispheric Estimate," in the journal *Current Anthropology*. Despite the carefully neutral title, his argument was thunderous, its impact long-lasting. In the view of James Wilson, the author of *The Earth Shall Weep* (1998), a history of indigenous Americans, Dobyns's colleagues "are still struggling to get out of the crater that paper left in anthropology." Not only anthropologists were affected. Dobyns's estimate proved to be one of the opening rounds in today's culture wars.

Dobyns began his exploration of pre-Columbian Indian demography in the early 1950s, when he was a graduate student. At the invitation of a friend, he spent a few months in northern Mexico, which is full of Spanish-era missions. There he poked through the crumbling leather-bound ledgers in which Jesuits recorded local births and deaths. Right away he noticed how many more deaths there were. The Spaniards arrived, and then Indians died—in huge numbers at incredible rates. It hit him, Dobyns told me recently, "like a club right between the eyes."

It took Dobyns eleven years to obtain his PhD. Along the way he joined a rural-development project in Peru, which until colonial times was the seat of the Incan empire. Remembering what he had seen at the northern fringe of the Spanish conquest, Dobyns decided to compare it with figures for the south. He burrowed into the papers of the Lima cathedral and read apologetic Spanish histories. The Indians in Peru, Dobyns concluded, had faced plagues from the day the conquistadors showed up—in fact, before then: smallpox arrived around 1525, seven years ahead of the Spanish. Brought to Mexico apparently by a single sick Spaniard, it swept south and eliminated more than half the population of the Incan empire. Smallpox claimed the Incan dictator Huayna Capac and much of his family, setting off a calamitous war of succession. So complete was the chaos that Francisco Pizarro was able to seize an empire the size of Spain and Italy combined with a force of 168 men.

Smallpox was only the first epidemic. Typhus (probably) in 1546, influenza and smallpox together in 1558, smallpox again in 1589, diphtheria in 1614, measles in 1618—all ravaged the remains of Incan culture. Dobyns was the first social scientist to piece together this awful picture, and he naturally rushed his findings into print. Hardly anyone paid attention. But Dobyns was already working on a second, related question: If all those people died, how many had been living there to begin with? Before Columbus, Dobyns calculated, the Western Hemisphere held ninety to 112 million people. Another way of saying this is that in 1491 more people lived in the Americas than in Europe.

His argument was simple but horrific. It is well known that Native Americans had no experience with many European diseases and were therefore immunologically unprepared—"virgin soil," in the metaphor of epidemiologists. What Dobyns realized was that such diseases could have swept from the coastlines initially visited by Europeans to inland areas controlled by Indians who had never seen a white person. The first whites to explore many parts of the Americas may therefore have encountered places that were already depopulated. Indeed, Dobyns argued, they must have done so.

Peru was one example, the Pacific Northwest another. In 1792 the British navigator George Vancouver led the first European expedition to survey Puget Sound. He found a vast charnel house: human remains "promiscuously scattered about the beach, in great numbers." Smallpox, Vancouver's crew discovered, had preceded them. Its few survivors, second lieutenant Peter Puget noted, were "most terribly pitted . . . indeed many have lost their Eyes." In *Pox Americana* (2001), Elizabeth Fenn, a historian at George Washington University, contends that the disaster on the northwest coast was but a small part of a continental pandemic that erupted near Boston in 1774 and cut down Indians from Mexico to Alaska.

Because smallpox was not endemic in the Americas, colonials, too, had not acquired any immunity. The virus, an equal-opportunity killer, swept through the Continental Army and stopped the drive into Quebec. The American Revolution would be lost, Washington and other rebel leaders feared, if the contagion did to the colonists what it had done to the Indians. "The small Pox! The small Pox!" John Adams wrote to his wife, Abigail. "What shall We do with it?" In retrospect, Fenn says, "One of George Washington's most brilliant moves was to inoculate the army against smallpox during the Valley Forge winter of '78." Without inoculation smallpox could easily have given the United States back to the British.

So many epidemics occurred in the Americas, Dobyns argued, that the old data used by Mooney and his successors represented population nadirs. From the few cases in which before-and-after totals are known with relative certainty, Dobyns estimated that in the first 130 years of contact about 95 percent of the people in the Americas died—the worst demographic calamity in recorded history.

Dobyns's ideas were quickly attacked as politically motivated, a push from the hate-America crowd to inflate the toll of imperialism. The attacks continue to this day. "No question about it, some people want those higher numbers," says Shepard Krech III, a Brown University anthropologist who is the author of *The Ecological Indian* (1999). These people, he says, were thrilled when Dobyns revisited the subject in a book, *Their Numbers Become Thinned* (1983)—and revised his own estimates upward. Perhaps Dobyns's most vehement critic is David Henige, a bibliographer of Africana at the University of Wisconsin, whose *Numbers from Nowhere* (1998) is a landmark in the literature of demographic fulmination. "Suspect in 1966, it is no less suspect nowadays," Henige wrote of Dobyns's work. "If anything, it is worse."

When Henige wrote *Numbers From Nowhere,* the fight about pre-Columbian populations had already consumed forests' worth of trees; his bibliography is ninety pages long. And the dispute shows no sign of abating. More and more people have jumped in. This is partly because the subject is inherently fascinating. But more likely the increased interest in the debate is due to the growing realization of the high political and ecological stakes.

Inventing by the Millions

On May 30, 1539, Hernando de Soto landed his private army near Tampa Bay, in Florida. Soto, as he was called, was a novel figure: half warrior, half venture capitalist. He had grown very rich very young by becoming a market leader in the nascent trade for Indian slaves. The profits had helped to fund Pizarro's seizure of the Incan empire, which had made Soto wealthier still. Looking quite literally for new worlds to conquer, he persuaded the Spanish Crown to let him loose in North America. He spent one fortune to make another. He came to Florida with 200 horses, 600 soldiers, and 300 pigs.

From today's perspective, it is difficult to imagine the ethical system that would justify Soto's actions. For four years his force, looking for gold, wandered through what is now Florida, Georgia, North and South Carolina, Tennessee, Alabama, Mississippi, Arkansas, and Texas, wrecking almost everything it touched. The inhabitants often fought back vigorously, but they had never before encountered an army with horses and guns. Soto died of fever with his expedition in ruins; along the way his men had managed to rape, torture, enslave, and kill countless Indians. But the worst thing the Spaniards did, some researchers say, was entirely without malice—bring the pigs.

According to Charles Hudson, an anthropologist at the University of Georgia who spent fifteen years reconstructing the path of the expedition, Soto crossed the Mississippi a few miles downstream from the present site of Memphis. It was a nervous passage: the Spaniards were watched by several thousand Indian warriors. Utterly without fear, Soto brushed past the Indian force into what is now eastern Arkansas, through thickly settled land—"very well peopled with large towns," one of his men later recalled, "two or three of which were to be seen from one town." Eventually the Spaniards approached a cluster of small cities, each protected by earthen walls, sizeable moats, and deadeye archers. In his usual fashion, Soto brazenly marched in, stole food, and marched out.

After Soto left, no Europeans visited this part of the Mississippi Valley for more than a century. Early in 1682 whites appeared again, this time Frenchmen in canoes. One of them was Réné-Robert Cavelier, Sieur de la Salle. The French passed through the area where Soto had found cities cheek by jowl. It was deserted—La Salle didn't see an Indian village for 200 miles. About fifty settlements existed in this strip of the Mississippi when Soto showed up, according to Anne Ramenofsky, an anthropologist at the University of New Mexico. By La Salle's time the number had shrunk to perhaps ten, some probably inhabited by recent immigrants. Soto "had a privileged glimpse" of an Indian world, Hudson says. "The window opened and slammed shut. When the French came in and the record opened up again, it was a transformed reality. A civilization crumbled. The question is, how did this happen?"

> **Swine alone can disseminate anthrax, brucellosis, leptospirosis, trichinosis, and tuberculosis. Only a few of Hernando de Soto's pigs would have had to wander off to infect the forest.**

The question is even more complex than it may seem. Disaster of this magnitude suggests epidemic disease. In the view of Ramenofsky and Patricia Galloway, an anthropologist at the University of Texas, the source of the contagion was very likely not Soto's army but its ambulatory meat locker: his 300 pigs. Soto's force itself was too small to be an effective biological weapon. Sicknesses like measles and smallpox would have burned through his 600 soldiers long before they reached the Mississippi. But the same would not have held true for the pigs, which multiplied rapidly and were able to transmit their diseases to wildlife in the surrounding forest. When human beings and domesticated animals live close together, they trade microbes with abandon. Over time mutation spawns new diseases: Avian influenza becomes human influenza, bovine rinderpest becomes measles. Unlike Europeans, Indians did not live in close quarters with animals—they domesticated only the dog, the llama, the alpaca, the guinea pig, and here and there, the turkey and the Muscovy duck. In some ways this is not surprising: the New World had fewer animal candidates for taming than the Old. Moreover, few Indians carry the gene that permits adults to digest lactose, a form of sugar abundant in milk. Non-milk-drinkers, one imagines, would be less likely to work at domesticating milk-giving animals. But this is guesswork. The fact is that what scientists call zoonotic disease was little known in the Americas. Swine alone can disseminate anthrax, brucellosis, leptospirosis, taeniasis, trichinosis, and tuberculosis. Pigs breed exuberantly and can transmit diseases to deer and turkeys. Only a few of Soto's pigs would have had to wander off to infect the forest.

Indeed, the calamity wrought by Soto apparently extended across the whole Southeast. The Coosa city-states, in western Georgia, and the Caddoan-speaking civilization, centered on the Texas-Arkansas border, disintegrated soon after Soto appeared. The Caddo had had a taste for monumental architecture: public plazas, ceremonial platforms, mausoleums. After Soto's army left, notes Timothy K. Perttula, an archaeological consultant in Austin, Texas, the Caddo stopped building community centers and began digging community cemeteries. Between Soto's and La Salle's visits, Perttula believes, the Caddoan population fell from about 200,000 to about 8,500—a drop of nearly 96 percent. In the eighteenth century the tally shrank further, to 1,400. An equivalent loss today in the population of New York City would reduce it to 56,000—not enough to fill Yankee Stadium. "That's one reason whites think of Indians as nomadic hunters," says Russell Thornton, an anthropologist at the University of California at Los Angeles. "Everything else—all the heavily populated urbanized societies—was wiped out."

Could a few pigs truly wreak this much destruction? Such apocalyptic scenarios invite skepticism. As a rule, viruses, microbes, and parasites are rarely lethal on so wide a scale—a pest that wipes out its host species does not have a bright evolutionary future. In its worst outbreak, from 1347 to 1351, the European Black Death claimed only a third of its victims. (The rest survived, though they were often disfigured or crippled by its effects.) The Indians in Soto's path, if Dobyns, Ramenofsky, and Perttula are correct, endured losses that were incomprehensibly greater.

One reason is that Indians were fresh territory for many plagues, not just one. Smallpox, typhoid, bubonic plague, influenza, mumps, measles, whooping cough—all rained down on the Americas in the century after Columbus. (Cholera, malaria, and scarlet fever came later.) Having little experience with epidemic diseases, Indians had no knowledge of how to combat them. In contrast, Europeans were well versed in the brutal logic of quarantine. They boarded up houses in which plague appeared and fled to the countryside. In Indian New England, Neal Salisbury, a historian at Smith college, wrote in *Manitou and Providence* (1982), family and friends gathered with the shaman at the sufferer's bedside to wait out the illness—a practice that "could only have served to spread the disease more rapidly."

Indigenous biochemistry may also have played a role. The immune system constantly scans the body for molecules that it can recognize as foreign—molecules belonging to an invading virus, for instance. No one's immune system can identify all foreign presences. Roughly speaking, an individual's set of defensive tools is known as his MHC type. Because many bacteria and viruses mutate easily, they usually attack in the form of several slightly different strains. Pathogens win when MHC types miss some of the strains and the immune system is not stimulated to act. Most human groups contain many MHC types; a strain that slips by one person's defenses will be nailed by the defenses of the next. But, according to Francis L. Black, an epidemiologist at Yale University, Indians are characterized by unusually homogeneous MHC types. One out of three South American Indians have similar MHC types; among Africans the corresponding figure is one in 200. The cause is a matter for Darwinian speculation, the effects less so.

In 1966 Dobyns's insistence on the role of disease was a shock to his colleagues. Today the impact of European pathogens on the New World is almost undisputed. Nonetheless, the fight over Indian numbers continues with undiminished fervor. Estimates of the population of North America in 1491 disagree by an order of magnitude—from 18 million, Dobyns's revised figure, to 1.8 million, calculated by Douglas H. Ubelaker, an anthropologist at the Smithsonian. To some "high counters," as David Henige calls them, the low counters' refusal to relinquish the vision of an empty continent is irrational or worse. "Non-Indian 'experts' always want to minimize the size of aboriginal populations," says Lenore Stiffarm, a Native American-education specialist at the University of Saskatchewan. The smaller the numbers of

Indians, she believes, the easier it is to regard the continent as having been up for grabs. "It's perfectly acceptable to move into unoccupied land," Stiffarm says. "And land with only a few 'savages' is the next best thing."

"Most of the arguments for the very large numbers have been theoretical," Ubelaker says in defense of low counters. "When you try to marry the theoretical arguments to the data that are available on individual groups in different regions, it's hard to find support for those numbers." Archaeologists, he says, keep searching for the settlements in which those millions of people supposedly lived, with little success. "As more and more excavation is done, one would expect to see more evidence for dense populations than has thus far emerged." Dean Snow, the Pennsylvania State anthropologist, examined Colonial-era Mohawk Iroquois sites and found "no support for the notion that ubiquitous pandemics swept the region." In his view, asserting that the continent was filled with people who left no trace is like looking at an empty bank account and claiming that it must once have held millions of dollars.

The low counters are also troubled by the Dobynsian procedure for recovering original population numbers: applying an assumed death rate, usually 95 percent, to the observed population nadir. Ubelaker believes that the lowest point for Indians in North America was around 1900, when their numbers fell to about half a million. Assuming a 95 percent death rate, the pre-contact population would have been 10 million. Go up one percent, to a 96 percent death rate, and the figure jumps to 12.5 million—arithmetically creating more than two million people from a tiny increase in mortality rates. At 98 percent the number bounds to 25 million. Minute changes in baseline assumptions produce wildly different results.

"It's an absolutely unanswerable question on which tens of thousands of words have been spent to no purpose," Henige says. In 1976 he sat in on a seminar by William Denevan, the Wisconsin geographer. An "epiphanic moment" occurred when he read shortly afterward that scholars had "uncovered" the existence of eight million people in Hispaniola. *Can you just invent millions of people?* he wondered. "We can make of the historical record that there was depopulation and movement of people from internecine warfare and diseases," he says. "But as for how much, who knows? When we start putting numbers to something like that—applying large figures like ninety-five percent—we're saying things we shouldn't say. The number implies a level of knowledge that's impossible."

Nonetheless, one must try—or so Denevan believes. In his estimation the high counters (though not the highest counters) seem to be winning the argument, at least for now. No definitive data exist, he says, but the majority of the extant evidentiary scraps support their side. Even Henige is no low counter. When I asked him what he thought the population of the Americas was before Columbus, he insisted that any answer would be speculation and made me promise not to print what he was going to say next. Then he named a figure that forty years ago would have caused a commotion.

To Elizabeth Fenn, the smallpox historian, the squabble over numbers obscures a central fact. Whether one million or 10 million or 100 million died, she believes, the pall of sorrow that engulfed the hemisphere was immeasurable. Languages, prayers, hopes, habits, and dreams—entire ways of life hissed away like steam. The Spanish and the Portuguese lacked the germ theory of disease and could not explain what was happening (let alone stop it). Nor can we explain it; the ruin was too long ago and too all-encompassing. In the long run, Fenn says, the consequential finding is not that many people died but that many people once lived. The Americas were filled with a stunningly diverse assortment of peoples who had knocked about the continents for millennia. "You have to wonder," Fenn says. "What were all those people *up* to in all that time?"

Buffalo Farm

In 1810 Henry Brackenridge came to Cahokia, in what is now southwest Illinois, just across the Mississippi from St. Louis. Born close to the frontier, Brackenridge was a budding adventure writer; his *Views of Louisiana,* published three years later, was a kind of nineteenth-century *Into Thin Air,* with terrific adventure but without tragedy. Brackenridge had an eye for archaeology, and he had heard that Cahokia was worth a visit. When he got there, trudging along the desolate Cahokia River, he was "struck with a degree of astonishment." Rising from the muddy bottomland was a "stupendous pile of earth," vaster than the Great Pyramid at Giza. Around it were more than a hundred smaller mounds, covering an area of five square miles. At the time, the area was almost uninhabited. One can only imagine what passed through Brackenridge's mind as he walked alone to the ruins of the biggest Indian city north of the Rio Grande.

To Brackenridge, it seemed clear that Cahokia and the many other ruins in the Midwest had been constructed by Indians. It was not so clear to everyone else. Nineteenth-century writers attributed them to, among others, the Vikings, the Chinese, the "Hindoos," the ancient Greeks, the ancient Egyptians, lost tribes of Israelites, and even straying bands of Welsh. (This last claim was surprisingly widespread; when Lewis and Clark surveyed the Missouri, Jefferson told them to keep an eye out for errant bands of Welsh-speaking white Indians.) The historian George Bancroft, dean of his profession, was a dissenter: the earthworks, he wrote in 1840, were purely natural formations.

Bancroft changed his mind about Cahokia, but not about Indians. To the end of his days he regarded them as "feeble barbarians, destitute of commerce and of political connection." His characterization lasted, largely unchanged, for more than a century. Samuel Eliot Morison, the winner of two Pulitzer Prizes, closed his monumental *European Discovery of America* (1974) with the observation that Native Americans expected only "short and brutish lives, void of hope for any future." As late as 1987 *American History: A Survey,* a standard high school textbook by three well-known historians, described the Americas before Columbus as "empty of mankind and its works." The story of Europeans in the New World, the book explained, "is the story of the creation of a civilization where none existed."

Alfred Crosby, a historian at the University of Texas, came to other conclusions. Crosby's *The Columbian Exchange: Biological Consequences of 1492* caused almost as much of a stir when it was published, in 1972, as Henry Dobyns's calculation of Indian numbers six years earlier, though in different circles. Crosby was a standard names-and-battles historian who became frustrated by the random contingency of political events. "Some trivial thing happens and you have this guy winning the presidency instead of that guy," he says. He decided to go deeper. After he finished his manuscript, it sat on his shelf—he couldn't find a publisher willing to be associated with his new ideas. It took him three years to persuade a small editorial house to put it out. *The Columbian Exchange* has been in print ever since; a companion, *Ecological Imperialism: The Biological Expansion of Europe, 900–1900,* appeared in 1986.

Human history, in Crosby's interpretation, is marked by two world-altering centers of invention: the Middle East and central Mexico, where Indian groups independently created nearly all of the Neolithic innovations, writing included. The Neolithic Revolution began in the Middle East about 10,000 years ago. In the next few millennia humankind invented the wheel, the metal tool, and agriculture. The Sumerians eventually put these inventions together, added writing, and became the world's first civilization. Afterward Sumeria's heirs in Europe and Asia frantically copied one another's happiest discoveries; innovations ricocheted from one corner of Eurasia to another, stimulating technological progress. Native Americans, who had crossed to Alaska before Sumeria, missed out on the bounty. "They had to do everything on their own," Crosby says. Remarkably, they succeeded.

When Columbus appeared in the Caribbean, the descendants of the world's two Neolithic civilizations collided, with overwhelming consequences for both. American Neolithic development occurred later than that of the Middle East, possibly because the Indians needed more time to build up the requisite population density. Without beasts of burden they could not capitalize on the wheel (for individual workers on uneven terrain skids are nearly as effective as carts for hauling), and they never developed steel. But in agriculture they handily outstripped the children of Sumeria. Every tomato in Italy, every potato in Ireland, and every hot pepper in Thailand came from this hemisphere. Worldwide, more than half the crops grown today were initially developed in the Americas.

Maize, as corn is called in the rest of the world, was a triumph with global implications. Indians developed an extraordinary number of maize varieties for different growing conditions, which meant that the crop could and did spread throughout the planet. Central and Southern Europeans became particularly dependent on it; maize was the staple of Serbia, Romania, and Moldavia by the nineteenth century. Indian crops dramatically reduced hunger, Crosby says, which led to an Old World population boom.

In the Aztec capital Tenochtitlán the Spaniards gawped like hayseeds at the side streets, ornately carved buildings, and markets bright with goods from hundreds of miles away.

Along with peanuts and manioc, maize came to Africa and transformed agriculture there, too. "The probability is that the population of Africa was greatly increased because of maize and other American Indian crops," Crosby says. "Those extra people helped make the slave trade possible." Maize conquered Africa at the time when introduced diseases were leveling Indian societies. The Spanish, the Portuguese, and the British were alarmed by the death rate among Indians, because they wanted to exploit them as workers. Faced with a labor shortage, the Europeans turned their eyes to Africa. The continent's quarrelsome societies helped slave traders to siphon off millions of people. The maize-fed population boom, Crosby believes, let the awful trade continue without pumping the well dry.

Back home in the Americas, Indian agriculture long sustained some of the world's largest cities. The Aztec capital of Tenochtitlán dazzled Hernán Cortés in 1519; it was bigger than Paris, Europe's greatest metropolis. The Spaniards gawped like hayseeds at the wide streets, ornately carved buildings, and markets bright with goods from hundreds of miles away. They had never before seen a city with botanical gardens, for the excellent reason that none existed in Europe. The same novelty attended the force of a thousand men that kept the crowded streets immaculate. (Streets that weren't ankle-deep in sewage! The conquistadors had never heard of such a thing.) Central America was not the only locus of prosperity. Thousands of miles north, John Smith, of Pocahontas fame, visited Massachusetts in 1614, before it was emptied by disease, and declared that the land was "so planted with Gardens and Corne fields, and so well inhabited with a goodly, strong and well proportioned people . . . [that] I would rather live here than any where."

Smith was promoting colonization, and so had reason to exaggerate. But he also knew the hunger, sickness, and oppression of European life. France—"by any standards a privileged country," according to its great historian, Fernand Braudel—experienced seven nationwide famines in the fifteenth century and thirteen in the sixteenth. Disease was hunger's constant companion. During epidemics in London the dead were heaped onto carts "like common dung" (the simile is Daniel Defoe's) and trundled through the streets. The infant death rate in London orphanages, according to one contemporary source, was 88 percent. Governments were harsh, the rule of law arbitrary. The gibbets poking up in the background of so many old paintings were, Braudel observed, "merely a realistic detail."

The Earth Shall Weep, James Wilson's history of Indian America, puts the comparison bluntly: "the western hemisphere was larger, richer, and more populous than Europe." Much of it was freer, too. Europeans, accustomed to the serfdom that thrived from Naples to the Baltic Sea, were puzzled and alarmed by the democratic spirit and respect for human rights in many Indian societies, especially those in North America. In theory, the sachems of New England Indian groups were absolute monarchs. In practice, the colonial leader Roger Williams wrote, "they will not conclude of ought . . . unto which the people are averse."

Pre-1492 America wasn't a disease-free paradise, Dobyns says, although in his "exuberance as a writer," he told me recently, he once made that claim. Indians had ailments of their own, notably parasites, tuberculosis, and anemia. The daily grind was wearing; life-spans in America were only as long as or a little longer than those in Europe, if the evidence of indigenous graveyards is to be believed. Nor was it a political utopia—the Inca, for instance, invented refinements to totalitarian rule that would have intrigued Stalin. Inveterate practitioners of what the historian Francis Jennings described as "state terrorism practiced horrifically on a huge scale," the Inca ruled so cruelly that one can speculate that their surviving subjects might actually have been better off under Spanish rule.

I asked seven anthropologists, archaeologists, and historians if they would rather have been a typical Indian or a typical European in 1491. Every one chose to be an Indian.

I asked seven anthropologists, archaeologists, and historians if they would rather have been a typical Indian or a typical European in 1491. None was delighted by the question, because it required judging the past by the standards of today—a fallacy disparaged as "presentism" by social scientists. But every one chose to be an Indian. Some early colonists gave the same answer. Horrifying the leaders of Jamestown and Plymouth, scores of English ran off to live with the Indians. My ancestor shared their desire, which is what led to the trumped-up murder charges against him—or that's what my grandfather told me, anyway.

As for the Indians, evidence suggests that they often viewed Europeans with disdain. The Hurons, a chagrined missionary reported, thought the French possessed "little intelligence in comparison to themselves." Europeans, Indians said, were physically weak, sexually untrustworthy, atrociously ugly, and just plain dirty. (Spaniards, who seldom if ever bathed, were amazed by the Aztec desire for personal cleanliness.) A Jesuit reported that the "Savages" were disgusted by handkerchiefs: "They say, we place what is unclean in a fine white piece of linen, and put it away in our pockets as something very precious, while they throw it upon the ground." The Micmac scoffed at the notion of French superiority. If Christian civilization was so wonderful, why were its inhabitants leaving?

Like people everywhere, Indians survived by cleverly exploiting their environment. Europeans tended to manage land by breaking it into fragments for farmers and herders. Indians often worked on such a grand scale that the scope of their ambition can be hard to grasp. They created small plots, as Europeans did (about 1.5 million acres of terraces still exist in the Peruvian Andes), but they also reshaped entire landscapes to suit their purposes. A principal tool was fire, used to keep down underbrush and create the open, grassy conditions favorable for game. Rather than domesticating animals for meat, Indians retooled whole ecosystems to grow bumper crops of elk, deer, and bison. The first white settlers in Ohio found forests as open as English parks—they could drive carriages through the woods. Along the Hudson River the annual fall burning lit up the banks for miles on end; so flashy was the show that the Dutch in New Amsterdam boated upriver to goggle at the blaze like children at fireworks. In North America, Indian torches had their biggest impact on the Midwestern prairie, much or most of which was created and maintained by fire. Millennia of exuberant burning shaped the plains into vast buffalo farms. When Indian societies disintegrated, forest invaded savannah in Wisconsin, Illinois, Kansas, Nebraska, and the Texas Hill Country. Is it possible that the Indians changed the Americas more than the invading Europeans did? "The answer is probably yes for most regions for the next 250 years or so" after Columbus. William Denevan wrote, "and for some regions right up to the present time."

Amazonia has become the emblem of vanishing wilderness—an admonitory image of untouched Nature. But the rain forest itself may be a cultural artifact—that is, an artificial object.

When scholars first began increasing their estimates of the ecological impact of Indian civilization, they met with considerable resistance from anthropologists and archaeologists. Over time the consensus in the human sciences changed. Under Denevan's direction, Oxford University Press has just issued the third volume of a huge catalogue of the "cultivated landscapes" of the Americas. This sort of phrase still provokes vehement objection—but the main dissenters are now ecologists and environmentalists. The disagreement is encapsulated by Amazonia, which has become *the* emblem of vanishing wilderness—an admonitory image of untouched Nature. Yet recently a growing number of researchers have come to believe that Indian societies had an enormous environmental impact on the jungle. Indeed, some anthropologists have called the Amazon forest itself a cultural artifact—that is, an artificial object.

Green Prisons

Northern visitors' first reaction to the storied Amazon rain forest is often disappointment. Ecotourist brochures evoke the immensity of Amazonia but rarely dwell on its extreme flatness. In the river's first 2,900 miles the vertical drop is only 500 feet. The river oozes like a huge runnel of dirty metal through a landscape utterly devoid of the romantic crags, arroyos, and heights that signify wilderness and natural spectacle to most North Americans. Even the animals are invisible, although sometimes one can hear the bellow of monkey choruses. To the untutored eye—mine, for instance—the forest seems to stretch out in a monstrous green tangle as flat and incomprehensible as a printed circuit board.

The area east of the lower-Amazon town of Santarém is an exception. A series of sandstone ridges several hundred feet high reach down from the north, halting almost at the water's

edge. Their tops stand drunkenly above the jungle like old tombstones. Many of the caves in the buttes are splattered with ancient petroglyphs—renditions of hands, stars, frogs, and human figures, all reminiscent of Miró, in overlapping red and yellow and brown. In recent years one of these caves, La Caverna da Pedra Pintada (Painted Rock Cave), has drawn attention in archaeological circles.

Wide and shallow and well lit, Painted Rock Cave is less thronged with bats than some of the other caves. The arched entrance is twenty feet high and lined with rock paintings. Out front is a sunny natural patio suitable for picnicking, edged by a few big rocks. People lived in this cave more than 11,000 years ago. They had no agriculture yet, and instead ate fish and fruit and built fires. During a recent visit I ate a sandwich atop a particularly inviting rock and looked over the forest below. The first Amazonians, though, must have done more or less the same thing.

In college I took an introductory anthropology class in which I read *Amazonia: Man and Culture in a Counterfeit Paradise* (1971), perhaps the most influential book ever written about the Amazon, and one that deeply impressed me at the time. Written by Betty J. Meggers, the Smithsonian archaeologist, *Amazonia* says that the apparent lushness of the rain forest is a sham. The soils are poor and can't hold nutrients—the jungle flora exists only because it snatches up everything worthwhile before it leaches away in the rain. Agriculture, which depends on extracting the wealth of the soil, therefore faces inherent ecological limitations in the wet desert of Amazonia.

As a result, Meggers argued, Indian villages were forced to remain small—any report of "more than a few hundred" people in permanent settlements, she told me recently, "makes my alarm bells go off." Bigger, more complex societies would inevitably overtax the forest soils, laying waste to their own foundations. Beginning in 1948 Meggers and her late husband, Clifford Evans, excavated a chiefdom on Marajó, an island twice the size of New Jersey that sits like a gigantic stopper in the mouth of the Amazon. The Marajóara, they concluded, were failed offshoots of a sophisticated culture in the Andes. Transplanted to the lush trap of the Amazon, the culture choked and died.

Green activists saw the implication: development in tropical forests destroys both the forests and their developers. Meggers's account had enormous public impact—*Amazonia* is one of the wellsprings of the campaign to save rain forests.

Then Anna C. Roosevelt, the curator of archaeology at Chicago's Field Museum of Natural History, re-excavated Marajó. Her complete report, *Moundbuilders of the Amazon* (1991), was like the anti-matter version of *Amazonia*. Marajó, she argued, was "one of the outstanding indigenous cultural achievements of the New World," a powerhouse that lasted for more than a thousand years, had "possibly well over 100,000" inhabitants, and covered thousands of square miles. Rather than damaging the forest, Marajó's "earth construction" and "large, dense populations" had *improved* it: the most luxuriant and diverse growth was on the mounds formerly occupied by the Marajóara. "If you listened to Meggers's theory, these places should have been ruined," Roosevelt says.

Meggers scoffed at Roosevelt's "extravagant claims," "polemical tone," and "defamatory remarks." Roosevelt, Meggers argued, had committed the beginner's error of mistaking a site that had been occupied many times by small, unstable groups for a single, long-lasting society. "[Archaeological remains] build up on areas of half a kilometer or so," she told me, "because [shifting Indian groups] don't land exactly on the same spot. The decorated types of pottery don't change much over time, so you can pick up a bunch of chips and say, 'Oh, look, it was all one big site!' Unless you know what you're doing, of course." Centuries after the conquistadors, "the myth of El Dorado is being revived by archaeologists," Meggers wrote last fall in the journal *Latin American Antiquity,* referring to the persistent Spanish delusion that cities of gold existed in the jungle.

The dispute grew bitter and personal; inevitable in a contemporary academic context, it has featured vituperative references to colonialism, elitism, and employment by the CIA. Meanwhile, Roosevelt's team investigated Painted Rock Cave. On the floor of the cave what looked to me like nothing in particular turned out to be an ancient midden: a refuse heap. The archaeologists slowly scraped away sediment, traveling backward in time with every inch. When the traces of human occupation vanished, they kept digging. ("You always go a meter past sterile," Roosevelt says.) A few inches below they struck the charcoal-rich dirt that signifies human habitation—a culture, Roosevelt said later, that wasn't supposed to be there.

For many millennia the cave's inhabitants hunted and gathered for food. But by about 4000 years ago they were growing crops—perhaps as many as 140 of them, according to Charles R. Clement, an anthropological botanist at the Brazilian National Institute for Amazonian Research. Unlike Europeans, who planted mainly annual crops, the Indians, he says, centered their agriculture on the Amazon's unbelievably diverse assortment of trees: fruits, nuts, and palms. "It's tremendously difficult to clear fields with stone tools," Clement says. "If you can plant trees, you get twenty years of productivity out of your work instead of two or three."

Planting their orchards, the first Amazonians transformed large swaths of the river basin into something more pleasing to human beings. In a widely cited article from 1989, William Balée, the Tulane anthropologist, cautiously estimated that about 12 percent of the nonflooded Amazon forest was of anthropogenic origin—directly or indirectly created by human beings. In some circles this is now seen as a conservative position. "I basically think it's all human-created," Clement told me in Brazil. He argues that Indians changed the assortment and density of species throughout the region. So does Clark Erickson, the University of Pennsylvania archaeologist, who told me in Bolivia that the lowland tropical forests of South America are among the finest works of art on the planet. "Some of my colleagues would say that's pretty radical," he said, smiling mischievously. According to Peter Stahl, an anthropologist at the State University of New York at Binghamton, "lots" of botanists believe that "what the eco-imagery would like to picture as a pristine, untouched Urwelt [primeval world] in fact has been managed by people for millennia." The phrase "built

environment," Erickson says, "applies to most, if not all, Neotropical landscapes."

"Landscape" in this case is meant exactly—Amazonian Indians literally created the ground beneath their feet. According to William I. Woods, a soil geographer at Southern Illinois University, ecologists' claims about terrible Amazonian land were based on very little data. In the late 1990s Woods and others began careful measurements in the lower Amazon. They indeed found lots of inhospitable terrain. But they also discovered swaths of *terra preta*—rich, fertile "black earth" that anthropologists increasingly believe was created by human beings.

Terra preta, Woods guesses, covers at least 10 percent of Amazonia, an area the size of France. It has amazing properties, he says. Tropical rain doesn't leach nutrients from *terra preta* fields; instead the soil, so to speak, fights back. Not far from Painted Rock Cave is a 300-acre area with a two-foot layer of *terra preta* quarried by locals for potting soil. The bottom third of the layer is never removed, workers there explain, because over time it will re-create the original soil layer in its initial thickness. The reason, scientists suspect, is that *terra preta* is generated by a special suite of microorganisms that resists depletion. "Apparently," Woods and the Wisconsin geographer Joseph M. McCann argued in a presentation last summer, "at some threshold level . . . dark earth attains the capacity to perpetuate—even *regenerate* itself—thus behaving more like a living 'super'-organism than an inert material."

In as yet unpublished research the archaeologists Eduardo Neves, of the University of São Paulo; Michael Heckenberger, of the University of Florida; and other colleagues examined *terra preta* in the upper Xingu, a huge southern tributary of the Amazon. Not all Xingu cultures left behind this living earth, they discovered. But the ones that did generated it rapidly—suggesting to Woods that *terra preta* was created deliberately. In a process reminiscent of dropping microorganism-rich starter into plain dough to create sourdough bread, Amazonian peoples, he believes, inoculated bad soil with a transforming bacterial charge. Not every group of Indians there did this, but quite a few did, and over an extended period of time.

When Woods told me this, I was so amazed that I almost dropped the phone. I ceased to be articulate for a moment and said things like "wow" and "gosh." Woods chuckled at my reaction, probably because he understood what was passing through my mind. Faced with an ecological problem, I was thinking, the Indians *fixed* it. They were in the process of terraforming the Amazon when Columbus showed up and ruined everything.

Scientists should study the microorganisms in *terra preta,* Woods told me, to find out how they work. If that could be learned, maybe some version of Amazonian dark earth could be used to improve the vast expanses of bad soil that cripple agriculture in Africa—a final gift from the people who brought us tomatoes, corn, and the immense grasslands of the Great Plains.

"Betty Meggers would just die if she heard me saying this," Woods told me. "Deep down her fear is that this data will be misused." Indeed, Meggers's recent *Latin American Antiquity* article charged that archaeologists who say the Amazon can support agriculture are effectively telling "developers [that they] are entitled to operate without restraint." Resuscitating the myth of El Dorado, in her view, "makes us accomplices in the accelerating pace of environmental degradation." Doubtless there is something to this—although, as some of her critics responded in the same issue of the journal, it is difficult to imagine greedy plutocrats "perusing the pages of *Latin American Antiquity* before deciding to rev up the chain saws." But the new picture doesn't automatically legitimize paving the forest. Instead it suggests that for a long time big chunks of Amazonia were used nondestructively by clever people who knew tricks we have yet to learn.

Environmentalists want to preserve as much of the world's land as possible in a putatively intact state. But "intact" may turn out to mean "run by human beings for human purposes."

I visited Painted Rock Cave during the river's annual flood, when it wells up over its banks and creeps inland for miles. Farmers in the floodplain build houses and barns on stilts and watch pink dolphins sport from their doorsteps. Ecotourists take shortcuts by driving motorboats through the drowned forests. Guys in dories chase after them, trying to sell sacks of incredibly good fruit.

All of this is described as "wilderness" in the tourist brochures. It's not, if researchers like Roosevelt are correct. Indeed, they believe that fewer people may be living there now than in 1491. Yet when my boat glided into the trees, the forest shut out the sky like the closing of an umbrella. Within a few hundred years the human presence seemed to vanish. I felt alone and small, but in a way that was curiously like feeling exalted. If that place was not wilderness, how should I think of it? Since the fate of the forest is in our hands, what should be our goal for its future?

Novel Shores

Hernando de Soto's expedition stomped through the Southeast for four years and apparently never saw bison. More than a century later, when French explorers came down the Mississippi, they saw "a solitude unrelieved by the faintest trace of man," the nineteenth-century historian Francis Parkman wrote. Instead the French encountered bison, "grazing in herds on the great prairies which then bordered the river."

To Charles Kay, the reason for the buffalo's sudden emergence is obvious. Kay is a wildlife ecologist in the political-science department at Utah State University. In ecological terms, he says, the Indians were the "keystone species" of American ecosystems. A keystone species, according to the Harvard biologist Edward O. Wilson, is a species "that affects the survival and abundance of many other species." Keystone species have a disproportionate impact on their ecosystems. Removing them,

Wilson adds, "results in a relatively significant shift in the composition of the [ecological] community."

When disease swept Indians from the land, Kay says, what happened was exactly that. The ecological ancient régime collapsed, and strange new phenomena emerged. In a way this is unsurprising; for better or worse, humankind is a keystone species everywhere. Among these phenomena was a population explosion in the species that the Indians had kept down by hunting. After disease killed off the Indians, Kay believes, buffalo vastly extended their range. Their numbers more than sextupled. The same occurred with elk and mule deer. "If the elk were here in great numbers all this time, the archaeological sites should be chock-full of elk bones," Kay says. "But the archaeologists will tell you the elk weren't there." On the evidence of middens the number of elk jumped about 500 years ago.

Passenger pigeons may be another example. The epitome of natural American abundance, they flew in such great masses that the first colonists were stupefied by the sight. As a boy, the explorer Henry Brackenridge saw flocks "ten miles in width, by one hundred and twenty in length." For hours the birds darkened the sky from horizon to horizon. According to Thomas Neumann, a consulting archaeologist to Lilburn, Georgia, passenger pigeons "were incredibly dumb and always roosted in vast hordes, so they were very easy to harvest." Because they were readily caught and good to eat, Neumann says, archaeological digs should find many pigeon bones in the pre-Columbian strata of Indian middens. But they aren't there. The mobs of birds in the history books, he says, were "outbreak populations—always a symptom of an extraordinarily disrupted ecological system."

Throughout eastern North America the open landscape seen by the first Europeans quickly filled in with forest. According to William Cronon, of the University of Wisconsin, later colonists began complaining about how hard it was to get around. (Eventually, of course, they stripped New England almost bare of trees.) When Europeans moved west, they were preceded by two waves: one of disease, the other of ecological disturbance. The former crested with fearsome rapidity; the later sometimes took more than a century to quiet down. Far from destroying pristine wilderness, European settlers bloodily *created* it. By 1800 the hemisphere was chockablock with new wilderness. If "forest primeval" means a woodland unsullied by the human presence, William Denevan has written, there was much more of it in the late eighteenth century than in the early sixteenth.

Cronon's *Changes in the Land: Indians, Colonists, and the Ecology of New England* (1983) belongs on the same shelf as works by Crosby and Dobyns. But it was not until one of his articles was excerpted in *The New York Times* in 1995 that people outside the social sciences began to understand the implications of this view of Indian history. Environmentalists and ecologists vigorously attacked the anti-wilderness scenario, which they described as infected by postmodern philosophy. A small academic brouhaha ensued, complete with hundreds of footnotes. It precipitated *Reinventing Nature?* (1995), one of the few academic critiques of postmodernist philosophy written largely by biologists. *The Great New Wilderness Debate* (1998), another lengthy book on the subject, was edited by two philosophers who earnestly identified themselves as "Euro-American men [whose] cultural legacy is patriarchal Western civilization in its current postcolonial, globally hegemonic form."

It is easy to tweak academics for opaque, self-protective language like this. Nonetheless, their concerns were quite justified. Crediting Indians with the role of keystone species has implications for the way the current Euro-American members of that keystone species manage the forests, watersheds, and endangered species of America. Because a third of the United States is owned by the federal government, the issue inevitably has political ramifications. In Amazonia, fabled storehouse of biodiversity, the stakes are global.

Guided by the pristine myth, mainstream environmentalists want to preserve as much of the world's land as possible in a putatively intact state. But "intact," if the new research is correct, means "run by human beings for human purposes." Environmentalists dislike this, because it seems to mean that anything goes. In a sense they are correct. Native Americans managed the continent as they saw fit. Modern nations must do the same. If they want to return as much of the landscape as possible to its 1491 state, they will have to find it within themselves to create the world's largest garden.

Critical Thinking

1. What is meant by the "pristine myth"? How has this colored our thinking about the modern day environment?

2. What possible influence could Hernando de Soto's pigs have had on the environment?

Massacre in Florida

Spain's attack on Fort Caroline and brutal slaughter of its inhabitants ended France's colonial interests on the East Coast.

ANDRÉS RESÉNDEZ

In June 1564, 300 French colonists arrived at the mouth of the St. Johns River near present-day Jacksonville, Florida, after an arduous voyage across the Atlantic. Among these *colons* were men from some of France's greatest noble houses, bedecked in bright clothes and suits of gilded armor, accompanied by a train of artisans and laborers. They built a triangular outer wall on the southern bank, dragged several cannon into it, and set about raising a village, which soon contained houses, a mill, and a bakery. At first the local Timucua were friendly, furnishing them with food and giving them advice about survival.

France had so far established only rugged outposts along what would become known as the St. Lawrence, to harvest fish and furs and probe for the Northwest Passage. Yet these lowly stations soon fell short of satisfying France's grand ambitions for the New World.

This new settlement—Fort Caroline—represented France's first permanent colony in what would later become the United States, a continental foothold in the strategic Florida peninsula. From here French colonists had access to the sugar plantations and gold fields of the Caribbean and a chance to prey on bullion-bearing Spanish galleons coming from Mexico and Peru. The French crown had big plans for that muddy bank in northeast Florida.

Like the English pilgrims, most of the French settlers were spirited Protestants—Huguenots who saw the New World as a refuge and an opportunity to establish a model community. But unlike their English counterparts, the French pioneers also counted on direct royal patronage. The Huguenots had come to occupy key positions under the monarchy, and the main backer of the venture, Gaspard de Coligny, was a close adviser to the royal family, admiral of the French navy, and the undisputed Huguenot leader. He moved swiftly to resupply Fort Caroline the following year, dispatching seven ships, a thousand men, and provisions. Meanwhile, the situation at Fort Caroline had become dire as relations with the Indians had grown strained and the incipient French settlement had experienced mutinies. Just as the colonists were about to leave, the relief expedition finally arrived in the summer of 1565.

Hearing of this intrusion, Spain had dispatched Pedro Menéndez de Avilés with an armada under sweeping orders to "take the Florida coast." After the two fleets brushed briefly, Menéndez prudently retreated southward, where he broke ground for a new stronghold, St. Augustine, which has gone on to prosper and is today the oldest European-founded town in the continental United States.

Luck favored the Spanish. The French ships, which were roughly twice as numerous and much better supplied, ran into a hurricane, which blew some out to sea and forced others aground. Meanwhile Menéndez sent his men overland against Fort Caroline. At dawn on September 20, 1565, he and 500 men armed with arquebuses, pikes, and targets surprised the fort and overran it. Such men over 15 not killed at the outset were summarily executed. Only women, girls, and young boys were spared. Over the next few weeks Spanish soldiers mopped up the Florida coast, putting to death any French sailors who had managed to survive the storm and shipwreck.

Men over 15 not killed at the outset were summarily executed.

The French would come back to the Florida coast and exact harsh retribution, slaughtering Spaniards. But the damage to French interests on the East Coast had already been done. The French had been driven into the distant north, leaving a vacuum of settlement on the Atlantic coast for the English, Dutch, and Swedish settlers who arrived half a century later when Spanish power was already passing into decline. Had Fort Caroline prospered, a sizable French-speaking area such as Quebec could well exist in Florida today. But the events of 1565 steered the history of North America in a different direction.

Critical Thinking

1. What did the French hope to accomplish by building Fort Caroline in what is now Florida?

2. Why did the Spanish oppose the French?

ANDRÉS RESÉNDEZ, author of *A Land So Strange: The Epic Journey of Cabeza de Vaca* (Basic Books 2009), is an associate professor of history at the University of California at Davis.

Jamestown Hangs in the Balance

Only by luck and happenstance did Britain's first permanent settlement in the New World survive.

JAMES HORN

Arriving at the English colony of Jamestown in late May 1610, Sir Thomas Gates was appalled by what he discovered. The fort's palisades had been torn down, the church ruined, and empty houses "rent up and burnt." Only 60 or so colonists remained alive of the more than 200 who had crowded into the fort the previous fall, and these were "Lamentable to behold." Those able to raise themselves from their beds to meet Gates and his men "Looked Like Anatomies" [skeletons]. They cried out, "We are starved We are starved." Yet Gates could do little to relieve them.

Jamestown, established in May 1607, had not prospered. By the end of 1608 a combination of dissension among the colony's leaders, Indian attacks, and food shortages had left it in true disarray. Hearing this, its sponsor, the Virginia Company of London, decided to put the colony on a completely new footing and launched a national appeal for support. Securing Virginia, the company argued, was the first step by which the English could take possession of North America, bring Protestantism to the Indians, and produce valuable commodities for sale at home and abroad.

In June 1609 a fleet commanded by Gates had set out from Plymouth, England, carrying 500 settlers, food, arms, and equipment to Jamestown, only to meet with disaster on July 24—St. James's Day—when a mighty hurricane burst upon the fleet little more than a week from its destination and scattered it upon the winds. Gates and most of the colony's leaders were aboard the flagship *Sea Venture,* which was wrecked upon the reefs surrounding Bermuda. One hundred fifty passengers scrambled ashore, thankful for their miraculous salvation, but had to spend nearly 10 months on the island before they were able to complete the construction of two small ships, the *Deliverance* and the *Patience,* and make their way to their original objective.

While Gates and his men rebuilt their boats, a number of events conspired to make Jamestown's existence even more perilous. In mid-July 1610 a small Spanish ship sent to reconnoiter from the garrison at St. Augustine, Florida, entered the Chesapeake Bay. While the ship got no farther than the mouth of the James River before being turned back by a larger English vessel, the Spanish now knew where the English were settled.

It could only be a matter of time, the English feared, before a Spanish fleet was dispatched against them from bases in the West Indies.

Later that fall the Powhatan Indians launched a full-scale war against them. Hundreds of English were killed along the James River Valley. Jamestown was besieged for six months. The colony disintegrated.

The Indians besieged Jamestown for six months and the colony disintegrated.

Horrified at the suffering of the colonists he found, Gates decided there was no option but to abandon the colony. His own provisions were running out, and there was no hope of getting any food from the Powhatan or any means of taking fish from the rivers in sufficient quantities to sustain the colony. To the great joy of the ragged survivors, who wanted nothing more than to return to England, he announced his decision to abandon Jamestown. Discharging a salute of small shot by way of farewell, the colonists embarked at midday on June 7, 1610, heading for the mouth of the Chesapeake Bay and the Atlantic. Seemingly, the Jamestown colony was at an end.

But an extraordinary reversal awaited them. The departing flotilla had barely dropped a dozen miles downriver before, as they were waiting for the tide to turn, they espied a boat making its way upriver. It proved to be an advance party of a relief expedition led by the colony's new governor, Lord De La Warr, which had just entered the bay with three ships and 150 colonists. To the utter dismay of Gates's men, who must have wished that they had burnt their fort down before leaving, Gates was ordered to return to Jamestown forthwith. From collapse and abandonment, the colony now passed to some 375 settlers and a renewed leadership, all adequately provisioned.

De La Warr's timely arrival did not bring about an immediate improvement in the colony's fortunes, however. The next four years would still be hard going, as the Virginia Company strove to raise resources for the venture and the colonists struggled to extend their settlements in the face of fierce resistance from the Powhatan. But never again would the colony come so close to being abandoned.

In the long term, the survival of Jamestown profoundly influenced the future of America. From its uncertain beginnings, Virginia emerged as the richest and most populous of the British mainland colonies, the first transatlantic site of an empire that would carry English language, laws, institutions, and the Protestant Church across the globe. Representative government, established at Jamestown in 1619, would blossom into a vibrant political culture and spread throughout the British colonies, leading in time to a new republican faith that would find its fulfillment in the founding of the United States.

Critical Thinking

1. What obstacles did the colonists at Jamestown have to contend with in establishing a successful settlement?

2. Give the state of medical knowledge and technology at the time, could they have been much better prepared?

JAMXES HORN, author most recently of *A Land As God Made It: Jamestown and the Birth of America* (Basic Books 2005) and the upcoming *A Kingdom Strange: The Brief and Tragic History of the Lost Colony of Roanoke* (Basic Books 2010), is the vice president of research for the Colonial Williamsburg Foundation.

From *American Heritage,* Winter 2010, pp. 26–27. Copyright © 2010 by American Heritage Publishing Co. Reprinted by permission.

A Pox on the New World

As much as nine-tenths of the indigenous population of the Americas died in less than a generation from European pathogens.

CHARLES C. MANN

In the summer of 1605 the French explorer Samuel de Champlain sailed along the coast of New England, looking for a likely spot to place a colony—a place more hospitable than the upper St. Lawrence River, which he had previously explored. Halfway down the Maine coast he began to find spots with good harbors, abundant supplies of freshwater, and big spreads of cleared land. The problem was that these parcels were already occupied. The peoples there were happy to barter with him and treat his sailors to fine dinners. But none were interested in providing free real estate. A skirmish in Nauset Bay, halfway down Cape Cod, convinced Champlain that he had no hope of starting a colony in this area. Too many people already lived there.

Fifteen years later, a band of English voyagers showed up in Massachusetts. The Pilgrims were everything that Champlain was not: inexperienced, poorly supplied, and lacking in basic survival skills. Arriving on the cusp of winter, they anchored offshore, planted their metaphorical flag on some choice land, and quickly set about the business of dying en masse. Surprisingly, the Pilgrims made it through the winter; within a few years, they were prospering. Why did the land's original inhabitants, so clear about their rejection of the French, allow the English company to stay?

Pilgrim writings provide the answer. Colonist William Bradford learned that three or four years before the *Mayflower* landed, shipwrecked French seamen had set up shop on Cape Cod. Unwilling to countenance a long-term foreign presence, no matter how unintended, the Indians of Nauset, Bradford recounted, "never left watching & dogging them till they got advantage, and *kild them all but 3. or 4*." Even this limited mercy proved a mistake. One of the French carried a disease not known in the Americas. He bequeathed it to his captors, who passed it on to their friends and families. As the epidemic spread, the healthy fled from the sick, unwittingly carrying the disease with them to neighboring communities. All along the New England coast, the English poet-adventurer Thomas Morton reported, Indians "died in heapes, as they lay in their houses." So many perished so quickly that the living had no time to bury the dead. Morton, who settled in Massachusetts in 1624,

found native skeletons still littering the woods. The Pilgrims fared better than Champlain because they were moving into land that was now largely unoccupied.

So many perished so quickly that the living had no time to bury the dead.

Their story was no exception. Although Europeans had firearms, steel blades, and horses, none of which existed in the Americas, their biggest weapon was biological. By a quirk of evolutionary history, the Western Hemisphere had few epidemic diseases—no smallpox, influenza, measles, or malaria. When these illnesses hitchhiked to the Americas aboard European ships, somewhere between two-thirds and nine-tenths of the native population of the Americas died. Arguably, this is the single most powerful explanatory fact in the entire history of the Americas post-1492.

Consider the two assaults by Hernán Cortés on Mexico's great Triple Alliance (many historians view the term "Aztec" as a 19th-century invention). A brilliant commander who wielded the advantages of guns, swords, horses, and battalions of Alliance-hating indigenous soldiers, Cortés was able to occupy the capital of Tenochtitlán by seizing the empire's supreme military leader. The Alliance was as stunned as Spain would have been if an Indian force had abducted the king of Spain. Eventually there was a counterattack in which most of the Spaniards died, along with their horses. Cortés was reported to have sat weeping at the ruin of his hopes. With no other options, he readied a second assault, this one with far fewer horses, swords, and guns. But he had acquired an additional weapon: smallpox, which was apparently brought over by a Spanish slave. Packed into crowded cities and carrying no resistance, the people of central Mexico died in huge numbers, including most of the imperial court. Cortés's second assault, launched in the wake of the epidemic, was successful.

Disease preceded successful European colonization of the Americas in almost every instance. But it played a later role, too. Carried over in the bodies of colonists from the feverish fens of southwest England, malaria rapidly became endemic from Virginia to Florida. Killing or driving away natives and newcomers alike, it helped to create a labor shortage that fed the demand for African slaves. (Most West Africans are genetically immune to the type of malaria that was imported from England.) During the American Revolution, British general Charles Cornwallis occupied the Carolinas, hoping to inspire a loyalist rebellion—the "southern strategy," as it was known. Alas, the Carolinas were filled with rice paddies, a recent introduction. Mosquitoes thrived in this new environment, as did the malaria parasite inside them. With half his army sick, Cornwallis was ordered to retreat to Yorktown, Virginia, which he regarded as an "unhealthy swamp." (Correctly—malaria was probably introduced in nearby Jamestown.) There the rest of his army fell prey to the disease. His surrender soon followed, effectively ending the war.

George Washington's courage, tenacity, and political deftness were vital to the successful outcome of the American Revolution.

No history would be complete without taking them into account. But equally vital was the grinding, constantly rising toll of mosquito-borne disease. Here, as in so many other instances, examination of the landmarks of human history reveals its inextricable entanglement with the nonhuman world.

Critical Thinking

1. Many historians and anthropologists have blamed the settlers from Europe for countless deaths in the Americas. Looking back, do you believe that the settlers should have anticipated this calamity, or should they have taken precautions—as few as there were in those days—to avoid the transmission of diseases to the innocent inhabitants of the Americas?

CHARLES C. MANN, author of *1491: New Revelations of the Americas Before Columbus,* is a correspondent for *Science* and *The Atlantic Monthly* living in Amherst, Massachusetts.

From *American Heritage,* Winter 2010, pp. 23–24. Copyright © 2010 by American Heritage Publishing Co. Reprinted by permission.

Champlain among the Mohawk, 1609

A Soldier-Humanist Fights a War for Peace in North America

David Hackett Fischer

A few generations ago, American colonial history centered on a single narrative that flowed from Jamestown in 1607 to the Declaration of Independence in 1776. Today early American history has blossomed into a braided narrative with many story lines.

A starting point might be four small beginnings, far apart in space but close in time. On April 26, 1607, Capt. John Smith and his comrades founded Jamestown in Virginia. Four months later, in mid-August 1607, Capt. George Popham established a New England colony near Pemaquid in Maine. The following year, during the spring and summer of 1608, Spanish colonists, led by Capt. Martínez de Montoya, built a permanent settlement at Santa Fe in the region they called New Mexico. And on July 3, 1608, Capt. Samuel de Champlain founded the first permanent colony in New France at Quebec. The stories that began to unfold at these places shaped much of modern North America.

One of the most interesting of those small beginnings was New France. For more than 30 years the central figure was the extraordinary Champlain. He left six fascinating books of travels, filled with many superb maps and illustrations. His writings tell much about his actions but little about the man, and nearly nothing about his inner life.

Champlain came from Brouage, a little town on the Bay of Biscay on the Atlantic coast of France. A busy place in his youth, it served as the center of a lucrative salt trade. Today this small seaport lies quietly a mile from the sea. Born around 1570 and probably baptized Protestant, he grew up in a prosperous maritime family and was schooled by his father, who had risen through the ranks from seaman, pilot, and master to captain, merchant, and ship owner. Champlain came of age in a dark period, when horrific wars of religion had shattered France.

The United States has experienced one civil war, in which 600,000 people died over four years. The French people suffered nine civil wars of religion in nearly 40 years (1562–98). More than 2 million died, and atrocities beyond description occurred. Champlain fought in the largest of these wars, following an extraordinary leader who would become Henry IV, founder of the Bourbon dynasty. The king became the young Champlain's mentor, model, patron, and friend. Both men converted to Catholicism but always defended toleration for Protestants.

War was their profession. While always keeping a soldier's creed of honor, duty, courage, and loyalty to a larger cause, their feelings about war changed with the horrors they encountered. These veteran campaigners came to hate war for its cruelly, destruction, and terrible waste. They knew, however, that some of the world's evils overshadow even war. In a world of cruelty and violence, they dedicated themselves to fighting for peace and humanity.

Henry and his army won their last great struggle in 1598, giving France the Peace of Vervins and toleration under the Edict of Nantes. Henry next set his sights on bringing a general peace to Europe. Soon a web of peace treaties opened the Atlantic to commerce and made North America accessible for those many colonial beginnings in 1607 and 1608. It was a pivot point in American history.

The king was deeply interested in America, particularly the large area labeled on world maps as Nova Francia, after voyages of Jacques Cartier in the 16th century. Henry intended to turn that geographical expression into an empire called la Nouvelle France. Champlain got a new job.

He had already begun to serve the king as a secret agent. In 1599 he traveled through Spanish America on a long espionage mission. Upon its completion, Champlain delivered a long report called a *Bref discours* that outlined the strengths and resources of the Spanish empire in detail. Champlain found the people he variously called *Indiens* or *sauvages* fascinating. Impressed by their high intelligence, he was shocked by the cruelty and violence they had suffered under the Spanish. To illustrate the report, Champlain added his own luminous watercolors of their sufferings: Indians burned alive for heresy; Indians cudgeled on the orders of priests for not attending mass; Indians and African slaves compelled to dive to lethal depths in the pearl fisheries of Margarita Island off the coast of Venezuela. Altogether the *Bref discours* was a report on how not to found an empire in America.

Impressed with the report, King Henry gave Champlain a pension and the assignment to work with other experts in the basement of the Louvre on the colonization of North America.

Champlain closely studied the history of earlier French settlements, which had all ended in disaster. He also traveled to the Atlantic ports of France, interviewing fishermen who knew about America and the dangerous waters of the North Atlantic. He composed what he called his *grand dessein* for France in North America, a plan in large part based on a dream of peace and humanity, of amity and concord among the peoples of Europe and America.

Champlain pulled many others into his grand design, moving in a number of circles, all of which revolved around Henry IV. One consisted of the men who would go eventually with him to America: Pierre Dugua, the sieur de Mons; Marc Lescarbot; Jean de Poutrincourt; and François Gravé du Pont, a grizzled mariner from Saint-Malo whom he called Pont-Gravé. His friends at court formed another circle: Pierre Jeannin, several Sillerys and Brularts, and his old commander, the Comte de Cossé-Brissac, who offered advice and urgent support.

These men all shared a common bond as Christian humanists. While a few were Protestants, most embraced the literal Catholic idea of a universal faith. Men of learning, they were full of curiosity about the world and all its peoples. In their broad spirit of humanity, they had inherited the values of the Renaissance; in time, their work would inspire the Enlightenment. In a difficult time, they kept the idea of humanism alive; in doing so, they became important world figures.

Together they carefully prepared for a new sort of European presence in America, one that stressed peaceful cohabitation with the Indians, trading actively, and exploring the continent together. Pont-Gravé made a voyage in 1602 and persuaded Indian leaders to allow two young Montagnais "princes," as the Pont-Gravé called them, to come to France, learn the language, and serve as translators. In 1603 they all sailed to the St. Lawrence on a voyage of reconnaissance, arriving on May 26, 1603, at the little port of Tadoussac near the Saguenay River. Champlain and Pont-Gravé looked across the river and saw a huge gathering of Indians from many nations, including Montagnais, Algonquian, and Etchemin, the latter being Champlain's name for the nations living in what is now the state of Maine.

The two Frenchmen and the young Montagnais translators crossed the river, walked unarmed into the camp, and were invited to join a *tabagie,* or tobacco feast. Champlain, Pont-Gravé, and the representatives of these many Indian nations talked together through the night and into the next day. The informal alliance they formed would last for many generations, and the legacy of this first *tabagie* still lives on. All were warriors in search of peace, who were open and candid, learned to respect each other's vital interests, and created an alliance founded on cohabitation, trade, and mutual support against attacks by others.

After this beginning, other voyages followed. Champlain helped to found French settlements on the St. Croix River in 1604, in Acadia (now Nova Scotia) in 1605–6, and at Quebec. He explored the country, met with many other Indian nations, and forged alliances with more than 50 of them—more than any European leader of his time.

Champlain's special pattern of relating with the Indians made the history of New France fundamentally different than those of New Spain, New England, New Netherland, and Virginia. The Spanish conquistadors sought to subjugate the Indians. The English pushed the Indians away, built a big "pale" in Virginia, and forbade Indians from crossing it unless they presented a special passport. Only the French established a consistent policy of peaceful cohabitation, and something of its spirit persists in North America to this day.

A major threat to Champlain's design for New France was incessant warfare among the Indian nations in the St. Lawrence Valley. Much of it pitted the Iroquois League, and especially the Mohawk nation, against the Algonquian and Montagnais to the north, the Huron to the west, and the Etchemin to the east. As long as it continued, there could be no peace in the St. Lawrence Valley, no security for trade, and no hope for the dream of American Indians and Europeans living together in peace.

Champlain believed that a major cause of war was fear, and his remedy was to seek peace through diplomacy. To that end he had built alliances among the Montagnais, Algonquian, Huron, and other nations. But the Iroquois League proved difficult to work with. One historian of the Iroquois observes that by the start of the 17th century they were "at odds with all their neighbors—Algonquin and Huron to the north, Mahican on the east, and Susquehannock to the south." Many Indian nations in the Northeast were at war with some of their neighbors. The Iroquois, however, were at war with nearly all of theirs. They had a reputation for skill in war, among many warrior nations; they were also known for cruelty in a cruel world.

In 1608 Champlain had promised to aid the Indian nations of the St. Lawrence Valley when the Iroquois attacked them. At the same time, he understood that the Iroquois were victims as well as aggressors, so he sent peace feelers through a captive Mohawk woman. These overtures accomplished nothing. Mohawk war parties continued to attack the St. Lawrence Indians.

After a long and difficult winter of 1608 and 1609 in Quebec, Champlain decided that peace could be achieved only by concerted military action against the Mohawk. He did not intend a war of conquest. Instead he envisioned that a coalition of Montagnais, Algonquian, and Huron, with French support, might deliver one or two sharp blows that could deter future Mohawk attacks by raising the cost of their raiding to the north.

When Champlain met Pont-Gravé at Tadoussac on June 7, he laid out a bold plan for "certain explorations in the interior" and made clear his intention to enter "the country of the Iroquois" with "our allies the Montagnais." Both men knew that this plan would mean a fight with some of the most formidable warriors in North America. It was an act of breathtaking audacity, considering the small size of Champlain's force. But what Champlain lacked in mass, he made up in acceleration. He also had the early firearm known as the arquebus, and the Mohawk did not. The sieur de Mons had sent him a few good men who were trained in the use of that difficult weapon. Champlain also had many Indian allies with hundreds of warriors.

On June 28, 1609, Champlain set out from Quebec with a party of French soldiers and hundreds of Indian warriors. A week later they entered "the country of the Iroquois." Champlain and his party paddled their canoes south from the St. Lawrence Valley up the river of the Iroquois, known today as the Richelieu River. He wrote, "No Christians but ourselves had ever penetrated this place." Eventually most of the French and Indians decided to turn back, daunted by what lay ahead, but Champlain pressed on with a war party of only 60 Indians and two Frenchmen at his side. It was a courageous decision. Others would have called it foolhardy to the point of madness.

Champlain and his allies made a portage of about a mile around the rapids on the Richelieu, well into Iroquois country. At the end of each day, the expedition built a semicircular fort on the edge of the river. Some took bark from trees to make wigwams, while others felled big trees to make an abatis of tangled branches around their camp, leaving only the riverbank open as a line of retreat. They sent forward a party of three canoes and nine men to search four or six miles ahead. The scouts found nothing, and all retired for the night. This was one of the first occasions when European soldiers traveled with a large Indian war party in North America.

Intent on battling the Mohawk, who threatened his grand plans for peace in the region, Champlain traveled south from Quebec in the summer of 1609, coming across the beautiful lake that he would give his name to. Here Champlain, two French soldiers, and his Indian allies confronted a powerful Mohawk party and defeated them convincingly with the aid of Hudson's wheelock arquebus, an early muzzle loading firearm.

On July 14, 1609, they reached the large lake from which the river flowed. Champlain exercised his right to name it Lake Champlain on his map, as he and his two French companions may have been the first Europeans to see it. He reckoned its length at 80 to 100 leagues, and later amended his estimate to 50 or 60 land leagues, which is roughly correct. He explored both sides of the lake, saw the Green Mountains of Vermont to the east, and to the west sighted the Adirondacks, which are visible from the eastern shore. On the many maps created by Champlain, this lake was the only place where he put his name on the land.

As they moved further south, tensions mounted. On the evening of July 29, 1609, they approached the lake's southern end; on their right they passed a low peninsula with willow trees and a sandy beach below a steep eroded bank. Beyond the beach Champlain saw a promontory projecting into the water. His Indian allies knew it well. The Iroquois called it "the meeting place of two waters": *tekontató:ken* or, to European ears, Ticonderoga. The name came from two big, beautiful lakes. Lake George to the south and west was 200 feet above Lake Champlain, draining into it from a height greater than Niagara Falls. The water flowed downward through a run of falls and rapids that the French called a *chute,* entering Lake Champlain at Ticonderoga. For many generations past and to come, Ticonderoga served as one of the most strategic locations in North America, a key to anyone who wanted to control the long chain of lakes and rivers running from the St. Lawrence to the Hudson. For the Mohawk, it was also a sacred and magical place.

In the night of July 29, as Champlain's party rounded the promontory of Ticonderoga, their bow paddlers saw shadows stirring on the water ahead of them. As they stared intently into the darkness, the shadows began to assume an earthly form. They were boats of strange appearance, larger than northern birch-bark canoes, and filled with men. The Indians instantly identified them: Mohawk!

Each group sighted the other at about the same time. Both taken by surprise, they turned away and moved in opposite directions. "We retreated into the middle of the lake," Champlain later wrote. The Mohawk landed on a sand beach between the promontory of Ticonderoga and Willow Point to the north, where a fringe of willow trees still flourishes near the water's edge, and built a small fort or barricade.

Champlain and his allies remained afloat on the lake and lashed their canoes together with poles so as not to become separated in the night. "We were on the water," he wrote, "within bow-shot of their barricades." Songs and cries pierced the night. The Mohawk shouted insults at their enemies. "Our side was not lacking in repartee," Champlain recalled. As dawn approached, both sides prepared for battle. In the darkness before first light, Champlain's Indian allies paddled around the promontory and landed in a secluded spot where they were not under observation. "My companions and I were always kept carefully out of sight, lying flat in the canoes," he wrote. His allies sent scouts ahead to watch the Mohawk fort. The rest assembled in their fighting formation and moved forward toward the Mohawk barricade.

The three Frenchmen remained carefully hidden behind them. Each prepared his weapon, a short-barreled, shoulder-fired arquebus à rouet, Champlain's highly developed wheel-lock weapon that did not require a smoldering matchlock, which might have betrayed their position. Champlain dangerously overloaded his arquebus with four balls. On Cape Cod in 1605, his weapon had exploded in his hands and nearly killed him. But overloading was highly effective in close combat, so he accepted the risk.

At first light the Mohawk warriors mustered quickly and came out of the fort, many of them wearing wooden armor that was proof against stone arrowheads. Both forces assembled in close formation on opposite sides of a clearing between the water and the woods.

Champlain peered through the ranks of his allies and studied the Mohawk as they emerged from their barricade. He counted 200 warriors, "strong and robust men in their appearance," and he watched as "they advanced slowly to meet us with a gravity and assurance that I greatly admired." The Mohawk were in tight ranks—a disciplined close-order forest phalanx that had defeated many foes. Their wooden armor and shields covered their bodies. In the front were two Mohawks, each wearing three high feathers above their heads. Champlain's Indians told him that the men with the big feathers were chiefs, and "I was to do what I could to kill them."

Champlain's Indian allies were now about 200 yards from the Mohawk, and they began to move forward also in close formation. Once again Champlain kept behind them, remaining invisible to the other side. On Champlain's orders, the other two Frenchmen slipped into the forest and crept forward around the right flank of the Mohawk.

When they were about 50 yards from their enemy, Champlain's allies parted. Champlain strode forward alone until 30 yards from the enemy. The Mohawk stopped in amazement and studied this astonishing figure who wore a burnished steel cuirass and helmet that glittered in the golden light of the morning sun. Then a Mohawk leader raised his bow.

Champlain tells us, "I put my arquebus against my cheek and aimed straight at one of the chiefs." As the Mohawk drew their bowstrings, Champlain fired. There was a mighty crash and a cloud of white smoke. Two chiefs fell dead, and another warrior was mortally wounded—three men brought down by one shot. Champlain's Indian allies raised a great shout, so loud that "one could not have heard the thunder."

The Mohawk were stunned and "greatly frightened." Even so, they fought back bravely. Both sides fired clouds of arrows, and Champlain reloaded his weapon. As he did so, his two French companions emerged on the edge of the forest. They appear to have been veteran fighters—skilled arquebusiers and highly disciplined soldiers. Using the trees for cover, they knelt side by side, steadied their weapons, and took aim. "As I was reloading my arquebus," Champlain wrote, "one of my companions fired a shot from the woods." This second blow was delivered into the flank of the Mohawk formation, and it had a devastating effect. A third chief went down. The tight Mohawk formation shuddered in a strange way and sudenly came apart. "It astonished them so much that, seeing their chiefs dead, they lost courage, took to their heels, and abandoned the field and their fort, fleeing into the depth of the forest." Champlain led his Indian allies in a headlong charge. "I pursued them, and laid low still more of them."

Many historians have criticized Champlain for going to war with the Iroquois. Some have written that he initiated hostilities that would continue for two centuries. In the late 20th century, ethnohistorians studying this question came to a different conclusion. They agreed that he did not start these wars, but that the fighting had been going on between the Mohawk and their neighbors to the north long before he arrived.

Further, Iroquois ethnologist William N. Fenton writes, "Nineteenth-century historians to the contrary, this incident did not precipitate a hundred years of Mohawk vengeance against New France." It put a stop to major fighting between the Mohawk and the French for a generation. An ethnologist of the Huron agrees. Bruce Trigger writes of the two battles: "This was the last time that the Mohawks were a serious threat along the St. Lawrence River until the 1630s. Having suffered serious losses in two successive encounters, they avoided armed Frenchmen."

After the battles at Ticonderoga and the Rivière des Iroquois, the Mohawk made several peace overtures to the French. Champlain, however, could not find a way to make lasting peace with the Iroquois without alienating the Montagnais, Algonquian, and Huron. Even so, he hoped for a modus vivendi between the French and the Mohawk, and he achieved it. A fragile quasi peace was won by force of arms, and it continued for a generation, until 1634. The leaders who followed Champlain in Quebec and Paris (also in Boston, Philadelphia, Williamsburg, and London) were unable to keep it going. They used too much force or too little. Champlain's policy effected a middle way of peace through the carefully calibrated use of limited force. We are only beginning to understand how he did it.

Critical Thinking

1. Analyze Champlain's attempt to create a new society in which the French would collaborate with native American tribes rather than try to subdue them.

2. Was his failure due to personal inadequacies, or to conditions over which he had no control?

From *Chaplain's Dream* by David Hackett Fischer (Simon & Schuster, 2008). Copyright © 2008 by David Hackett Fischer. Reprinted by permission of Simon & Schuster.

New Amsterdam Becomes New York

The British seize Manhattan from the Dutch—and alter the trajectory of North American history.

RUSSELL SHORTO

On September 5, 1664, two men faced one another across a small stretch of water. Onshore, just outside the fort at the southern tip of Manhattan Island, stood Peter Stuyvesant, director-general of the Dutch colony of New Netherland, his 52-year-old frame balanced on the wooden stump where he had lost a leg in battle a quarter century earlier. Approaching him aboard a small rowboat flying a flag of truce was John Winthrop, governor of the Connecticut colony, until very recently a man Stuyvesant had called his friend.

For 17 years Stuyvesant had managed the Dutch settlement in North America. The colony's origins dated to 1609, when Englishman Henry Hudson had charted the area on behalf of the Dutch East India Company and the Dutch had laid claim to a wide swath of the East Coast. At its height, New Netherland covered an area encompassing all or parts of five future states: New York, New Jersey, Connecticut, Pennsylvania, and Delaware. From its second city, Beverwijck—the future Albany—residents traded for beaver pelts and other furs with Indians. Goods traveled down the Hudson River to the capital of New Amsterdam on Manhattan Island for transshipment to Europe. The colonists also grew tobacco for the European market, and New Amsterdam functioned as a port for English ships from Virginia and New England.

The colony existed in a state of constant struggle. Indians threatened it, and so did the English. Thanks largely to the English Civil Wars, people had fled England in large numbers for the colonies in New England and Virginia, and as their numbers swelled they encroached on the boundaries of New Netherland.

Stuyvesant, meanwhile, had to work with an unusually mixed society. In the 1640s the 500 colonists in New Amsterdam communicated in 18 languages. To deal with this diversity, the city's elders formulated an official policy of tolerance, a genuine anomaly in Europe at the time. Along with tolerance, the Dutch also introduced 17th-century capitalism. The inhabitants were vigorous traders: carpenters, wheelwrights, and even prostitutes bought shares in shipments of goods being transported to the home country.

In addition to mediating between inhabitants and the company officials, Stuyvesant found himself begging Amsterdam for soldiers and ships to protect the colony from encroachment. Failing to get these, he negotiated treaties with the New England governors; his most trusted ally became Winthrop.

He had believed Winthrop's claim in 1661 that the English had no designs on the colony. But in London other plans were afoot. In the wake of the restoration of the Stuart monarchy, Charles II had set about reorganizing the American colonies. He intended to restrict the power of the Puritans and also to make a play for the Dutch colony. The Puritan Winthrop found the first part of this strategy hard to swallow. But he understood the new political reality, fell in line behind the king, and agreed to be an emissary for the crown. Charles granted his brother James, the Duke of York, title over the land that encompassed the Dutch colony. He sent a flotilla of four ships and 2,000 men.

Stuyvesant was clearly outmatched: he could muster only 150 soldiers and had no gunpowder for his cannons. A letter arrived from Richard Nicolls, commander of the flotilla, demanding surrender. Despite the odds, Stuyvesant wanted to fight.

At that moment, Winthrop rowed ashore and handed his former friend a letter granting generous terms. When the townsfolk learned of the offer, they wanted to surrender. Stuyvesant argued against it, but he was forced to capitulate in the end.

As it happened, it was fortunate for the city—whose name was changed forthwith to New York after the duke's title—that it had gotten its start under the Dutch. The Dutch imprinted their tolerance and free trading into its DNA, ensuring that New York would grow along a different trajectory from the rest of British North America. In time these dynamics would lead to New York's distinctively multiethnic, upwardly mobile culture. And because New York would have a vast impact on the growing United States, the seeds of that Dutch influence would take root in places thousands of miles from where they had originally been sown, and grow in ways that Stuyvesant and Winthrop, as they came together on that late summer day in 1664, could not possibly have foreseen.

Critical Thinking

1. What were the characteristics of New Amsterdam (renamed New York) that made it different from other cities along the Atlantic Coast?

2. How did these differences result in a more liberal society?

RUSSELL SHORTO, author of *Island at the Center of the World: The Epic Story of Dutch Manhattan and the Forgotten Colony That Shaped America* (Random House 2004), is the director of the John Adams Institute in Amsterdam.

From *American Heritage,* Winter 2010, pp. 28–29. Copyright © 2010 by American Heritage Publishing Co. Reprinted by permission.

Taken by Indians

Kevin Sweeney

At sunrise on this cold winter's day, 39-year-old Mary Rowlandson awoke to the sound of musket fire rippling across her remote town in north central Massachusetts. A peek out of her family's fortified house revealed her worst nightmare: a large number of Indians descending on the small village of 50 to 60 families, firing houses and killing anyone who set foot outside. A wounded man pleaded for his life. The Indians "knocked [him] in [the] head, and stripped him naked, and split open his bowels," she recalled. Methodically, the Indians moved toward her house.

For two hours, "they shot against the House, so that the Bullets seemed to fly like hail . . . [and] "wounded one man among us, then another, and then a third." The Indians set fire to flax and hemp they had jammed against the house's outer walls. Her housemates found themselves "fighting for their lives, others wallowing in their blood, the House on fire over our heads, and the bloody Heathen ready to knock us on the head, if we stirred to [go] out."

But they had no choice as the fire roared up behind them, so Rowlandson, cradling her six-year-old daughter, Sarah, stepped over the threshold only to see her brother-in-law cut down in front of her in a fusillade of bullets; a ball pierced her side, another penetrated her daughter's bowels. "Thus we were butchered by those merciless heathen, standing amazed, with the blood running down to our heels." The house's front compound now contained "many Christians lying in their blood, some here, and some there, like a company of sheep torn by wolves, all of them stripped naked by a company of hell-hounds, roaring, singing, ranting, and insulting, as if they would have torn our very hearts out." In all, 14 men, women, and children staying in Rowlandson's garrison house perished, "some shot, some stab'd with their Spears, some knock'd down with their Hatchets."

Rowlandson, mother of three and wife of the town's absent minister, the Reverend Joseph Rowlandson, was one of a score of survivors who now found themselves force-marched to the Nipmuc town of Menamest, about 25 miles southwest of Lancaster. The Indians and their captives spent the first night upon a hill within sight of the town. "Oh the roaring, and singing and dancing, and yelling of those black creatures in the night, which made the place a lively resemblance of hell," she remembered. Over the next 82 days, Rowlandson's trek through a "vast and howling Wilderness" in midwinter would cover more than 150 miles. Each "Remove," as she called a stage of her forced journey, took her farther from her familiar world and into that of her captors: "My Children gone, my Relations and Friends gone, our House and home

and all our comforts within door, and without all gone (except my life) and I knew not but the next moment that might go too."

Her captors were Algonquian Indians: Wampanoags from Plymouth Colony; neighboring Nipmucs from central Massachusetts; and Narragansetts from what is today southern Rhode Island. In June 1675, Plymouth Colony's mounting threats to Wampanoag lands and independence had set off a series of raids that erupted into sustained warfare. Some Nipmuc warriors and other tribesmen combined to attack colonial villages, and the conflict, later called King Philip's War after the Wampanoag leader, spread to the colonies of Massachusetts and Connecticut. A preemptive assault on the Narragansett by colonial militiamen in December 1675 brought the Indians and the colony of Rhode Island into the war. In January the Indian allies had resolved to regain the initiative and strike a decisive blow by attacking five frontier towns, beginning with the February assault on Lancaster.

For Rowlandson, raised in Puritan New England and married to a minister, her journey into the "desolate wilderness" was spiritual as well as physical. On the ninth day of her captivity, during their "Third Remove," her daughter Sarah died "in this miserable condition, without any refreshing of one nature or other, except a little cold water." Rowlandson wrote, "I have thought since of the wonderful goodness of God to me in preserving me in the use of my reason and senses in that distressed time, that I did not use wicked and violent means to end my own miserable life."

Rowlandson's captors soon turned northward, heading cross-country toward a point on the Connecticut River not far from where it traverses the northern border of Massachusetts. During this "Fourth Remove" she was separated from the other Lancaster captives. Alone and despairing, she saw her journey as a test of her faith in "the Sovereignty and Goodness of God," who had decided whether she would live or die. Her actions, and even those of her captors, were determined—actually predestined—by Him. Calling to mind the words of Psalm 27, she resolved to "Wait on the Lord: be of good courage, and He shall strengthen thine heart: wait, I say, on the Lord."

Wounded, starving, but still strong, Mary Rowlandson carried her six-year-old daughter, Sarah, for the first nine days of the march before the child died. Her powerful autobiographical narrative of her 82-day captivity inspired James Fenimore Cooper to write.

—*The Last of the Mohicans*

And wait she did, trusting in the Lord, refusing to contemplate escape, and advising others not to run off. Sustained by her faith, Rowlandson displayed iron strength and firmness of spirit, overcoming the exhaustion and disorientation of long hunger, the wearying strain of constant travel over hard ground, the sleepless grief of Sarah's lingering death, and the plain terror of not knowing what her captors might do. She traveled over mountains and through swamps, often sleeping directly on the frozen earth, at times thinking that "my heart and legs, and all would have broken, and failed me." But she survived.

At the same time, to a degree she did not always realize or later acknowledge, Rowlandson stayed alive due to the actions and restraint of her captors and her own ability to adapt and negotiate. The Indians heaped verbal and physical abuse on her and, having little food for themselves, gave her even less. Still, they had a stake in keeping her and the other captives alive. By taking and keeping these prisoners, the Indians humiliated the seemingly impotent English, and gained valuable pledges that could be bartered for desperately needed gunpowder or, possibly, exchanged for the Nipmuc and other Indians imprisoned by Massachusetts authorities on Deer Isle in Boston Harbor. As the wife of a minister, Rowlandson was particularly valuable, and from the outset received special treatment. Her captors placed her and Sarah on a horse during the first part of their journey, and one of them gave her a stolen Bible, a "wonderful mercy of God to me in those afflictions." Rowlandson was surprised that "not one of them offered the least imaginable miscarriage to me," not realizing that Algonquian customs guarded her from sexual assault. Because she was unaware of these protections, she took seriously every threat that she would "be knockt in [the] head."

Her diet included raw horse liver, boiled horses' hooves, and bear meat.

As she was trekked northwest to the Connecticut River on her fourth through seventh "Removes" in late February and early March, Rowlandson learned, for instance, to eat whatever food came her way. "The first week of my being among them, I hardly ate any thing; the second week, I found my stomach grow very faint for want of something; and yet it was very hard to get down their filthy trash." Her diet included raw horse liver, boiled horses' hooves, raw corn on the cob, peas and groundnuts in broth thickened with bark; and bear meat, the very thought of which at first made her "tremble." By the third week they were all "sweet and savory to my taste."

In some ways, Rowlandson, who was used to being mistress of her own home, found it hard to adjust socially. Soon after being taken prisoner, she had been sold by her captor to Quinnapin, a prominent Narragansett, whom she soon came to regard as "her master," and his three wives as her mistresses. Among the latter was the "severe and proud" Weetamoo, a Wampanoag and a leader in her own right, who was in the opinion of one colonist "next to Philip in respect of the mischief she hath done." Rowlandson studied the women's moods and learned, if not to show them respect, to avoid displaying any disrespect that might bring a blow with fist or stick. By playing one wife against another, she moderated Weetamoo's often abusive behavior. She also knitted stockings for one wife and sewed a shirt for the young child of another. She even made a shirt for the Wampanoag leader Metacom (King Philip); in return, he gave her a shilling that she used to buy "a piece of Horse flesh." Trading upon her skills as a needlewoman, she obtained other things—including a knife—which she presented to Quinnapin and Weetamoo as gifts. Gradually she came to look upon Quinnapin as her protector and "the best friend that I had of an *Indian*," even acknowledging that "glad I was to see him" after one period of separation.

This period of separation ended some days after the Indians reversed course on their "Thirteenth Remove" and headed east from the Connecticut River toward central Massachusetts. Short of food and ammunition, harried by Mohawk raiders in the west, and confronted by colonial militiamen now reinforced by native allies, Rowlandson's captors found themselves back near Lancaster in late April. There the Nipmuc leaders opened negotiations to trade their prisoners. After some hesitation, Rowlandson set the price of her own ransom at 20 pounds and effectively dispensed gifts brought to her by an English negotiator to accelerate the process.

After three anxious days, her captors released her on May 2, 1676. Eventually she was reunited with her husband and children, Mary and Joseph, who had survived their own captivities. Six years later, Rowlandson wrote an account of her captivity, *A True History of the Captivity & Restoration of Mrs. Mary Rowlandson*—part adventure story, part spiritual autobiography, but mostly an extended sermon reminding New Englanders of the power and mercy of Him who had saved one so unworthy.

Mary Rowlandson, who lived to 73, saw her book go through four printings in one year to become the first and perhaps most powerful example of the captivity narrative, an American genre that would influence future generations of American writers and moviemakers, from James Fenimore Cooper to John Ford.

Critical Thinking

1. Why did the Algonquins take Mary Rowlandson and others prisoner instead of killing them?

2. Why were they released from captivity?

Blessed and Bedeviled

Tales of remarkable providences in puritan New England.

HELEN MONDLOCH

On October 31, 2001, Massachusetts Gov. Jane Swift signed a bill exonerating the last five souls convicted of witchcraft during the infamous Salem witch trials of 1692. Rectifying a few of history's wrongs on this Halloween day, the governor's conciliatory gesture was arguably ill-timed, given the frivolous revelry associated with this annual celebration of superstition and frights. In the real-life horror of the witch scare, at least 150 people were imprisoned, including a four-year-old girl who was confined for months to a stone dungeon. Twenty-three men and women, all of whom have now been cleared of their crimes, were hanged or died in prison, and one man was pressed (crushed) to death for his refusal to stand trial.

In probing the underpinnings of this tragic and incredible chapter of American history, New England observers past and present have agreed that the nascent Massachusetts Bay Colony provided a fertile ground for the devil's plagues. Among others, folklore scholar Richard Dorson, author of *America in Legend and American Folklore,* has argued that the frenzy culminating in the witch-hunt was fueled by legends that flourished among the Puritans, a populace that imagined itself both blessed and bedeviled. Of key importance was belief in phenomena called "providences" (more commonly called "remarkable providences"). These were visible, often terrifying, signs of God's will that forged themselves onto the fabric of daily life.

As Dorson explains, "Since, in the Puritan and Reformation concept, God willed every event from the black plague to the sparrow's fall, all events held meaning for errant man." The providences brought rewards or protection for the Lord's followers (generally the Puritans themselves) or vengeance upon His enemies. Sprung from European roots and embraced by intellectuals and common folk alike, they became the subject of a passionate story tradition that enlarged and dramatized events in the manner of all oral legends.

The pursuit of providences was greatly reinforced by those who felt compelled to record their occurrence, including John Winthrop, longtime theocratic governor of Massachusetts Bay Colony. Two prominent New England ministers, Increase Mather and his son Cotton, became the most zealous popularizers of such tales. In 1684 the elder Mather set forth guidelines for their documentation in *An Essay for the Recording of Illustrious*

Providences, a study that Cotton Mather would later extend in his own works. The Essay defined "illustrious" providences as the most extraordinary of divinely ordained episodes: "tempests, floods, earthquakes, thunders as are unusual, strange apparitions, or whatever else shall happen that is prodigious." The directives for recording the providences—a duty over which the elder Mather would preside in order to preserve the stories for all posterity—are likened by Dorson to methods observed by modern folklore collectors.

The flip side of the providences were the witchcrafts of the devil, who poised himself with a special vengeance against this citadel of God's elect. Where faith and fear converged, the tales of remarkable providences heightened both.

A 'City upon a Hill'

In his *Book of New England Legends and Folklore in Prose and Poetry* (1901), Samuel Adams Drake called New England "the child of a superstitious mother." Dorson acknowledges that folk legends in the colonies were "for the most part carbon copies of the folklore in Tudor and Stuart England." But in grafting themselves onto a New World setting, says Dorson, the old beliefs took on a special intensity in the realm of the Puritans.

Many have credited the Mathers with projecting and magnifying this Puritan zeal. Writing at the turn of the last century, historian Samuel McChord Crothers, quoted in B.A. Botkin's *Treasury of New England Folklore,* captured the fervency of the younger Mather, who became a principal driver of the witch-hunt:

> Even Cotton Mather could not avoid a tone of pious boastfulness when he narrated the doings of New England . . .
>
> . . . New England had the most remarkable providences, the most remarkable painful preachers, the most remarkable heresies, the most remarkable witches. Even the local devils were in his judgment more enterprising than those of the old country. They had to be in order to be a match for the New England saints.

Perhaps we can gain the proper perspective on the Puritans' passion when we consider the enormous pains they undertook to escape persecution in England and establish their new covenant across the sea. Upholding that covenant was now critical, as evidenced in the lofty proclamations of a sermon delivered in 1630 by John Winthrop. Excerpted in Frances Hill's *Salem Witch Trials Reader,* the governor's words resound with poignant irony given the events that rocked Salem sixty-two years later: "We shall be as a City upon a Hill, the eyes of all people . . . upon us; so if we shall deal falsely with our God in this work we have undertaken and to cause Him to withdraw His present help from us, we shall be made a story . . . through the world . . . and . . . we shall shame the faces of . . . God's worthy servants, and cause their prayers to be turned into curses upon us."

Clearly, the task of maintaining this sinless "City upon a Hill" wrought insecurity among the Puritans, and so, says Dorson, they "searched the providences for continued evidence of God's favor or wrath." As he reveals, popular legends spurred their confidence: "Marvelous escapes from shipwreck, Indian captivity, or starvation reassured the elect that the Lord was guarding their fortunes under His watchful eye."

Cotton Mather recorded many such episodes in his 1702 chronicle titled *Magnalia Christi Americana: The Ecclesiastical History of New England.* In one renowned tale, a spectral ship appeared to an ecstatic crowd of believers in New Haven harbor in 1647. Six months earlier the heavily freighted vessel was presumed lost, after it had sailed from that harbor and never returned. According to Mather's account, quoted by Botkin, the community lost "the best part of their tradable estates . . . and sundry of their eminent persons." Mather quotes an eyewitness who believed that God had now "condescended" to present the ship's ghostly image as a means of comforting the afflicted souls of the mourners, for whom this remarkable providence affirmed not only their fallen friends' state of grace but also their own.

The Puritans also gleaned affirmation from providences in which the Lord exacted harsh punishments on the enemies of His elect. According to Dorson, the Puritans apparently relished most these tales of divine judgment. Those scourged in the tales included Indians, Quakers, and anyone else deemed blasphemous or profane. In the *Magnalia,* Cotton Mather correlates providential offenses to the Ten Commandments. He cites the destruction of the Narragansett Indian nation by a group of white settlers as retribution for the Indians' foul contempt for the Gospel. Oral legends also relayed the fate of Mary Dyer, a Quaker who was sent to the gallows around 1659; Dyer was said to have given birth to a monster, a common curse meted out to nefarious women. Even members of the elect might be struck down by plague or fatal lightning bolts for lapses ranging from the omission of prayer to adultery and murder. The *Magnalia* narrates the doom suffered by various "heretics" who quarreled with village ministers or voted to cut their salaries.

In addition to these ancient themes of reward and punishment, the providence tales incorporated a host of familiar spectacles from an Old World tradition, including apparitions, wild tempests, and corpses that communicated with blood—all magnanimous instruments of an angry but just Lord. Like the spectral ship, apparitions offered hope and solved mysteries; the apparition of a murder victim often disclosed the identity of his killer, a belief that came into play during the witch trials. The age-old notion that a corpse bleeds at the murderer's touch also surfaced abundantly in the tales.

Increase Mather devoted a whole chapter of his *Essay* to thunder and lightning, perceiving in them signs of God's consternation over the advent of secularism in Massachusetts Bay Colony. Mather declared that thunder and lightning had been observed ever since "the English did first settle these American deserts," but warned that only in recent years had they wrought "fatal and fearful slaughters . . . among us." In the *Magnalia,* Cotton Mather, too, expounded on thunder, a phenomenon that the Harvard scholar and scientist, quoted in Dorson, astutely attributed to the "laws of matter and motion [and] . . . divers weighty clouds" in collision; lightning, he postulated, derived from "subtil and sulphureos vapours." Like his erudite father, however, Cotton maintained that God was the omnipotent "first mover" of these and other natural forces.

Tales of Witchcraft

Dorson explains that "providences issued from God and witchcrafts from the devil, and they marked the tide of battle between the forces of Christ and the minions of Satan." Tales of witchery had their own illustrious elements, including menacing poltergeists, enchantments, and innocent creatures who became possessed and tormented by wicked sorcerers.

He and others have argued that the widely circulated tales of remarkable providences, wherein the Puritans sealed their identity of chosenness, created a fertile climate for witch tales and the witch-hunt. According to Dorson, "Other Protestants in New York and Virginia, and the Roman Catholics in Maryland, spoke of witchery, but the neurotic intensity of the New England witch scare . . . grew from the providential aura the Puritans gave their colonial enterprise."

Cotton Mather himself, quoted in Dorson, described the devil's vengeful plot to "destroy the kingdom of our Lord Jesus Christ" in this region that had once been "the Devil's territories" (that is, inhabited by Indians). Both Mathers were implicated as early as the mid-eighteenth-century for promoting bloodlust over witchcraft with their recordings of providence tales. Thomas Hutchinson, governor of Massachusetts Bay in 1771–74, lamented the witch debacle in his *History of the Colony of Massachusetts Bay* (1765). According to Hill, who refers to the governor as a "man of the Enlightenment," Hutchinson's chronicle suggests "that there was widespread disapproval of hanging witches until the *Illustrious Providences and Memorable Providences* [Cotton's later work] . . . changed the climate of opinion."

Providence lore undoubtedly played a part in the actions of those who spearheaded the witch scare with their clamorous cries of demonic possession. The trouble began in January 1692 when two girls, Betty Parris, the nine-year-old daughter of Salem Village minister Samuel Parris, and her cousin Abigail Williams, age eleven, began experiencing spells of bizarre behavior. In these alarming episodes, the girls convulsed and ranted incoherently. Within a month other neighborhood girls began having similar spells; soon they all began accusing various members of the community of bewitching them.

The cause of these disturbing bouts—which would continue for ten months, until the last of the condemned was pulled down from the gallows—has been the topic of much scholarly speculation and simplistic analysis. Some have theorized, at least as an initiating factor, that the girls suffered from temporary mental illness engendered by eating ergot-infected rye (a theory to which the growing conditions and agricultural practices of the time lend credence, according to Hill). Others have postulated a conspiracy theory incorporating the fierce factionalism that emerged in large part over arguments related to the Reverend Parris' salary and living arrangements.

The most prevalent theory suggests that the girls' hysteria grew from feelings of paranoia and guilt at having dabbled in fortune-telling and other occult practices with Tituba, a native of Barbados who served as the Parris family's slave (and who later confessed, albeit under dubious circumstances, to having engaged in such activities with her young charges). Perhaps one falsehood led to another as the girls struggled to cover up their forbidden deeds; perhaps one or another girl actually believed, for a period, that she had been bewitched; perchance the girls also were pressured by their elders, who were eager to avoid scandal, to reveal the cause of their afflictions. Quite possibly, too, some combination of these factors set into motion the outbursts and subsequent accusations. In any case, as Hill argues, the girls very likely started out as victims of "human suggestibility" and at some point later became perpetrators of fraud.

This view is supported by the fact that the girls had been reared abundantly on tales of providences and demonic possession. In his popular *Memorable Providences,* quoted by Hill, Mather provided a detailed description of four children who suffered "strange fits, beyond those that attend an epilepsy," as a result of a wicked washerwoman's sorcery. In addition, Hill reveals that Puritans young and old "devoured" sensational pamphlets describing similar demonic episodes, a fact that is hardly surprising, she says, since secular reading was prohibited. In his account of the witch trials, Governor Hutchinson charges that the similarities between these well-known accounts of demonic possession and those of the "supposed bewitched at Salem . . . is so exact, as to leave no room to doubt the stories had been read by the New England persons themselves, or had been told to them by others who had read them."

One case in particular demonstrates the far-reaching influence of the providence legends: that of Giles Corey, who suffered an excruciating death by pressing for his refusal to stand trial for witchcraft. According to Dorson, as the executions mounted with dreadful fury, the fatal torture of this "sturdy, uncowed farmer" aroused the people's sympathy. Some wondered whether his only crime had been his stubborn silence. Public opinion shifted, however, thanks to the actions of Thomas Putnam, a prominent citizen and the father of twelve-year-old Anne Putnam, one of the principal accusers.

The elder Putnam wrote a letter to Samuel Sewall, one of the trial judges who would later become a famous diarist. The letter reported that on the previous night, Anne had witnessed the apparition of a man who had lived with Giles Corey seventeen years earlier. This "Natural Fool"—perhaps a mentally disabled man—had died suddenly in Corey's house; his ghost now claimed that Corey had murdered him by pressing him to death, causing "clodders of blood about his heart." The apparition reported, moreover, that Corey had escaped punishment for his crime by signing a pact with the devil, whose protective powers were now being usurped by a God who meted out His just desserts—that is, a ghastly punishment precisely matching the crime. Hence, Putnam's letter, now filed by Cotton Mather as an official court document, helped sanctify Corey's execution in the eyes of the citizenry.

By the fall of 1692 the witch crisis had begun to die down. Hill explains that the girls had apparently "overreached themselves by naming as witches several prominent people, including Lady Phipps, the wife of the governor." As the executions began drawing public criticism, Phipps dissolved the witch court and later granted reprieves to the remaining accused. Twelve years later, a sullen Anne Putnam, now twenty-four years old, stood before the congregation in Salem Village Church while the minister read aloud her apology, quoted in Hill, for the "great delusion of Satan" that had caused her to "bring upon . . . this land the guilt of innocent blood."

A Dark Legacy

With his strangely circular reasoning, Mather, reflecting on the witch crisis in a 1697 chronicle excerpted by Hill, shaped the tragedies into one great remarkable providence. Oblivious to any possibility of delusion or fraud, he attributed the calamities to God's wrath on New England, ignited by the "little sorceries" practiced by its youth as well as the "grosser" witchcrafts of those condemned: "Although these diabolical divinations are more ordinarily committed perhaps all over the world than they are in the country of New England, yet, that being a country devoted unto the worship and the service of the Lord Jesus Christ above the rest of the world, He signaled His vengeance against such extraordinary dispensations, as have not often been seen in other places."

While post-Enlightenment scholars have generally dismissed Mather's arguments as the rantings of a self-righteous fanatic, his thoughts and actions have left their mark on us. In 1953, the "Red Scare" of the McCarthy era inspired playwright Arthur Miller to re-create the Salem witch-hunt in *The Crucible.* Miller remarked in a 1996 *New Yorker* article, quoted by Hill, that the play's enduring relevance lies in its core subject: "human sacrifice to the furies of fanaticism and paranoia that goes on repeating itself forever."

In our own time, such furies seem painfully present. The era of remarkable providences leaves as its dark legacy a number of lessons not easily reckoned. Now, as the world grapples with the bane of terrorism, Hill's analysis of the Salem trials strikes a contemporary nerve: "The more a group idealizes itself, its own values, and its god, the more it persecutes both other groups and the dissenters in its midst."

Today the American government is repeatedly challenged to implement policies that will prevent the current conflict from turning into a witch-hunt. Moreover, our democratic principles still face the perennial threat of an arrogant religious impulse that has never totally died out. Even now, those among us who boldly stake their claim to the mind of God—like the self-appointed prophets who construed the events of last September 11 as a kind of remarkable providence—risk the resurrection of demons similar to the forces that once ravaged a New England community. The calamities of 1692 entreat us to conquer those demons by loving our neighbor and consigning the will of Providence to the realm of mystery.

Additional Readings

B.A. Botkin, ed., *A Treasury of New England Folklore,* Crown Publishers, Inc., New York, 1967.

Richard Dorson, *American Folklore,* University of Chicago Press, Chicago, 1967.

——, *America in Legend: Folklore from the Colonial Period to the Present,* Pantheon Books, New York, 1973.

Samual Adams Drake, *A Book of New England Legends and Folklore in Prose and Poetry,* Little, Brown, 1901.

Frances Hill, *The Salem Witch Trials Reader,* DeCapo Press, Boston, 2000.

Increase Mather, *An Essay for the Recording of Remarkable Providences,* Scholars' Facsimiles and Reprints, Inc., Delmar, N.Y., 1977. Reprint of the 1684 edition printed by J. Green for J. Browning, Boston.

Critical Thinking

1. Analyze the following sentence with regard to the Salem Witch Trials: "The more a group idealizes itself, its own values, its own God, the more it persecutes both other groups and dissenters in its midst."

2. How does this apply to more recent situations such as the McCarthy era and present day attitudes toward Muslims?

HELEN MONDLOCH is a freelance writer and frequent contributor to the Culture section.

Pontiac's War

A Great Lakes Indian rebellion against the British changed the balance forever between Indian and colonist.

ALAN TAYLOR

The dead woman was one of the lowly Indian slaves known as Panis. Near Detroit in August 1762, she had helped another Pani to murder their master, a British trader. The outraged British commander in North America, Baron Jeffery Amherst, ordered them executed "with the utmost rigor and in the most publick manner." By putting them publicly to death, Amherst meant to demonstrate that the Indians had become colonial subjects answerable to British law. Earlier in the year, the French provincial authorities had surrendered their forts around the Great Lakes to the British under the Treaty of Paris that ended the Seven Years' War. Emboldened by victory, Amherst vowed to impose a harsh peace on the Indians who had so long and ably supported their French allies. The Pani man broke his leg irons and escaped, leaving the woman to hang in late April 1763.

Amherst had no idea that her execution would set off a bloody and widespread rebellion two weeks later, which would remake the continent and lead to revolution. The nearby Ottawa dreaded the British execution of an Indian as an implicit assertion that they were now subordinate. They already felt insulted by Amherst's cutting off the flood of trade goods customarily paid by the French for permission to occupy the forts. No longer could the Indians play one European nation off the other to maintain their own independence, maximize their presents, and ensure trade competition. Meanwhile British colonists poured across the frontier to take lands from them.

Amherst had no idea that his execution order would set off a bloody and widespread rebellion two weeks later.

Setting aside old rivalries, the chiefs of many nations developed a new cooperation by exchanging covert messages from Illinois to Niagara and from Pennsylvania to Lake Superior. But someone had to act first; it was to be the Ottawa, led by their chief, Pontiac, who were pressed to the point of violence by the hanging.

During the spring of 1763, the tribes surprised and captured most of the British forts around the Great Lakes and in the Ohio Valley. In June a band of Ojibwa playing lacrosse outside of Fort Michilimackinac pursued the ball into the surprised fort and slaughtered most of the garrison. Through the summer and fall, the rebels raided the Pennsylvania, Maryland, and Virginia frontiers, killing or capturing about two thousand colonists, but failing to take the three strongest British forts: Detroit, Niagara, and Fort Pitt.

Embarrassed by the expensive war, the British sought peace by making concessions. Blaming Amherst for the crisis, the crown recalled him in disgrace. The new commander, Thomas Gage, followed the conciliatory advice of the crown's northern superintendent for Indian affairs, Sir William Johnson, who understood that diplomacy was cheaper than war. By lavishing presents and deference upon the Indians, Johnson enticed them to sign several peace treaties between 1764 and 1766.

The British rebuilt their forts but had to adopt a new, more generous policy, treating the Indians as allies rather than foes. In 1766 Pontiac assured Johnson that "if you expect to keep these Posts, we will expect to have proper returns from you." Johnson and Gage covertly agreed to exempt the Great Lakes Indians from British law. During the next decade, an Indian who murdered a colonist could settle the matter by customary tribal procedure—by giving presents to the victim's kin. And the British crown laid out comparable goods to cover the Indians whom the settlers had killed.

To further mollify the Indians, the crown mandated a new boundary line along the crest of the Appalachian Mountains, in the hope that holding settlers to the east would avert conflict. The policy failed. It proved unenforceable because the British lacked the troops to patrol thousands of square miles of forest; it also angered the colonists, already less bound to the empire by the elimination of the French threat. While drawing the British and the Indians closer together, the resolution of Pontiac's Rebellion deepened the clash between the Indians and the colonists. In 1775–76, when the colonists launched their own rebellion, most of the tribes defended the British forts that they had tried to destroy under Pontiac's leadership a mere half-generation before.

Critical Thinking

1. Why did so many Indian tribes fight on the side of the British during the Revolutionary War?

2. Did the western movement of American colonists make conflict with Native Americans inevitable?

ALAN TAYLOR, winner of the 1996 Pulitzer Prize for *William Cooper's Town: Power and Persuasion on the Frontier of the Early American Republic* (Vintage Books 1995), is a professor of history at the University of California at Davis.

UNIT 2
Revolutionary America

Unit selections

Learning Outcomes

After reading this Unit, you will be able to:

• Discuss the differences between those colonists who wished to pry concessions from the British but who still wanted to remain in the empire, and those who sought nothing less than independence. How and why did the latter group prevail?

• Explain what purposes the Declaration of Independence was supposed to serve, both within the colonies and abroad.

• Analyze the immediate causes of the Boston Tea Party. What larger issues than the price of tea were involved? Were the colonists' grievances against the British justified?

Student Website
www.mhhe.com/cls

Internet References

The Early America Review
    www.earlyamerica.com/review
House of Representatives
    www.house.gov
National Center for Policy Analysis
    www.public-policy.org/web.public-policy.org/index.php
Supreme Court/Legal Information Institute
    http://supct.law.cornell.edu/supct/index.html
U.S. Senate
    www.senate.gov
The White House
    www.whitehouse.gov
The World of Benjamin Franklin
    www.fi.edu/franklin

We live in an age of instant communication. Our call to complain about a credit card may be answered by someone in India. Television satellites permit the simultaneous viewing of events all over the world. Imagine what it was like in the eighteenth century when it took weeks for a message to be delivered from London to one of the colonies, and weeks more to receive a reply. Under such circumstances the British understandably gave wide latitude to royal governors who were on the scene and who knew more about local conditions than could the bureaucrats at home. The fact that the American colonies were but part of the British world empire also discouraged attempts to micromanage their affairs.

According to economic theory at the time, an empire could be likened to an organism with each part functioning in such a way as to benefit the whole. The ideal role of a colony, aside from helping to defend the empire when the need arose, was to serve as a protected market for the mother country's manufactured goods and as a provider of raw material for its mills and factories. Because imperial rivalries often led to war, particular emphasis was placed on achieving self-sufficiency. An imperial power did not wish to be dependent on another empire for materials, especially those of strategic value such as shipbuilding materials that might be cut off if the two came into conflict.

With regard to the American colonies, those in the South most nearly fit the imperial model. Southern colonies produced goods such as cotton and tobacco that could not be grown in Great Britain, and Southerners were disinclined to become involved in activities that would compete with British manufactures. The New England and the middle colonies were another matter. Individuals in both areas often chafed at imperial restrictions that prevented them from purchasing products more cheaply from other countries or from engaging in manufacturing their own. What served to temper discontent among these colonists was the knowledge that they depended on the British army and navy against threats by other powers, most notably the French.

During the middle decades of the 1700s, London permitted the colonists to exercise a great deal of control over their own internal affairs so long as they played their designated economic role within the empire. This attitude, which came to be known as "benign neglect," meant that colonies for all practical purposes became nearly autonomous. The passage of time and the great distances involved combined to make British rule more of an abstraction than a day-to-day relationship. Most colonists never visited the mother country, and they might go months or years without seeing any overt signs of British authority. They came to regard this as the normal order of things.

This casual relationship was altered in 1763 when what the colonists called the French and Indian War came to an end after seven years of fighting. The peace brought two results that had enormous consequences. First, British acquisition of French possessions in North America meant that the military threat to the colonists had ended. Second, the war had been enormously costly to the British people who were suffering under staggering tax burdens. The government in London, taking the understandable view that the colonists ought to pay their fair share of the costs, began levying a variety of new taxes and enforcing shipping regulations that previously had been ignored.

© Library of Congress, Prints and Photographs Division (LC-USZC2-3793)

The new British crackdown represented to the colonists an unwarranted assault on the rights and privileges they had long enjoyed. "The Sparck of Rebellion" discusses the causes and results of what became known as the Boston Tea Party. Disputes over economic matters escalated into larger concerns about rights and freedoms in other areas. Many colonists who regarded themselves as loyal subjects of the crown at first looked upon the situation as a family quarrel that could be smoothed out provided there was good will on both sides. When clashes escalated instead, more and more people who now regarded themselves as "Americans" began calling for independence from the motherland. "The Gain from Thomas Paine" analyzes the impact of his pamphlet "Common Sense." The British, of course, had no intention of handing over portions of their hard-won empire to the upstarts. War became inevitable.

Most accounts of the Revolutionary War, for good reason, focus on those "patriots" who fought against the British. "One Revolution Two Wars" tells the story of the "Loyalists" who remained faithful to the crown. "God and the Founders" discusses a dispute that arose at the meeting of the first Continental Congress over whether it should be opened with a prayer. The issue was resolved in such as way as to acknowledge religion without permitting it to become divisive.

Even after the early battles of the Revolutionary War, many colonists sought a negotiated settlement with Great Britain rather than to embark on the uncertain quest for independence. They were defeated by those who wished to sever all ties with Great Britain. "A Day to Remember: July 4, 1776" tells how the Declaration of Independence emerged in its final form from the second Continental Congress. "The Patriot Who Refused to Sign the Declaration of Independence" describes the position taken by John Dickenson, a man who had opposed the British on numerous occasions in the past.

"America's Worst Winter Ever" describes the incredible hardships George Washington's troops had to endure in Morristown, New Jersey, during the winter of 1780. Very little has been written about this ordeal compared with the attention paid to the winter at

Valley Forge two years earlier. The author of this essay suggests that the reason for this disparity is that the soldiers at Valley Forge suffered quietly whereas those at Morristown threatened to mutiny.

"Franklin Saves the Peace" analyzes Benjamin Franklin's brilliant diplomatic strategies toward the end of the Revolutionary War. Despite the British surrender at Yorktown, American prospects remained dim. The Continental Congress had gone bankrupt and threatened to fall apart. Franklin managed to get the British to agree to a peace treaty and the French to extend greatly needed financial aid.

"The Sparck of Rebellion"

Badly disguised as Indians, a rowdy group of patriotic vandals kicked a revolution into motion.

DOUGLAS BRINKLEY

On the evening of December 16, 1773, in Boston, several score Americans, some badly disguised as Mohawk Indians, their faces smudged with blacksmith's coal dust, ran down to Griffin's Wharf, where they boarded three British vessels. Within three hours, the men—members of the Sons of Liberty, an intercolonial association bent on resisting British law—had cracked open more than 300 crates of English tea with hatchets and clubs, then poured the contents into Boston Harbor.

News of the "Boston Tea Party" quickly spread throughout the colonies, and other seaports soon staged their own tea parties. While tensions between the Americans and the British had simmered for the past several years, there had been few acts of outright rebellion. The tea party lit the smoldering coals of discontent and ignited events that would lead to rebellion, war, and, finally, independence.

The first bloodshed of the Revolution had occurred nearly three years earlier, on March 5, 1770. A continual source of tension was the taxes levied by the British government on the colonists. Although British Prime Minister Lord North tried to placate the colonists with a pledge of no new taxes from London, on March 5 a mob of radical Americans, unaware of the announcement, had attacked the customhouse in Boston, prompting a confrontation with British redcoats. The crowd had begun to throw hard-packed snowballs at the British sentries guarding the customhouse. Goaded beyond endurance, the soldiers began to fire, killing five people and wounding several others in what came to be known as the Boston Massacre.

But North's concessions had dampened the rebellious attitude that had been spreading through the colonies, causing a backlash among moderates who believed that the Sons of Liberty presented a greater danger to America than did British taxes and troops. By October 1770 Boston's merchants announced that they would no longer honor the patriots' boycott of British imports, and it looked as though the flames of rebellion had been snuffed out. Although some of the more ardent revolutionaries kept in contact through committees of correspondence that issued statements of colonial rights and grievances—Samuel Adams pledging that "Where there is a Spark of patriotic fire, we will enkindle it"—no more significant incidents of violence would occur until late 1773.

During this reprieve North became more concerned with Britain's economic policies than with colonial discontent. The behemoth of British international trade, the East India Company, teetered on the verge of insolvency. Because many leading British politicians were company shareholders, saving it was of particular concern to Parliament. One potential solution seemed at hand: the company's London warehouse held more than 17 million pounds of tea. If these stores could be sold, the East India Company might survive. North concocted an ingenious plan to sell the tea in America at much lower prices than those offered by smugglers such as John Hancock, who brought in goods from Dutch possessions in the West Indies. Even with the British tax, the company's tea would still be cheaper than any imported from the Dutch. If everything went according to plan, the Americans would concede England's right to tax them in order to get inexpensive tea, and the East India Company would be saved in the bargain.

But things did not go according to North's plan. The Sons of Liberty believed it reeked of subterfuge, an underhanded attempt to force the colonists to continue to pay taxes. Hancock, who hated the British as much as he loved his profits, finally saw a chance to strike at the former while preserving the latter. On December 16, 1773, he and Samuel Adams directed a group, most of whom were members of the Sons of Liberty, to board the British tea ships and destroy their cargoes.

London was shocked and angered. Parliament bristled with loose, vengeful talk of sending a large expeditionary force to America to hang the rebels, level the settlements, and erect a blockade in the Atlantic to starve the ungrateful colonists. A few voices of reason, such as Charles James Fox and Edmund Burke, rose in the House of Commons to endorse punishing those directly involved but warning against a blanket indictment of all Americans.

In March 1774 Parliament passed the Boston Port Act, mandating that the city's harbor be closed until the colony paid Britain 9,570 pounds for the lost tea. (The bill was not paid.) A firestorm of protest exploded in the colonies, where radical leaders sneered at the new laws as "the Intolerable Acts" or "the Coercive Acts." Sympathetic demonstrations took place in many cities. Samuel Adams demanded action from the committees of correspondence in the form of a complete embargo on British goods. In Virginia Thomas Jefferson burst upon the revolutionary scene when he published his *Summary View of the Rights of British America,* which took issue with Parliament's right to legislate colonial matters on the grounds that "The God who gave us life, gave us liberty at the same time."

On September 5 representatives from every colony except Georgia met in Philadelphia at what came to be known as the first Continental Congress. Radicals called for Samuel Adams's trade embargo, while moderates led by John Jay of New York and Joseph Galloway of Pennsylvania supported a strongly worded protest. All agreed that some form of action had to be taken. On behalf of the radicals, Joseph Warren of Massachusetts introduced the Suffolk Resolves, declaring the Intolerable Acts to be in violation of the colonists' rights as English citizens and urging the creation of a revolutionary colonial government. Much to his surprise, the resolves passed, if just barely. George III was infuriated at the whole business. To him, the very calling of the Continental Congress was proof of perfidy. "The New England governments are in a state of rebellion," he told North.

Gen. Thomas Gage, the British commander and now Massachusetts governor, received orders to strike a blow at the New England rebels. Gage learned of their whereabouts and sent troops to seize them and then destroy the supply facility at Concord. But that night Boston silversmith Paul Revere rode the 20 miles to Lexington to warn the radical leaders and everyone else along the way that the British were coming. When British troops reached the town on April 19, 1775, they encountered an armed force of 70, some of them "minutemen," a local militia formed by an act of the provincial congress the previous year. Tensions were high and tempers short on both sides, but as the Lexington militia's leader, Capt. John Parker, would state after the battle,

he had not intended to "make or meddle" with the British troops. In fact it was the British who were advancing to form a battle line when a shot rang out—whether it was from a British or colonial musket, no one knows to this day. At the time neither side realized it was the first blast of the American Revolution.

The lone shot was followed by volleys of bullets that killed eight and wounded 10 minutemen before the British troops marched on to Concord and burned the few supplies the Americans had left there. But on their march back to Boston, the British faced the ire of local farmers organized into a well-trained embryo army, which outnumbered the British five to one and shot at them from every house, barn, and tree. By nightfall total casualties numbered 93 colonists and 273 British soldiers, putting a grim twist on Samuel Adams's earlier exclamation to John Hancock, "What a glorious morning for America is this!"

A declaration of independence was no longer a pipe dream but a revolutionary plan in the making. From the Tea Party to the bloody fields of Concord, the thirteen colonies had proved that direct action was the surest way to free themselves from British tyranny.

Critical Thinking

1. What was the "Boston Tea Party" all about?
2. Make the best case you can for British actions during this period.

DOUGLAS BRINKLEY, author of *The American Heritage History of the United States* (Viking 1998), is a professor of history at Rice University and recently wrote *The Wilderness Warrior: Theodore Roosevelt and the Crusade for America* (Harper 2009).

The Gain from Thomas Paine

Thomas Paine, who died 200 years ago, inspired and witnessed the revolutions that gave birth to the United States and destroyed the French monarchy. A genuinely global figure, he anticipated modern ideas on human rights, atheism, and rationalism. David Nash looks at his enduring impact.

DAVID NASH

At the end of President Obama's inaugural address in January 2009, he alluded to a small passage that appeared in Thomas Paine's pamphlet *Common Sense.* Faced with an American economy wracked by nervousness and self-doubt Obama noted Paine's rallying cry that galvanised and gave hope to the despairing:

> "Let it be told to the future world . . . that in the depth of winter, when nothing but hope and virtue could survive . . . that the city and the country, alarmed at one common danger, came forth to meet [this danger]."

Unique among radicals, the 200th anniversary of the death of Thomas Paine will be marked in England, in France and across the Atlantic. This is a measure of the impact of Paine's ideas both in his own country and in parts of the world that became the centre of revolutionary political change at the end of the 18th century. Paine was perhaps fortunate to live in such invigorating times and to be able to think about them so constructively. Yet what is remarkable is that his message has been capable of speaking with immediacy to each successive generation, providing radical inspiration and comfort in troubled times. This is because Paine was a persuasive author with a gift for penetrating, lucid and memorable language. However, he was also actively participating in the revolutions he wished to inspire. Both through word and deed he could justly claim "the world is my country and my religion to do good."

Thomas Paine's origins were anything but promising. He was born in Thetford in Norfolk in 1737 and was apprenticed to his father as a corset- and stay-maker, a trade that he followed intermittently. Some commentators would not let him forget this and later a number of cartoons portrayed his radicalism as an attempt forcibly to lace the English constitution in the shape of Britannia into an uncomfortable corset. After a spell in the capital, Paine embarked on a similarly lacklustre career as an excise officer. In 1768 he moved to Lewes, but debt and disillusion with this career led to his emigration to America in 1774.

Arriving in Philadelphia with a letter of introduction from Benjamin Franklin, Paine immediately began to mix with radical journalists and to make his mark. His first venture into radical journalism, as the editor of the *Pennsylvania Magazine,* was a success. The magazine focused on American colonial opposition to high-handed British policies and it flourished. From this success, Paine distilled his arguments for American independence into one of his most important pamphlets, *Common Sense:*

> . . . many strong and striking reasons may be given, to shew, that nothing can settle our affairs so expeditiously as an open and determined declaration of independence.

The pamphlet appeared in the first month of 1776 and by the end of the year had sold 150,000 copies in 56 separate editions. So impassioned was Paine that he enlisted himself in the colonists' fight for freedom, serving as aide-de-camp to an American general. He became a trusted adviser to Washington, coming to the practical and ideological defence of the colonists with a series of pamphlets under the umbrella title of *The Crisis.* These galvanised resistance and were responsible for stabilising the army's morale when it was on the point of collapse. Paine received the gratitude of the American nation and a number of states granted him pensions or gave him gifts in kind.

In the 1780s, after the defeat of the British forces and the gaining of American independence, Paine returned to England where he briefly switched his attention to scientific and engineering projects, in particular the construction of a single-span iron bridge. The movement between political science and pure science was not uncommon among Enlightenment thinkers. Just as mechanics and magnetism were mysteries of the natural world, the study of which would yield their significance, so too could similar analysis be applied to man's political instincts and relationships.

When the French Revolution ignited in 1789 Paine, though still a political animal, was initially preoccupied with other business. However, when in November 1790 Edmund Burke published *Reflections on the Revolution in France,* his shocked reaction to the violence in Paris, a response from Paine was guaranteed. Paine must have been surprised at Burke's apparent change of heart since Burke had also supported the American colonists. The two had met in 1788 and corresponded. Paine swiftly replied with what was to be his most famous and widely read work *Rights of Man,* published in early 1791. Written in an immediate and engaging style, it was spectacularly popular, selling in the region of 250,000 copies within the space of two years. Although Paine hoped for open debate, he found himself a wanted man for views that incited revolution and unrest and which threatened the established monarchical order in England. While he continued to lecture on constitutional change, government reaction was rising against him and in September 1792 he eventually fled to France, where he had been made an honorary citizen the previous month, missing the order for his arrest at Dover by some 20 minutes. In France he was feted as a defender and promoter of liberty.

"Government by kings was first introduced into the world by the Heathens . . . It was the most prosperous invention the Devil ever set foot for the promotion of idolatry"

Thomas Paine, *Common Sense*

Paine now took a role in the revolutionary government of France and was one of only two foreigners to be elected to the country's National Convention. He was instrumental in ensuring Louis XVI was tried but also argued against his execution. Meanwhile, in England Paine had been convicted in his absence of seditious libel and this effectively ended his relationship with the land of his birth. He also fell out of favour in his adopted country, falling victim to the factionalism and political upheavals that wracked France. He was imprisoned at the end of 1793, possibly on the fabricated grounds that he was an enemy alien. Indeed, several Americans in post-revolutionary Paris petitioned for Paine's release on the grounds that he was an American citizen and was deserving of that country's protection. Narrowly escaping execution when others imprisoned with him went to the guillotine, his American connections eventually saved him and he was freed with the help of the American ambassador James Monroe on November 4th, 1794. Within a few years Paine was rehabilitated by the Convention and was voted a pension.

During the troubled early years of the 1790s Paine wrote another of his most enduring works, *The Age of Reason.* This was intended to undermine the pretensions of established religion and the structures associated with it.

Paine eventually returned to America in 1802 to discover that he was no longer a hero. He had quarrelled with Washington and this was remembered by those who revered the country's first president after his death in 1799. Paine's anti-Christian views were also extremely unpopular and were more readily recalled than his earlier exertions for the young republic. His last years were characterised by ill-health exacerbated by his periods of imprisonment. His mood was not helped by a series of small slights and the refusal of financial support which he took to be poor recompense for all he had done for the cause of American freedom. He died in 1809 a somewhat bitter man. Even his dying wish to be interred in a Quaker cemetery was refused. His funeral was a miserable affair and he was mourned by a tiny group of friends and two African-Americans who wanted to pay tribute to one of the few founding fathers of the United States who had argued against slavery.

Paine's story might have belonged solely to the 18th century were it not for the importance of his ideas, the captivating nature of his writing and its dramatic appeal. Paine's skill at producing political tracts for specific purposes was aided by his ability to write quickly when the mood took him. He was also adept at creating memorable phrases that enlivened his major works, ensuring them a wide audience. Paine's fame and legacy largely rests on the ideas and concepts conveyed in his three central works, *Common Sense, Rights of Man* and *The Age of Reason.* In a sense these represent a fitting trio since each was written in one of the three countries whose welfare preoccupied his life: America, Britain and France, and each addressed the particular problems those countries faced at a historic moment in time.

Common Sense conveys a breathless energy and appetite for change. In its first few pages Paine urges the American people to form a government from scratch, a chance almost without precedent, which the colonists should grasp with both hands since it was likely this would be their best opportunity. The fact that this would lead to conflict and a swift call to arms was a dramatic consequence that should be recognised:

> By referring the matter from argument to arms, a new era for politics is struck; a new method of thinking hath arisen. All plans, proposals . . . are like the almanacks of the last year, which though proper then, are superseded and useless now.

Paine argued that the American colonists had right and justice on their side in their struggle for independence. He also suggested that the colonies could afford such a break with Britain since they were prosperous and economically independent. However, he did not simply offer these as arguments for freedom, but went further to ask Americans to think about what they wished to do with their independence once they had gained it. Paine demonstrated that American freedom was wholly justified since the ancient, corrupt and privilege-ridden British monarchy had dispensed with fairness and justice in favour of coercing the colonies into submission.

By seeking independence the colonies could cast off such tyranny and look forward to the creation of a new society that would be governed by properly elected and accountable representatives of the people. Paine sketched the form this government might take and also suggested crucial social reforms to promote and sustain the common good. This blend of radical political ideals with concrete schemes for reforms of everyday life was a theme he would return to. Nonetheless, his immediate intention in *Common Sense* was to show how a break with the forms of organisation of the old world was essential. In so doing he unashamedly urged republican thinking: "Government by kings was first introduced into the world by Heathens", he wrote, "from whom the children of Israel copied the custom. It was the most prosperous invention the Devil ever set on foot for the promotion of idolatry." Individuals were not protected or

When Paine came to write in defence of English liberty his thoughts upon the subject were able to be couched as replies and refutations to the arguments presented in Burke's *Reflections*. Outraged and alarmed by the consequences of the French Revolution, Burke argued for a retention of what was antique, tried and tested. The destruction of the apparatus of the *ancien régime* clearly alarmed those who felt civilisation itself would be compromised in France and beyond. Burke argued that the English constitution was robust and should be defended because it had stood the test of time and had conveyed benefits upon its citizens. It operated through a system of checks and balances that always represented a control on each area of government, ensuring against overmighty subjects or tyrannical kings.

Burke argued this system had evolved organically and had thus been able to incorporate gradual change and newly developing interests. Moreover, it was capable of recognising that those who had a stake in the welfare of society were those best able to govern and those most likely to govern justly and for the benefit of the community. Burke focused upon the Glorious Revolution of 1688 as a dramatic illustration of his case. The tyrannical James II had been persuaded to abdicate in favour of the reforming William of Orange. Not surprisingly, many have seen this as a blueprint for more modern forms of conservatism that see society protected by property ownership and trust in governing institutions.

Paine challenged Burke's arguments, suggesting that they were an overblown defence of vested interests and privileges. His anger towards Burke's position played out in a carping personal attack on his writing style in the opening sections of *Rights of Man*. Paine noted that the so-called legitimate monarchy Burke was so fond of rested on the actions of an "armed banditti" led by someone who in his own land had been known as "William the Bastard". In this Paine was stoking the radical idea of the "Norman Yoke" which posited that freeborn Englishmen had been dispossessed by the Anglo-French interlopers who had taken control of the country after the Conquest of 1066.

Rejecting Burke's view that a country's government was organic and preordained by providence, Paine saw this tradition as an intolerable burden, one which fostered what he called "Old Corruption", a conspiracy in which those who produced little or nothing defrauded those who created the nation's wealth. Paine argued instead that individuals were not born to their position in life but came into the world with certain basic, indestructible rights. These gave individuals freedom to make choices about everything, including the type of government they wished for themselves. No previous generation had any right to predetermine the nature of this government or to commit subsequent generations to its will. "Man has no property in man, neither has one generation a property in the generations that are to follow", Paine wrote.

Age of Reason has attracted attention from some rather different quarters. Paine was a vociferous opponent of organised religion, writing that "All national institutions of churches, whether Jewish, Christian or Turkish [Islamic], appear to me no other than human inventions, set up to terrify and enslave mankind, and monopolise power and profit." But he was anxious to

Edmund Burke before Marie Antoinette, 1790 satire (Library of Congress)

privileged by birth or position in the society he envisaged. He answered those who wondered where America might find its future monarch with the telling phrase "the Law is King". The accountability of people for their actions was seen as a central core of the new society, a reflection of wider Enlightenment thinking that increasingly viewed humankind in terms of the individual.

Having given the American colonists the reason to fight, *The American Crisis* offered support when their backs were against the wall:

These are times that try men's souls. The summer soldier and the sunshine patriot will shrink from the service of their country; but he that stands now, deserves the love and thanks of man and woman . . . What we obtain too cheap, we esteem too lightly; it is dearness only that gives everything its value. Heaven knows how to put a proper price upon its goods; and it would be strange indeed if so celestial an article as freedom should not be highly rated.

save the French nation from its collapse into destructive anti-clericalism and atheism. Paine stopped short of holding this extreme position, seeing instead the hand of a creator at work in the universe. Much of the *Age of Reason* explored the effect of applying rational thought to the stories and accounts of the Old and New Testaments. Paine subjected these texts to the test of reason and concluded that their claim to ultimate truth was suspect. Facts appeared implausible and the textual consistency they would require if they were the truthful word of God was lacking, inviting not belief and reverence but ridicule. Importantly for his own deism Paine's *Age of Reason* pushed God and established religion further and further apart. This was apparent in his suggestion that a moral God who had created the universe as it was bore no relation to the God portrayed in the Bible, who was by turns jealous, devious and tyrannical.

Paine's ideas did not melt away after his death. For generations, his analysis made sense and inspired confidence in those whose Christian faith was wavering. *Age of Reason* has been regularly republished in cheap editions in both Britain and the United States up until the present day.

In the first years of the 19th century political radicals latched onto Paine's attacks on "Old Corruption" and how they might dismantle the privileged aristocratic rule inherited from the 18th century. These ideas spoke to artisans and small producers and laid the foundations for 19th-century examinations of wealth and its distribution, even if Paine's analysis which attacked the landed aristocrat would later be replaced by an indictment of the capitalist.

Although Paine's critique did not fit the analysis of later Marxist socialism he had an influence on social democratic ideals. With the collapse and discredit of Marxism in the years after 1989 interest in Paine, with his undiluted focus upon individual rights surrounded by a network of enabling social mechanisms, was to some extent revived. Yet some socialists never lost sight of Paine's meritocratic messages. E.P. Thompson saw him as a great publicist of the issues associated with freedom and wove him centrally into the narrative of his 1963 classic, *The Making of the English Working Class*. Thompson also acknowledged a debt to Paine for lessons about activism and writing for a purpose. Thompson's involvement in the Campaign for Nuclear Disarmament (CND) echoed Paine's desire to get actively involved in the politics he wrote about. Similarly Thompson's *Writing by Candlelight* (1980), in which he despaired about the superpowers' relentless arms race and diplomatic posturing, was written for a purpose. Thompson may equally have concluded that, like Paine, he was living through a "time to try men's souls".

Similarly Tony Benn throughout his parliamentary career as a radical socialist has often referred to Paine's punchy political language and his inspirational quest for accountable government. When Benn met world leaders he would ask them three questions: Who had elected them? Were such elections fair? And, finally, did the people have a chance of getting rid of them? All these sentiments echo Paine and reflect the influence of a voice that speaks across the centuries. It might even be argued that Paine created the idea of the global village where individuals co-exist as citizens; certainly he was the first to make the message of individual and natural rights traverse boundaries in what, for the 18th century, was the blink of an eye.

Further Readings

G. Claeys, *Thomas Paine: Social and Political Thought* (Unwin Hyman, 1989)

I. Dyck, *Citizen of the World: Essays on Thomas Paine* (St Martin's Press, 1988)

J. Fruchtman, *Thomas Paine: Apostle of Freedom* (Four Walls Eight Windows, 1994)

J. Keane, *Tom Paine: A Political Life* (Little, Brown, 1995)

B. Kuklick, *Thomas Paine* (Ashgate, 2006)

T. Paine and J. Dos Passos, *The Essential Thomas Paine* (David & Charles, 2008)

M. Philip, *Thomas Paine* (OUP, 2007)

B. Vincent, *The Transatlantic Republican: Thomas Paine and the Age of Revolutions* (Penguin, 2005)

Critical Thinking

1. Thomas Paine's *Common Sense* argued that the colonists had the right to declare independence from Great Britain. On what grounds?

2. What benefits did he believe would accrue from such a separation?

DAVID NASH is Professor of History at Oxford Brookes University and the author of *Blasphemy in the Christian World: A History* (Oxford University Press, 2007).

One Revolution Two Wars

Redcoats were not the only enemies of American Independence.

THOMAS B. ALLEN

The Declaration of Independence said that by July 1776 the time had come "for one people to dissolve the political bands which have connected them with another." But the signers knew they did not speak for "one people" but for a people including Americans who opposed the Revolution. The latter called themselves Loyalists; the Patriots called them Tories. Thousands of them armed themselves and began a civil war whose savagery shocked even battle-hardened Redcoats and Hessians. That war all but vanished in the glory that enfolds the grand story of the American Revolution. But those men and women who fought for the king were Americans, and they live on as reminders that within the tapestry known as "We the People," there will always be strands of a defiant, fervent minority.

There were truly and clearly two Americas—one governed by the British military operating from New York and the other a group of colonies in rebellion but not quite governed. Every American now had a choice: to remain a subject of King George III and thus a traitor to a new regime called the United States of America or to support the rebellion and become a traitor to the Crown.

Loyalists by the thousands signed oaths administered by Royal Governor of New York William Tryon, who traveled to territory occupied by British troops. Few refused to swear allegiance to the Crown.

And those who chose the king had another way to show their choice. In taverns and meeting halls throughout New York City, Tryon's recruiters signed up wealthy, well-connected young men for commissions in Loyalist regiments. The Loyalist recruits were issued weapons and uniforms, usually designed by their regimental commanders. Ultimately, New York would send more men into Loyalist regiments than into the Continental Army.

As soon as the British army took root on Long Island, scores of young Connecticut men sailed across the sound to enlist. Many described themselves as churchmen, Anglicans who equated service to the king with their religious beliefs. Their names appeared on the musters of the Queens Rangers, the King's American Regiment and the Prince of Wales' American Volunteers.

The latter unit was the creation of Montfort Browne, former governor of His Majesty's Bahamas. Browne fell into enemy hands in March 1776 at Nassau, New Providence, when Esek Hopkins, commander in chief of the fledgling Continental Navy, led its first amphibious operation, landing some 270 Marines and sailors from whaleboats. No one offered resistance when the Continentals cleared the island's fort of military stores—including dozens of cannon and a ton of gunpowder—and took Browne prisoner.

Despite being placed under house arrest in Middletown, Conn., Browne managed to raise the Prince of Wales' Volunteers by smuggling out invitations to Tory friends, much as he might have arranged a dinner party on New Providence. Freed in a prisoner exchange that September, Browne set up his headquarters in Flushing, Long Island, and began issuing warrants to recruiters.

In New Jersey, Cortlandt Skinner, a member of one of the state's oldest and wealthiest families and a longtime spy for the British, accepted a brigadier general's commission from British Commander in Chief William Howe. Skinner raised four 400-man battalions of volunteers. Outfitted in green—a common color choice for Loyalist units—his men became known as Skinner's Greens. They would fight battles from New Jersey to Virginia.

In Hackensack, N.J., Continental Commander in Chief General George Washington was racing time as well as British Lt. Gen. Charles Cornwallis, for the enlistments of many Continentals would soon expire. With the addition of Maj. Gen. Nathanael Greene's men—who had abandoned Fort Lee and moved down to Hackensack—Washington had a force of about 3,000 troops. But they were "much broken and dispirited men."

Washington bid farewell to Peter Zabriskie, a Patriot in whose mansion the American general had been staying. According to family tradition, Zabriskie asked the general where he was heading. And, the story goes, Washington leaned down from his saddle and whispered, "Can you keep a secret?" Zabriskie assured him that he could, and Washington replied, "I can, too."

The story underlined the Patriots' distrust of New Jersey people. "A large part of the Jerseys," Washington bitterly observed, "have given every proof of disaffection that a people can do."

As soon as Washington's troops left Hackensack, young men from local homes and outlying areas began to converge on the village green. They were Loyalists, who had secretly enlisted in the 4th Battalion of New Jersey Volunteers. Formed in 1776, it was the state's first Loyalist regiment and one of New Jersey's three major Loyalist units. Most enlisted men were Scotch-Irish; the officers scions of old Dutch families, known as the Tory Dutch.

Local Patriots, especially farmers, led worrisome lives, trying to earn a living while wondering where and when Tory raiders might strike. Sometimes the latter staged small-scale raids, picking up some cattle here, a few horses there. Or they might launch a major foraging expedition, with several hundred British troops and members of the 4th Battalion, who would first jail the Patriots and then plunder their homes and farms. The Patriots retaliated by ambushing the smaller foraging parties. Each side lost men to sudden skirmishes on this strange, unexpected battlefield called the "Neutral Ground."

As Washington retreated into New Jersey, taking the war westward, citizens' allegiance also began to turn. In parts of New Jersey, as Washington would learn, Tories were in the majority and in control. Back in New York, there were so many Loyalists in some areas that they pinned down Patriot militiamen who otherwise might be aiding Washington in New Jersey. New Jersey's government was under Patriot control, but its population included thousands of Tories.

In flight with Washington's army across New Jersey was Tom Paine, whose *Common Sense* had stirred the Rebels and thrust them toward independence. Now, in a dark December of defeats, in "times that try men's souls," when the "summer soldier and the sunshine patriot . . . shrink from the service of their country," he looked around and began to envision what he soon would write in *The Crisis*. He noted an infestation of Tories and realized the time had come when Rebels and Tories would fight each other, regardless of whether the British army was present.

Loyalists in Bergen County, New Jersey, provided the British in New York City with not only food but also spies and recruits, many of whom Tryon secretly signed up aboard the ship of the line HMS *Duchess of Gordon,* where he sought refuge in the fall of 1775 when Rebels controlled the city. Those shipboard enlistees were instructed to return home and tell no one about their enlistments until British troops arrived in New Jersey. This was an unprecedented move, going beyond usual British military doctrine by setting up advance Loyalist units in places the British army had yet to invade.

Volunteers for Loyalist regiments were given equipment and paid in British money, not in the ever-declining currency printed by the Continental Congress. Some Loyalist recruiters promised prospective soldiers a 5 guinea signing bonus, rather than the advertised 40 guineas, but added the lure of 200 acres of land, with an extra 100 acres for his wife and 50 for each child. A Patriot enlisting in a Rebel militia typically had to provide his own musket and bayonet, a sword or tomahawk, cartridge box and belt, 23 cartridges, 12 flints, a knapsack, 1 pound of gunpowder and 3 pounds of bullets in reserve. All this was an expensive outlay for a poor farmer.

Each Tory battalion had, in addition to its commissioned officers, a surgeon and a chaplain, all drawn from New York and New Jersey. The most distinguished of the chaplains was the Rev. Charles Inglis, assistant minister at Trinity Church, New York City's most esteemed Anglican congregation. Inglis was a passionate Loyalist who, after the occupation of the city, became an eloquent propagandist.

Loyalists who enlisted or were commissioned in areas under Patriot control had to make their way to safe ground in New York City or Long Island. Patriots regarded these traveling new soldiers of the Provincial Corps (as the British army collectively termed the Loyalist units) as either spies or armed foes.

New York's Ulster County fielded one of the largest Loyalist units, numbering about 50 men. In April 1777, Patriots spotted this group at Wallkill, about 85 miles north of New York City. In the brief firefight that followed, the Loyalists wounded three Rebels before slipping away. Patriots spread the alarm through the countryside, so the recruits, aided by local Loyalists, hid out in the woods or in the cellars or barns of sympathizers by day and traveled by night. They had not gone far before a militia patrol caught up to them and captured about 30. Eleven were charged with "levying war against the United States of America," five for "aiding and assisting [and] giving comfort" to the enemy. They were brought before a court-martial ordered by Brig. Gen. George Clinton, a former member of the Continental Congress and soon to become governor of New York.

The court-martial, after listening to Patriots who told of encounters with the armed Tories, resolved that "an immediate example was necessary and requisite to deter intestine enemys [*sic*] from continuing treasonable practices against the state." Fourteen men "were adjudged to suffer the pains and penalties of death by being hanged by the neck until they are dead." After hearing petitions and statements, the Convention of the Representatives of the State of New York, the provisional state government, ruled that only the leader and his assistant were to be executed. The others received various sentences, ranging from parole to confinement through war's end.

In October 1775, the New York Provincial Congress had described widespread Tory recruiting as a "conspiracy from Haverstraw [New York] to Hackensack [New Jersey]," roughly encompassing what became known as the "Neutral Ground." It stretched along both banks of the Hudson River from above the New York–New Jersey border south to Sandy Hook. In Westchester County, the term referred to the land between the British-held Bronx and American-held Peekskill. The label was ironic, for on this so-called Neutral Ground both sides would fight, not to gain territory but to forage for food and firewood, demand loyalty oaths, kill each other in skirmishes—and spy.

On this so-called Neutral Ground both sides would fight, not to gain territory but to forage for food and firewood, demand loyalty oaths, kill each other in skirmishes—and spy.

James Fenimore Cooper made famous the label "spy" in his Revolutionary War novel *The Spy,* published in 1821 with the subtitle *A Tale of the Neutral Ground.* Cooper wrote the book while living in Scarsdale, a Westchester County town that had been part of the Neutral Ground. Cooper's hero, Harvey Birch, was based in part on Enoch Crosby, a true spy of the Neutral Ground. Crosby, masquerading as a Tory recruiter, secretly worked for John Jay, chairman of the New York State Committee and Commission for Detecting and Defeating Conspiracies. Jay had the power to send Tories to the notorious "fleet prison," a string of former privateer ships anchored off Kingston, N.Y.

Cooper never publicly linked the real Crosby and the fictional Birch. But he did say that Jay had told him spy stories, and presumably Cooper learned about Loyalist activities from his wife and in-laws, descendants of a powerful Tory family. In his petition for a federal pension, Crosby told his own story, which began in the summer of 1776, when his eight-month enlistment in a Connecticut regiment ended and he found himself in the Neutral Ground. On his way to join another regiment, he met a stranger who took him to be a Tory. Realizing the stranger "intended to go to the British," Crosby instantly decided to string along the Tory. The talkative stranger told Crosby where and by whom a Loyalist regiment was secretly being raised.

Crosby took his information to a member of the Westchester County Committee of Safety. Once vetted by the committee, Crosby became an agent. Among the Tories he exposed were some 30 men recruited by Lt. Col. Beverley Robinson, son of the Tory commander of the Loyal American Regiment.

Patriot officials withheld Crosby's true status from Captain Micah Townsend of Westchester, commander of Townsend's Rangers and the principal hunter of Tory spies in the area. Townsend later detained Crosby on suspicion of spying, and Crosby genuinely escaped, risking his life to preserve his secret identity. The escape helped secure his reputation among Tories.

Crosby's real and staged escapes, under various names and in various Neutral Ground locales, did not raise suspicion. In the Neutral Ground war, many real Tories were captured and later able to escape from inept Rebel guards. But the ruse could not last forever, and after nine months as a secret agent, Crosby enlisted in a new regiment and served as a sergeant on regular service.

While Crosby was hunting Tories in the Neutral Ground, a small but brutal civil war was heating up between New Jersey's Dutch Tories and Dutch Rebels. British forces, Loyalist volunteers and Patriot militiamen took turns at hit-and-run raids, keeping residents jittery. No one knew when a Tory or a Rebel might shatter the night. Bergen County was particularly divided due to a schism in the Dutch Reformed Church—some congregations supporting American-trained clergy and the Rebels, others backing more conservative factions and the Loyalists.

In New York's Orange County, which bordered New Jersey on the north, a militia leader reported that "matters are come to such a height that they who are friends of the American cause must (for their own safety) be cautious how they speak in public" and that some of those "who have been active in favor of our cause, will soon (if an opportunity offers) be carried down to New York." Patriots carried down to New York City faced confinement in a prison ship or in the Sugar House, a sugar refinery turned dank stone prison.

Matters are come to such a height that they who are friends of the American cause must . . . be cautious how they speak in public, for I make no doubt but we have often spies amongst us

At anchor in a small Brooklyn bay rode several British prison ships—dreaded dungeons for thousands of captured Continental Army soldiers, Rebel militiamen and Patriot civilians. Joshua Loring, commissary of American prisoners, showed little interest in his captives, except as a source of income from contractors' kickbacks. Prisoners were jammed into holds, where so many died of disease or starvation that each day guards would open the hatches and yell down, "Turn out your dead!" The British either tossed the bodies into the sea or buried them ashore in shallow graves. Estimates of the total death toll ran as high as 11,500.

The Sugar House, although less notorious than the prison ships, was as horrifying. "Cold and famine were now our destiny," a survivor wrote. "Not a pane of glass, nor even a board to a single window in the house, and no fire but once in three days to cook our small allowance of provision. There was a scene that truly tried body and soul. Old shoes were bought and eaten with as much relish as a pig or a turkey; a beef bone of 4 or 5 ounces, after it was picked clean, was sold by the British guard for as many coppers."

Thomas Jones, who lived in New York and knew Loring, wrote that "[he] was determined to make the most of his commission and, by appropriating to his own use nearly two-thirds of the rations allowed the prisoners, he actually starved to death about 300 of the poor wretches before an exchange took place." Noting General Howe's fondness for Mrs. Loring, Jones wrote, "Joshua made no objections. He fingered the cash; the general enjoyed Madam."

As Cornwallis pursued Washington across New Jersey, a guerrilla war was declared. In a special order, Howe empowered his own troops, including Loyalist forces, to treat their retreating foes as outlaws: "Small straggling parties, not dressed like soldiers and without officers, not being admissible in war, who presume to molest or fire upon soldiers, or peaceable inhabitants of the country, will be immediately hanged without tryal [sic] as assassins."

Vicious little actions, hardly noticed in the chronicles of the Washington–Cornwallis saga, took uncounted lives. Kidnappings were all too common. One claimed a famous Patriot as its victim: Richard Stockton, a member of Congress and a signer of the Declaration of Independence.

As the British set their sights on Princeton in late 1776, Stockton fled with his family to a friend's house in Monmouth County, N.J., where Loyalists soon betrayed him to the British. A descendant of an old and distinguished Quaker family and a member of Princeton's first graduating class, Stockton was a prize catch. The British jailed him as a criminal, mistreating him until he broke under duress and signed an oath of allegiance to the king—an act that disavowed his signature on the Declaration.

Sometime around mid-March, 1777, Stockton was released without any public explanation and returned to his magnificent Princeton home. The mansion—Cornwallis' headquarters during his occupation of Princeton—lay in ruin. Tories blamed Hessians for making firewood of fine furniture, drinking their way through the wine cellar, bayoneting family portraits and stealing Stockton's horses and livestock. But the Tories had led looters to hastily buried silver plate and other treasures. Stockton had returned from captivity under a cloud, as congressmen possessed unpublicized knowledge that he had foresworn the Declaration. Later, an ailing Stockton tried to recant his oath to the king by signing oaths of adjuration and allegiance prescribed by the New Jersey legislature as a way to redeem tainted citizens.

Tryon, New York's provincial governor, participated in the Neutral Ground guerrilla conflict by organizing a troop of Westchester County cavalry raiders under the command of Colonel James De Lancey. The cavalry soon became known as De Lancey's Cow-boys, a dubious term with origins in cattle and horse rustling.

A typical raid, as reported in an October 1777 edition of the Loyalist *New-York Gazette:* "Last Sunday Colonel James De Lancey, with 60 of his Westchester Light Horse, went from Kingsbridge to the White Plains, where they took from the Rebels 44 barrels of flour, two ox teams, near 100 head of black cattle and 300 fat sheep and hogs."

The following month Patriots savagely retaliated against De Lancey's Cow-boys by attacking Oliver De Lancey's country home at Blooming dale, about seven miles up the Hudson from New York City. As victims later recounted, strange noises awakened De Lancey's teenage daughter Charlotte and her friend Elizabeth Floyd, daughter of a Long Island Loyalist. They ran to a window, opened it and shouted, "Who is there?" From below a gruff voice answered, "Put in your heads, you bitches!"

Men entered the house from front and rear and, prodding the teenagers with muskets, ordered them out of the house. The girls fled to a swampy wood and spent the night "sitting upon their feet to keep a little warmth in them" and watching the house burn to the ground. The elder Mrs. De Lancey managed to hobble from the house and hid in a dog kennel beneath the stoop.

De Lancey's horsemen also foraged on Long Island, the site of frequent clashes between mounted Tories and amphibious Rebels. Earlier that year, in one of the biggest whaleboat attacks, Colonel Return Jonathan Meigs led 170 Patriots across the Sound to Sag Harbor and pounced on the foragers, killing six of them. After burning the Tory boats and forage, Meigs returned to Connecticut with 90 prisoners. The entire operation took 25 hours. Congress rewarded Meigs with a commendation and a sword.

Governor Tryon, commissioned a major general of provincials, waged what he called "desolation warfare," sending the Cow-boys and Emmerich's Chasseurs, another mounted Loyalist unit, to torch the homes of leading Patriots. In the fall of 1777, during one of the horsemen's harshest raids, they burned down sections of Tarrytown, a Hudson River community split between Loyalists and Patriots.

German native Andreas Emmerich's Chasseurs unit added a European element to Loyalist guerrilla forces. Emmerich had emigrated to England, then to America, where he secured a lieutenant colonel's commission and raised the corps of light troops named after himself. About half of his officers were Europeans and did not get along with their American counterparts.

Mutinous American officers asked Lt. Gen. Sir Henry Clinton (brother of Governor George Clinton) to court-martial Emmerich "for employing soldiers, negroes, and [Tory] refugees, to robb [*sic*] and plunder the inhabitants of Westchester County" and for taking a cut of the loot from the looters. The officers also accused him of "imprisoning, whipping and cruelly beating the inhabitants without cause or tryal [*sic*]," selling British army horses and stealing from the army payroll. Clinton sidestepped the court-martial by transferring the officers into other regiments. Emmerich somehow managed to keep his colonelcy.

For a time Continental Army Maj. Gen. Israel Putnam kept his headquarters at Peekskill, N.Y. Putnam tried to rein in Tory raiders by sending Colonel Meigs down the Hudson to attack the pillagers. Rumors circulated that, in retaliation, Tryon planned to kidnap Putnam. Coincidentally, Patriots reported a sudden surge of Tory spies in the area. One of them, a Loyalist lieutenant named Nathan Palmer, managed to infiltrate the headquarters encampment. Soldiers discovered him, and Putnam brought him before a court-martial to be tried as a spy. Tryon tried to intercede, threatening Putnam personally if he did not release Palmer.

Putnam replied:

Sir—Nathan Palmer, a lieutenant in your king's service, was taken in my camp as a spy, he was tried as a spy, he was condemned as a spy, and you may rest assured, sir, that he shall be hanged as a spy.

I have the honor to be, &c,

Israel Putnam

PS. Afternoon. He is hanged.

Critical Thinking

1. Who were the "Loyalists"? Why did they believe they were the true patriots?

2. In what ways did the Loyalists contribute to the British war effort?

For further reading, Tom Allen recommends: *The Price of Loyalty,* by Catherine S. Crary, and *Divided Loyalties,* by Richard M. Ketchum.

From *Military History,* June 20, 2011, pp. 58–63. Copyright © 2011 by Weider History Group. Reprinted by permission.

God and the Founders

Battles over faith and freedom may seem never-ending, but a new book, '*American Gospel*,' argues that history illuminates how religion can shape the nation without dividing it.

JON MEACHAM

America's first fight was over faith. As the Founding Fathers gathered for the inaugural session of the Continental Congress on Tuesday, September 6, 1774, at Carpenters' Hall in Philadelphia, Thomas Cushing, a lawyer from Boston, moved that the delegates begin with a prayer. Both John Jay of New York and John Rutledge, a rich lawyer-planter from South Carolina, objected. Their reasoning, John Adams wrote his wife, Abigail, was that "because we were so divided in religious sentiments"—the Congress included Episcopalians, Congregationalists, Presbyterians, and others—"we could not join in the same act of worship." The objection had the power to set a secular tone in public life at the outset of the American political experience.

Things could have gone either way. Samuel Adams of Boston spoke up. "Mr. S. Adams arose and said he was no bigot, and could hear a prayer from a gentleman of piety and virtue who was at the same time a friend to his country," wrote John Adams. "He was a stranger in Philadelphia, but had heard that Mr. Duche (Dushay they pronounce it) deserved that character, and therefore he moved that Mr. Duche, an Episcopal clergyman, might be desired to read prayers to the Congress tomorrow morning." Then, in a declarative nine-word sentence, John Adams recorded the birth of what Benjamin Franklin called America's public religion: "The motion was seconded and passed in the affirmative."

The next morning the Reverend Duche appeared, dressed in clerical garb. As it happened, the psalm assigned to be read that day by Episcopalians was the 35th. The delegates had heard rumors—later proved to be unfounded—that the British were storming Boston; everything seemed to be hanging in the balance. In the hall, with the Continental Army under attack from the world's mightiest empire, the priest read from the psalm: "'Plead my cause, O Lord, with them that strive with me: fight against them that fight against me.'"

Fight against them that fight against me: John Adams was at once stunned and moved. "I never saw a greater effect upon an audience," he told Abigail. "It seemed as if Heaven had ordained that Psalm to be read on that morning." Adams long tingled from the moment—the close quarters of the room, the mental vision in every delegate's head of the patriots supposedly facing fire to the north, and, with Duche's words, the summoning of divine blessing and guidance on what they believed to be the cause of freedom.

As it was in the beginning, so it has been since: an American acknowledgment of God in the public sphere, with men of good will struggling to be reverent yet tolerant and ecumenical. That the Founding Fathers debated whether to open the American saga with prayer is wonderfully fitting, for their conflicts are our conflicts, their dilemmas our dilemmas. Largely faithful, they knew religious wars had long been a destructive force in the lives of nations, and they had no wish to repeat the mistakes of the world they were rebelling against. And yet they bowed their heads.

More than two centuries on, as millions of Americans observe Passover and commemorate Easter next week, the role of faith in public life is a subject of particularly pitched debate. From stem cells and science to the Supreme Court, from foreign policy and the 2008 presidential campaign to evangelical "Justice Sundays," the question of God and politics generates much heat but little light. Some Americans think the country has strayed too far from God; others fear that religious zealots (from the White House to the school board) are waging holy war on American liberty; and many, if not most, seem to believe that we are a nation hopelessly divided between believers and secularists.

History suggests, though, that there is hope, for we have been fighting these battles from our earliest days and yet the American experiment endures.

However dominant in terms of numbers, Christianity is only a thread in the American tapestry—it is not the whole tapestry. The God who is spoken of and called on and prayed to in the public sphere is an essential character in the American drama, but He is not specifically God the Father or the God of Abraham. The right's contention that we are a "Christian nation" that has fallen from pure origins and can achieve redemption by some kind of return to Christian values is based on wishful thinking, not convincing historical argument. Writing to the Hebrew Congregation in Newport, Rhode Island, in 1790, George Washington assured his Jewish countrymen that the American government "gives to bigotry no sanction." In a treaty with the Muslim nation of Tripoli initiated by Washington, completed by John Adams, and ratified by the Senate in 1797, we declared "the Government of the United States is not, in any sense, founded on the Christian religion. . . ." The Founders also knew the nation would grow ever more diverse; in Virginia, Thomas Jefferson's bill for religious freedom was "meant to comprehend, within the mantle of its protection, the Jew and the Gentile, the Christian and the Mahometan, the Hindoo and infidel of every denomination." And thank God—or, if you choose, thank the Founders—that it did indeed.

In Jefferson's words, 'The God who gave us life gave us liberty'—including the liberty to believe or not to believe.

Understanding the past may help us move forward. When the subject is faith in the public square, secularists reflexively point to the Jeffersonian "wall of separation between church and state" as though the conversation should end there; many conservative Christians defend their forays into the political arena by citing the Founders, as though Washington, Adams, Jefferson, and Franklin were cheerful Christian soldiers. Yet to claim that religion has only recently become a political force in the United States is uninformed and unhistorical; in practice, the "wall" of separation is not a very tall one. Equally wrongheaded is the tendency of conservative believers to portray the Founding Fathers as apostles in knee britches.

The great good news about America—the American gospel, if you will—is that religion shapes the life of the nation without strangling it. Driven by a sense of providence and an acute appreciation of the fallibility of humankind, the Founders made a nation in which faith should not be singled out for special help or particular harm. The balance between the promise of the Declaration of Independence, with its evocation of divine origins and destiny, and the practicalities of the Constitution, with its checks on extremism, remains the most brilliant of American successes.

The Founding Fathers and presidents down the ages have believed in a God who brought forth the heavens and the earth, and who gave humankind the liberty to believe in Him or not, to love Him or not, to obey Him or not. God had created man with free will, for love coerced is no love at all, only submission. That is why the religious should be on the front lines of defending freedom of religion.

Our finest hours—the Revolutionary War, abolition, the expansion of the rights of women, hot and cold wars against terror and tyranny, Martin Luther King Jr.'s battle against Jim Crow—can partly be traced to religious ideas about liberty, justice, and charity. Yet theology and scripture have also been used to justify our worst hours—from enslaving people based on the color of their skin to treating women as second-class citizens.

Still, Jefferson's Declaration of independence grounded America's most fundamental human rights in the divine, as the gift of "Nature's God." The most unconventional of believers, Jefferson was no conservative Christian; he once went through the Gospels with a razor to excise the parts he found implausible. ("I am of a sect by myself, as far as I know," he remarked.) And yet he believed that "the God who gave us life gave us liberty at the same time," and to Jefferson, the "Creator" invested the individual with rights no human power could ever take away. The Founders, however, resolutely refused to evoke sectarian—specifically Christian—imagery: the God of the Declaration is largely the God of Deism, an Enlightenment-era vision of the divine in which the Lord is a Creator figure who works in the world through providence. The Founding Fathers rejected an attempt to rewrite the Preamble of the Constitution to say the nation was dependent on God, and from the Lincoln administration forward presidents and Congresses refused to support a "Christian Amendment" that would have acknowledged Jesus to be the "Ruler among the nations."

At the same time, the early American leaders were not absolute secularists. They wanted God in American public life, but in a way that was unifying, not divisive. They were politicians and philosophers, sages and warriors, churchmen and doubters. While Jefferson edited the Gospels, Franklin rendered the Lord's Prayer into the 18th-century vernacular, but his piety had its limits: he recalled falling asleep in a Quaker meeting house on his first day in Philadelphia. All were devoted to liberty, but most kept slaves. All were devoted to virtue, but many led complex—the religious would say sinful—private lives.

The Founders understood that theocracy was tyranny, but they did not feel they could—or should—try to banish religion from public life altogether. Washington improvised "So help me, God" at the conclusion of the first presidential oath and kissed the Bible on which he had sworn it. Abraham Lincoln issued the Emancipation Proclamation, he privately told his cabinet, because he had struck a deal with "my Maker" that he would free the slaves if the Union forces triumphed at Antietam. The only public statement Franklin D. Roosevelt made on D-Day 1944 was to read a prayer he had written drawing on the 1928 Episcopal Book of Common Prayer. John Kennedy said that "on earth, God's work must truly be our own," and Ronald Reagan was not afraid to say that he saw the world as a struggle between light and dark, calling the Soviet empire "the focus of evil in the modern world." George W. Bush credits Billy Graham with saving him from a life of drift and drink, and once said that Christ was his favorite philosopher.

Sectarian language, however, can be risky. In a sermon preached on the day George Washington left Philadelphia to take command of the Continental Army, an Episcopal priest said: "Religion and liberty must flourish or fall together in America. We pray that both may be perpetual." The battle to preserve faith and freedom has been a long one, and rages still: keeping religion and politics in proper balance requires eternal vigilance.

Our best chance of summoning what Lincoln called "the better angels of our nature" may lie in recovering the true sense and spirit of the Founding era and its leaders, for they emerged from a time of trial with a moral creed which, while imperfect, averted the worst experiences of other nations. In that history lies our hope.

Critical Thinking

1. Is it fair to call the United States a Christian nation? On what grounds?

2. How did the Founding Fathers deal with this potentially divisive issue?

A Day to Remember: July 4, 1776

CHARLES PHILLIPS

On Independence Day every year, millions of Americans turn out for myriad parades, public and backyard barbecues, concerts of patriotically stirring music and spectacular pyrotechnic displays, and they do so to celebrate the day on which we declared our independence from Great Britain.

But America did not declare its independence on July 4, 1776. That happened two days earlier, when the second Continental Congress approved a resolution stating that "these United Colonies are, and of a right ought to be, free and independent States." The resolution itself had first been introduced back on June 7, when Virginia's Richard Henry Lee rose in the sweltering heat of the Congress' Philadelphia meeting house to propose an action many delegates had been anticipating—and not a few dreading—since the opening shots of the American Revolution at Lexington and Concord.

Lee asked for a newly declared independent government, one that could form alliances and draw up a plan for confederation of the separate Colonies. The need for some such move had become increasingly clear during the last year, especially to George Washington, if for no other reason than as a rallying cry for his troops. The Virginia soldier chosen by Congress to general its Continental Army languished in New York, short of supplies, short of men and short of morale while facing the threat of a massive British offensive.

But many in Congress, some sent with express instructions against independence, were leery of Lee's proposal despite the growing sentiment for independence stirred up by such rebel rousers as Boston's Samuel Adams and the recent émigré Thomas Paine. Paine's political pamphlet, Common Sense, openly attacked King George III and quickly became a bestseller in the Colonies; Paine donated the proceeds to the Continental Congress. Lee was so closely associated with Adams that critics charged Lee with representing Massachusetts better than he did Virginia. On the night before Lee offered up his resolution, Adams boasted to friends that Lee's resolution would decide the most important issue Americans ever had faced.

Little wonder that the more conservative delegates, men such as Pennsylvania's John Dickinson and South Carolina's Edward Rutledge, balked. Treaty with France? Surely. Draw up articles of confederation? Fine. But why declare independence? The Colonies, they argued, were not even sure they could achieve it. To declare their intent now would serve merely to warn the British, and hence forearm them. Dickinson wanted to postpone the discussion—forever if he could—and he managed to muster support for three weeks of delay. At the same time, Lee's faction won approval to appoint committees to spend the three weeks preparing drafts on each point of the resolution.

Sam Adams was named to the committee writing articles of confederation. His cousin, John Adams, a great talker, headed the committee drawing up a treaty with France. John Adams also was appointed to help draft a declaration of independence along with the inevitable choice, the celebrated author and internationally renowned philosopher Benjamin Franklin. Congress also assigned New York conservative Robert Livingston and Connecticut Yankee Roger Sherman to the committee but fell to arguing over a fifth member.

Southern delegates wanted one of their own to achieve balance. But many in Congress disfavored the two obvious candidates, considering Lee too radical and his fellow Virginian Benjamin Harrison too conservative. There was another Virginian, however, a 32-year-old lanky, red-haired newcomer named Thomas Jefferson, who had a reputation for learning in both literature and science. Though he seemed to shrink from public speaking, the Adamses liked him, and John pushed so effectively for Jefferson to join the committee that, when the votes were counted, he tallied more than anyone else.

Franklin's health was clearly failing, and he wouldn't be able to draft the declaration. Adams was busy with what he probably considered at the time the more important work of drafting an alliance with France (though he would live to regret such an opinion). Neither Livingston nor Sherman evidently had the desire nor, most probably, the talent to pen the kind of document needed. To Jefferson, then, with his reputation as a fine writer, fell the task of drafting a resolution whose language, edited and approved by the committee, would be acceptable to all the delegates.

Jefferson worried about his sick wife, Martha, back home and longed to be in Virginia working on the colony's new constitution, then under debate in Williamsburg. Nevertheless, he set to work and quickly produced what, given the time constraints, was a remarkable document. A justification to the world of the action being taken by Britain's American Colonies assembled in Congress, the declaration was part bill of indictment and part philosophical assertion, the latter an incisive summary of Whig political thought.

With the document's key sentiments much inspired, say some, by such Scottish Enlightenment figures as Francis Hutcheson, and its thinking much influenced, say many, by John Locke's Two Treatises of Government, the declaration summarized common notions expressed everywhere in the Colonies in those days. Many such notions could be found in numerous local proclamations. Especially relevant, because it was on Jefferson's mind, was the language of the new Virginia constitution with its elaborate Bill of Rights penned by his cohort, George Mason. Indeed, Jefferson's assignment was to capture the sense of the current rebellion in the 13 Colonies and distill its essence into a single document.

In this, as everyone recognized, he greatly succeeded, though he did not do it alone. Despite what Jefferson himself later wrote, and John Adams, too, when age and the glory of the Revolution led them both to embroider their accounts, the committee reviewed Jefferson's work, and then he ran it past both senior members, Adams and Franklin. He incorporated suggested changes before writing a clean copy. Still, Jefferson personally was quite proud of the draft he laid before Congress on June 28, 1776.

On the first day of July, with Jefferson's manuscript at the ready, the delegates once more took up Richard Henry Lee's resolution to openly declare independence. Lee was off in Virginia, where Jefferson wished to be, so he was not there to see John Dickinson's last protest seemingly cow the Congress, before an eloquent rebuttal by a determined John Adams carried the motion. Congress on July 2 without dissent voted that the American Colonies were from that day forward free and independent states.

That evening an exultant John Adams wrote home to his wife that July 2, 1776, would "be celebrated by succeeding generations as the great anniversary festival." It was his day of triumph, as well he knew, and he imagined it "commemorated as the day of deliverance by acts of devotion to God Almighty. It ought to be solemnized with pomp and parade, with shows, games, sports, guns, bells, bonfires and illuminations from one end of the continent to the other, from this time forward forever more."

Congress immediately turned to consider Jefferson's document. It would have to serve as a sort of early version of a press release—an explanation that could be disseminated at home and around the globe by broadside and to be read aloud at gatherings. Its statements had to inspire the troops and garner public support for the action Congress had just taken. Not surprisingly, Congress paid close attention to the document's language.

The delegates took the time to spruce it up a little and edit out what they found objectionable. In general the Congress was fine with the vague sentiments of the early paragraphs that have since become the cornerstone of American democracy: "We hold these truths to be self-evident: that all men are created equal, that they are endowed by their Creator with certain unalienable rights; that among these are life, liberty, and the pursuit of happiness; that to secure these rights, governments are instituted among men, deriving their just powers from the consent of the governed" and so on.

What the delegates were more interested in, however, and what they saw as the meat of the document, were the more concrete declarations. For years, they had based their resistance to England on the belief they were not fighting a divinely chosen king, but his ministers and parliament. But during the previous 14 months the Crown had waged war on them, and King George had declared the Colonials in rebellion, that is, outside his protection. Common Sense had gotten them used to thinking of the king as that "royal brute" and this document was supposed to explain why he should be so considered. Thus Jefferson had produced a catalog of George III's tyrannies as its heart and soul.

Congress at length struck out some sentimental language in which Jefferson tried to paint the British people as brothers indifferent to American suffering and a paragraph where he ran on about the glories the two people might otherwise have realized together. But more substantive changes were especially telling. Among George's crimes, Jefferson had listed the slave trade, contending that the king had "waged a cruel war against human nature" by assaulting a "distant people" and carrying them into slavery in "another hemisphere." This was too much for Jefferson's fellow slaveholders in the South, especially South Carolina, and certain Yankee traders who had made fortunes from what Jefferson called the "execrable commerce." Together, representatives of these Southern and Yankee interests deleted the section.

For the rest, the delegates also changed a word here and there, usually improving some of the hasty writing. They worked the language of Lee's resolution into the conclusion and added a reference to the Almighty, which Jefferson would have been happier without. "And," the document now concluded, "for support of this Declaration, with a firm reliance on the protection of divine Providence, we mutually pledge to each other our lives, our fortunes, and our sacred honor."

None of this sat well with the young author. He made a copy of the declaration as he submitted it and the "mutilated" version Congress approved, and sent both to his friends and colleagues, including Richard Henry Lee, who agreed the original was superior, though most historians since have concluded otherwise.

In any case, after more than two days of sometimes-heated debate, on July 4, 1776, the Continental Congress approved the revised document that explained its declaration of independence of July 2. The approval was not immediately unanimous, since the New York delegates had to await instructions from home and did not assent until July 9. At the time of approval, Congress ordered the document "authenticated and printed," and that copies "be sent to several assemblies, conventions and committees, or councils of safety, and to the several commanding officers of the Continental troops; that it be proclaimed in each of the United States, and at the head of the army." If any delegates officially signed the approved document on the glorious Fourth, they were President John Hancock and Secretary Charles Thomson.

Within days the printed document was circulated across the land. The declaration was read aloud in the yard of the Philadelphia State House to much loud cheering. When New York formally accepted the declaration, the state celebrated by releasing its debtors from prison; Baltimoreans burned George III in effigy; the citizens of Savannah, Ga., gave him an official funeral.

The carefully engrossed copy we see reproduced everywhere today, with its large handwritten calligraphy, was not ordered prepared until July 19, and it was not ready for signing until August 2. Delegates probably dropped in throughout the summer to add their names to the bottom of the document. In any event, since the proceedings were secret and the signers all in danger of their lives, the names were not broadcast.

Even before the engrossed copy was ready, and long before it was signed by all, the legends were growing—how Hancock signed the parchment so boldly that John Bull could read his name without spectacles. How Hancock remarked to Benjamin Franklin: "We must be unanimous. There must be no pulling in different ways. We must all hang together." And how Franklin replied, "Yes, we must indeed all hang together, or most assuredly we shall hang separately."

Almost from the start, confusion blurred the distinctions between the July 2 act of declaring independence, the July 4 approval of the document explaining that declaration, and the actual signing of the Declaration. That confusion might best be represented by John Trumbull's famous 1819 painting, which now hangs in the Capitol Rotunda and appears on the back of the $2 bill. Thought by most Americans to represent the signing of the Declaration of Independence, it was intended by Trumbull "to preserve the resemblance of the men who were the authors of this memorable act," not to portray a specific day or moment in our history.

The Fourth of July was not as widely celebrated during the heat of the Revolutionary War or during the period of confederation as it was afterward. It became much more popular as a national holiday in the wake of the War of 1812 and with the passing of the Revolutionary generation.

And then four score and seven years after that July 4, 1776, President Abraham Lincoln used the lofty ideas and flowing words of the Declaration as the basis for his famous Gettysburg Address to sanctify the country's sacrifices in the Civil War and, in so doing, he redefined the nation as a land of equality for all. Ever since, those early paragraphs of the Declaration, with their beautifully phrased abstractions and sentiments, have served virtually to define the American faith in secular democracy. His well-chosen remarks and our July 4 Independence Day celebrations, like Trumbull's painting, honor not a single event but, rather, the democratic process, the ideas proposed back then and the men who directly made them possible.

Critical Thinking

1. Analyze the statement that the Declaration Independence was a "sort of early version of a press release."
2. To whom did the statement "all men are created equal" apply?

CHARLES PHILLIPS is the author and co-author of numerous works of history and biography. These include *What Every American Should Know About American History, The Macmillan Dictionary of Military Biography; Cops, Crooks, and Criminologists; What Everyone Should Know About the Twentieth Century, Tyrants, Dictators, and Despots;* and *The Wages of History.* Phillips has edited several multivolume historical reference works, including the *Encyclopedia of the American West, the Encyclopedia of War* and *the Encyclopedia of Historical Treaties.*

From *American History,* August 2006, pp. 15–16. Copyright © 2006 by Weider History Group. Reprinted by permission.

The Patriot Who Refused to Sign the Declaration of Independence

John Dickinson believed it was foolhardy to brave the storm of war in a skiff made of paper.

JACK RAKOVE

In the decade before the American colonies declared independence, no patriot enjoyed greater renown than John Dickinson. In 1765 he helped lead opposition to the Stamp Act, Britain's first effort to get colonists to cover part of the mounting cost of empire through taxes on paper and printed materials. Then, after Parliament rescinded the Stamp Act but levied a new set of taxes on paint, paper, lead and tea with the Townshend Duties of 1767, Dickinson galvanized colonial resistance by penning *Letters From a Pennsylvania Farmer,* a series of impassioned broadsides widely read on both sides of the Atlantic. He even set his political sentiments to music, borrowing the melody from a popular Royal Navy chantey for his stirring "Liberty Song," which included the refrain: "Not as slaves, but as freemen our money we'll give."

Yet on July 1, 1776, as his colleagues in the Continental Congress prepared to declare independence from Britain, Dickinson offered a resounding dissent. Deathly pale and thin as a rail, the celebrated Pennsylvania Farmer chided his fellow delegates for daring to "brave the storm in a skiff made of paper." He argued that France and Spain might be tempted to attack rather than support an independent American nation. He also noted that many differences among the colonies had yet to be resolved and could lead to civil war. When Congress adopted a nearly unanimous resolution the next day to sever ties with Britain, Dickinson abstained from the vote, knowing full well that he had delivered "the finishing Blow to my once too great, and my Integrity considered, now too diminish'd Popularity."

Indeed, following his refusal to support and sign the Declaration of Independence, Dickinson fell into political eclipse. And 234 years later, the key role he played in

American resistance as the leader of a bloc of moderates who favored reconciliation rather than confrontation with Britain well into 1776 is largely forgotten or misunderstood.

To be a moderate on the eve of the American Revolution did not mean simply occupying some midpoint on a political line, while extremists on either side railed against each other in frenzied passion. Moderation for Dickinson and other members of the founding generation was an attitude in its own right, a way of thinking coolly and analytically about difficult political choices. The key decision that moderates ultimately faced was whether the dangers of going to war against Britain outweighed all the real benefits they understood colonists would still enjoy should they remain the king's loyal subjects.

Dickinson and his moderate cohorts were prudent men of property, rather than creatures of politics and ideology. Unlike the strong-willed distant cousins who were leaders of the patriot resistance in Massachusetts—John and Samuel Adams—moderates were not inclined to suspect that the British government was in the hands of liberty-abhorring conspirators. Instead, they held out hope well into 1776 that their brethren across the Atlantic would come to their senses and realize that any effort to rule the colonies by force, or to deny colonists their due rights of self-government, was doomed to failure. They were also the kind of men British officials believed would choose the benefits of empire over sympathy for suffering Massachusetts, the colony that King George III, his chief minister, Lord North, and a docile Parliament set out to punish after the Boston Tea Party of December 1773. Just as the British expected the Coercive Acts that Parliament directed against Massachusetts in 1774 would teach the other colonies the costs of defying the empire, so they assumed that sober men of property, with a lot at stake, would never endorse the hot-headed proceedings of the mob in Boston. Yet in practice, exactly the opposite happened. Dickinson and other moderates ultimately proved they were true patriots intent on vindicating American rights.

Men of moderate views could be found throughout America. But in terms of the politics of resistance, the heartland of moderation lay in the middle colonies of New York, New Jersey, Pennsylvania and Maryland. Unlike Massachusetts, where a single ethnic group of English descent predominated and religious differences were still confined within the Calvinist tradition, the middle colonies were a diverse melting pot where differences in religion, ethnicity and language heightened the potential for social unrest. This was also the region where a modern vision of economic development that depended on attracting free immigrants and harnessing their productive energy shaped the political view of moderate leaders. Let Samuel Adams indulge his quaint notion of turning the town of Boston into "the Christian Sparta." The wealthy landowners of the middle colonies, as well as the merchant entrepreneurs in the bustling ports of Philadelphia, New York, Annapolis and Baltimore, knew that the small joys and comforts of consumption fit the American temperament better than Spartan self-denial and that British capital could help fund many a venture from which well-placed Americans could derive a healthy profit.

Dickinson, the son of a land baron whose estate included 12,000 acres in Maryland and Delaware, studied law at the Inns of Court of London as a young man in the 1750s. An early trip to the House of Lords left him distinctly unimpressed. The nobility, he scoffed in a letter to his parents, "drest in their common cloths" and looked to be "the most ordinary men I have ever faced." When Thomas Penn, the proprietor of Pennsylvania, took him to St. James for a royal birthday celebration, Dickinson was struck by the banal embarrassment King George II showed, staring at his feet and mumbling polite greetings to his guests. Yet Dickinson's memory of his sojourn in cosmopolitan London laid a foundation for his lasting commitment to reconciliation on the eve of the Revolution. Whatever the social differences between the colonies and the mother country, England was a dynamic, expanding and intellectually creative society. Like many moderates in the mid-1770s, Dickinson believed that the surest road to American prosperity lay in a continued alliance with the great empire of the Atlantic.

Another source of Dickinson's moderation lay in his complicated relation to the Quaker faith. Dickinson's parents were both Quakers and so was his wife, Mary Norris,

the daughter and heiress of a wealthy Pennsylvania merchant and landowner. Dickinson balked at actively identifying with the Friends and their commitment to pacifism. Even though he worried as much as any moderate about resistance escalating to all-out warfare, he supported the militant measures Congress began pursuing once the British military clampdown began in earnest. But at the same time, Dickinson's rearing and close involvement with Quaker culture left him with an ingrained sense of his moral duty to seek a peaceful solution to the conflict.

Dickinson's Quaker rearing left him with an ingrained sense of his moral duty to seek a peaceful solution to the crisis.

Dickinson's belief that the colonists should make every feasible effort at negotiation was reinforced by his doubts as to whether a harmonious American nation could ever be built on the foundation of opposition to British misrule. Remove the superintending authority of empire, Dickinson worried, and Americans would quickly fall into internecine conflicts of their own.

General outrage swept through the colonies after the British closed the port of Boston in May 1774. When the First Continental Congress convened in Philadelphia in September in response to the crisis, John and Samuel Adams immediately began courting Dickinson, whose writings as the Pennsylvania Farmer made him one of the few men renowned across the colonies. At their first meeting, John Adams wrote in his diary, Dickinson arrived in "his coach with four beautiful horses" and "Gave us some Account of his late ill Health and his present Gout. . . . He is a Shadow—tall, but slender as a Reed—pale as ashes. One would think at first Sight that he could not live a Month. Yet upon a more attentive Inspection, he looks as if the Springs of Life were strong enough to last many Years." Dickinson threw his support behind a compact among the colonies to boycott British goods, but by the time the Congress ended in late October, Adams was growing exasperated with his sense of moderation. "Mr. Dickinson is very modest, delicate, and timid," Adams wrote.

Dickinson and other moderates shared an underlying belief with more radical patriots that the colonists' claims to be immune from the control of Parliament rested on vital principles of self-government. Even if Boston had gone too far with its tea party, the essential American pleas were just. But the moderates also desperately hoped that the situation in Massachusetts would not spin out of control before the government in London had a fair opportunity to gauge the depth of American resistance and respond to the protests Congress submitted to the Crown.

That commitment to conciliation was sorely tested after fighting broke out at Lexington and Concord on April 19, 1775. "What human Policy can divine the Prudence of precipitating Us into these shocking Scenes," Dickinson wrote to Arthur Lee, the younger, London-based brother of Richard Henry Lee of Virginia. "Why have we been so rashly declared Rebels?" Why had General Thomas Gage, the royal governor of Massachusetts, not waited "till the sense of another Congress could be collected?" Some members were already resolved "to have strain'd every nerve of that Meeting, to attempt bringing the unhappy Dispute to Terms of Accommodation," he observed. "But what Topicks of Reconciliation" could they now propose to their countrymen, what "Reason to hope that those Ministers & Representatives will not be supported throughout the Tragedy as They have been thro the first Act?"

Dickinson's despair was one mark of the raw emotions triggered throughout the colonies as the news of war spread. Another was the tumultuous reception that the Massachusetts delegates to the Second Continental Congress enjoyed en route to Philadelphia in early May. The welcome they received in New York amazed John Hancock, the delegation's newest member, to the point of embarrassment. "Persons appearing with proper Harnesses insisted upon taking out my Horses and Dragging me into and through the City," he wrote. Meanwhile no matter what direction delegations from other colonies took as they headed to Philadelphia, they were hailed by well-turned-out contingents of militia. The rampant martial fervor of the spring of 1775 reflected a groundswell of opinion that Britain had provoked the eruption in Massachusetts and Americans could not flinch from the consequences.

Military preparations became the first task of the new session of Congress, and a week passed before any attempts to negotiate with the British were discussed. Many delegates felt that the time for reconciliation had already passed. The king and his ministers had received an "olive branch" petition from the First Congress and ignored it. Dickinson delivered a heartfelt speech in which he acknowledged that the colonists must "prepare vigorously for War," but argued that they still owed the mother country another chance. "We have not yet tasted deeply of that bitter Cup called the Fortunes of War," he said. Any number of events, from battlefield reverses to the disillusion that would come to a "peaceable People jaded out with the tedium of Civil Discords" could eventually tear the colonies apart.

John Jay: A Moderate Destined for Political Greatness

John Jay, a New York lawyer, was a political novice when he went to the First Continental Congress in September 1774. Yet at age 28, he was not shy about making his opinions known, taking the floor three times during the first heated debate about colonial rights. It was Jay who moved that Congress offer to pay for the tea dumped in Boston Harbor on December 16,1773. Although he believed in the moral rightness of the American cause, he argued vehemently that it was more prudent to seek conciliation than war with Britain. When independence was declared, Jay was in New York helping his wife, Sally, recover after the birth of their first son. But when he returned to Congress in December 1778, he was immediately elected its president. Jay later was the key American negotiator in the peace talks of 1782, served as a postwar secretary for foreign affairs, contributed five essays on the Constitution to *The Federalist Papers* and was the first chief justice of the Supreme Court.

— Jack Rakove

Dickinson and other moderates prevailed on a reluctant Congress to draft a second olive branch petition to George III. The debate, recorded only in the diary of Silas Deane of Connecticut, was heated. Dickinson insisted not only that Congress should petition anew, but that it should also send a delegation to London, authorized to initiate negotiations. Dickinson's plans were attacked "with spirit" by Thomas Mifflin of Pennsylvania and Richard Henry Lee of Virginia, and dismissed with "utmost contempt" by John Rutledge of South Carolina, who declared that "Lord North has given Us his Ultimatum, with which We cannot agree." At one point tempers rose so high that half of Congress walked out.

In the end, the mission idea was rejected, but Congress did agree to a second olive branch petition for the sake of unity, which, John Adams and others sneered, was an exercise in futility.

Over the next two months Congress took a series of steps that effectively committed the colonies to war. In mid-June, it began the process of transforming the provisional forces outside Boston into the Continental Army to be led by George Washington. Washington and his entourage left for Boston on June 23, having learned the day before of the carnage at the Battle of Bunker Hill on June 17. Meanwhile, John Adams chafed at the moderates' diversionary measures. His frustration came to a boil in late July. "A certain great Fortune and piddling Genius whose Fame has been trumpeted so loudly has given a silly Cast to our whole Doings," he grumbled in a letter to James Warren, president of the Massachusetts Provincial

Robert Morris: A Calculated Risk Taker with Deep Pockets

"Great Britain may thank herself for this event," wrote Robert Morris as the Continental Congress moved toward declaring independence. As a wealthy Philadelphia merchant for whom the calculation of risk was a daily concern, Morris held out hope that the British would relent in their stubborn refusal to negotiate and save the colonies from risking everything by going to war. When he joined John Dickinson in abstaining from the initial vote on independence on July 2, 1776, he expected to be drummed out of the Pennsylvania delegation. Instead he was invited back. He signed the Declaration and was soon running the three-member executive committee Congress left in Philadelphia in December when the British advance across New Jersey sent the delegates scurrying to Baltimore for safety. Morris combined patriotism and profit-seeking during the war, increasing his personal wealth by selling the cargo of English ships seized by American privateers. In 1781 Congress made him its superintendent of finance, and Morris sketched the first serious plan for giving the national government its own independent sources of revenue.

— Jack Rakove

Congress. Adams obviously meant Dickinson, and he then went on to complain that "the Farmer's" insistence on a second petition to the king was retarding other measures Congress should be taking. But a British patrol vessel intercepted the letter and sent it on to Boston, where General Gage was all too happy to publish it and enjoy the embarrassment it caused.

John Adams called Dickinson a 'piddling Genius' whose moderation 'has given a silly Cast to our whole Doings.'

Adams received his comeuppance when Congress reconvened in September 1775. Walking to the State House in the morning, he encountered Dickinson on the street. "We met, and passed near enough to touch Elbows," John wrote to his wife, Abigail, back home. "He passed without moving his Hat, or Head and Hand. I bowed and pulled off my Hat. He passed haughtily by. The Cause of his Offence, is the Letter no doubt which Gage has printed." Adams was loath to admit that his original letter to Warren had been as unfair in its judgment as it was ill-advised in its shipment. Dickinson sincerely thought a second petition was necessary, not only to give the British government a last chance to relent, but also to convince Americans that their Congress was acting prudently.

Having pushed so hard to give peace a chance, Dickinson felt equally obliged to honor his other commitment to "prepare vigorously for War." He joined Thomas Jefferson, a newly arrived Virginia delegate, in drafting the Declaration of the Causes and Necessity for Taking up Arms, which Washington was instructed to publish upon his arrival in Boston. Meanwhile Dickinson undertook another ploy to try to slow the mobilization for war. He wrote a set of resolutions, which the Pennsylvania legislature adopted, barring its delegates from approving a vote for independence. The instructions were a barrier to separation, but only so long as many Americans throughout the colonies hesitated to take the final step.

That reluctance began to crack after Thomas Paine published *Common Sense* in January 1776. Paine's flair for the well-turned phrase is exemplified in his wry rejoinder to the claim that America still needed British protection: "Small islands not capable of protecting themselves, are the proper objects for kingdoms to take under their care, but there is something very absurd, in supposing a continent to be perpetually governed by an island." Public support for more radical action was further kindled as Britain indicated that repression was the only policy it would pursue. Township and county meetings across the country adopted pro-independence resolutions that began flowing into Congress, as John Adams remarked, "like a torrent." In May 1776, Adams and other delegates moved to break the logjam in Pennsylvania by instructing the colonies to form new governments, drawing their authority directly from the people. Soon the authority of the Pennsylvania legislature collapsed, and the instructions Dickinson had drawn lost their political force.

In the weeks leading up to the vote on independence, Dickinson chaired the committee that Congress appointed to draft Articles of Confederation for a new republican government. Meanwhile, he remained the last major foe of separation. Other moderates, like Robert Morris of Pennsylvania and John Jay of New York, (see box p. 63) also had hoped that independence could be postponed. Yet having grown increasingly disenchanted with Britain's intransigence, they accepted the congressional consensus and redoubled their commitment to active participation in "the cause."

Only Dickinson went his own way. Perhaps his Quaker upbringing left him with a strong conscience that prevented him from endorsing the decision that others now found inevitable. Perhaps his youthful memories of England still swayed him. In either case, conscience and political judgment led him to resist independence at the final moment, and to surrender the celebrity and influence he had enjoyed over the past decade.

Pennsylvania's new government quickly dismissed Dickinson from the congressional delegation. In the months that followed, he took command of a Pennsylvania militia battalion and led it to camp at Elizabethtown, N.J. But Dickinson had become an opportune target of criticism for the radicals who now dominated Pennsylvania politics. When they got hold of a letter he had written advising his brother Philemon, a general of the Delaware militia, not to accept Continental money, their campaign became a near vendetta against the state's once eminent leader. Dickinson protested that he meant only that Philemon should not keep money in the field, but in the political upheaval of 1776 and 1777, the fiercely independent Dickinson was left with few allies who could help him salvage his reputation.

Eventually Dickinson returned to public life. In January 1779, he was appointed a delegate for Delaware to the Continental Congress, where he signed the final version of the Articles of Confederation he had drafted. He subsequently served as president of the Delaware General Assembly for two years before returning to the fray in Pennsylvania, where he was elected president of the Supreme Executive Council and General Assembly in November 1782. He was also a delegate to the Constitutional Convention in 1787 and promoted the resulting framework for the young republic in a series of essays written under the pen name Fabius.

Despite his accomplishments late in life, Dickinson never fully escaped the stigma of his opposition to independence. But upon hearing of Dickinson's death in February 1808, Thomas Jefferson, for one, penned a glowing tribute: "A more estimable man, or truer patriot, could not have left us," Jefferson wrote. "Among the first of the advocates for the rights of his country when assailed by Great Britain, he continued to the last the orthodox advocate of the true principles of our new government, and his name will be consecrated in history as one of the great worthies of the Revolution."

A few years later, even John Adams sounded a note of admiration for his erst-while adversary in a letter to Jefferson. "There was a little Aristocracy, among Us, of Talents and Letters," Adams wrote. "Mr. Dickinson was *primus inter pares*"—first among equals.

Critical Thinking

1. Analyze John Dickenson's contribution to the patriot cause prior to the Declaration of Independence.
2. On what grounds did he oppose independence?

Historian **JACK RAKOVE** won a Pulitzer Prize for *Original Meanings: Politics and Ideas in the Making of the Constitution*. His most recent book is *Revolutionaries: A New History of the Invention of America*.

America's Worst Winter Ever
And Why Mythmakers Chose to Forget It

RAY RAPHAEL

In January 1780, fighting in the Revolutionary War came to a standstill as Mother Nature transformed America into a frigid hell. For the only time in recorded history, all of the saltwater inlets, harbors and sounds of the Atlantic coastal plain, from North Carolina northeastward, froze over and remained closed to navigation for a period of a month or more. Sleighs, not boats, carried cords of firewood across New York Harbor from New Jersey to Manhattan. The upper Chesapeake Bay in Maryland and the York and James rivers in Virginia turned to ice. In Philadelphia, the daily *high* temperature topped the freezing mark only once during the month of January, prompting Timothy Matlack, the patriot who had inscribed the official copy of the Declaration of Independence, to complain that "the ink now freezes in my pen within five feet of the fire in my parlour, at 4 o'clock in the afternoon."

The weather took an especially harsh toll on the 7,460 patriot troops holed up with General George Washington in Morristown, N.J., a strategic site 30 miles west of the British command in New York City. On January 3, the encampment was engulfed by "one of the most tremendous snowstorms ever remembered," army surgeon James Thacher wrote in his journal. "No man could endure its violence many minutes without danger of his life." When tents blew off, soldiers were "buried like sheep under the snow . . . almost smothered in the storm." The weather made it impossible to get supplies to the men, many of whom had no coats, shirts or shoes and were on the verge of starvation. "For a Fortnight past the Troops both Officers and Men, have been almost perishing for want," George Washington wrote in a letter to civilian officials dated January 8.

The winter at Valley Forge two years earlier is a celebrated part of America's Revolutionary mythology, while its sequel at Morristown is now largely forgotten. And therein lies a paradoxical tale. The climatic conditions the Continental Army faced at Valley Forge and a year later at Middlebrook, N.J., were mild compared to those they endured at Morristown during the harshest winter in American history. "Those who have only been in Valley Forge and Middlebrook during the last two winters, but have not tasted the cruelties of this one, know not what it is to suffer," wrote Baron Johann de Kalb, a German soldier who served as a major general in the Continental Army.

So why do we remember Valley Forge and not Morristown? The answer, in a nutshell, is that Valley Forge better fits the triumphal story of the Revolution passed down from generation to generation, while Morristown is viewed as an embarrassment. At Valley Forge, the story goes, soldiers suffered quietly and patiently. They remained true to their leader. At Morristown, on the other hand, they threatened to mutiny.

Nobody celebrated either Valley Forge or Morristown during the Revolution itself. The sorry plight of the poor men and teenage boys who comprised the Continental Army was a guarded secret, kept from the British, who must not know their vulnerability, and from the French, who might deny aid to a weak ally. Further, the failure of civilian governments to supply troops was just that—a failure, not to be publicized.

By the early 19th century, however, writers who looked to the Revolutionary War to inspire a new wave of patriotism developed a storyline that transformed the troubled winter at Valley Forge into a source of pride. Soldiers had endured their sufferings without complaint, drilled obediently under the instructions of Baron Von Steuben, and emerged strong and ready to fight. "How strong must have been their love of liberty?" Salma Hale asked rhetorically in a romanticized history written in 1822 for schoolchildren as well as adults. If Valley Forge was the low point of the war, the story went, it was also the turning point. After that, things got better.

For the Valley Forge story to work, a climatically normal winter was transformed into one of the most severe—something akin to the one soldiers experienced at Morristown two years later. Historical memory of Morristown was conveniently suppressed, in part because it revealed that the soldiers' hardships continued throughout the war, virtually unabated. Even worse, Morristown afforded clear proof that the soldiers' suffering was not always so silent.

At Morristown "we were absolutely, literally starved," Private Joseph Plumb Martin recalled after the war. "I do solemnly declare that I did not put a single morsel of victuals into my mouth for four days and as many nights, except a little black birch bark which I gnawed off a stick of wood, if that can be called victuals. I saw several of the men roast their old shoes and eat them, and I was afterwards informed by one of the officers' waiters, that some of the officers killed and ate a favorite little dog that belonged to one of them."

The prospect of mass desertions worried General Nathanael Greene. "Here we are surrounded with Snow banks, and it is well we are, for if it was good for traveling, I believe the Soldiers would take up their pack and march," he reported on January 5. The following day, Greene's fears were almost realized. "The Army is upon the eve of disbanding for want of Provisions," he wrote. Although the army did not break up as Greene feared, men deserted almost daily, about at the same rate as they had been leaving throughout the war, including the winter spent at Valley Forge. The rest toughed it out, and most of those survived.

Ironically, the largest threat to the continued existence of the Continental Army came in the spring, with the passing of harsh weather. Then, soldiers hoped for better fare at their mess, and they did get some food—but not with the regularity they would have preferred. The army's supply line continued to experience periodic lapses. When nature was to blame, soldiers found the inner strength to endure, but when human error was the cause of their discontent, they were less tolerant. So when little meat turned to no meat in the middle of May, many felt it was time to force the issue.

"The men were now exasperated beyond endurance; they could not stand it any longer," Private Martin recalled. "They saw no alternative but to starve to death, or break up the army, give all up and go home. This was a hard matter for the soldiers to think upon. They were truly patriotic, they loved their country, and they had already suffered everything short of death in its cause; and now, after such extreme hardships to give up all was too much, but to starve to death was too much also. What was to be done?"

Finally, on May 25, Martin and his fellow soldiers in the Connecticut line snapped. It was a "pleasant day," Martin recalled, but as the troops paraded, they started "growling like soreheaded dogs." That evening they disregarded their officers and acted "contrary to their orders." When an officer called one of the soldiers "a mutinous rascal," the rebel defiantly pounded the ground with his musket and called out, "Who will parade with me?" Martin reported the response: "The whole regiment immediately fell in and formed" with the dissenter. Then another regiment joined in, and they both started marching to the beat of the drums—without orders. Officers who stepped in to quell the incipient mutiny found bayonets pointed at their chests. Meanwhile, the defiant troops continued parading and "venting our spleen at our country and government, then at our officers, and then at ourselves for our imbecility in staying there and starving in detail for an ungrateful people who did not care what became of us."

Two days after the men had so dramatically registered their complaints, a shipment of pork and 30 head of cattle arrived in camp. The immediate crisis was over, but a series of escalating protests occurred in and around Morristown the following winter as well. Throughout the war, American soldiers did not suffer in silence, as the Valley Forge myth suggests. They kept themselves fed and alive however they could, even when that meant speaking out. By remembering Morristown, we acknowledge the can-do, rambunctious spirit that characterized Revolutionary soldiers and helped them carry on.

Critical Thinking

1. Compare the conditions George Washington's troops faced at Valley Forge with those they faced at Morristown two years later.
2. Analyze the reasons why the situation at Morristown has received so little attention in the history books.

RAY RAPHAEL is the author of *Founding Myths* and *Founders*.

From *American History*, April 2010, pp. 52–55. Copyright © 2010 by Weider History Group. Reprinted by permission.

Franklin Saves the Peace

Shrewd negotiating by America's premier diplomat forced the British to sign an anything-but-inevitable peace treaty with the new republic.

THOMAS FLEMING

Most people think that George Washington's 1781 triumph at York town ended the American Revolution. In fact the victory set in motion a peace process that imperiled America's independence as virulently as the invading armies George III had dispatched in 1776. No one understood this more clearly than 76-year-old Benjamin Franklin, the American ambassador to Paris.

Franklin had first rescued the infant nation in 1777, when he persuaded the wary French to sign a treaty of alliance, a coup that revived the Revolution's faltering hopes and transformed the contest into a global war from the West Indies to distant India. But as 1782 began, France was teetering on bankruptcy and ready to sign a face-saving peace that might not include American independence. As an ominous sign of their intentions, French diplomats had browbeaten the Continental Congress into ordering Franklin to keep them fully informed of any peace negotiations and to sign nothing without French approval.

The British were not merely indifferent to America's independence; they were still set on aborting it. When peace negotiations began in April 1782, Lord Shelburne, the double-talking secretary of state for home, Irish, and American affairs, simultaneously dispatched letters to his generals in America, directing them to send envoys to the leaders of the 13 rebel states, urging each to consider reconciliation with the mother country. The commission of the British envoy to the peace conference, Richard Oswald, omitted any mention of a United States of America. Instead Oswald was empowered to negotiate "with the said colonies or any of them or any parts thereof."

Redoubling Franklin's problems was the knowledge that his country was totally bankrupt and dependent on loans and gifts from France to keep even a semblance of a government and army operating. His desk was thick with frantic dispatches from Congress begging him to raise another multimillion-dollar loan. He also had to deal with his fellow negotiators, John Adams and John Jay, contentious lawyers determined to take no advice or guidance, from France, no matter how instructed by Congress.

The ambassador decided to live dangerously. While maintaining a cordial face-to-face relationship with the French foreign secretary, the Comte de Vergennes, he told Adams and Jay: "I am of your opinion and will go on [with the negotiations] without consulting this court."

The Americans swiftly agreed on four goals: certifying their "full and complete" independence; designating the Mississippi River as the western border of the United States; determining the new nation's northern and southern borders; and obtaining the right to fish on the Grand Banks of Newfoundland, vital to New England's prosperity.

The British began the talks in an aggressive mood. In the West Indies, the Royal Navy had recently shattered the French fleet that had trapped Cornwallis at Yorktown. In India their army had routed the French and their allies. But the Americans blustered the British into conceding all four of their primary goals.

Finally, just one thorny issue divided the antagonists: compensation for the colonial loyalists who had lost millions of dollars' worth of property to confiscation by the rebel states, a concession the British were determined to exact. For a few days the conference teetered on the edge of dissolution. Franklin broke the impasse with a letter that he read aloud, which declared that the Americans would insist on a counterclaim for all the damages the British army and navy had inflicted since 1775. He listed burned towns such as Norfolk, Virginia, and Falmouth, Massachusetts, and reviewed the thousands of wrecked and looted houses in New Jersey, Pennsylvania, and the southern states. The British negotiators sat in stunned silence for a long time—and then agreed to sign.

Now came the great unanswered question: what would the French do when Franklin sent them the treaty? For several days nothing but frigid silence emanated from Versailles. Undeterred, Franklin visited Vergennes, who icily informed him there was "little in [the document] that could be agreeable to the king."

Franklin pointed out that, in the preface, the Americans said they would not sign a final treaty until France had negotiated a satisfactory separate peace. He then asked Vergennes for another loan of 6 million livres—a considerable sum considering the tiny American economy of 1782.

Franklin heard nothing for a week, whereupon he wrote a letter telling Vergennes that the appropriately named American vessel *Washington* was going home with a copy of the treaty. Could it possibly also carry the first installment of the 6-million-livre loan? "I fear Congress will be reduced to despair when they find that nothing is yet obtained."

Vergennes fired off a furious letter denouncing the Americans' conduct as a betrayal of France. Franklin pondered this missive for 36 hours and replied with his ultimate diplomatic master-piece. He admitted that, in failing to inform France about the treaty in advance, America had neglected a point of *bienséance* (propriety), but not out of any lack of respect for King Louis XVI, "whom we all love and honor." Should Vergennes refuse any further assistance, "the whole edifice sinks to the ground immediately."

Franklin would hold the *Washington* until the end of the week, awaiting the foreign minister's reply. Then came a threat, deliv-ered in the same smooth style, and underlined: *the English, I just now learn, flatter themselves that they have already divided us*—all the more reason to hope that this "little misunderstanding" would be kept secret until George III and his followers found themselves "totally mistaken."

A few days later the *Washington* sailed for America with 600,000 gold livres in her hold. The ship's passport was made out to the United States of America and contained George III's signature—his first written acknowledgment of American independence.

That was when everyone realized the United States was going to happen.

Critical Thinking

1. Despite the British defeat at Yorktown, the American cause seemed very much in doubt at the time. Why?

2. Analyze Benjamin Franklin's role in playing off the British against the French to achieve peace and to secure French financial aid.

THOMAS FLEMING, author most recently of *The Intimate Lives of the Founding Fathers* (Harper 2009), has served as president of the Society of American Historians.

UNIT 3

National Consolidation and Expansion

Unit Selections

Learning Outcomes

After reading this Unit, you will be able to:

- Analyze the debates during the Constitutional Convention over what kind of government the various delegates hoped to create.

- Discuss the opposing visions of Alexander Hamilton and Thomas Jefferson as the new government got underway, and how this played out following the Wall Street crash of 1792.

- Consider the notion that the Louisiana Purchase constituted a "revolution" in American history. Discuss the ramifications of this acquisition at the time and for the future.

- Compare and contrast the status of white women and black slaves during the early Republic. White women obviously had certain advantages, but what were the similarities?

- Trace the evolution of manufacturing in the United States from the home, to the shop, to the factory. Evaluate the impact of Samuel Slater's systems on the lives of workers.

Student Website

www.mhhe.com/cls

Internet References

Consortium for Political and Social Research
www.icpsr.umich.edu

Department of State
www.state.gov

Mystic Seaport
http://amistad.mysticseaport.org

Social Influence Website
www.workingpsychology.com/intro.html

University of Virginia Library
www.lib.virginia.edu/exhibits/lewis_clark

Women in America
http://xroads.virginia.edu/~HYPER/DETOC/FEM

Women of the West
www.wowmuseum.org

The individuals who wrote the American Constitution could only provide a general structure under which the government would work. Those involved in actually making the system function had to venture into uncharted territory. There were no blueprints as to exactly which body had what powers, or what their relationships with one another would be. If disputes arose, which individual or group would act as arbiter? "Madison's Radical Agenda" analyzes the proposals put forward by James Madison, rightly considered the "father" of the Constitution. He was defeated on some issues and had to compromise on others, but got most of what he sought.

Officials during the first few years after 1789 were conscious that practically everything they did would be regarded as setting precedents for the future. Even such apparently trivial matters as the proper form of addressing the president caused debate. From hindsight of more than 200 years, it is difficult to appreciate how tentative they had to be in establishing this newborn government.

The most fundamental question about the Constitution arose over whether it should be interpreted strictly or loosely. That is, should governmental powers be limited to those expressly granted in the document, or were there "implied" powers that could be exercised as long as they were not expressly prohibited? Many of the disputes were argued on principles, but the truth is that most individuals were trying to promote programs that would benefit the interests they represented. "Wall Street's First Collapse" describes the first financial crisis of the new government and how it came to embody the struggle between Thomas Jefferson and Alexander Hamilton over the future course of the United States.

George Washington, as first president, was a towering figure who provided a stabilizing presence during the seemingly endless squabbles. He believed that he served the entire nation, and that there was no need for political parties (he disdainfully referred to them as "factions"), which he regarded as divisive. Despite his disapproval, nascent political parties did begin to develop fairly early on in his first administration. By the time of John Adams' presidency the party system was almost fully established. "Adams Appoints Marshall" analyzes Chief Justice John Marshall's brilliant performance in steering between the parties to establish the Supreme Court as a coequal arm of the federal government.

The United States already was a large country by 1803, stretching from the Atlantic Ocean to the Mississippi River. Some said it was too large. Propertied Easterners complained that the western migration lowered property values and raised wages, and they feared population shifts would weaken their section's influence in government. Others thought that the great distances involved might cause the system to fly apart, given the primitive means of communication and transportation at the time. When Thomas Jefferson had the unexpected opportunity to double the nation's size by purchasing the huge Louisiana Territory, as discussed in "The Revolution of 1803," he altered the course of American history.

What we call the War of 1812 did not go well for the United States at first. It began the conflict with virtually no army and

a tiny navy. Except for a few isolated naval victories, American forces suffered defeat after defeat. Indeed, by the summer of 1814, British forces invaded Washington, DC, and burned the White House. Through all of this, Dolley Madison stood like a rock. "I have always been an advocate of fighting when assailed," she said, and acted as a kind of cheerleader to keep up morale in the face of such adversity. Her heroic performance in saving national treasures from British seizure made her a symbol of patriotism.

At the time the Declaration of Independence was being created, Abigail Adams wrote to her husband that if "perticular care and attention is not paid to the Laidies," women "will not hold ourselves bound by any laws in which we have no voice or representation." Nothing came of her entreaty at the time, but years later she showed her disdain for laws that privileged men by writing her own will in which she left most of her assets to other women. It had no legal standing but, to his credit, John carried it out to the letter.

The invention of the cotton gin in the 1790s had an enormous impact on the institution of slavery. "The Everyday Life of Enslaved People in the Antebellum South" describes how it resulted in the large-scale migration of slaves from the Upper South to states such as Mississippi and Alabama. Working conditions in the new areas were extremely harsh and many slave families were broken apart in the process.

Manufacturing in the early years moved from the home to small shops, which in turn gave way to factories employing relatively large numbers of people. At first some owners of these factories attempted to retain customs and relationships characteristic of the earlier period. In time these efforts were abandoned and workers were treated impersonally as just another cost of production. "Liberty Is Exploitation: The Force of Tradition in Early Manufacturing" describes this process.

Much has been written about the Underground Railway and its part in spiriting runaway slaves to freedom. "From Detroit to the Promised Land" describes an 1833 case in which a Detroit judge ruled that a young black couple which had escaped must be returned to their owners. His decision touched off a number of riots in Detroit. When both husband and wife escaped again, this time to Canada, demands were made that they be extradited back to the United States. These demands were refused, thereby serving notice that Canada would be a refuge for slaves seeking their freedom.

Accounts of settling the west have changed over the years. Once presented in the relatively simplistic terms of "taming the wilderness," the westward movement was far more complicated than the story of hardy pioneers overcoming obstacles. One of the tragedies of this expansion was the forcible removal of the so-called Southern Tribes from their homes to west of the Mississippi. "The Holdouts" tells the story of two leaders of the Cherokee Nation and how they tried to prevent the Cherokees from being displaced. The election of Andrew Jackson to the presidency dashed their hopes.

The Mexican War, dubbed "Polk's War," because President James K. Polk had precipitated it, was a divisive and costly conflict. When a treaty with Mexico was negotiated that was very favorable to the United States, Polk submitted it to the Senate for approval. The problem was that the President had earlier dismissed the man who negotiated the treaty. "Polk's Peace" describes how the treaty finally went through and thereby increased the size of the United States by nearly one-third.

Madison's Radical Agenda

A diminutive, persuasive Virginian hijacked the Constitutional Convention and forced the moderates to accept a national government with vastly expanded powers.

Joseph J. Ellis

On May 5, 1787, James Madison arrived in Philadelphia. He was a diminutive young Virginian—about five feet three inches tall, 130 pounds, 36 years old—who, it so happened, had thought more deeply about the political problems posed by the current government under the Articles of Confederation than any other American.

Madison had concluded that the loose confederation of states was about to collapse, that the full promise of the American Revolution—liberty and order in an independent American nation—was about to be lost, and that only the wholesale replacement of the feeble authority of the Articles by a central government of vastly expanded, truly national powers could rescue the infant republic from anarchy, possible civil and petty interstate war, and the likely return of predatory European powers to American soil. He was poised to make that case to the other delegates gathering in Philadelphia for the Constitutional Convention, most of whom were moderates who presumed they were there to reform the Articles, whereas Madison was one of the radical minority that regarded the Articles as beyond repair and wished to replace them altogether.

He quickly discovered that he was the beneficiary of two pieces of good luck. The first was that the leading member of the Virginia delegation—none other than George Washington—agreed with his political diagnosis. "The situation of the General Government (if it can be called a government) is shaken to its foundations," Washington declared upon his arrival in Philadelphia. "In a word, it is at an end, and unless a remedy is soon applied, anarchy and confusion will inevitably ensue."

Madison's second stroke of good fortune was that the entire Virginia delegation had arrived on time, while the other state delegations took three weeks to gather and create a quorum. This meant that Madison enjoyed a providential interval during which he could lobby his fellow Virginians about the acute character of the political crisis and the radical reforms necessary to avert it.

There are no records of the many conversations that occurred in the boarding houses and taverns between May 5 and May 29, when the Constitutional Congress officially assembled. But going by the document that emerged from these deliberations—known as the Virginia Plan—Madison most probably conducted a nonstop seminar. He had all the information at his fingertips: the sorry history of all European confederacies; the abject failure of the state governments to maintain fiscal discipline; the inability of the Confederation Congress to raise revenue to pay off debts incurred during the war; the lack of any coherent foreign policy.

All of these concerns resulted in the fifteen-point plan, which recommended a fully empowered central government consisting of three branches—executive, legislative, and judicial. In effect it posited the wholesale replacement of a confederation where sovereignty resided in the states by a truly national government. Madison pushed hard for a provision that gave the new federal government a veto over state laws, but Edmund Randolph and George Mason insisted on softening this bold assertion of federal power with more ambiguous language. As a result, when the Constitutional Convention officially assembled on May 29, Madison's extraordinary diligence enabled the Virginia delegation to seize the initiative. No one on the moderate side of the argument had come to Philadelphia with equivalently clear proposals for a simple tinkering with the Articles, so the radical agenda embodied in the Virginia Plan commanded the field by default.

From the moderate point of view, and even more so from that of those delegates who opposed any reform of the Articles, Madison's maneuvers behind the scenes represented an orchestrated coup de main, a remarkably deft hijacking of the debate by a minority of radical nationalists. Over the next three months Madison was forced into repeated compromises. His proposal for a federal power to override state laws never gained any traction. And his insistence that both branches of the legislature be based on population was rejected in favor of a state-based Senate and population-based House. Madison took both of these defeats hard, and when the convention adjourned, he departed Philadelphia fearful that the final document would prove inadequate to sustain the United States as a coherent union.

He was wrong about that, at least until 1861, when the core question of federal against state sovereignty became necessary to resolve on the battlefield. But by defining the terms of the debate with his Virginia colleagues in late May of 1787, Madison had established a framework that placed advocates of modest reform on the defensive throughout the convention, and thereby made some kind of consolidated American nation not only possible but likely.

In retrospect, the most important conversations that occurred during that sweltering summer took place before the delegates convened. This was "little Jemmy Madison's" most influential and consequential moment, because it defined the terms of the debate in collective terms that made the federal government a supportive embodiment of "us," or "We the People," rather than an alien embodiment of "them."

Madison had almost 50 years of public service before him, to include the secretaryship of state under Thomas Jefferson and the presidency in his own right. His constitutional posture shifted on several occasions over those years, and he had the misfortune to be the only sitting president to have the national capital laid waste by invaders' fire during his tenure. Life during the most formative phase of a nation's identity, especially political life at the highest level, is always hard. But looking back, with all the advantages of hindsight, we can say without much doubt that May 1787 was Madison's finest hour.

Critical Thinking

1. Analyze the debates during the Constitutional Convention over what kind of government the various delegates hoped to create.

2. What was Madison's "radical agenda"?

JOSEPH J. ELLIS, winner of the 2001 Pulitzer Prize in History for *Founding Brothers: The Revolutionary Generation* (Knopf 2000), is the Ford Foundation Professor of History at Mount Holyoke College.

From *American Heritage*, Winter 2010, pp. 39–40. Copyright © 2010 by American Heritage Publishing Co. Reprinted by permission.

Wall Street's First Collapse

Speculators caused a stock market crash in 1792, forcing the federal government to bail out New York bankers—and the nation.

THOMAS FLEMING

Wall Street's first bubble swelled and burst in the spring of 1792, exerting a profound effect on American politics and society. Nine years after the Treaty of Paris and the acknowledgment of the former colonies' independence, both Europe and America lay in turmoil. The French Revolution was showing its first symptoms of radical violence. In March an assassin's bullet felled Sweden's King Gustav III, who had called for a crusade against France. In the United States, President Washington struggled to fight a war against British-backed Indians in the Midwest. Closer to home, a savage feud had exploded between his secretary of state, Thomas Jefferson, and his secretary of the treasury, Alexander Hamilton.

In spite of strenuous opposition by the supporters of Jefferson, Hamilton had persuaded Congress to set up a financial system designed to rescue the Republic from the humiliating bankruptcy that had almost destroyed the nation after the Revolution. In 1791 Congress chartered the Bank of the United States with the intention that it would buy up the millions of dollars in promissory notes issued by the Continental Congress when its paper money became worthless in the final years of the Revolution. "A public debt," Hamilton said, "was a public blessing." It could be used to pump new life into the all-but-dormant American economy. The Jeffersonians accused the secretary of trying to turn the new nation into a mirror image of Great Britain, which was not far from the truth.

Hamilton did not inspire confidence in average Americans. Born illegitimate in the West Indies, he had served as General Washington's chief aide-de-camp during the Revolution. The public neither saw nor appreciated his contributions. As the war ended, he married a daughter of Gen. Philip Schuyler, one of the nation's richest men. In the struggle to create a new constitution and federal government, he had displayed a no-holds-barred political style and a disdain, even contempt, for popular government. Hamilton regarded democracy as a "disease," dangerous to the nation's stability.

After winning the brawl over the bank, Hamilton and his followers clashed further with the Jeffersonians over how to deal with the debt. Haunted by the memory of the financial collapse of the 1780s, Hamilton decided to concentrate the wealth of the new republic in the hands of a relatively few men so that the nation would have capital when and if it was needed. He decided to buy at par value the millions of dollars in promissory notes that the bankrupt Continental Congress and state governments had issued to soldiers, farmers, and others who had supported the Revolution.

Hamilton knew that much of this federal debt was already in the hands of speculators. Most of the original holders of government paper had long since given up any hope of being paid its full value. They had either stuffed their certificates in drawers and forgotten them or sold them at heavy discounts. Hamilton permitted—and perhaps collaborated in—leaking his plan to numerous wealthy Americans. Chief among the leakers was almost certainly William Duer, the assistant secretary of the treasury, who combined government service with a passion for quick profits.

The son of a rich West Indies planter, Duer had come to New York on business in 1768 and stayed. He had joined the American side in the Revolution and served ably in the Continental Congress, where he had won Hamilton's friendship by defending General Washington against his critics. Later Duer became secretary of the Confederation government's Treasury Board. In 1779 he married Catherine Alexander, daughter of Maj. Gen. William Alexander of New Jersey, also known as Lord Stirling thanks to his somewhat dubious claim to a Scottish title. "Lady Kitty," as she was called, liked a splendid lifestyle as much as did Duer. They rode around New York in a coach and four with a coat of arms emblazoned on the doors, and they often served 15 different wines at their dinner parties.

Duer and his friends saw Hamilton's plan as a way to make a killing. There were still certificates from the speculative cites of New York and Philadelphia waiting for aggressive buyers—especially in state debts, which had seemed even worse bets than the federal notes. Duer leaked word that Hamilton intended to consolidate these debts with the federal debt to strengthen the people's attachment to the new government. Pennsylvania Senator Robert Morris, former superintendent of finance during the Revolution and considered the nation's wealthiest man, sent agents galloping into the western reaches of New York, Pennsylvania, and other states to buy up state paper at a few cents on the dollar. Former army contractor James Wadsworth, now a congressman from Connecticut, dispatched two vessels to South Carolina, loaded with cash to do likewise. Duer, ignoring a law that forbade Treasury employees from speculating in government securities, was another major player in this greedy game.

Some 78 New Yorkers, many of them friends or partners of the assistant secretary, bought $2,717,754 of southern state certificates, with eight accounting for more than $1,500,000 of this potential bonanza. Add to this the $4,949,253 in the federal debt held by New Yorkers, and it is clear why New York's well-to-do had a feverish interest in Congress's approval of Hamilton's funding system.

These numbers also reveal why Jefferson and his followers wanted to get Congress out of New York City. In return for backing the funding bill, the Jeffersonians demanded Hamiltonians' support for the transfer of the capital to yet unbuilt Washington, DC, in 1800. Meanwhile, Philadelphia became the temporary capital.

Hamilton made most of his payments in government bonds with a par value of $400, paying 6 percent interest. These notes were soon being traded on America's first stock exchange, under a buttonwood tree at the foot of Wall Street. Alas for Secretary Hamilton's vision of an orderly prosperous future, too many newly rich titans declined to devote their magically multiplied wealth to launching new businesses. Instead they started looking for ways to double and quadruple their paper profits.

On July 4, 1791, the Treasury began selling stock in the new Bank of the United States. Noting that speculation was already brisk in government 6 percents, Hamilton attempted to check a similar fever in the bank's stock by making it expensive to buy. A $400 share required $100 down, the rest to be paid in four semi-annual installments. (In modern money, this was roughly $6,000 a share and $1,500 down.) Laborers earned about $200 a year in 1792. Even skilled craftsmen, who earned ten times that much, would hesitate to part with $400. Hamilton's goal was still to concentrate stock ownership among "the better sort."

Congress, already demonstrating an eagerness to please as many people as possible, reduced the opening payment to $25. For this amount, the purchaser received a certificate, soon nicknamed a "scrip," which entitled him to buy the full share at par. Hamilton had intended to offer the stock only in the nation's capital, Philadelphia, but Congress ordered him to give speculators in New York, Boston, Baltimore, and Charleston a chance to buy as well.

In less than an hour, the $8 million first issue was oversubscribed by $1.6 million. In five weeks, the value of the scrip soared from $25 to $325. The low opening price enabled almost everyone to get into the game. "Scrippomania" swept the nation. Newspapers began printing daily stock quotations. Six-percent government bonds also levitated in the bubble, soaring from 75 cents on the dollar to 130. Other bonds, called deferred sixes, because they would not come due for 10 years, went from 40 cents to par.

In Philadelphia an angry Thomas Jefferson wrote to a friend: "Stock and scrip are the sole domestic subjects of conversation. . . . Ships are lying idle at the wharfs, buildings are stopped, capital withdrawn from commerce, manufacturers, arts and agriculture to be employed in gambling." Hamilton was almost as dismayed at the speculation. He knew the rise could not last. On August 11, 1791, the market broke, and a wave of frantic selling swept the major cities, leaving a great many people poorer than they had been on Independence Day.

Anticipating Henry Paulson, Hamilton struggled to calm the situation. Utilizing a $1,000,000 sinking fund he had created for this purpose, he bought some of the plummeting stock on the government's account and publicly declared that scrip should be selling at 195 and 6 percents at 110. The market stabilized around these figures, averting a crash.

The wildest speculation boiled up in New York, led by Duer, who had resigned his post in government to devote full time to his investments. Hamilton warned him stiffly to exercise more public responsibility: "I have serious fears for you—for your purse and for your reputation." For unknown reasons, however, Hamilton still trusted Duer enough to involve him in the next phase of his plan to turn the United States into an economic powerhouse. The secretary called for the creation of a Society for the Establishment of Useful Manufactures (S.U.M.); he asked Duer to become its governor and chief salesman, even though Duer had mishandled his government accounts, occasionally using Treasury warrants to cover his private speculations and generally leaving his books a mess. Already regarded as a man with a golden touch, Duer easily raised $600,000 in a stock offering to capitalize the S.U.M.

The mania for paper profits had only been checked, not eliminated. Across the country, state banks were being founded, primarily to loan money for speculation in stock and land. "Bank mania" joined "scrippomania" as part of the national vocabulary. The market in government securities soon resumed its rise. By October 1791, 6 percents were selling at $500, or $100 over par, and scrip had risen similarly.

Duer had learned nothing from the summer's close call. He now decided to plunge on a grand scale. Forming a partnership with Alexander McComb, a New York businessman and land speculator, he set out to corner the market in government 6 percents. Duer soon drew in many of the leading S.U.M. investors forming what later would be called the "6 percent club." They hoped to achieve a corner by July 1792, when the next installment on stock in the Bank of the United States was due.

They also bought "on time" as many shares in the bank as they could find. If they brought off the corner, Duer and McComb planned to sell the 6 percents at huge markups to European investors eager to buy American securities. With revolutionary France on the brink of exploding, the United States looked far more stable than any country on their continent. With this wealth, Duer and McComb hoped to buy enough shares to take control of the Bank of the United States.

Another part of the Duer-McComb strategy called for winning early control of the Bank of New York, a private institution Hamilton had helped to found. The partners spread a rumor that the Bank of New York would soon combine with the local branch of the Bank of the United States. To depress the price of the Bank of New York's shares, they launched a bogus entity, the Million Bank, which they capitalized at $1.8 million. Duer and McComb soon had contracts to buy 400 of the Bank of New York's outstanding shares.

As news of Duer's schemes circulated through New York, people rushed to entrust their savings to him; he cheerfully promised to double their money in six months. Even the madam of one of the city's premier brothels pulled dollars from beneath her much-used mattresses to pour into the bonanza. Duer also dipped into the funds of the S.U.M. and persuaded numerous merchant friends to cosign notes to expand his credit.

As with so many other attempted corners, Duer's ploy looked better on paper than in reality. Bringing off such a coup required not only nerve but also the ability to keep track of a plethora of details, which was not Duer's strong suit. He also had a manic tendency to get involved in more speculations than even the most gifted financier could handle. While impossibly leveraged by buying government stock with McComb, he was also the absentee contractor for the U.S. Army as they fought the western Indians. Simultaneously, he was heavily involved in the Scioto Company, an immense land speculation entity that had agents in Europe trying to unload 1 million acres of the Ohio wilderness.

Nor did Duer and McComb expect to run into difficulties in their 6 percent project. A group of speculators more or less aligned with New York Governor George Clinton, Hamilton's political rival and Jefferson's ally, got into the game on the bear side, selling all the stock they could find to Duer and his partners at a future date. Their goal was to depress stock prices, so that they could make a killing on the day of delivery.

Their timing was good. In the spring, much of the specie in New York went into the country to buy produce for export. This put a squeeze on the banks, which began calling in their loans. With the price of their stocks remaining flat, Duer and other members of the 6 percent club scurried around New York in search of money, paying interest as high as 1 percent per day—365 percent per year.

These desperate measures staved off disaster—temporarily. Watching from Philadelphia, Hamilton became increasingly dismayed. Duer and his friends were making a mockery of the system Hamilton had created to give America financial stability. He was keenly aware that Jefferson and his colleague James Madison were looking for an opportunity to strike him down. "The enemies to banks and credit are in a fair way to having their utmost malignity gratified," the secretary lamented.

Oliver Wolcott Jr. of Connecticut, the meticulous comptroller of the treasury, had been toiling over the books Duer left behind. He had found a shortfall of $239,000 from that resourceful fellow's tenure on the old Treasury Board. Duer had long acknowledged the deficiency but ignored Wolcott's demands that he make it good. Rumors of his financial overextension reached Wolcott, who called upon the U.S. attorney in New York, Richard Harison, to sue Duer.

The frantic Duer begged Hamilton to block a suit that would cripple his power to borrow. For the secretary of the treasury, it was a painful clash between private friendship and public duty. Hamilton met the test, grimly consigning Duer to his fate: "'This time there should be a line of separation between honest men and knaves.'"

On March 9, 1792, Duer failed to meet a number of payments on loans, and his paper pyramid began to crumble. He claimed that the notes had been issued by his agent in his absence and required "investigation." No one believed a word of this, but it bought Duer a little more time.

> To pay soldiers and suppliers during the Revolution, the Continental Congress issued millions of dollars worth of promissory notes known as "scrip," which were bought cheaply by speculators and fueled a bubble.

By March 15, 6 percents were in precipitous decline and deferreds were also showing signs of galloping anemia. The bears were throwing all the stock they could find into the market to accelerate the downward plunge. Duer faced a crescendo of demands for payments of stocks that would soon be delivered, and the falling market combined with the government's lawsuit made it impossible for him to raise another cent. He was soon in serious danger of physical harm from what one speculator called "the lower class of his creditors," who were threatening that if they did not get their money they would "rise to extremities."

On March 23 Duer took refuge in the city jail—a place to which most debtors went reluctantly, but which he now saw as far safer than his mansion on Broadway. In a letter a New York businessman ticked off the names of a veritable gallery of top merchants to whom Duer owed large sums—$80,000 to one man alone. He also owed "shopkeepers, widows, orphans—butchers, carmen, gardners, market women." Another writer reported: "The town has rec'd a shock which it will not get over for many years. Men look as if some general calamity had taken place."

Soon one of Duer's partners, Walter Livingston of the powerful Hudson River Valley clan, joined him in debtors' prison. He had cosigned 28 of Duer's notes for a total of $203,875.80. Stock prices continued to fall in spite of Hamilton's attempts to stabilize the market with government money. Public unrest grew. On April 15 Alexander McComb defaulted on half a million dollars in stock purchased from the bears. The following day he joined Duer and Livingston in the city prison.

On the night of April 17 a large mob gathered around the jail but was dispersed by a sudden rain shower. A few days later another angry crowd gathered, determined to do someone harm, but they lacked leadership. One jittery Connecticut visitor wrote that all the city needed was a "small riot" to burst into a "general flame" that would "consume the prison & D-r and McComb with it." The city fathers equipped the jailers with small arms and cannon, which may have chilled the impulse to violence.

Hamilton's attempts to quell the cascading stock market with infusions from his sinking fund were repeatedly overwhelmed by the escalating panic. Even the bears were swallowed in the general collapse. One of their chiefs, Brockholst Livingston, was reported as "nearly ruined," and his fellows were not in much better shape. The commerce of New York all but stopped functioning. An upriver merchant with several tons of wheat on ships refused to unload them because no one could pay him in specie, and he did not trust the notes of the people who offered to store it. Philadelphia also felt the shock. Land prices throughout Pennsylvania dropped by two-thirds.

On April 17 a gloating Jefferson reported that in New York "bankruptcy is become general, every man concerned in paper being broke." He estimated that the total loss was $5 million, roughly the value of all the buildings in the city. It was the equivalent, Jefferson said, "of the whole town [being] burnt to the ground."

His unconcealed satisfaction was the signal for a ferocious onslaught upon Hamilton by the secretary of state's followers in Congress and elsewhere. Writing in the National Gazette, Philip Freneau, Jefferson's favorite mouthpiece, assailed the funding system as evil. He blamed it for "the scenes of speculation calculated to aggrandize the few and the wealthy, while oppressing the great body of the people." Never hesitant about replying to critics, Hamilton blasted back under numerous pseudonyms, accusing Jefferson of being, among other things, a secret enemy of the Constitution.

The total loss was $5 million, roughly the value of all the buildings in the city.

Another series of letters in Freneau's newspaper assailed the S.U.M. Alas for the immediate future of American industry, the society was an easy target. Its treasury had been depleted by Duer's illegal transfers into the speculative whirlwind. Many of its board of governors were either in jail or in hiding, and the few who showed up for meetings nursed grievous financial wounds inflicted by the 6 percent club.

The congressional elections in the fall of 1792 reflected the success of the newspaper and congressional clamors, giving the Jeffersonians a clear majority in the House of Representatives. It was the death knell of the S.U.M., although the wake and interment took three more years. A corporate ghost remained alive for another century, leasing land it owned on the Passaic River to entrepreneurs, but it no longer resembled Hamilton's enterprise.

New York City, however, rode out Jefferson's apocalyptic predictions. By June 1792, thanks in large part to new infusions from the sinking fund, stability had returned to the stock market and city.

For the rest of the decade, speculative fever abated on Wall Street. William Duer, still in prison, remained a kind of living reminder of what could go wrong. But the appetite for a fast buck was not purged from the American psyche. Robert Morris and other wealthy men continued to speculate in land. Vast stretches of wilderness in the West and North became a new bubble that collapsed at the end of the decade, bankrupting Morris and many others. For a year a small army of creditors and sheriffs' deputies camped on the lawn of Morris's mansion. He sold off furniture, silver, and rugs to satisfy those who shouted loudest. But in February 1798, without wood or coal to keep warm, the once richest American surrendered and was escorted to Philadelphia's debtors' prison.

The failures of America's first group of financiers had not a little to do with the election of Thomas Jefferson in 1800, beginning decades of a federal government that was ideologically hostile to banks, industrial development, and the accumulation of capital. Only when a new generation of businessmen and financiers demonstrated that they could combine profit seeking with self-restraint and concern for the general welfare did American voters and politicians begin to unlearn the harsh conclusions that had been drawn as Wall Street's first bubble burst in fear and misery in the spring of 1792.

Critical Thinking

1. Analyze Alexander Hamilton's financial program for the new nation.
2. Analyze the views of Thomas Jefferson and his followers who opposed Hamilton's plan.

From *American Heritage*, Winter 2009, pp. 55–60. Copyright © 2009 by American Heritage Publishing Co. Reprinted by permission.

Adams Appoints Marshall

Critical decisions by the Chief Justice saved the Supreme Court's independence—and made possible its wide-ranging role today.

GORDON S. WOOD

Most jurists and constitutional scholars today would probably contend that the most controlling precedent to be set in the early republic was laid down in the 1803 *Marbury v. Madison* decision. While a formidable ruling, it was not, however, the decisive moment—at least not to people at the time. The hinge event in the early history of the judiciary was President John Adams's appointment of John Marshall as chief justice of the Supreme Court in 1801. More important than Marshall's *Marbury* decision, which was incidental and scarcely as momentous in 1803 as it later came to be, was his campaign to save not just the Court's role in interpreting the Constitution but its independent existence. Without Marshall's shrewd maneuvering in the decade or so following his appointment, the Court would have turned out a substantially different and much weaker institution than it became.

When Marshall took office, the Federalist-dominated Supreme Court was a beleaguered institution, increasingly vulnerable to attacks by the Jeffersonian Republicans as aristocratic and out of touch with the popular majority. Consequently, it had become difficult to find able nominees for vacancies. Between 1789 and 1801, 12 men had sat on the bench, of whom five, including two chief justices, had resigned. The Court even had trouble mustering a quorum, forcing cases to be carried over and sometimes compelling sessions to be cancelled entirely. In 1801 President John Adams had initially wanted to reappoint John Jay, the first chief justice in 1789. But Jay declined, explaining that the Court had none of the necessary "Energy, weight and Dignity" to support the national government and little likelihood of acquiring any.

More alarming, the Jeffersonian Republicans who had just seized the White House and control of Congress were set on yet further reducing the power of the Federalist-dominated judiciary, the only branch of the federal government they did not control. The Congress attempted to use impeachment as a crude but effective method of clearing away obnoxious Federalist judges. Having put matters to the test by impeaching and removing an alcoholic and partisan New Hampshire federal district judge, it turned to Associate Justice Samuel Chase, the Court's most overbearing Federalist. If Chase were convicted,

many Republicans hoped to move next against the other justices, including Marshall. Although the Senate narrowly failed to convict Chase, the Republican threat to the judiciary remained.

These were the dangerous circumstances that Marshall had to deal with; and deal with them he did, superbly. In the end his greatest achievement was maintaining the Court in the amplitude of its authority and asserting its independence within so hostile a climate. He began by changing the Court's lordly image. Using his extraordinary charm, he persuaded his fellow justices to shed their feudal scarlet and ermine robes in favor of a plain republican black. He then sought to solidify the Court by restricting the previous practice of each justice issuing his own opinion seriatim, customary in both 18th-century English courts and American state benches. Instead he convinced the associate justices to reach in most cases a collective decision, which was usually written by him, thus enhancing the Court's authority by making it speak with one voice. During the first four years of Marshall's tenure, the Court handed down 46 written decisions, all of them unanimous. Marshall participated in 42, in each of which he wrote the Court's opinion. Even after 1810, when there were more Republican than Federalist justices, somehow Marshall maintained his good-natured dominance.

> **Marshall persuaded his fellow justices to shed their feudal scarlet and ermine robes in favor of plain republican black.**

Most important, he sought to reach some sort of accommodation with the other branches of government, which he attained by avoiding direct confrontation. Under his amiable leadership, the Court retreated from some of the advanced positions that the Federalists had tried to establish for the judiciary in the 1790s. He rejected the contentious idea that the common law of crimes ran in the federal courts, and repudiated the broad definition of treason that the Federalists had brought down upon the Whiskey and Fries rebels in the 1790s. Even Marshall's assertion of the Court's role in interpreting the Constitution in *Marbury v. Madison* was so subtle and indirect that it aroused little Republican hostility. It was the Federalists who were the angriest at the *Marbury* decision, having wanted to declare the Republicans' repeal of the Judiciary Act of 1801 unconstitutional. But Marshall knew better. That would have brought down the full fury of the Republican Congress.

In a variety of ways, therefore, Marshall sought to escape the partisan politics of the 1790s. All of his evasion and caution, he said, was based on a quite reasonable fear that otherwise he and his brethren would have been "condemned as a pack of consolidating aristocratic." He did much more than affirm the Court's authority to oversee the Constitution. He actually saved the Court's independence and thereby made possible its subsequent vast-ranging role in American history.

Critical Thinking

1. Analyze John Marshall's conduct as Chief Justice of the Supreme Court.
2. How did he help establish the court's legitimacy?

GORDON S. WOOD, winner of the 1993 Pulitzer Prize for *The Radicalism of the American Revolution* (Knopf 1992), is the Alvo O. Way Professor of History emeritus at Brown University.

The Revolution of 1803

The Louisiana Purchase of 1803 was "the event which more than any other, after the foundation of the Government and always excepting its preservation, determined the character of our national life." So said President Theodore Roosevelt on the 100th anniversary of this momentous acquisition. As we celebrate the 200th anniversary, it's clear that the extraordinary real estate deal also shaped America's perception of its role in the world.

PETER S. ONUF

If there was one thing the United States did not seem to need in 1803, it was more land. The federal government had plenty to sell settlers in the new state of Ohio and throughout the Old Northwest (stretching from the Ohio and Mississippi rivers to the Great Lakes), as did New York, Pennsylvania, and other states. New Englanders were already complaining that the westward exodus was driving up wages and depressing real estate prices in the East.

The United States then consisted of 16 states: the original 13, strung along the Atlantic seaboard, and three recent additions on the frontier: Vermont, which had declared its independence from New York during the Revolution, was finally recognized and admitted in 1791, and Kentucky and Tennessee, carved out of the western reaches of Virginia and North Carolina in 1792 and 1796, respectively, extended the union of states as far as the Mississippi River. The entire area east of the Mississippi had been nominally secured to the United States by the Peace of Paris in 1783, though vast regions remained under the control of Indian nations and subject to the influence of various European imperial powers.

Many skeptical commentators believed that the United States was already too big and that the bonds of union would weaken and snap if new settlements spread too far and too fast. "No paper engagements" could secure the connection of East and West, Massachusetts congressman Rufus King wrote in 1786, and separatist movements and disunionist plots kept such concerns alive in subsequent years. Expansionists had a penchant for naturalistic language: At best, the "surge" or "tide" of white settlement might be channeled, but it was ultimately irresistible.

Though President Thomas Jefferson and the American negotiators who secured the Louisiana Purchase in 1803 had not even dreamed of acquiring such a vast territory, stretching from the Mississippi to the Rockies, the expansion of the United States has the retrospective feel of inevitability, however much some modern Americans may bemoan the patriotic passions and imperialistic excesses of "Manifest Destiny" and its "legacies of conquest." Indeed, it's almost impossible for us to imagine any other outcome now, or to recapture the decidedly mixed feelings of Americans about their country's expansion at the start of the 19th century.

Jefferson and his contemporaries understood that they were at a crossroads, and that the American experiment in republican self-government and the fragile federal union on which it depended could easily fail. They understood that the United States was a second-rate power, without the "energy" or military means to project—or possibly even to defend—its vital interests in a world almost constantly at war. And they understood all too well that the loyalties of their countrymen—and, if they were honest with themselves, their own loyalties—were volatile and unpredictable.

There were good reasons for such doubts about American allegiances. Facing an uncertain future, patriotic (and not so patriotic) Americans had only the dimmest sense of who or what should command their loyalty. The Union had nearly collapsed on more than one occasion, most recently during the presidential succession crisis of 1800–01, which saw a tie in the Electoral College and 36 contentious ballots in the House of Representatives before Jefferson was elevated to the presidency. During the tumultuous 1790s, rampant partisan political strife between Federalists and Jefferson's Republicans roiled the nation, and before that, under the Articles of Confederation (1781–89), the central government ground to a virtual halt and the Union almost withered away before the new constitution saved it. Of course, everyone professed to be a patriot, dedicated to preserving American independence. But what did that mean? Federalists such as Alexander Hamilton preached fealty to a powerful, consolidated central government capable of doing the people's will (as they loosely construed it); Republican oppositionists championed a strictly construed federal constitution that left power in the hands of the people's (or peoples') state governments. Each side accused the other of being subject to the corrupt influence of a foreign power: counterrevolutionary England in the case of Federalist "aristocrats" and "monocrats"; revolutionary France for Republican "Jacobins."

In Jefferson's mind, and in the minds of his many followers, the new Republican dispensation initiated by his ascension to power in "the Revolution of 1800" provided a hopeful answer to all these doubts and anxieties. Jefferson's First Inaugural Address, which the soft-spoken, 57-year-old president delivered to Congress in a nearly inaudible whisper in March 1801, seemed to his followers to herald a new epoch in American affairs. "We are all republicans, we are all federalists," he insisted in the speech. "Let us, then, unite with one heart and one mind." The president's inspiring vision of the nation's future augured, as he told the English radical Joseph Priestley, then a refugee in republican Pennsylvania, something "new under the sun."

While Jefferson's conciliatory language in the inaugural address famously helped mend the partisan breach—and, not coincidentally, helped cast Hamilton and his High Federalist minions far beyond the republican pale—it also anticipated the issues that would come to the fore during the period leading up to the Louisiana Purchase.

First, the new president addressed the issue of the nation's size. Could an expanding union of free republican states survive without jeopardizing the liberties won at such great cost by the revolutionary generation? Jefferson reassured the rising, post-revolutionary generation that it too had sufficient virtue and patriotism to make the republican experiment work and to pass on its beneficent legacy. "Entertaining a due sense of our equal right to the use of our own faculties" and "enlightened by a benign religion, professed, indeed, and practiced in various forms, yet all of them inculcating honesty, truth, temperance, gratitude, and the love of man; acknowledging and adoring an over-ruling Providence, which by all its dispensations proves that it delights in the happiness of man here and his greater happiness hereafter," Americans were bound to be "a happy and a prosperous people."

Jefferson congratulated his fellow Americans on "possessing a chosen country, with room enough for our descendants to the thousandth and thousandth generation," a vast domain that was "separated by nature and a wide ocean from the exterminating havoc of one quarter of the globe." Jefferson's vision of nationhood was inscribed on the American landscape: "An overruling Providence, which by all its dispensations proves that it delights in the happiness of man here and his greater happiness hereafter" provided this fortunate people with land enough to survive and prosper forever. But Jefferson knew that he was not offering an accurate description of the nation's current condition. Given the frenzied pace of westward settlement, it would take only a generation or two—not a thousand—to fill out the new nation's existing limits, which were still marked in the west by the Mississippi. Nor was the United States as happily insulated from Europe's "exterminating havoc" as the new president suggested. The Spanish remained in control of New Orleans, the key to the great river system that controlled the continent's heartland, and the British remained a powerful presence to the north.

Jefferson's vision of the future was, in fact, the mirror opposite of America's present situation at the onset of the 19th century. The nation was encircled by enemies and deeply divided by partisan and sectional differences. The domain the president envisioned was boundless, continent-wide, a virgin land waiting to be taken up by virtuous, liberty-loving American farmers. In this providential perspective, Indian nations and European empires simply disappeared from view, and the acquisition of new territory and the expansion of the Union seemed preordained. It would take an unimaginable miracle, acquisition of the entire Louisiana territory, to begin to consummate Jefferson's inaugural promise.

Jefferson's expansionist vision also violated the accepted axioms of contemporary political science. In his *Spirit of the Laws* (1748), the great French philosopher Montesquieu taught that the republican form of government could survive only in small states, where a virtuous and vigilant citizenry could effectively monitor the exercise of power. A large state, by contrast, could be sustained only if power were concentrated in a more energetic central government; republicanism in an expanding state would give way to more "despotic," aristocratic, and monarchical regimes. This "law" of political science was commonly understood in mechanical terms: Centrifugal forces, pulling a state apart, gained momentum as territory expanded, and they could be checked only by the "energy" of strong government.

James Madison had grappled with the problem in his famous *Federalist* 10, in which he argued that an "extended republic" would "take in a greater variety of parties and interests," making it "less probable that a majority of the whole will have a common motive to invade the rights of other citizens." Modern pluralists have embraced this argument, but it was not particularly persuasive to Madison's generation—or even to Madison himself a decade later. During the struggle over ratification of the Constitution, Antifederalists effectively invoked Montesquieu's dictum against Federalist "consolidationism," and in the 1790s, Jeffersonian defenders of states' rights offered the same arguments against Hamiltonian High Federalism. And Jefferson's "Revolution of 1800," vindicating the claims of (relatively) small state-republics against an overly energetic central government, seemed to confirm Montesquieu's wisdom. Montesquieu's notion was also the basis for the popular interpretation of what had caused the rise of British tyranny in the colonies before the American Revolution.

At the same time, however, Montesquieu's logic posed a problem for Jefferson. How could he imagine a continental republic in 1801 and negotiate a land cession that doubled the country's size in 1803? To put the problem somewhat differently, how could Jefferson—who had, after all, drafted the controversial Kentucky Resolutions of 1798, which threatened state nullification of federal authority—overcome his own disunionist tendencies?

Jefferson's response in his inaugural was to call on his fellow Americans to "pursue our own federal and republican principles, our attachment to union and representative government," with "courage and confidence." In other words, a sacred regard for states' rights ("federal principles") was essential to the preservation and strength of a "union" that depended on the "attachment" of a people determined to secure its liberties ("republican principles"). This conception of states as republics would have been familiar and appealing to many Americans, but Jefferson's vision of the United States as a *powerful* nation, spreading across the continent, was breathtaking in its boldness. How could he promise Americans that they could have it both ways, that they could be secure in their liberties yet have a federal government with enough "energy" to preserve itself? How could he believe that the American government, which had only recently endured a near-fatal succession crisis and which had a pathetically small army and navy, was "the strongest Government on earth"?

Jefferson responded to these questions resoundingly by invoking—or perhaps more accurately, inventing—an American people or nation, united in devotion to common principles, and coming together over the course of succeeding generations to constitute one great family. Thus, the unity the president imagined was prospective. Divided as they might now be, Americans would soon come to realize that they were destined to be a great nation, freed from "the throes and convulsions of the ancient world" and willing to sacrifice everything in defense of their country. In Jefferson's vision of progressive continental development, the defensive vigilance of virtuous republicans, who were always ready to resist the encroachments of power from any and every source, would be transformed into a patriotic devotion to the transcendent community of an inclusive and expanding nation, "the world's best hope." "At the call of the law," Jefferson predicted, "every man . . . would fly to the standard of the law, and would meet invasions of the public order as his own personal concern."

Jefferson thus invoked an idealized vision of the American Revolution, in which patriotic citizen-soldiers rallied against British tyranny, as a model for future mobilizations against internal as well as external threats. (It was an extraordinary—and extraordinarily influential—exercise in revisionist history. More dispassionate observers, including those who, unlike Jefferson, actually had some military experience, were not inclined to give the militias much, if any, credit for winning the war.)

Jefferson's conception of the American nation imaginatively countered the centrifugal forces, the tendency toward anarchy and disunion, that republicanism authorized and unleashed. Devotion to the Union would reverse this tendency and draw Americans together, even as their private pursuits of happiness drew them to the far frontiers of their continental domain. It was a paradoxical, mystifying formulation. What seemed to be weakness—the absence of a strong central government—was, in fact, strength. Expansion did not attenuate social and political ties; rather, it secured a powerful, effective, and affective union. The imagined obliteration of all possible obstacles to the enactment of this great national story—the removal of Indians and foreigners—was the greatest mystification of all, for it disguised how the power of the federal state was to be deployed to clear the way for "nature's nation."

In retrospect, the peaceful acquisition of the Louisiana Territory, at the bargain-basement price of $15 million, seemed to conform to the expansionist scenario in Jefferson's First Inaugural Address. The United States bought land from France, just as individuals bought land from federal and state land offices, demonstrating good intentions (to be fruitful and multiply, to cultivate the earth) and their respect for property rights and the rule of law. Yet the progress of settlement was inexorable, a "natural" force, as the French wisely recognized in ceding their claims.

The threat of armed conflict was, nonetheless, never far below the surface. When the chilling news reached America in 1802 that Spain had retroceded Louisiana to France, under pressure from Napoleon Bonaparte, some Federalists agitated for a preemptive strike against New Orleans before Napoleon could land troops there and begin to carry out his plan for a reinvigorated French empire in the Western Hemisphere. As if to provide a taste of the future, Spanish authorities in New Orleans revoked the right of American traders to store goods in the city for export, thereby sending ripples of alarm and economic distress through farms and plantations of the Mississippi valley. Americans might like to think, with Jefferson, that the West was a vast land reserve for their future generations, but nature would issue a different decree if the French gained control of the Mississippi River system.

As Senator William Wells of Delaware warned the Senate in February 1803, if Napoleon were ensconced in New Orleans, "the whole of your Southern States" would be at his mercy; the French ruler would not hesitate to foment rebellion among the slaves, that "inveterate enemy in the very bosom of those States." A North Carolina congressman expected the French emperor to do even worse: "The tomahawk of the savage and the knife of the negro would confederate in the league, and there would be no interval of peace." Such a confederation—a powerful, unholy alliance of Europeans, Indians, and slaves—was the nightmarish antithesis of the Americans' own weak union. The French might even use their influence in Congress to revive the vicious party struggles that had crippled the national government during the 1790s.

Jefferson had no idea how to respond to the looming threat, beyond sending his friend and protégé James Monroe to join U.S. Minister to France Robert R. Livingston in a desperate bid to negotiate a way out of the crisis. At most, they hoped that Napoleon would sell New Orleans and the Floridas to the United States, perhaps with a view to preempting an Anglo-American alliance. Jefferson dropped a broad hint to Livingston (undoubtedly for Napoleon's edification) that if France ever took "possession of N. Orleans . . . we must marry ourselves to the British fleet and nation." For the Anglophobe Jefferson this must have been a horrible thought, even if it was a bluff. But then, happily for Jefferson—and crucially for his historical reputation—fortune intervened.

Napoleon's intentions for the New World hinged on control of Saint-Domingue (now Haiti), but a slave revolt there, led by the brilliant Toussaint L'Ouverture, complicated the emperor's plans. With a strong assist from yellow fever and other devastating diseases, the rebels fought a French expeditionary force of more than 20,000 to a standstill. Thwarted in his western design and facing the imminent resumption of war in Europe, Napoleon decided to cut his losses. In April 1803, his representative offered the entire Louisiana Territory to a surprised Livingston. By the end of the month, the negotiators had arrived at a price. For $15 million, the United States would acquire 828,000 square miles of North America, stretching from the Mississippi River to the Rocky Mountains and from the Gulf of Mexico to the Canadian border. Over time 13 states would be carved from the new lands.

When the news reached America in July, it proved a great deal more than anyone had been contemplating but was met with general jubilation. There was widespread agreement that national security depended on gaining control of the region around New Orleans; and Spanish Florida, occupying the critical area south of Georgia and the territory that the state had finally ceded to Congress in 1802, was high on southern planters' wish list of territorial acquisitions. But it was hard to imagine any immediate use for the trans-Mississippi region, notwithstanding Jefferson's inspiring rhetoric, and there was some grumbling that the negotiators had spent more than Congress had authorized. A few public figures, mostly New England Federalists, even opposed the transaction on political and constitutional grounds.

The Lewis and Clark expedition, authorized before the Purchase was completed, testifies to Americans' utter ignorance of the West in 1803. The two explorers were sent, in effect, to feel around in the dark. Perhaps, Jefferson mused, the trans-Mississippi region could be used as a kind of toxic waste dump, a place to send emancipated slaves beyond harm's way. Or, a more portentous thought, Indian nations might be relocated west of the river—an idea President Andrew Jackson later put into effect with his infamous removal policy.

What gripped most commentators as they celebrated the news of the Purchase in 1803 was simply that the Union had survived another awful crisis. They tended to see the new lands as a buffer. "The wilderness itself," Representative Joseph Nicholson of Maryland exclaimed, "will now present an almost insurmountable barrier to any nation that inclined to disturb us in that quarter." And another congressman exulted that America was now "insulated from the rest of the world."

David Ramsay, the South Carolina historian and devout Republican, offered the most full-blown paean to the future of the "chosen country" as Jefferson had envisioned it. Echoing Jefferson's First Inaugural, he asked, "What is to hinder our extension on the same liberal principles of equal rights till we have increased to twenty-seven, thirty-seven, or any other number of states that will conveniently embrace, in one happy union, the whole country from the Atlantic to the Pacific ocean, and from the lakes of Canada to the Gulf of Mexico?" In his Second Inaugural, in 1805, Jefferson himself would ask, "Who can limit the extent to which the federative principle may operate effectively?" Gone were his doubts about the uses to which the new lands could be put. "Is it not better that the opposite bank of the Mississippi should be settled by our own brethren and children, than by strangers of another family?"

Jefferson's vision of the American future has ever since provided the mythic master narrative of American history. In the western domains that Jefferson imagined as a kind of blank slate on which succeeding generations would inscribe the image of American nationhood, it would be all too easy to overlook other peoples and other possibilities. It would be all too easy as well to overlook the critical role of the state in the progress of settlement and development. When Americans looked back on events, they would confuse effects with causes: War and diplomacy eliminated rival empires and dispossessed native peoples; an activist federal state played a critical role in pacifying a "lawless" frontier by privatizing public lands and promoting economic development. In the mythic history of Jefferson's West, an irresistible westward tide of settlement appears to be its own cause, the manifest destiny of nature's nation.

Yet if the reality of power remains submerged in Jefferson's thought, it's not at any great depth. The very idea of the nation implies enormous force, the power of a people enacting the will of "an overruling Providence." In Jefferson's Declaration of Independence, Americans claimed "the separate & equal station to which the laws of nature and of nature's God entitle them." The first law of nature, the great natural law proclaimed by writers of the day, was self-preservation, and the defining moment in American history was the great mobilization of American power to secure independence in the Revolution. President Jefferson's vision of westward expansion projected that glorious struggle into the future and across the continent. It was a kind of permanent revolution, reenacting the nation's beginnings in the multiplication of new, self-governing republican states.

Born in war, Jefferson's conception of an expanding union of free states constituted a peace plan for the New World. But until it was insulated from Europe's "exterminating havoc," the new nation would remain vulnerable, unable to realize its historic destiny. By eliminating the clear and present danger of a powerful French presence at the mouth of the Mississippi, the Louisiana Purchase guaranteed the survival of the Union—for the time being, at least. By opening the West to white American settlers, it all but guaranteed that subsequent generations would see their own history in Jefferson's vision of their future, a mythic, nation-making vision yoking individual liberty and national power and promising a future of peace and security in a dangerous world. Two hundred years later, that vision remains compelling to many Americans.

Critical Thinking

1. How did the Louisiana Purchase come about?
2. Analyze the arguments of those who believed a republican form of government could survive only in a small state.

PETER S. ONUF is a professor of history at the University of Virginia. His most recent book is *Jefferson's Empire: The Language of American Nationhood* (2001). Copyright © 2003 by Peter Onuf.

From *Wilson Quarterly,* Winter 2003, pp. 22–29. Copyright © 2003 by Peter S. Onuf. Reprinted by permission of the author.

Dolley Madison Saves the Day

In August 1814, with invading British soldiers only a few hours away, the First Lady took command of the White House to save the young nation's treasures.

THOMAS FLEMING

In the years leading up to America's second war with Britain, President James Madison had been unable to stop his penny-pinching secretary of the treasury, Albert Gallatin, from blocking Congressional resolutions to expand the country's armed forces. The United States had begun the conflict on June 18, 1812, with no Army worth mentioning and a Navy consisting of a handful of frigates and a fleet of gunboats, most armed with a single cannon. In 1811, Congress had voted to abolish Alexander Hamilton's Bank of the United States, making it nearly impossible for the government to raise money Worst of all, the British and their European allies had engaged (and would ultimately defeat) Napoleon's France in battles across Europe in 1812 and 1813, which meant the United States would have to fight the world's most formidable army and navy alone.

In March 1813, Gallatin told the president, "We have hardly money enough to last till the end of the month." Along the Canadian border, American armies stumbled into ruinous defeats. A huge British naval squadron blockaded the American coast. In Congress, New Englanders sneered at "Mr. Madison's War," and the governor of Massachusetts refused to allow any of the state's militiamen to join the campaign in Canada. Madison fell ill with malaria and the aged vice president, Elbridge Gerry, grew so feeble that Congress began arguing about who would become president if both men died. The only good news came from victories over lone British warships by the tiny American Navy.

Dolley Madison's White House was one of the few places in the nation where hope and determination continued to flourish. Although she was born a Quaker, Dolley saw herself as a fighter. "I have always been an advocate for fighting when assailed," she wrote to her cousin, Edward Coles, in a May 1813 letter discussing the possibility of a British attack on the city. Spirits had risen when news of an American victory over the British frigate *Macedonian,* off the Canary Islands, reached the capital during a ball given in December 1812 to celebrate Congress' decision to enlarge the Navy at last. When a young lieutenant arrived at the ball carrying the flag of the defeated ship, senior naval officers paraded it around the floor, then laid it at Dolley's feet.

At social events, Dolley strived, in the words of one observer, "to destroy rancorous feelings, then so bitter between Federalists and Republicans." Members of Congress, weary of flinging curses at each other during the day, seemed to relax in her presence and were even willing to discuss compromise and conciliation. Almost all their wives and daughters were Dolley's allies. By day Dolley was a tireless visitor, leaving her calling cards all over the city Before the war, most of her parties attracted about 300 people. Now attendance climbed to 500, and young people began calling them "squeezes."

Dolley undoubtedly felt the stress of presiding over these crowded rooms. "My head is dizzy!" she confessed to a friend. But she maintained what an observer called her "remorseless equanimity," even when news was bad, as it often was. Critics heaped scorn on the president, calling him "Little Jemmy" and reviving the smear that he was impotent, underscoring the battlefield defeats over which he had presided. But Dolley seemed immune to such slander. And if the president looked as if he had one foot in the grave, Dolley bloomed. More and more people began bestowing a new title on her: first lady, the first wife of a U.S. president to be so designated. Dolley had created a semipublic office as well as a unique role for herself and those who would follow her in the White House.

She had long since moved beyond the diffidence with which she had broached politics in her letters to her husband nearly a decade before, and both had jettisoned any idea that a woman should not think about so thorny a subject. In the first summer of his presidency in 1809, Madison had been forced to rush back to Washington from a vacation at Montpelier, his Virginia estate, leaving Dolley behind. In a note he wrote to her after returning to the White House, he said he intended to bring her up to date on intelligence just received from France. And he sent her the morning newspaper, which had a story on the subject. In a letter two days later, he discussed a recent speech by the British prime minister; clearly, Dolley had become the president's political partner.

The British had been relentless in their determination to reduce Americans to obedient colonists once more. Checked by an American naval victory on Lake Erie on September 10, 1813, and the defeat of their Indian allies in the West, almost a month later, the British concentrated their assault on the coastline from Florida to Delaware Bay. Again and again their landing parties swarmed ashore to pillage homes, rape women, and burn public and private property. The commander of these operations was Sir George Cockburn, a strutting, red-faced rear admiral, widely considered to be as arrogant as he was ruthless.

Even as many Washington residents began packing up families and furniture, Dolley, in correspondence at the time, continued to insist that no British Army could get within 20 miles of the city. But the drumbeat of news about earlier landings—British troops had sacked Havre de Grace, Maryland, on May 4, 1813, and tried to take Craney Island, near Norfolk, Virginia, in June of that year—intensified criticism of the president. Some claimed that Dolley herself was planning to flee Washington; if Madison attempted to abandon the city as well, critics threatened, the president and the city would "fall" together. Dolley wrote in a letter to a friend: "I am not the least alarmed at these things but entirely disgusted & determined to stay with him."

On August 17, 1814, a large British fleet dropped anchor at the mouth of the Patuxent River, only 35 miles from the nation's capital. Aboard were 4,000 veteran troops under the command of a tough professional soldier, Maj. Gen. Robert Ross. They soon came ashore in Maryland without a shot being fired and began a slow, cautious advance on Washington. There was not a single trained American soldier in the vicinity to oppose them. All President Madison could do was call out thousands of militia. The commander of these jittery amateurs was Brig. Gen. William Winder, whom Madison had appointed largely because his uncle, the governor of Maryland, had already raised a sizable state militia.

Winder's incompetence became obvious, and more and more of Dolley's friends urged her to flee the city. By now thousands of Washingtonians were crowding the roads. But Dolley, whose determination to stay with her husband was unwavering, remained. She welcomed Madison's decision to station 100 militiamen under the command of a regular Army colonel on the White House lawn. Not only was it a gesture of protection on his part, it was also a declaration that he and Dolley intended to stand their ground. The president then decided to join the 6,000 militiamen who were marching to confront the British in Maryland. Dolley was sure his presence would stiffen their resolve.

After the president had ridden off, Dolley decided to show her own resolve by throwing a dinner party, on August 23. But after *The National Intelligencer* newspaper reported that the British had received 6,000 reinforcements, not a single invitee accepted her invitation. Dolley took to going up to the White House roof to scan the horizon with a spyglass, hoping to see evidence of an American victory. Meanwhile, Madison sent her two scribbled messages, written in quick succession on August 23. The first assured her that the British would easily be defeated; the second warned her to be ready to flee on a moment's notice.

Her husband had urged her, if the worst happened, to save the cabinet papers and every public document she could cram into her carriage. Late in the afternoon of August 23, Dolley

began a letter to her sister Lucy describing her situation. "My friends and acquaintances are all gone," she wrote. The army colonel and his 100-man guard had also fled. But, she declared, "I am determined not to go myself until I see Mr. Madison safe." She wanted to be at his side "as I hear of much hostility toward him . . . disaffection stalks around us." She felt her presence might deter enemies ready to harm the president.

At dawn the next day, after a mostly sleepless night, Dolley was back on the White House roof with her spyglass. Resuming her letter to Lucy at midday, she wrote that she had spent the morning "turning my spy glass in every direction and watching with unwearied anxiety, hoping to discern the approach of my dear husband and his friends." Instead, all she saw was "groups of military wandering in all directions, as if there were a lack of arms, or of spirit to fight for their own firesides!" She was witnessing the disintegration of the army that was supposed to confront the British at nearby Bladensburg, Maryland.

Although the boom of cannon was within earshot of the White House, the battle—five or so miles away at Bladensburg—remained beyond the range of Dolley's spyglass, sparing her the sight of American militiamen fleeing the charging British infantry. President Madison retreated toward Washington, along with General Winder. At the White House, Dolley had packed a wagon with the red silk velvet draperies of the Oval Room, the silver service and the blue and gold Lowestoft china she had purchased for the state dining room.

Resuming her letter to Lucy on that afternoon of the 24th, Dolley wrote: "Will you believe it, my sister? We have had a battle or skirmish . . . and I am still here within sound of the cannon!" Gamely, she ordered the table set for a dinner for the president and his staff, and insisted that the cook and his assistant begin preparing it. "Two messengers covered with dust" arrived from the battlefield, urging her to flee. Still she refused, determined to wait for her husband. She ordered the dinner to be served. She told the servants that if she were a man, she would post a cannon in every window of the White House and fight to the bitter end.

The arrival of Maj. Charles Carroll, a close friend, finally changed Dolley's mind. When he told her it was time to go, she glumly acquiesced. As they prepared to leave, according to John Pierre Sioussat, the Madison White House steward, Dolley noticed the Gilbert Stuart portrait of George Washington in the state dining room. She could not abandon it to the enemy, she told Carroll, to be mocked and desecrated. As he looked anxiously on, Dolley ordered servants to take down the painting, which was screwed to the wall. Informed they lacked the proper tools, Dolley told the servants to break the frame. (The president's enslaved White House footman, Paul Jennings, later produced a vivid account of these events; see box on page 89.) About this time, two more friends—Jacob Barker, a wealthy ship owner, and Robert G. L. De Peyster—arrived at the White House to offer whatever help might be needed. Dolley would entrust the painting to the two men, saying they must conceal it from the British at all costs; they would transport the portrait to safety in a wagon. Meanwhile, with remarkable self-possession, she completed her letter to Lucy: "And now, dear sister, I must leave this house . . . where I shall be tomorrow, I cannot tell!"

As Dolley headed for the door, according to an account she gave to her grandniece, Lucia B. Cutts, she spotted a copy of the Declaration of Independence in a display case; she put it into one of her suitcases. As Dolley and Carroll reached the front door, one of the president's servants, a free African-American named Jim Smith, arrived from the battlefield on a horse covered in sweat. "Clear out! Clear out," he shouted. The British were only a few miles away. Dolley and Carroll climbed into her carriage and were driven away to take refuge at his comfortable family mansion, Belle Vue, in nearby Georgetown.

The British arrived in the nation's capital a few hours later, as darkness fell. Admiral Cockburn and General Ross issued orders to burn the Capitol and the Library of Congress, then headed to the White House. According to Lt. James Scott, Cockburn's aide-de-camp, they found the dinner Dolley had ordered still on the table in the dining room. "Several kinds of wine in handsome cut glass decanters sat on the sideboard," Scott would later recall. The officers sampled some of the dishes and drank a toast to "Jemmy's health."

Soldiers roamed the house, grabbing souvenirs. According to historian Anthony Pitch, in *The Burning of Washington,* one man strutted around with one of President Madison's hats on his bayonet, boasting that he would parade it through the streets of London if they failed to capture "the little president."

Under Cockburn's direction, 150 men smashed windows and piled White House furniture in the center of the various rooms. Outside, 50 of the marauders carrying poles with oil-soaked rags on the ends surrounded the house. At a signal from the admiral, men with torches ignited the rags, and the flaming poles were flung through the smashed windows like fiery spears. Within minutes, a huge conflagration soared into the night sky. Not far away the Americans had set the Navy Yard on fire, destroying ships and warehouses full of ammunition and other materiel. For a time, it looked as if all Washington were ablaze.

The next day, the British continued their depredations, burning the Treasury, the State and War departments and other public buildings. An arsenal on Greenleaf's Point, about two miles south of the Capitol, exploded while the British were preparing to destroy it. Thirty men were killed and 45 were injured. Then a freak storm suddenly erupted, with high winds and violent thunder and lightning. The shaken British commanders soon retreated to their ships; the raid on the capital had ended.

Meanwhile, Dolley had received a note from Madison urging her to join him in Virginia. By the time they were finally reunited there on the night of August 25, the 63-year-old president had barely slept in several days. But he was determined to return to Washington as soon as possible. He insisted that Dolley remain in Virginia until the city was safe. By August 27, the president had reentered Washington. In a note written hastily the next day, he told his wife: "You cannot return too soon." The words seem to convey not only Madison's need for her companionship but also his recognition that she was a potent symbol of his presidency.

On August 28, Dolley joined her husband in Washington. They stayed at the home of her sister Anna Payne Cutts, who had taken over the same house on F Street that the Madisons had occupied before moving to the White House. The sight of the ruined Capitol—and the charred, blackened shell of the White House—must have been almost unbearable for Dolley. For several days, according to friends, she was morose and tearful. A friend who saw President Madison at this time described him as "miserably shattered and woebegone. In short, he looks heartbroken."

Madison also felt betrayed by General Winder—as well as by his Secretary of War, John Armstrong, who would resign within weeks—and by the ragtag army that had been routed. He blamed the retreat on low morale, the result of all the insults and denunciations of "Mr. Madison's War," as the citizens of New England, the center of opposition, labeled the conflict.

In the aftermath of the British rampage through the nation's capital, many urged the president to move the government to a safer place. The Common Council of Philadelphia declared its readiness to provide housing and office space for both the president and Congress. Dolley fervently maintained that she and her husband—and Congress—should stay in Washington. The president agreed. He called for an emergency session of Congress to take place on September 19. Meanwhile, Dolley had persuaded the Federalist owner of a handsome brick dwelling on New York Avenue and 18th Street, known as the Octagon House, to let the Madisons use it as an official residence. She opened the social season there with a crowded reception on September 21.

Dolley soon found unexpected support elsewhere in the country. The White House had become a popular national symbol. People reacted with outrage when they heard that the British had burned the mansion. Next came a groundswell of admiration as newspapers reported Dolley's refusal to retreat and her rescue of George Washington's portrait and perhaps also a copy of the Declaration of Independence.

On September 1, President Madison issued a proclamation "exhorting all the good people" of the United States "to unite in their hearts and hands" in order "to chastise and expel the invader." Madison's former opponent for the presidency, DeWitt Clinton, said there was only one issue worth discussing now: Would the Americans fight back? On September 10, 1814, the *Niles' Weekly Register,* a Baltimore paper with a national circulation, spoke for many "The spirit of the nation is roused," it editorialized.

The British fleet sailed into the port of Baltimore three days later, on September 13, determined to batter Fort McHenry into submission—which would allow the British to seize harbor ships and to loot waterfront warehouses—and force the city to pay a ransom. Francis Scott Key, an American lawyer who had gone aboard a British flagship at the request of President Madison to negotiate the release of a doctor seized by a British landing party, was all but certain that the fort would surrender to a nightlong bombardment by the British. When Key saw the American flag still flying at sunrise, he scribbled a poem that began, "Oh say can you see by the dawn's early light?" Within a few days, the words, set to the music of a popular song, were being sung all over Baltimore.

Good news from more distant fronts also soon reached Washington. An American fleet on Lake Champlain won a surprise victory over a British armada on September 11, 1814.

Witness to History

The First Memoir by a White House Slave Recreates the Events of August 23, 1814

The tale of Dolley Madison's rescue of the Gilbert Stuart portrait of George Washington is known mainly through Dolley's own letters and diary. But another firsthand account, by Paul Jennings, a slave who served as President Madison's footman, is getting new attention. Beth Taylor, a historian at Montpelier, Madison's Virginia estate, arranged for nearly two dozen descendants of Jennings to view the painting at the White House this past August.

Jennings believed misperceptions had arisen over time. "It has often been stated in print," he recalled years after the fact, "that when Mrs. Madison escaped from the White House, she cut out from the frame the large portrait of Washington . . . and carried it off. This is totally false." Jennings continued: "She had no time for doing it. It would have required a ladder to get it down. All she carried off was the silver in her reticule, as the British were . . . expected every moment."

Jennings said White House staffers John Sioussat, a steward, and Thomas McGraw, a gardener, removed the canvas "and sent it off on a wagon, with some large silver urns and such other valuables as could be hastily got hold of."

Jennings had come to the White House in 1809, at about age 10, from Montpelier. Dolley kept Jennings until 1846, when, by then an impoverished widow, she sold him to Pollard Webb, an insurance agent, for $200. Six months later, Massachusetts Senator Daniel Webster purchased Jennings' freedom for $120, an amount Jennings agreed to work off as Webster's servant. In 1851, Webster recommended Jennings for a job at the Pension Office. In 1865, his recollections were published in *A Colored Man's Reminiscences of James Madison*—believed to be the first published account by a White House slave as well as the first White House staff memoir. But it attracted little notice.

Taylor has unearthed the only known photograph of Jennings (who died in 1874) and discovered details of his marriage to Fanny Gordon, a slave on the plantation next to Montpelier. "It was the [Jennings] memoir that inspired me," Taylor says. She plans to complete a book about him this year.

The discouraged British had fought a halfhearted battle there and retreated to Canada. In Florida, after a British fleet arrived in Pensacola Bay, an American Army commanded by Gen. Andrew Jackson seized Pensacola (under Spanish control since the late 1700s) in November 1814. Thus, the British were deprived of a place to disembark. President Madison cited these victories in a message to Congress.

But the House of Representatives remained unmoved; it voted 79–37 to consider abandoning Washington. Still, Madison resisted. Dolley summoned all her social resources to persuade the congressmen to change their minds. At Octagon House, she presided over several scaled-down versions of her White House galas. For the next four months, Dolley and her allies lobbied the legislators as they continued to debate the proposal. Finally, both houses of Congress voted not only to stay in Washington but also to rebuild the Capitol and White House.

The Madisons' worries were by no means over. After the Massachusetts legislature called for a conference of the five New England states to meet in Hartford, Connecticut, in December 1814, rumors swept the nation that the Yankees were going to secede or, at the very least, demand a semi-independence that could spell the end of the Union. A delegate leaked a "scoop" to the press: President Madison would resign.

Meanwhile, 8,000 British forces had landed in New Orleans and clashed with General Jackson's troops. If they captured the city, they would control the Mississippi River Valley. In Hartford, the disunion convention dispatched delegates to Washington to confront the president. On the other side of the Atlantic, the British were making outrageous demands of American envoys, headed by Treasury Secretary Albert Gallatin, aimed at reducing the United States to subservience. "The prospect of peace appears to get darker and darker," Dolley wrote to Gallatin's wife, Hannah, on December 26.

On January 14, 1815, a profoundly worried Dolley wrote again to Hannah: "The fate of N Orleans will be known today—on which so much depends." She was wrong. The rest of January trickled away with no news from New Orleans. Meanwhile, the delegates from the Hartford Convention reached Washington. They were no longer proposing secession, but they wanted amendments to the Constitution restricting the president's power, and they vowed to call another convention in June if the war continued. There was little doubt that this second session would recommend secession.

Federalists and others predicted New Orleans would be lost; there were calls for Madison's impeachment. On Saturday, February 4, a messenger reached Washington with a letter from General Jackson reporting that he and his men had routed the British veterans, killing and wounding about 2,100 of them with a loss of only 7. New Orleans—and the Mississippi River—would remain in American hands! As night fell and the news swept through the nation's capital, thousands of cheering celebrants marched along the streets carrying candles and torches. Dolley placed candles in every window of Octagon House. In the tumult, the Hartford Convention delegates stole out of town, never to be heard from again.

Ten days later, on February 14, came even more astonishing news: Henry Carroll, secretary to the American peace delegation, had returned from Ghent, Belgium. A buoyant Dolley urged her friends to attend a reception that evening. When they arrived, they were told that Carroll had brought a draft of a peace treaty; the president was upstairs in his study, discussing it with his cabinet.

The house was jammed with representatives and senators from both parties. A reporter from *The National Intelligencer* marveled at the way these political adversaries were congratulating each other, thanks to the warmth of Dolley's smile and rising hopes that the war was over. "No one . . . who beheld the radiance of joy which lighted up her countenance," the reporter wrote, could doubt "that all uncertainty was at an end." This was a good deal less than true. In fact, the president had been less than thrilled by Carroll's document, which offered little more than an end to the fighting and dying. But he decided that accepting it on the heels of the news from New Orleans would make Americans feel they had won a second war of independence.

Dolley had shrewdly stationed her cousin, Sally Coles, outside the room where the president was making up his mind. When the door opened and Sally saw smiles on every face, she rushed to the head of the stairs and cried: "Peace, Peace." Octagon House exploded with joy. People rushed to embrace and congratulate Dolley. The butler began filling every wineglass in sight. Even the servants were invited to drink, and according to one account, would take two days to recover from the celebration.

Overnight, James Madison had gone from being a potentially impeachable president to a national hero, thanks to Gen. Andrew Jackson's—and Dolley Madison's—resolve. Demobilized soldiers were soon marching past Octagon House. Dolley stood on the steps beside her husband, accepting their salutes.

Critical Thinking

1. What actions did Dolley Madison take in the face of the British threat?

2. Why did her conduct make her a symbol of patriotism?

Abigail Adams' Last Act of Defiance

Our nation's most outspoken founding mother fired the final salvo of her revolutionary quest for women's rights when she scratched out her will.

WOODY HOLTON

Weeks before the Continental Congress issued the Declaration of Independence in 1776, Abigail Adams penned a now famous letter to her husband, John, admonishing him to "Remember the Ladies" when drawing up a new code of laws. "If perticuliar care and attention is not paid to the Laidies," she wrote, "we are determined to foment a Rebelion, and will not hold ourselves bound by any Laws in which we have no voice, or Representation." Within a few years of writing these words, Adams did something that has never been revealed until now. She carried out a mini-revolution in the arena that mattered to her the most: her own household.

In the new Code of Laws which I suppose it will be necessary for you to make I desire you would Remember the Ladies, and be more generous and favourable to them than your ancestors.

Of all the means by which the Founding Fathers and other men lorded it over women, none annoyed Adams more than the legal degradation that women had to submit to the moment they got married. Single women, including widows, were allowed to own and control property. Yet as Adams complained to her husband in a June 1782 letter, wives' property was "subject to the controul and disposal of our partners, to whom the Laws have given a soverign Authority." Historians have studied Abigail Adams' denunciations of married women's inability to control property for decades. But what they have overlooked is that she did not simply complain about the government's denial of married women's property rights. She defied it.

As the Revolutionary War drew to a close, Adams started setting aside a portion of her husband's property and declaring it her own. She added more and more to this stash over the ensuing decades, and she invested it wisely. By the end of 1815 her "pocket money," as she sometimes called it, had grown to more than $5,000—which would be about $100,000 today.

Finally in 1816, racked with pain and convinced she was dying, Adams delivered the parting shot in her household revolution. On January 18, she sat down to write a will. Since she had no legal right as a married woman to own property in her name and her husband was still very much alive, scratching out the four-page document was the ultimate act of rebellion. Moreover, a close look at the will reveals a curious fact that historians have mostly ignored. Apart from a couple of token gifts to her two sons, all the people Adams chose to bequeath money to were women. And many of those women were married.

You know my situation, and that a rigid oeconomy is necessary for me to preserve that independancy which has always been my ambition.

Adams' personal property rights revolution had its roots in her struggle to shield her family from the financial destruction that accompanied the Revolutionary War. Of all the patriot soldiers and statesmen who were forced to abandon their families for long periods, few stayed away as long as John Adams, who saw very little of his Braintree, Mass., farm from 1774 to 1784. John put Abigail in charge of all of the Adams family finances, and she ended up handling her husband's money much better than he ever had, primarily because she was more open to risk. During the course of the war she became an import merchant and then a speculator in depreciated government securities and Vermont land titles. And as she repeatedly reinvested her profits, she increasingly thought of the money she earned as her own.

Abigail lived by the credo "nothing venture nothing have"—a notion that John found somewhat alarming. While he was an envoy in France, the couple confronted a seemingly mundane problem. How could he remit a portion of his salary home? Her solution was audacious. If he shipped her trunkloads of merchandise from Europe, she could extract the few items

What Would Abigail Do?

Americans struggling to weather the economic recession could learn a few things from Abigail Adams, who made money during one of the rockiest periods of our nation's history. If you were to hire her as your financial adviser, here's some advice she might offer.

- **Invest with your head, not your heart.** John Adams wanted to invest all his savings in real estate. But his farmland returned as little as 1 percent annually, and Abigail proved she could earn as much as 25 percent each year speculating in depreciated government securities.
- **Wait for the motivated seller.** In 1785 the Adamses daughter, Abigail, jilted her fiancé, Royall Tyler, who then stopped making payments on the home they planned to move into after they wed. The frustrated seller agreed to sell the house at a bargain price to Abigail and John Adams.
- **Stay coy while bargaining.** When buying real estate, Abigail instructed her business agent not to reveal that he was representing her until a hard bargain was struck. She worried that a seller who knew he was dealing with the wealthy Adams would demand a higher price.
- **Negotiate with the taxman.** After John became president, a tax collector tried to pay him the compliment of giving the Adams mansion in Quincy, Mass., the highest valuation in town. When Abigail protested, the assessed value of the house was lowered and they paid less tax.
- **Be fearless.** When the Dow dipped below 7,000 a year ago, many Americans dumped their stocks, only to kick themselves when the market later rallied. Abigail would not have joined the panic. Shays' Rebellion, a farmers' revolt in Massachusetts, sent bond prices plummeting in late 1786, but she ignored advice from her uncle Cotton Tufts to sell her federal securities and instead instructed him to buy more. "Do not be affraid," she wrote.
- **Keep a close eye on your spouse.** While the Adamses were living in Europe, Abigail routinely read letters John sent from Europe to his business agent in America. As a result, she discovered that her husband planned to purchase a notoriously unproductive farm near their own. She talked him out of it.
- **Share the credit.** Abigail never objected when John took credit for investment decisions that she had actually made. And she tended to portray herself as just the passive consumer of the investment advice she received from her uncle—though she actually managed her portfolio quite aggressively.

—Woody Holton

her family needed and arrange to sell the rest to New England shopkeepers whose shelves were nearly empty because of the war. She convinced John the scheme would allow her to avoid having to "pay extravagant prices" for basic necessities, downplaying that she could also turn a healthy profit by selling the imported goods at an enormous markup. When some of these shipments were captured by the British, John wanted to abandon the whole thing, but she wrote back, "If one in 3 arrives I should be a gainer."

In the fall of 1781, Abigail decided to turn some income from her import business into productive capital. As she later reported to John, she placed 100 pounds sterling "in the hands of a Friend"—her uncle, Cotton Tufts—to invest for her. John, who had seen wartime inflation devastate his, savings, reacted with the curt instruction: "Don't trust Money to any Body." But she chose not to call in the loan. She even speculated in depreciated government securities that had been inveigled from Continental Army soldiers at a fraction of their face value. John hated bond speculators, and used anti-Semitic language against them, but Abigail turned him into one, and she got him an annual return of as much as 24 percent.

By the winter of 1782, Adams had her sights on a new commercial venture. She set about purchasing a 1,650-acre tract in the projected town of Salem, Vt., near the Canadian border. The purchase would be highly speculative, for the sellers had a less than perfect right to the land. Moreover, the town charter prohibited anyone from buying more than 330 acres, but Adams was able to obtain one grant for her husband and one each in the name of four straw men, who then deeded their tracts to the Adams children. The only member of the family who received no parcel was Abigail herself, since as a married woman she was not allowed to purchase real estate in her own name. John thought the venture was far too risky and told Abigail in no uncertain terms, "Don't meddle any more with Vermont." But after the war, she pressed him to expand the family holdings there.

There was scarce ever any such thing under the Sun as an inconsolable widow.

Out of all the money Abigail made for her husband, she set aside some of it and declared it "my own pocket money," "my pin money" and "this money which I call mine." She used it to help out her kids, her sisters, her father's former slave Phoebe Abdee, and other needy neighbors. Even though Abigail believed she had full authority over these funds, she often concealed her activities from her husband. For example, since John had an annoying habit of opening her mail, she once devised a way for her correspondent to enclose her message in a letter addressed to her daughter, Nabby. "It will then fall into no hands but my own," she explained.

But she didn't always conceal her savings from her husband. Once, in December 1783, she tried to use some of this money to bribe John, who had spent the previous five years in Europe as an American diplomat, into coming home to her.

There was a farm he wanted to buy, but he didn't have enough money on hand to complete the deal. So Abigail wrote him, "If my dear Friend you will promise to come home, take the Farm into your own hands and improve it, let me turn dairy woman, and assist you in getting our living this way; instead of running away to foreign courts and leaving me half my Life to mourn in widowhood, then I will run you in debt for this Farm." Most of Abigail's biographers quote this statement, since it went against Abigail and John's shared abhorrence for borrowing money. But they haven't noticed *who it was* that she was proposing John borrow money from. It was Abigail herself. Even though in the eyes of the law she owned *no* personal property, here she was offering to lend her husband a portion of what was technically his own money—but only if he would come home to her. John insisted on staying in Europe, and Abigail held on to the money.

Nearly all of Abigail Adams' biographers mention her will, but they usually move on, overlooking not only the remarkable fact of its existence but its contents. In it, she made token gifts to her two surviving sons, but she gave nothing to her grandsons, nephews or male servants. Everything went to her granddaughters, nieces, female servants and daughters-in-law. In addition to gowns and small sums of cash to pay for mourning rings, Abigail handed out more than $4,000 worth of bank stock, a $1,200 IOU and a total of seven shares of stock in the companies managing the Weymouth and Haverhill toll bridges.

Each granddaughter received clothing, jewelry and a cash payment of anywhere from $400 to $750, depending on how wealthy she was. Her granddaughters Caroline De Windt and Susanna Adams each received $750. Susanna also got a gold watch, several gowns, "the upper part of my pearl Earings" and a share in the Haverhill toll-bridge company. The smallest bequests, $400 each, went to her son Thomas' daughters, both of whom were still children. The cluster of granddaughters that headed up Abigail's roll call of heirs contained one anomaly: Adams included Louisa Smith in this list, even though she was actually a niece. Having never married, Smith had become her aunt's steadiest companion, her most faithful nurse—and her honorary granddaughter. Indeed, her inheritance was the largest of all. In addition to transferring the $1,200 promissory note to her, Abigail gave her a share in the company managing the Haverhill toll bridge. Additional bequests went to Adams' nieces, her sister-in-law Catherine Smith, a pair of distant cousins who were sisters, and two female servants.

There is no indication that Adams had any animus against her male relatives. So why did she exclude all but two of them from her will? Having spent three decades asserting control over land and ownership of personal property despite being married, Adams now bequeathed the bulk of her estate to her granddaughters, nieces, daughters-in-law and female servants in order to enable them, as far as lay in her power, to make the same claim.

To her own surprise, Abigail held on for another year and a half after writing her will. She died about 1 P.M. on October 28, 1818, a few weeks shy of her 74th birthday. Abigail's will was not a legal document that any court was bound to respect, and John would have been within his rights in throwing it in the fire. But he honored it to the letter.

Whilst you are proclaiming peace and good will to Men, Emancipating all Nations, you insist upon retaining an absolute power over Wives.

Abigail had assigned her son Thomas the responsibility of supervising the distribution of her property. Thomas' brother, John Quincy Adams, and their father assisted him in carrying out Abigail's wishes. On November 9, less than two weeks after her death, John transferred the $1,200 promissory note to Louisa Smith, just as Abigail had directed. The former president's compliance with the provisions of his wife's will transformed it into a legally valid document. In the eyes of the law, she had acted as his agent and distributed property that belonged to him. In 1819 John Quincy replaced the promissory note he had given his mother years earlier with a new one made out to Louisa herself. No one could ever challenge his cousin's legal right to recover these funds, for she had never married.

In January 1819, when Louisa Catherine Adams, John Quincy's wife, learned that Abigail had left her an inheritance of $150, she set aside half of the bequest to be divided equally among her three sons, who seemed "to have a better title to it than I could boast." By passing this money on to Abigail's grandsons, Louisa may have indicated disapproval of her mother-in-law's decision to exclude all male descendants other than her own sons from her will. Yet it seems unlikely that Abigail would have considered the younger woman's gift a defeat. After all, by deciding on her own authority to present the money to her children instead of her husband, Louisa acknowledged what the law of the land denied and Abigail had always affirmed: that the money was hers to give.

Critical Thinking

1. Analyze Abigail Adams' views on the rights of women.
2. What was the significance of her writing a will?

WOODY HOLTON, an associate professor of history at the University of Richmond, is the author of *Abigail Adams* and *Unruly Americans*. For a glimpse of a woman's life at the other end of the economic spectrum in early America, see the online extra "Abigail Adams and Phoebe Abdee" at www.historynet.com.

The Everyday Life of Enslaved People in the Antebellum South

CALVIN SCHERMERHORN

Coming of age in a nation that hungered for black labor, antebellum America's slaves were driven relentlessly to toil in fields and factories. Their bodies weakened by fatigue and hunger, wracked by chronic illnesses and injury and, in the case of women of childbearing age, strained by near constant pregnancy, daily existence often came down to an endless struggle of will and endurance. Yet that was not the sum of the challenges and tribulations that burdened black people's lives, for they lived in the shadow of an agricultural revolution. Beginning in the 1790s, short-staple cotton became a profitable commodity owing to the introduction of efficient cotton gins (which separated the sticky seeds from the valuable lint) and a growing demand from British textile mills. To take advantage of new economic opportunities, migrating masters forcibly moved hundreds of thousands of enslaved women, children, and men from the Upper South onto the cotton and sugar frontiers of Mississippi, Texas, Arkansas, Louisiana, and Alabama. This agricultural revolution rapidly changed the shape and face of a young nation. It also profoundly altered the lives of America's slaves as owners and traders separated families, parted friends, and orphaned children. Though enslaved women and men worked as hard to repair the damage done to their families and friendships as they worked for their owners—meeting, marrying, raising babies, and forming all sorts of social institutions—few could escape the human cost of agricultural and national expansion. As Virginia native Madison Jefferson later recalled, "we [had] dread constantly on our minds," never knowing "how long master might keep us, "nor into whose hands we may fall".[1]

Such fears were especially acute among slaves who lived in the upper South states of Maryland and Virginia. In these areas where much of the domestic (or internal) migration originated, owners increasingly came to value their slaves not for the work they might perform but for the cash they could bring at auction. A decline in the profitability of tobacco, combined with a steady growth in the population of slaves, encouraged such recalculation. Between 1790 and 1860 some 1.1 million enslaved people—the majority of them between the ages of 15 and 30— found themselves forced onto the roads. Often plucked away by traders called "Georgia men" and bound together in coffles, black women and men marched south and west, footsore, forlorn, and

"Auction & Negro Sales," Whitehall Street, Atlanta, 1864. Illustrating the immense human cost of slavery, auction houses such as this one wrecked families, separated friends, and orphaned children. (Image courtesy of Library of Congress, LC-DIG-cwpb-03351.)

often missing their families. Later, as the machinery of the slave market grew more elaborate, traders packed slaves into railroad cars and the holds of ships, reducing the duration of the journey though not its harmful effects. The bulk of this traffic took place in the winter, a choice that would deliver fresh workers just in time for spring planting. Some would be dispatched at one of the many auction houses that sprang up in New Orleans, Natchez, and Memphis. Others would be marched through new neighborhoods and sold away in ones or twos by the trader. About 6o percent of America's forced migrants went that way, sold by traders and mixed in with strangers. The remainder moved along with their owners, bundled together with horses, cattle, wagons, and supplies by men (and women) eagerly seeking their fortunes on the southern frontier.[2]

Given the propensity of traders and free migrants to select the strongest, the healthiest, and the most fertile of slaves for transshipment to Deep South plantations—after all, what planters wanted were slaves who could both produce and reproduce—the impact on black families was extensive. Upper South slave communities in Virginia and Maryland were especially hard hit. There, in what amounted to the headwaters of a great forced migration, as many as one half of all sales separated parents from children. One-quarter took husbands from wives[3]. Each season that passed without the sale of a friend or relative brought considerable relief, but slaves worried and prepared for the near inevitable arrival of a trader or his agent. In anticipation of such an eventuality, Henry "Box" Brown's mother took her son "upon her knee and, pointing to the forest trees which were then being stripped of their foliage by the winds of autumn, would say to me, my son, as yonder leaves are stripped from off the trees of the forest, so are the children of the slaves swept away from them by the hands of cruel tyrants".[4] Other parents tried to delay the day of forced departure, hiding their children in the woods as did North Carolina native Moses Grandy's mother, in a heartbreaking and usually futile attempt "to prevent master selling us".[5]

Planters and masters were quick to capitalize on black people's desperate efforts to keep their families intact. Recognizing a new means to wring obedience out of their laborers, sale became a way to "domesticate" those who, like Josiah Henson's father, proved immune to more conventional forms of slave discipline. Recounting how his father had been severely beaten for having intervened to protect his wife from an overseer's assault, Henson described a punishment that failed to achieve its intended effect. "My father became a different man," Henson later wrote, but not an obedient man. Despite a hundred lashes and the amputation of his right ear, he turned "morose, disobedient, and intractable." So much so that the owner gave up on the more conventional modes of control and eventually rid himself of a difficult slave by selling Henson's father to "Alabama; and neither my mother nor I, ever heard of him again".[6]

Sale as punishment was but just one of the many reasons slaves witnessed loved ones being bound away. Slaveowners frequently balanced their personal accounts and paid off their debts by selling excess slaves. Others dismembered longstanding slave families and communities when they divided their property among heirs or gave away a slave to celebrate a child's marriage. These were practices that made enslaved women and men acutely conscious of the ambitions, health, and financial condition of those who claimed to own them. "A bankruptcy, a death, or a removal, may produce a score or two of involuntary divorces," recalled Virginia native Henry Goings. Husbands and wives who belonged to different owners and who had married "abroad" suffered disproportionately from owners' changing

fortunes. Maria Perkins learned this first hand when her owner determined to sell away a number of his slaves. "Dear Husband," Maria opened her letter, "I write . . . to let you know of my distress. my master has sold [our son] albert to trader on Monday court day and myself and other child is for sale also." "I don't want a trader to get me," Maria cried, before asking her husband to approach his own master about buying Maria and the couple's remaining child.[7]

Slaves could do little, however, to slow the rushing tide of forced migration. Swept up in a current that would deposit 285,000 people on Deep South plantations in the 1830s alone, enslaved men and women soon found themselves hard at work in their new homes, creating cotton and sugar economies one field and furrow at a time. The earliest arrivals faced the worst work, much of which involved the back-breaking labor of carving plantations from forests and building the most basic features of an agricultural infrastructure. But those who arrived later had no easy time of it. Sold away from his native Virginia, J. H. Banks arrived in Alabama by rail in the 1830s to find that his new owner "had purchased a new farm, and had taken a contract to finish three miles of railroad," which he intended his slaves to build before putting them to work making cotton.[8] Viewing the fields from his drafty and ramshackle slave quarters—a cabin with "no chinking or daubing," Banks recalled seeing the toll the work took. Despite their location "in the midst of the cotton paradise," young men who were no more "than nineteen or twenty" looked easily twice their age.[9] Along the Oconee and Savannah rivers in Georgia, the Coosa and Tombigbee rivers in Alabama, and along the banks of the Tennessee and Mississippi, conditions were no better. Young women and men labored from before dawn to after dark, usually under the supervision of overseers and horse-mounted patrollers.[10] In places where "sugar wuz king," as one former Louisiana slave recalled it, the work regime pressed even harder, mirroring the volatile Caribbean slave societies that served as models for these factories in the fields. Because of the physically demanding nature of the work slaves performed on America's sugar estates, sex balances remained far out of balance. Men, planters believed, swung the heavy cane knives more effectively than did women. As a consequence, sugar plantations were characterized by disproportionately more men than women, fewer families, and birth rates that lagged behind those of other regions, where despite the trauma of forced migration, strangers gradually came to be friends, married, and had children.[11]

Labor posed plenty of dangers, but it was not the only danger inherent to slavery. There was another side to daily life in bondage, one which women and girls especially confronted. The antebellum South was a landscape characterized by sexual violence against African American women.[12] Harriet Jacobs knew this too well, having learned this particular terrain the day her owner "began to whisper foul words" into her ear.[13] Some women tried to turn the tables and use their sexuality strategically. Though a few may have succeeded, failure could exact a deadly high price. Take Eliza, for example. The concubine of a Maryland planter, Eliza had borne the man a daughter named Emily. When jealous relatives intervened, the arrangement abruptly unraveled. Carried to Washington D.C. by her master's son-in-law Eliza realized too late that she had been badly deceived. Rather than receiving her freedom as she had been promised, the finely attired and petted Eliza found herself lodged in jail and discovered that her so-called freedom paper was actually a bill of sale.[14] Mary, too, suffered grievously when a vengeful mistress sold the Alabama woman away from the baby she had borne her master. The child, only eleven months old, went to a Kentucky owner while Mary ended up in the hands of a Maryland master. Sale did not end Mary's troubles. Subjected to the sexual harassment of her new owner's son, Mary fought back, as did the slave who had been courting her. In a rage, he murdered Mary's attacker. Neighborhood slaves were forced to watch the man who had defended Mary burned alive, and Mary—in a fit of desperation—ended her own life in the waters of the Chesapeake Bay.[15]

Day-to-day life involved more than growing the South's staple crops. Besides constructing and maintaining miles of fence and out-buildings, tending owners' livestock, splitting firewood, and performing a near endless assortment of chores associated with antebellum agricultural enterprise, slaves grew a wide range of crops. In the cotton South, for example, Henry Goings recalled, "a good hand is supposed to cultivate 15 acres of cotton and 10 acres of corn," besides "potatoes and other vegetables," which were grown "for home consumption".[16] After a day sowing, weeding, chopping, or picking cotton, slaves would also often tend to their own garden patches where they would raise vegetables, keep chickens and small livestock, and sometimes even produce commodities on marginal land. In many corners of the South—particularly in or near urban centers—enslaved people became small property owners, accumulating small amounts of wealth by peddling extra eggs, homemade confections, and homegrown produce to townspeople. A few even sold small crops of cotton or tobacco back to their owners, some of whom occasionally found themselves in perpetual debt to their slaves. Others, however, promoted slaves' productive activities as a way to shift some of the burden of support from owners to the owned. Nevertheless, slaves' home enterprises produced some advantages. In creating informal economies, enslaved people developed their own concepts of property, and in rare cases, earned enough from their entrepreneurial and agricultural activities to finance their own freedom or that of a loved one.[17]

Stretching the workday into the nights exposed slaves to a different kind of risk. Again, in the words of Henry Goings—who had been born a slave in Virginia before traveling much of the cotton South with a peripatetic owner—long work days and heavy work loads "often showed themselves in fevers and other miasmatic diseases".[18] Besides aging the nation's slaves before their time, the labor regimes that produced the South's great staples exposed workers to infectious diseases like hookworm, which was endemic on some plantations. Infected slaves grew anemic, lost weight, and succumbed to infections. The sufferers' symptoms began with a dermatitis, "ground itch" or "dew poison," when the hookworm larvae penetrated the skin en route to the small intestine. A raft of other diseases also plagued slaves. Mosquitoes spread yellow fever and malaria. Unwashed

hands and undercooked meat introduced food poisoning and dysentery. Infections transmitted through exposure to soil and fecal matter (workers often went without shoes and babies went without diapers) were common and debilitating. To combat illness, enslaved people cultivated knowledge of folk remedies and sometimes used spiritual medicine. Enslaved women exchanged information on contraception and abortion and became expert midwives. But often even experienced doctors could do little. Outbreaks of viral hepatitis or cholera might tear through a neighborhood at any time, carried on occasion by coffles of the newly arrived slaves. Not surprisingly, the average life expectancy for slaves in antebellum America was just over thirty years.[19]

In addition to being sick, enslaved people were perennially hungry and ill-clothed, especially infants, toddlers, and preteens who made up over 43 percent of the enslaved population in 1820.[20] In the upper South, insufficient quantities of food complemented poor quality, as owners stinted children, reserving calories for slaves in their most productive years. Partly as a consequence, adult slaves tended to be shorter than other Americans.[21] Frederick Douglass recalled being "so pinched with hunger" as a child that he had "fought with the dog" for the "smallest crumbs".[22] Scanty clothing compounded children's problems. Virginia native John Brown recalled that youngsters "of both sexes usually run about quite naked, until they are from ten to twelve years of age".[23] Young Moses Grandy was "compelled to go into the fields and woods to work, with my naked feet cracked and bleeding from extreme cold." To warm them he would "rouse an ox or hog, and stand on the place where it had lain".[24]

Ill-health, hunger, and the raw winds of winter rarely excused slaves from their daily labors. Indeed, in a system as heavily dependent on slaves' labor as were the cotton, sugar, tobacco, and rice crops that enriched their owners—and the nation—any deviance brought summary and often severe punishment. Whips were the favored weapon of choice, falling on slaves' backs and gouging out flesh in retaliation for the smallest infractions. But virtually anything could become an instrument of discipline and control. Masters, mistresses, overseers, and agents routinely relied on sticks, pistols, knives, fists, feet, shovels, and tongs to terrorize and subdue their slaves. Hanna Fambro's mistress beat her mother to death with a broomstick. Ira Jones's aunt died of tetanus after her owner nailed her hands to a barrel.[25] When a young mother arrived late to the fields one morning, fellow slave Charles Ball recalled, the overseer "compelled her to remove her old tow linen shift, the only garment she wore, so as to expose her hips," whereupon he "gave her ten lashes, with his long whip, every touch of which brought blood, and a shriek from the sufferer".[26] Children were not spared their owners' rods. Determined that the youngest slaves mature into the most obedient slaves, masters and mistresses beat children for crying, for failing to do their chores, and sometimes for no reason at all.[27] As one survivor recalled years after the Civil War, slavery "wuz hell".[28]

Family—whether remembered or reconstructed—gave slaves the strength to continue. Whether calling on one another

A Slave Named Gordon and the Power of Historical Images

A wood engraving from *Harper's Weekly* was drawn from a widely distributed and shocking photograph of Gordon, a runaway slave, as he received a medical examination during his induction into the Union army in March 1863. Two months earlier Gordon had been severely beaten by his overseer. While recuperating, he plotted his escape. Pursued by slavecatchers, Gordon showed particular cunning by rubbing onions on his body to disorient the pack of bloodhounds that chased him. The tactic worked. Although muddy, tired, and tattered, he reached the Union encampment at Baton Rouge after covering 80 miles in ten days. Upon learning that Lincoln had recently granted African Americans the opportunity to fight in segregated units, Gordon decided to enlist. He was among the first of nearly 200,000 black Americans to fight during the Civil War.

In the coming weeks, the photographers who took the picture of Gordon's scarred back soon realized the image's potential. They mass produced and sold copies of it around the country. Within months commercial photographers in Philadelphia, Boston, New York, and London were also reproducing the image. The photograph became the latest evidence in the abolitionist outcry over the horrors of slavery. A journalist for the *New York Independent* wrote: "This photograph should be multiplied by 100,000, and scattered over the States. It tells the story in a way that even Mrs. [Harriet Beecher] Stowe [author of *Uncle Tom's Cabin* (1852)] can not approach, because it tells the story to the eye." Abolitionist William Lloyd Garrison also repeatedly referenced Gordon's story and the famous photograph in his crusade against slavery. The photograph received its widest distribution in the July 4, 1863 edition of *Harper's Weekly.* The popular magazine recounted Gordon's story of courage, fortitude, and patriotism. This effort transformed him into a symbol that inspired many free blacks in the North to enlist.

What happened to Gordon after enlisting remains murky. The *Liberator* reported that he served as a sergeant in a black regiment that fought bravely at the siege of Port Hudson, an important Confederate stronghold on the Mississippi River twenty miles north of Baton Rouge. This battle on May 27, 1863 marked the first time that black soldiers played a leading role in an assault on a major Confederate position. Their heroism was widely noted and helped convince many skeptics to accept the enlistment of African Americans into the U.S. Army. Although little more is known about Gordon, the image lives on. By influencing the national debate about slavery, and testifying to the courage displayed by African Americans in the face of terrible brutality, Gordon's photograph not only tells an important story about slavery's history, but also reveals the power of an image in the making of that history.

to stave off an overseer's blows, sharing their meals in the sooty darkness of a plantation cabin, or as Maria Perkins attempted to do, keeping the slave trader at bay, husbands and wives, parents and children, sisters and brothers found in their affective and domestic relations the means to deflect some of the worst of slavery's impositions. For many of those who were transported out of the upper, older, and seaboard South and onto cotton and sugar's new plantations, this often meant starting their families anew. One of probably hundreds of thousands of enslaved women and men who attempted to bring order out of chaos through marriage, Virginia-born Philip Joiner met and wed Henrietta when both were enslaved in south Georgia. By the Civil War, the couple had two daughters, Lucy Ann and Mary Jane, named as so many enslaved children were after grandparents and other close kin.[29]

Despite the calloused advice of owners who told grieving husbands and wives that if they wanted a spouse "so badly, stop your crying and go and find another," many resisted forming new families while their closest kin remained alive in old homes.[30] Charles Ball, for example, joined an enslaved family on his master's South Carolina plantation—sharing a roof, helping out, and contributing food to a collective table—but he never forgot the woman and children he had been made to leave behind in Maryland. As he later explained, "a firm conviction settled upon my mind, that by some means, at present incomprehensible to me, I should yet again embrace my wife, and caress my children." At length Ball did, escaping and making his way back to Maryland, where he was recaptured and reenslaved.[31]

Countless others relied solely on memory, keeping alive in their minds those heartfelt affections. These images did little to shield slaves from owners' blows, but they did remind enslaved people that they were far more than mere tools of agricultural and industrial production. They belonged not only to masters and mistresses, but also to each other. Thus it was that when Hawkins Wilson was sold away from Virginia in 1843, he carried with him a rich set of memories that kept him in mental touch with a family he hoped to see again someday. After the Civil War and emancipation, that day seemed to be fast approaching and Wilson wrote home from Texas that he was "anxious to learn about my sisters, from whom I have been separated many years—I have never heard from them since I left Virginia twenty four years ago—I am in hopes that they are still living and I am anxious to hear how they are getting on." Lest the recipient (an agent of the Bureau of Refugees, Freedmen, and Abandoned Lands) deliver his letter into the wrong hands, Wilson offered a detailed description of his family as he had last known them:

One of my sisters belonged to Peter Coleman in Caroline County and her name was Jane—Her husband's name was Charles and he belonged to Buck Haskin and lived near John Wright's store in the same county—She had three children, Robert, Charles and Julia, when I left—Sister Martha belonged to Dr. Jefferson, who lived two miles above Wright's store—Sister Matilda belonged to Mrs. Botts, in the same county—My dear uncle Jim had a wife at Jack Langley's and his wife was named Adie and his oldest son was named buck and they all belonged to Jack

ANNUAL EDITIONS

Langley—These are all my own dearest relatives and I wish to correspond with them with a view to visit them as soon as I can hear from them—My name is Hawkins Wilson and I am their brother, who was sold at Sheriff's sale.[32]

Hawkins Wilson never reconnected with his family. Neither did hundreds of thousands of other slaves, men and women whose lives had been roughly transformed by cotton's and sugar's antebellum revolutions. Whether left behind in the upper South—unsure of where their loved ones went and how they fared—or deposited among strangers on a Deep South plantation, America's last generation of slaves experienced deep and wrenching change. Many, indeed, lived their lives in near perpetual motion. Subject to repeated sales and migrations, handed off from one owner to the next, burdened with heavy demands on their labor, and haunted by the chronic terror of losing a close friend or kinsman to a trader's coffle, America's enslaved women and men struggled continuously to maintain their health, their strength, and, above all, their humanity. Theirs were day-to-day experiences that involved a hierarchy of concerns: for nourishment, for health, and for whatever security they could eke out of a system that repeatedly visited them with the incremental terrors of forced labor and enforced separations.

Notes

1. John Blassingame, *Slave Testimony: Two Centuries of Letters, Speeches, Interviews, and Autobiographies* (Baton Rouge: Louisiana State Press, 1977), 218.

2. Steven Deyle, *Carry Me Back: The Domestic Slave Trade in American Life* (New York: Oxford University Press, 2005), 288.

3. Brenda E. Stevenson, *Life in Black & White: Family and Community in the Slave South* (New York: Oxford University Press, 1996), 204–05, 223–25; Michael Tadman, *Speculators and Slaves: Masters, Traders, and Slaves in the Old South* (Madison: University of Wisconsin Press, 1996), 147.

4. Henry "Box" Brown, *Narrative of the Life of Henry Box Brown, Written by Himself* (Manchester: Lee and Glynn, 1851), 2. Available at http://docsouth.unc.edu/neh/brownbox/brownbox .html.

5. Moses Grandy, *Narrative of the Life of Moses Grandy, Late a Slave in the United States of America* (London: C. Gilpin, 1843), 8. Available at http://docsouth.unc.edu/fpn/grandy/ grandy.html.

6. Josiah Henson, *The Life of Josiah Henson, Formerly a Slave, Now an Inhabitant of Canada, as Narrated by Himself* (Boston: Arthur D. Phelps, 1849), 1–2. Available at http://docsouth.unc .edu/neh/henson49/henson49.html.

7. Maria Perkins to Richard Perkins, October 7, 1852, Folder 47, Box 3, U. B. Phillips Papers, Manuscripts and Archives, Yale University Library.

8. J. W. C. Pennington, *A Narrative of Events of the Life of J. H. Banks, an Escaped Slave, from the Cotton State, Alabama, in America* (Liverpool: Rourke, 1861), 48. Available at http://docsouth.unc.edu/neh/penning/penning.html.

9. Ibid., 49, 50–51.

10. Steven F. Miller, "Plantation Labor Organization and Slave Life on the Cotton Frontier: The Alabama-Mississippi Black Belt, 1815–1840," in *Cultivation and Culture: Labor and the Shaping of Slave Life in the Americas,* Ira Berlin and Philip D. Morgan, eds. (Charlottesville: University of Virginia Press, 1993), 155–69.

11. Richard J. Follett, *The Sugar Masters: Planters and Slaves in Louisiana's Cane World, 1820–1860* (Baton Rouge: Louisiana State University Press, 2005), 11.

12. Walter Johnson, *River of Dark Dreams: Slavery, Capitalism, and Imperialism in the Mississippi Valley's Cotton Kingdom* (Cambridge: Harvard University Press, forthcoming).

13. Harriet Jacobs, *Incidents in the Life of a Slave Girl. Written by Herself,* Jean Fagan Yellin, ed. (Cambridge: Harvard University Press, 1987), 27.

14. Solomon Northup, *Twelve Years a Slave* (London: Sampson, Low, Son & Co., 1853), 50. Available at http://docsouth.unc .edu/fpn/northup/northup.html.

15. Jacob D. Green, *Narrative of the Life of J. D. Green, a Runaway Slave, from Kentucky, Containing an Account of His Three Escapes, in 1839, 1846, and 1848,* 16. Available at http://docsouth.unc.edu/neh/greenjd/greenjd.html.

16. Henry Goings, *Rambles of a Runaway from Southern Slavery* (Stratford: J. M. Robb, 1869).

17. Dylan C. Penningroth, *The Claims of Kinfolk: African American Property and Community in the Nineteenth-Century South* (Chapel Hill: University of North Carolina Press, 2003), 45–109.

18. Goings, *Rambles of a Runaway from Southern Slavery,* xx.

19. Philip R. P. Coelho and Robert A. McGuire, "Biology, Diseases, and Economics: An Epidemiological History of Slavery in the American South," *Journal of Bioeconomics 1* (November 1999): 151–90, 160; Herbert C. Covey, *African American Slave Medicine: Herbal and Non-Herbal Treatments* (New York: Rowan and Littlefield, 2007); Sharla Fett, *Doctoring the South: Southern Physicians and Everyday Medicine in the Mid-Nineteenth Century* (Chapel Hill: University of North Carolina Press, 2003); Historical Census Browser, Geospatial and Statistical Center, University of Virginia, www.lib .virginia.edu/scholarslab/resources/index.html.

20. Historical Census Browser, Geospatial and Statistical Center, University of Virginia, www.lib.virginia.edu/scholarslab/ resources/index.html.

21. Wilma King, *Stolen Childhood: Slave Youth in Nineteenth-Century America* (Bloomington: Indiana University Press, 1997); Richard H. Steckel, "Work, Disease, and Diet in the Health and Mortality of American Slaves," in *Without Consent or Contract: Technical Papers, vol. II,* Robert W. Fogel and Stanley Engerman, eds. (New York: W. W. Norton, 1992), 498–507; Marie Jenkins Schwartz, *Born in Bondage: Growing Up Enslaved in the Antebellum South* (Cambridge: Harvard University Press, 2001).

22. Frederick Douglass, *My Bondage and My Freedom. Part I.—Life as a Slave. Part II.—Life as a Freeman* (New York: Miller, Orton, and Mulligan, 1855), 75. Available at http://docsouth .unc.edu/neh/douglass55/douglass55.html.

23. John Brown, *Slave Life in Georgia: A Narrative of the Life, Sufferings, and Escape of John Brown, a Fugitive Slave, Now in England,* L. A. Chamerovzow, ed. (London, 1855), 4–5. Available at http://docsouth.unc.edu/neh/jbrown/jbrown .html.

24. Grandy, *Narrative,* II. Available at http://docsouth.unc.edu/fpn/grandy/grandy.html.

25. Thavolia Glymph, *Out of the House of Bondage: The Transformation of the Plantation Household* (Cambridge: Oxford University Press, 2008), 55–56.

26. Charles Ball, *Slavery in the United States: A Narrative of the life and Adventures of Charles Ball, a Black Man* (New York: John S. Taylor, 1837), 159. Available at http://docsouth.unc.edu/neh/ballslavery/ball.html.

27. Blassingame, *Slave Testimony,* 217–18.

28. Glymph, *Out of the House of Bondage,* 33.

29. Susan Eva O'Donovan, *Becoming Free in the Cotton South* (Cambridge: Harvard University Press, 2007), 42.

30. Elizabeth Keckley, *Behind the Scenes, or, Thirty years a Slave, and Four Years in the White House* (New York: G. W. Carleton & Co., 1869), 24–25. Available at http://docsouth.unc.edu/neh/keckley/keckley.html.

31. Ball, *Slavery in the United States,* 36, 71.

32. Ita Berlin and Leslie S. Rowland, eds., *Families and Freedom: A Documentary History of African-American Kinship in the Civil War Era* (New York: The New Press, 1997), 17–18.

Critical Thinking

1. Analyze the "machinery of the slave market."
2. Why was slave life in the lower South generally harsher than that in the upper South?

CALVIN SCHERMERHORN is assistant professor of history at Arizona State University. His research and teaching focuses on American slavery, history of the American South, and nineteenth-century African American history.

Liberty Is Exploitation

The Force of Tradition in Early Manufacturing

Barbara M. Tucker

The industrial revolution represented a watershed in American history. The transition from agriculture to manufacturing was neither an even nor an easy process. The factory floor became a contested and negotiated place, in which the very shape of the work-place depended upon the outcome of struggles between management and labor and between the demands of the factory system and traditional values observed by families. Change occurred at a different pace in various industries as production moved from the household to the workshop and then to the factory. It was the factory system, however, that had the most dramatic impact on the production process and helped to change the economic and social direction of the new nation.

In the historiography of the early republic, the rise of the factory system has received considerable scholarly attention. Beginning in the 1970s, a plethora of monographs were published on the economic and social transformation of such industries as boots and shoes, textiles, paper, and armaments. The customary concerns of economic and business historians, however, did not dominate the discussion; instead, a "new labor history" emerged. These scholars emphasized the impact of the new industrial order on the people who worked in the shops and factories that appeared between 1790 and 1860 and followed them from their workplaces to their communities, homes, churches, and social activities. Issues of paternalism, class, and gender informed their works.

Alan Dawley and Paul Faler were among the most significant innovators in this changing field. Their work on the boot and shoe industry of Lynn, Massachusetts, partly focused on the stress caused when laborers and shoe manufacturers ceased to share a common work space or ideology. This simple change in manufacturing relations profoundly affected the town of Lynn, its neighborhoods, churches, and political structure.[1]

Other scholars turned to the textile industry, in particular Thomas Dublin, who authored a work that challenged the romanticized view of the Lowell system. With eleven investors, Francis Cabot Lowell had formed the Boston Manufacturing Company in 1813. This was one of the most innovative companies organized during the early republic, a corporation characterized by professional management, large-scale production of yarn and cloth, and a unique labor force comprised of girls and women. Dublin challenged the sentimental view of labor-management relations advanced by others. He argued that the relationship between labor and management was an economic one and that the female workers recognized it as such. Whatever community of interests emerged in Waltham and later Lowell and Lawrence, Massachusetts, was among the girls and women themselves and not between labor and management. "When women workers spoke of independence," Dublin writes, "they referred at once to independence from their families and from their employers."[2] While the Lowell system embraced a new production system, its development did not overspread the entire textile industry and remained largely confined to the regions north of Boston. Throughout most of the country, cloth continued to be produced in homes and shops on hand looms. And spinning mills, not integrated corporations, supplied workers with the necessary yarn. Many of these processes were patterned after the system introduced by Samuel Slater.

Born in England and trained under the progressive factory master Jedediah Strutt, Samuel Slater brought the Arkwright system of yarn manufacturing to the United States. Around 1790 he formed a partnership with William Almy and Obadiah Brown to build a factory for the production of yarn. (Parenthetically, most accounts link Almy with Moses Brown, who placed the ad to which Slater responded. Actually, in this partnership Smith Brown, not Moses Brown, first entered the agreement and was later replaced by Obadiah Brown.) Under their arrangement, Slater built carding engines, water frames, and a carding and roving machine which he temporarily installed in a clothier's shop in nearby Pawtucket, Rhode Island, while Almy and Brown supplied the capital. Boys were hired to operate the equipment; within weeks, he doubled his labor force and eventually moved his operations to a specially built factory. Following a practice adopted in England, young children between seven and twelve years of age were employed to operate the new equipment. Initially they were drawn from local families, but as the need for workers increased. Slater turned to the apprentice system. In 1794 he advertised for "four or five active Lads, about 15 Years of Age to serve as Apprentices in the Cotton Factory."[3]

Local poor law officials answered Slater's advertisement and sent indigent boys to the mills. But apprentices proved problematic. Some resented Slater's control over them and his disciplinary style, while others were appalled by the demanding schedule that required them to work from twelve to sixteen hours a day, six days a week. They learned few skills, received room and board in lieu of wages, and were forced to attend Sunday Schools operated by Slater where they received educational training. Many ran away. By 1797 Slater noted that one Rehoboth boy ran away and another followed, and "again If it is suffered to pass, another will go tomorrow & so on until they are all gone."[4] Another form of labor had to be found.

Slater now turned to poor families throughout the area and invited them to send their children to the mill. This form of pauper labor also presented problems. Slater needed the children but not their parents, who resented Slater's control over their children and complained about the irregularity of wage payments and the lack of light and heat in the factories. Some threatened to keep their children home while others entered the factory and withdrew their children without notice, thereby stopping the machines. Slater was exasperated. He had little control over some of the complaints voiced by the parents. Almy and Brown were responsible for paying the families in cash or in kind, but often they were not able to keep their commitments. Slater protested: "You must not expect much yarn until I am better supplied with hands and money to pay them with several are out of corn and I have not a single dollar to buy any for them." The situation was not rectified and Slater again pleaded with Almy and Brown. Send "a little money if not I must unavoidably stop the mill after this week." He could not "bear to have people come round me daily if sometimes hourly and saying I have no wood nor corn nor have not had any several days. Can you expect my children to work if they have nothing to eat?[5] In desperation, he threatened to close the mill and sell the machinery.

Pauper labor was not the answer, and Slater turned to the family system. In New England the family was the basic economic unit. The householder still dominated the family economy, and he retained considerable authority within it to discipline wife and children, protect kin, lead the family in prayer, and supervise the educational and moral training of sons and daughters. Men fought and children resisted attempts by Slater to encroach on these prerogatives. To recruit and retain a labor force of children. Slater had to find common ground with householders. He had to effect some sort of compromise with parents whereby their customary values and their social and economic position within the family and the wider society would be safeguarded and respected. Slater sought to strengthen patriarchy, not challenge it. He recruited entire families to work for him, and a division of labor developed based on age and gender. Householders were brought under the control of the factory master, but they were not required to enter the factory and work alongside their children. Instead, Slater employed them in traditional jobs such as night watchman, painter, mason, and later farm hand. He strengthened their position within the family by having householders negotiate and sign contracts for the employment of their children and personally receive all wages earned by them.

Labor contracts suggest the strength and influence householders exerted over manufacturers. At the Slater and Kimball factory, contracts usually were signed annually beginning April 1. Abel Dudley, for example, agreed to work in 1827, and he put five children in the mill: Sumner, Mary, Eliza, Abigail, and Caroline. He stipulated, however, that "Mary and Caroline have the privilege of going to school two months each one at a time and Amos is to work at 4/pr week when they are out."[6] Some contracts included other stipulations: a child was allowed to work with the mule spinner and taught his trade; either party had to give two weeks notice before quitting; householders were to receive extra pay for Sunday work. Thus, in order to recruit and retain a stable labor force, Samuel Slater struck a compromise with New England householders. If Slater respected their traditional prerogatives, they would provide him with a plentiful, tractable supply of workers. For those families who failed to adhere to this understanding. Slater had a solution. The case of Obadiah Greenhill was typical. On April 1, 1827, Greenhill placed five children from nine to seventeen years of age in Slater's factory. On October 6, the family was "Dismissed for manifesting a disposition to make disturbance in the mills amongst the help and for misconduct in general."[7]

The force of tradition that operated in the factories was extended to village, home, and church. The new factory villages Slater established reflected the needs of New England families. Slatersville was one of the first mill villages developed by Slater and served as a model for later manufacturers:

> Like many of the towns of colonial New England, it was built around a broad road that traversed the town center. The smithy, the dry goods stores, the church, and the school were on this road. Predictably, the Congregational church stood in the geographic center of the village and was surrounded by a broad common. Toward the outskirts of the village lived more than six hundred textile workers, farm laborers, merchants, and mechanics. Their homes were one- and two-story detached and semi-detached dwellings that were built parallel to the main road and separated from one another by garden plots. Each dwelling was occupied by a single family. No house stood isolated from the central community. The mill and its outbuildings . . . did not disturb the traditional sense of community. They were built at a short distance from the village and were surrounded by fenced and tilled fields belonging to the company.[8]

The family and the church were the predominant forces in the lives of many residents. Familial and religious doctrines and discipline served as the basis for a well-ordered society and also a well-run factory. Values taught in the home and the church served the needs of the factory masters.

In the nineteenth century, the home became a training ground for a generation of factory hands. The first law of childhood, the one necessary for the proper maintenance of good family government and obviously the one necessary for the proper maintenance of good order within the factory, was unquestioning obedience. All commands had to be immediately and, in fact, cheerfully obeyed. If obedience was the first law of childhood, then deference was the second. According to nineteenth-century educator Heman Humphrey, "children must early be brought under absolute parental authority, and must submit to all the rules and regulations of the family during the whole period of their minority, and even longer, if they choose to remain at home."[9] These values were reinforced by the church.

Samuel Slater was one of the first manufacturers to establish schools for factory children. Called Sunday Schools, they later were brought under the supervision of local churches. In Webster, Massachusetts—a Slater company town—the Methodist Church played a leading role in the discipline of factory children. The written tracts, hymns, and sermons found in the church advanced a familiar message: obedience, deference, industry, punctuality, and temperance. Such lessons prepared the child and adolescent operatives for salvation and also trained them to be good, obedient factory hands. The Webster Sabbath School Constitution reinforced these notions. In part it read:

> To be regular in attendance, and punctually present at the hour appointed to open school.
>
> To pay a strict and respectful attention to whatever the teacher or Superintendent shall say or request.
>
> To avoid whispering, laughing and any other Improper conduct.[10]

Manufacturers throughout New England and the Mid-Atlantic states adopted many of the features developed by Slater. Philadelphia, for example, became a center for hand-loom weaving. This occurred even after power looms had been installed in Waltham and Lowell. In the Kensington section of Philadelphia, weavers "turned out cotton cloth on hand frames in tiny red-brick cottages lined up in monotonous rows on grid-like streets." A local resident of the area observed that the "sound of these looms may be heard at all hours in garrets, cellars, and out-houses, as well as in the weavers' apartments."[11] Among these weavers a distinct culture emerged. Workers generally owned their own looms, regulated their own time, and observed traditional feasts and holidays. They were a group of especially independent and proud men. Their craft world was "a man's dominion, the weaver's prowess an element in the constitution of patriarchal family relations."[12] But by the 1840s the industry began to change. Adjacent to their dwellings, some men constructed wooden buildings or sheds, either purchased looms outright and hired weavers to operate them, or opened their sheds to weavers who brought their own equipment with them. By the Civil War, a weaver earned from $3.00 to $4.50 per week, a wage insufficient to support a family.[13] Their children often had to work in the spinning mills. Slater's efforts to preserve the patriarchy of the fathers in effect reduced their offspring to permanent children—as opposed to the apprenticeship model that implied growth and eventual maturity.

While the spinning mills that supplied yarn to the weavers of Kensington were patterned after those started by Slater, there were differences. This was especially true for the treatment of labor. In Philadelphia, where hand loom weaving persisted well into the mid-century, the treatment of young child operatives in textile mills caused a public scandal. In 1837 a Select Committee was formed by the Pennsylvania Senate to investigate conditions of labor, especially the employment of children under twelve in the state's textile mills. One adult worker, William Shaw, commented extensively on the work and treatment of children. Most of the youngest children were employed at carding and spinning and worked from twelve to fourteen hours per day. Shaw commented further: "I have known children of nine years of age to be employed at spinning[;] at carding, as young as ten years. Punishment, by whipping, is frequent; they are sometimes sent home and docked for not attending punctually." Another witness, Joseph Dean, offered similar testimony. At his factory one-third to one-half of the operatives were under the age of twelve. He described the attitudes toward the children: "The children were occasionally punished by a blow from the hand; does not know that the strap was used. . . . Males and females were provided with separate water closets, when provided at all; no pains taken on the subject: sometimes none were provided." Another witness, Robert Craig, described some of the working conditions experienced by the young workers:

> "the children must stand all the time at their work, walking backwards and forwards; the children often complain of fatigue; witness has been many of them neglect their work, from exhaustion, and seek repose in sleep; for this, they are generally punished. . . . The greatest evil, in my mind, is that the children, from nine to eleven years old, are required to carry up from one to four stories, a box of bobbins; these boxes weight about sixteen pounds; they are carried on the head."[14]

Some labor leaders and educators—Seth Luther, Horace Mann, and Henry Barnard, among others—called for an end to child labor. While legislation was passed, it failed to solve the problem. In 1842 Massachusetts declared that children under twelve could not work more than ten hours per day. Six years later Pennsylvania passed laws stating that minors could not work over ten hours a day or sixty hours per week. But by special contract, boys and girls over fourteen could work longer.[15] And then, of course, enforcement of these laws became problematic. Who was to enforce the laws and who was to be the final arbiter in determining the age of the children?

By the time child labor laws were passed, conditions within the industry had begun to change. The industry experienced several economic downturns, especially in 1829 and chronically from 1836 to 1844. Companies took the opportunity to reorganize, and Samuel Slater was no exception. In 1829 Slater feared insolvency. He had endorsed notes and was not able to pay them without first liquidating and reorganizing his holdings. He relinquished partial control of his business to his three sons and formed Samuel Slater and Sons. Other changes included the introduction of cost accounting, the employment of paid professional managers, and incorporation. The labor force was not exempt. Family labor and many of the traditional prerogatives associated with it ended. Each hand was hired, paid, assigned jobs, and disciplined by the factory manager. Young people now could contract for themselves, and this had an important impact on the family. Economically independent now, adolescents could negotiate with parents over the price of room and board, education, discipline, dress, marriage partners, and life style. Some left home and moved into boarding houses or traveled to other mill towns looking for work. If men wanted to remain with the company, they now had to enter the mills and labor alongside their women and children, suffering an implicit loss of status. This trend spread throughout the textile industry. The paternalism that once served the needs of labor and management was discarded by manufacturers; increasingly, the Slater system came to resemble Lowell.

Less expensive hands could be found, and by the 1840s French Canadian and Irish immigrants replaced many Yankee families in the mills. Factory owners no long felt compelled to accommodate adults. Next to their factories they erected multi-family tenements and boarding houses. Built side by side along a roadway, the small wooden tenements housed from three to four families plus their boarders. Rooms were small, windows were few, storage space was limited, and garden plots were eliminated altogether. Physically the tenements, boarding houses, and factory now formed a distinct unit; the factory dominated work and home life. Overcrowding occurred, health deteriorated, and mortality rates increased. Deaths from dysentery, convulsions, lung fever, delirium tremors, dropsy, erysipelas, typhus, and of course consumption or tuberculosis were recorded. In the 1840s typhus reached epidemic proportions, striking Webster, Massachusetts, first in 1843, then again in 1844 and 1846. Consumption was endemic, and children often were its victims. Indeed, child mortality rates were high, and young children even succumbed to convulsions and "teething."[16] Several possibilities could account for such infant deaths. To quiet a crying child, parents might give him or her a drug such as laudanum; some of these children could have overdosed on opiates. Or vitamin and mineral deficiencies, including a lack of calcium, magnesium, and vitamin D, might have caused convulsions and resulted in death. As two historians suggest, however, "teething is suspect because nineteenth century physicians observed that the convulsions which ravaged babies often occurred during the teething process and concluded that the sprouting of teeth was somehow responsible—hence 'teething' as a cause of death." It has been argued that the primary source of calcium for children came from mother's milk; during teething, some women ceased to breast feed children and turned to bovine milk. This abrupt shift sometimes triggered convulsions, but people mistakenly blamed the child's death on teething.[17]

By the 1850s manufacturers with clear economic interests and goals considered labor just another cost of production. Paternalism and the force of traditional social relations gave way under changing conditions. Individual hands replaced family units in the mills; manufacturers enlarged their mills and increased their labor supply. Little attention was given to the quality of life in the factory towns. Overcrowding, disease, high mortality rates, frequent labor turnover, crime, and illiteracy came to characterize life in these communities. The factories and villages of 1850 bore scant resemblance to traditional rural manufacturing communities of 1800. In the end, neither innovators such as Lowell nor conservative paternalists such as Slater had been able to prevent the transformation of factory labor into a commodity with a price—the living wage—to be set by supply and demand.

Notes

1. Alan Dawley, *Class and Community: The Industrial Revolution in Lynn* (Cambridge, MA: Harvard University Press, 1976) and Paul G. Faler, *Mechanics and Manufacturers in the Early Industrial Revolution: Lynn, Massachusetts, 1780–1860* (Albany: State University of New York Press, 1981).

2. Thomas Dublin, *Women at Work: The Transformation of Work and Community in Lowell, Massachusetts, 1826–1860* (New York: Columbia University Press, 1979), 95.

3. *Providence Gazette,* October 11, 1794, quoted in Brendan F. Gilbane, "A Social History of Samuel Slater's Pawtucket, 1790–1830" (PhD diss., Boston University Graduate School, 1969), 247. Much of this essay is based on the author's book; see Barbara M. Tucker, *Samuel Slater and the Origins of the American Textile Industry, 1790–1860* (Ithaca, NY: Cornell University Press, 1984).

4. Ibid., 78.

5. Ibid., 84.

6. Slater and Kimball vol. 3, contract. Abel Dudley, 1827. Samuel Slater Collection. Baker Library, Harvard University, Cambridge, Massachusetts.

7. Ibid., Obadiah Greenhill, 1827.

8. Tucker, *Samuel Slater and the Origins of the American Textile Industry,* 126.

9. Heman Humphrey, *Domestic Education* (Amherst, MA; J, S. & C. Adams, 1840), 41.

10. "Constitution of the Methodist Episcopal Church Sabbath School," 1861–1863, United Church of Christ, Webster, Massachusetts.

11. Bruce Laurie, *Working People of Philadelphia, 1800–1850* (Philadelphia: Temple University Press, 1980), IL. See also, Edwin T. Freedley, *Philadelphia and Its Manufactures: A Handbook Exhibiting the Development, Variety, and Statistics of the Manufacturing Industry of Philadelphia in 1857* (Philadelphia: Edward Young, 1859), 253.

12. Philip Scranton, *Proprietary Capitalism: The Textile Manufacture at Philadelphia, 1800–1885* (Cambridge: Cambridge University Press, 1983), 195.

13. Freedley, *Philadelphia and Its Manufactures,* 254.

14. Pennsylvania General Assembly. Senate, *Report of the Select Committee Appointed to Visit the Manufacturing Districts of the Commonwealth, for the Purpose of Investigating the Employment of Children in Manufactories, Mr. Peltz, Chairman* (Harrisburg, PA: Thompson & Clark, Printers. 1838), 12–16.

15. Elizabeth Otey, *Beginnings of Child Labor Legislation in Certain States: a Comparative Study,* vol. VI of *Report on Condition of Woman and Child Wage-Earners in the United*

States. Prepared under the direction of Chas. P. Neill, Commissioner of Labor. 61st Cong., 2nd Sess. (Washington, DC: Government Printing Office, 1910), 207–8.

16. Tucker, *Samuel Slater and the Origins of the American Textile Industry,* 232. See also Webster, Massachusetts. Vital Statistics, Deaths. Emory Hough, November 1853 and Lewis Johnson, 1844, 1845.

17. Kenneth F. Kiple and Virginia H. Kiple, "Slave Child Mortality: Some Nutritional Answers to a Perennial Puzzle." *Journal of Social History* 10 (March 1977): 291–92. The Kiples believe that convulsions and teething as a cause of death were misunderstood. The children had tetany, a disease not recognized at the time.

Critical Thinking

1. Discuss the working conditions many children encountered in the factory system.

2. Why was work in the factory system generally more grueling that that in a small shop?

BARBARA M. TUCKER is Professor of History and Director of the Center for Connecticut Studies at Eastern Connecticut State University. She is the author of *Samuel Slater and the Origins of the American Textile Industry, 1790–1860* and has published articles in such journals as *Labor History, Business History Review, Agricultural History* and *Journal of the Early Republic*.

From *OAH Magazine of History,* May 2005, pp. 21–24. Copyright © 2005 by Organization of American Historians. Reprinted by permission via the Copyright Clearance Center.

From Detroit to the Promised Land

**Two escaped slaves from Kentucky touched off riots
in Detroit and set an international legal precedent.**

KAROLYN SMARDZ FROST

Detroit Sheriff John M. Wilson glanced anxiously upward. From the courtroom balcony came the sounds of angry muttering and restless shuffling. Peering down over the railing were dozens of black faces.

Before him stood a young couple, well-dressed and respectful toward Judge Henry Chipman, who occupied the bench of the Wayne County, Courthouse that Saturday morning in 1833. Thornton Blackburn, 21, and his beautiful wife, Ruthie, some nine years his senior, were accused of being fugitives from slavery. According to Michigan law, those claimed as runaways had to prove themselves entitled to free status before a judge or magistrate. While no black could testify on his or her own behalf against a white claimant, the law guaranteed a legal defense to ensure that the genuinely free could not be carried off to a life of bondage. After all, slave catchers, the unscrupulous bounty hunters who captured runaways and returned them to their Southern owners, had been known to kidnap free blacks and sell them into slavery. Detroit city attorney Alexander D. Frazier was tasked with defending the accused.

Despite an impassioned defense by Frazier, the case was not going well for the Blackburns. They had been unable to produce certificates of manumission, the documentation registered in a local courthouse when a Southern slave was legally freed by his or her owner. On the other hand, the Kentucky attorney employed by the Blackburns' owners, Benjamin G. Weir, and Talbot Clayton Oldham, the nephew of Thornton's owner who had traveled to Detroit to identify him, had presented signed affidavits stating that the Blackburns were both "fugitives from labor."

The Blackburns had lived in Detroit for two years after a harrowing escape from Kentucky. Ruthie had been auctioned off to a Louisville merchant named Virgil McKnight—who was suspected of buying groups of Kentucky slaves to then sell to Southern markets. The couple fled in a bold and incredibly dangerous escape in broad daylight. Traveling up the Ohio River by steamboat as far as Cincinnati, they reached free soil on July 4, Independence Day, 1831, before continuing on to Michigan Territory where they settled down. Thornton had trained as a stonemason in his youth and soon found employment. The couple became both respected and popular in Detroit's tiny black community.

**A slave's heavy iron shackles, sometimes
used as a punishment for running away,
weighed down body and spirit.**

Shortly after the fugitives reached Michigan, a Louisville native visiting Detroit had recognized Thornton Blackburn on the street. Thomas Rogers knew that Blackburn was Susan Brown's escaped slave but, inexplicably, he withheld information about his discovery for almost two years. When he finally disclosed the Blackburns' whereabouts in late May 1833, Judge John Pope Oldham, Brown's brother-in-law, and McKnight hired Weir, a prominent lawyer and member of the Louisville City Council, to travel to Detroit and present their claim to the Blackburns before the Michigan courts.

Weir and Judge Oldham's son, Talbot, arrived in Detroit on June 13 and demanded the return of Thornton and Ruthie Blackburn. Judge Chipman had little choice in the matter. The federal Fugitive Slave Law of 1793 required that he hand the hapless couple over to their claimants. Likewise, the Northwest Ordinance of 1787, which forbade slavery north and west of the Ohio River, guaranteed that Southern fugitives apprehended in those territories would be returned to their owners. Runaway slaves like the Blackburns faced terrible punishment: Whippings, brandings and mutilation were well-known consequences of flight. Then, most likely, one or both of them would be "sold down the river." Thousands of Kentucky slaves, worth less in the cooler climate of that border state than in the great markets at the mouth of the Mississippi River, had been sold over the years to feed the unending appetite of King Cotton for labor.

Black Detroit was incensed at the prospect. When Judge Chipman pronounced his fateful sentence sending the Blackburns back to bondage, the mood turned ugly. Observers in the courtroom that day later testified that the blacks there threatened to burn Detroit to the ground.

Weir and Oldham had booked passage for themselves and the Blackburns on the steamboat Ohio, scheduled to leave for Buffalo the next day, Sunday. Legally, the Detroit courts and keepers of the peace had no further responsibility in the matter.

But Sheriff Wilson quite rightly feared the rising racial tension in the city and took the unprecedented step of incarcerating the Blackburns in the city jail. He then set about convincing Ohio's captain to delay sailing until Monday afternoon when most in the black community would be back at work.

Wilson's actions further enraged blacks in the city. They considered him to be acting in the interests of the slaveholders, above and beyond his responsibilities as sheriff. Furthermore, rumors spread that both Wilson and the city jailer, Lemuel Goodall, had been promised $50 by Weir for the safe delivery of Thornton and Ruthie Blackburn to the docks.

By the early 1830s, there were already numerous former slaves living in the nominally free territory of Michigan. Detroit was an important station on what would soon be called the Underground Railroad. If the judge and sheriff willingly handed over the Blackburns to slave agents, then no black man, woman or child living in Michigan Territory was safe. The more militant elements of the community immediately armed themselves and took to the streets.

Angry crowds milled around the jail on Gratiot Street well into Saturday evening. People came from as far away as Fort Malden, Upper Canada, to lend their support. The sheriff's deputy, Alexander McArthur, later testified:

> There were assembled around the said jail a large number of blacks and mulattoes armed with sticks, clubs, knives, pistols, swords, and other unlawful weapons avowing with loud threats their determination to rescue the said Prisoner Thornton Blackburn then in the custody of the said John M. Wilson, Sheriff of the said County. The Sheriff . . . endeavored reasoning with them to persuade them to disperse, but without effect, they telling him that they expected some of them would be killed but that they were determined to rescue the prisoner at all hazards.

Saturday night, after the case had been decided, concerned men and women met at the home of respected local businessman Benjamin Willoughby. Willoughby was an emancipated slave from Kentucky who had lived very close to the place Thornton had been born. He brought his family to Detroit in about 1826, and he and his wife wielded considerable influence within the black community.

Several other people who would later become leaders in the Underground Railroad activities along the Detroit River shore were also present: Madison J. Lightfoot and his wife, Tabitha; George and Caroline French; and John Cook, who owned a profitable hairdressing establishment that served a largely white clientele. Frazier, the white attorney who had defended the Blackburns, and his friend Charles Cleland, the white publisher of the Detroit Courier and also an attorney, were there, too. The group hatched a daring plot to rescue the Blackburns and, at the same time, send a strong message to Michigan's territorial government that returning fugitive slaves to bondage would not be tolerated.

The next day, Sunday, June 16, crowds of armed blacks flocked to the district near the jail. They also gathered at the steamboat docks at the foot of Randolph Street where Ohio bobbed gently at its berth. That afternoon, Tabitha Lightfoot and Caroline French approached Sheriff Wilson. Could they possibly visit Mrs. Blackburn in her cell to pray with her and comfort her before her journey? Wilson, concerned about the possibility of civil unrest, quite likely saw granting the visit as one means for diffusing the tension and agreed.

It was well after dark when two very distressed ladies, covering their faces with veils as they wept, emerged from the jail and hurried home. When the jailer entered Ruthie Blackburn's cell the next morning, he found Caroline French in her place. The editor of the Detroit Courier of June 19 wrote, "By a contrivance that demonstrates that Negroes are not wholly wanting in shrewdness, the female was rescued from jail on Sunday evening and made her escape to Canada where she is now." It was later revealed that she had been taken across the Detroit River on the advice of Frazier, who had visited the Blackburns in their cells and informed them that their only safety lay in reaching the British colony of Upper Canada.

When Weir and Talbot Oldham learned of Blackburn's flight, they approached Judge Chipman to claim Mrs. French in lieu of their rightful prisoner. They intended to sell her as a slave so Ruthie Blackburn's owner, McKnight, could recoup his losses. Fortunately for French, her husband George and Madison Lightfoot worked at the popular Steamboat Hotel in downtown Detroit. Many members of the legal profession frequented the hotel bar, including Judge Charles Larned, who sympathized with French's situation. Larned immediately issued a writ of habeas corpus protecting French and she was freed, but she soon crossed the river and remained in Canada for some months after the incident.

By now, Ruthie Blackburn was safely ensconced with friends at Amherstburg in what is now Ontario, but her husband still remained in prison awaiting his imminent return to slavery.

About 4 o'clock on the same day that Ruthie's escape was discovered, Monday, June 17, Thornton was brought in chains to the door of the jail flanked by Sheriff Wilson and Jailer Goodall. Deputy McArthur and Oldham were also present; Weir had already boarded [the] Ohio. Only a few black men and women were outside the jail, but they were armed and very agitated.

One account, published years later in the February 7, 1870, Detroit Daily Post and probably much embellished, presents an inspiring image of what happened as the carriage arrived to take Thornton to the docks. A crowd of about 200 angry blacks marched up Gratiot Street toward the jail. At their head strode an elderly woman carrying a stake with a white rag tied around it and pointed forward like a spear. The sheriff tried to take the prisoner back inside the jail, but Thornton offered to calm the crowd. Oldham, who had grown up with his aunt's former slave, said that he thought Blackburn might have more influence than would the sheriff. As Thornton came forward, a black man in the crowd tossed him a pistol and said, "Shoot the rascal," meaning Wilson, who then tried to wrest the gun from his prisoner. Thornton fired in the air, igniting what came to be known as the Blackburn Riots of 1833, the first racial riots in Detroit history.

Although no one suspected it at the time, the whole event had been carefully orchestrated. Well known local blacks such as the Lightfoots, Frenches and Willoughbys stayed in the background while a daring group of young men prepared to grab Thornton and carry him off to a boat waiting by the river. All but one were fugitive slaves themselves, and all were readily identified by Wilson and the other officials. The rescuers knew that if they were successful in rescuing Thornton, they could never return from the Upper Canadian shore.

Eminent Detroit historian Norman McRae pieced together the following account of the riot:

> Seeing Blackburn in difficulty, members of the mob attacked Sheriff Wilson, while Lewis Austin took Blackburn into the stagecoach that was waiting to transport Blackburn, his captor and the sheriff to the dock. Earlier several women had removed the linchpin from the vehicle in order to disable it. As a result Blackburn was kept inside the coach until two elderly blacks. Daddy Grace and Sleepy Polly, could remove him. Then . . . Blackburn was placed into a horse-drawn cart that disappeared into the nearby woods.

Considering discretion the better part of valor, Goodall, Oldham and McArthur retreated into the jail, leaving Wilson to face the furious crowd alone. The sheriff fired several shots in an effort to halt the violence, but he was pulled to the ground and terribly beaten. Afterward, Wilson could remember little of the day's events, and he died of his injuries a year later. Neither did the rescuers all escape unscathed. According to the Detroit Daily, Post's 1870 retrospective edition—published at the time that Michigan blacks were finally awarded the right to vote—"One Negro, named Louis Austin, was shot in the breast, the ball penetrating the lung, and lodging in the shoulder blade. . . . After two years of long suffering, Louis died, attributing his death to the effects of the wound."

The Daily Post also gave the following description of the escape in which Daddy Grace (or Daddy Walker, accounts vary) took center stage. The numbers are much exaggerated, with most contemporary accounts recording that only 30 or 40 people actually took part in the fray.

> During the melee, an old colored man, named "Daddy Walker," who, with his cart and a blind horse, had been impressed into the service, backed up his vehicle to the jail steps, while an old colored woman by the name of "Sleepy Polly," and who never before nor after showed signs of activity, seized hold of Blackburn and dragged him into the cart. . . . Daddy Walker, and the mob, which had been swelled to 400 or 500 persons, immediately drove, post-haste, up Gratiot road with the evident intention of turning toward the river as soon as practicable. . . .

> The driver was somewhat reluctant about his task, but a Negro in the cart, holding a drawn sword over his head, urged him and his blind horse to respectable speed. The crowd continued to push up Gratiot road and in answer to inquiries whither the fugitive had been taken, pointed forward and said, "further on." But the cart entered the woods on the north side of the road, about where Russell street now is, and disappeared.

The sound of barking dogs alerted the Blackburn party that a posse had been formed and was in pursuit. They devised a clever ruse to put the dogs off the scent. Sending Daddy Grace and his cart off in one direction as a decoy, the rescuers broke the manacles on Thornton's feet with an axe and wrapped his

chains in bandanas to stop them from rattling. Together they ran through the woods toward the river. They paid the waiting boatman with a gold watch and were safely conveyed across to Sandwich (now part of Windsor), Upper Canada.

Back in Detroit, all was chaos. General Friend Palmer was a youthful eyewitness to the event. "Great excitement ensued; the Presbyterian Church bell rang an alarm, the cry 'To Arms' was shouted through the streets and men with guns, pistols and swords were seen coming from all directions," Palmer wrote in 1906. Wilson lay bleeding and alone on the jailhouse steps until McArthur, Goodall and Oldham ventured out to bring the sheriff inside and dress his wounds. There they remained until the entire mob had dispersed, about 8 o'clock that night.

In the aftermath of the riot, many of the city's African-American residents were rounded up and jailed. Their cases were heard before the mayor's court. Those who were judged innocent still had to provide bail to ensure their good behavior, and then they were freed. At least 10 men, including the aged Daddy Grace, were sentenced to hard labor and served several months in municipal roadwork gangs.

Madison Lightfoot and George French, surely the ringleaders of the plot along with Willoughby, were incarcerated for only a short time, even though Lightfoot was suspected of supplying Thornton with the pistol. Upon his release, French crossed to Upper Canada and remained there with his wife for months; he later returned to Detroit. No suspicion seems to have fallen on the Willoughbys or on Cook, and their names were never mentioned in formal records of the affair. Tabitha Lightfoot was fined $25 as "the prime mover of the riot," a charge she did not dispute.

A curfew was maintained in Detroit for some weeks, and the militia, under War of 1812 veteran General John Williams, was charged with patrolling the streets. Lewis Cass, a former governor of Michigan and President Andrew Jackson's secretary of war, happened to be in town when the incident occurred. He declared martial law and called out federal troops from Fort Gratiot to assist the militia.

Rumors abounded. It was widely believed that blacks from Upper Canada (what is now Ontario) were planning to cross the river en masse and invade Detroit. Contemporary letters attested to the fear felt by the white citizens and made comparisons to the early days of Michigan Territory, when they worried about Indian attacks. A night watch of 16 men was appointed, with orders not to allow any black person to approach the Detroit River bank. Their only catches were a smuggler plying his clandestine trade along the river and the mayor himself who was prowling the streets in search of miscreants and was apprehended by an overzealous picket.

There was a terrible backlash against black Detroiters for the community's support of Thornton and Ruthie Blackburn. People were attacked in the streets, and homes were burned to the ground. Many blacks sold their property for less than it was worth or simply abandoned what they had and fled across the river to Upper Canada. Detroit lost all but a few of its black residents as a result of the 1833 riots and their aftermath, and the population did not again increase until after 1837, when

Looking for Clues

Researching the early lives of fugitive slaves is extremely difficult. Slaveholders' records are usually limited to describing the labor slaves could perform and their potential market value. Furthermore, although African Americans often adopted surnames, part of the intentional dehumanizing process was that slaves were addressed only by their first names, as one would address a child or a pet.

Fortunately for researchers, the Blackburn family had an illustrious surname redolent of old Virginia. The Blackburns of Rippon Lodge, Prince William County, Va., who owned Thornton's mother, Sibby, at the time of her birth were intimate friends of George Washington. Sibby and her children consistently used the name after they were taken to Kentucky as part of the vast westward migration and it was occasionally recorded by whites.

Still, for my first foray into African-American genealogy, I found myself searching for a young man named only "Thornton." To complicate matters, he had been owned, successively, by Kentuckians named "Smith" and "Brown." The search for the Blackburn family's individual members took 20 years, and encompassed information located in more than a dozen states as well as Ontario, Canada.

The most fruitful source was the court records. The Blackburns' escape by steamboat up the Ohio River in 1831 was both bold and perilous. The steamboat captain and the boat's owners were prosecuted for their part in the escape in a case that lasted 15 years and went all the way to the U.S. Supreme Court. The Blackburns' recapture in Detroit and the ensuing civil unrest resulted in a vast array of civil and diplomatic documentation, copies of which were found in the Michigan state archives as well as in the official records of the province of Upper Canada (Ontario). Details of the Blackburns' ownership, their earlier lives as slaves and even their personal appearance come from these all-important records, a unique window on a past that has in so many ways shaped modern North American attitudes to race.

—Karolyn Smardz Frost

Michigan became a state and ratified a constitution repudiating slavery and safeguarding personal liberty.

Immediately after the riots, Detroit's municipal government established a citizens' committee to investigate the events. Its report was published in the Detroit Journal and Advertiser of Friday, July 19, 1833, and included resolutions that reaffirmed support for the federal law regarding fugitive slaves:

> That while we hold personal liberty to be a sacred and unalienable right, yet when the property of the master is clearly proven in the slave, it becomes our duty to see that the laws be maintained and that no riotous mob be allowed to violate them.

The report also acknowledged the role of Canadian authorities:

> Resolved: that we duly appreciate the prompt and efficient measures adopted by the Civil Authority of the Province of Upper Canada and by our British neighbors in arresting and securing the negroes concerned in the riotous proceedings which occurred in this city.

That statement referred to the fact that the mayor of Detroit had sent a letter to the sheriff of the Western District in Upper Canada, whose administrative center was at Sandwich, demanding the arrest of Thornton Blackburn and his rescuers on the grounds that they had incited a riot and tried to kill the Wayne County sheriff. Blackburn and his friends were arrested and jailed, and Ruthie Blackburn was also taken into custody.

What followed was the first extradition case between Canada and the United States over the thorny issue of fugitive slaves. Sir John Colborne, Upper Canada's abolitionist lieutenant governor, and his attorney general, Robert Simpson Jameson, defended the Blackburns on the grounds that even if they were acquitted of the criminal charges in Michigan, they would still be condemned to a lifetime of slavery. Canada, under British colonial law, could not extradite people to a jurisdiction that imposed harsher penalties than they would have received for the same offense in Canada. Thornton and Ruthie Blackburn remained in Ontario, and the landmark decision set the precedent for all future runaway slave disputes. More than any other incident, the Blackburn case established Upper Canada as the main terminus of the fabled Underground Railroad.

Critical Thinking

1. What was the "Underground Railroad"?
2. What was the significance of Canada's refusal to return runaway slaves to their masters?

The Holdouts

Under the unique leadership of John Ross and Major Ridge, the Cherokee Indians fought to keep their traditional homelands. And then Andrew Jackson was elected president.

BRIAN HICKS

John Ross made an unlikely looking Cherokee chief. Born in 1790 to a Scottish trader and a woman of Indian and European heritage, he was only one-eighth Cherokee by blood. Short, slight and reserved, he wore a suit and tie instead of deerskin leggings and a beaver-skin hat. His trading post made him more prosperous than most Indians—or white men. But his mother and grandmother raised him in a traditional household, teaching him the tribe's customs and legends. When the Cherokees embraced formal education—they were adapting quickly to a world they knew was changing—he attended school with their children. After his mother died, in 1808, Ross worked at his grandfather's trading post near present-day Chattanooga, an important way station on the road to the West. There he encountered white settlers moving onto Cherokee land.

To a degree unique among the five major tribes in the South, the Cherokees used diplomacy and legal argument to protect their interests. With the help of a forward-looking warrior named Major Ridge, Ross became the tribe's primary negotiator with officials in Washington, D.C., adept at citing both federal law and details from a dozen treaties the Cherokees signed with the federal government between 1785 and 1819. In the 1820s, as they enjoyed one of the most promising periods in their history—developing a written language, adopting a constitution and building a capital city—Ross became the Cherokees' principal chief, and Ridge was named his counselor.

All the while, white settlers kept coming.

The state governments did little to discourage them, ignoring federal treaties and even abetting the taking of Indian land through bribery, fraud and coercion. When the tribes turned to Washington for redress, federal officials proved ineffectual or hostile, depending on the administration. One by one the other major Southern tribes—the Chickasaws, the Choctaws, the Creeks and the Seminoles—signed treaties that required them to uproot to the far side of the Mississippi River. But the Cherokees held out.

They finally succumbed in 1838, when they were marched 800 miles into an extremely bitter winter. The survivors of the journey to what is now Oklahoma would call it the Trail of Tears. The exodus was a communal tragedy, as it had been for the other tribes. But in the case of the Cherokees, their resistance and defeat were reflected as well in the rise and collapse of the extraordinary partnership between Ross and Ridge.

The two had met in 1813, the year Ross had a political awakening while on a trading trip to the Alabama Territory. A Creek chief named Big Warrior told him a faction of his tribe had become openly hostile to European customs and settlers. These Red Sticks, as the faction called itself, were threatening civil war. Ross, only 22, recognized a hazard to the Cherokees: such a war would likely endanger white settlers, and given that whites scarcely distinguished between tribes, any retaliatory move they made would threaten every Indian. So he wrote an urgent note to the local U.S. Indian agent: "The intelligence received from the Creek Nation at this present crisis is very serious. The hostile party is said to be numerous and if assistance is not given to the Big Warrior and his party by the U.S. it is apprehensive that they will be conquered from the Superior force of the rebels."

> ## "The intelligence received from the Creek Nation at this present crisis is very serious," Ross told an Indian agent.

When Tennessee militiamen intervened that fall, the Cherokees joined them, both to protect their own interests and to curry favor with whites. Ross, whose early record shows not even a fistfight, was among the 500 Cherokees who enlisted. So was Ridge, already a renowned warrior.

The Cherokees called him "the man who walks on the mountaintop," for his preferred means of traversing the woods; white men interpreted that as "ridge." He would appropriate the rank he was given during the Creek War as a first name. Born in 1770 or 1771, Ridge straddled two generations: in his youth he had fought white settlers, but as a man he welcomed

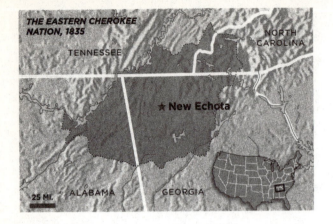

THE EASTERN CHEROKEE NATION, 1835

★ New Echota

TENNESSEE
NORTH CAROLINA
ALABAMA
GEORGIA
25 MI.

European traditions. "He appears very anxious that all his people should receive instruction, and come into the customs of the whites," the missionary William Chamberlin would write in 1822. Indeed, Ridge was one of the first Cherokees to send his children to missionary schools.

Ridge's embrace of change was initially unpopular among his tribesmen, but few questioned his loyalty. In 1807 he had helped kill the powerful Cherokee chief Doublehead for selling tribal hunting grounds for personal profit. And in 1808, when white U.S. Indian agents enticed principal chief Black Fox into proposing that the tribe move west, Ridge had been the first to protest. "As a man he has a right to give his opinion," Ridge declared before the Cherokees' ruling council, "but the opinion he has given as the chief of this nation is not binding; it was not formed in council in the light of day, but was made up in a corner—to drag this people, without their consent, from their own country, to the dark land of the setting sun."

By 1813, Ridge had seen enough of politics to understand the diplomatic advantage to be gained from joining the Tennesseans against the Red Sticks. The Cherokees might even have realized that advantage had it not been for the militia leader they fought under: Andrew Jackson.

As a boy in the 1770s, Jackson had listened to stories of Indian violence toward settlers, and with no apparent understanding of their motives, he developed prejudices that he—like many Americans of his day—held throughout his life. He routinely called Indians "savages" and people of mixed heritage "half-breeds," and he was unshakable in his conviction that Indians should be removed from the South. When news that the Red Sticks were attacking settlers reached him in Nashville, he asked: "Is a citizen of the United States, to remain under the barbarous lash of cruel and unrelenting savages?"

In March 1814, Jackson tracked the Red Sticks to Horseshoe Bend, a peninsula formed by the Tallapoosa River in the Alabama Territory, and launched a frontal assault on their breastworks. His troops might have been repulsed had the Cherokees not crossed the river and attacked from the rear. Caught between two attacking forces, the Red Sticks lost nearly 900 warriors in what proved to be the decisive battle of the war.

That day, a Cherokee named Junaluska saved Jackson from an attacker, prompting the Tennessean to declare, "As long as the sun shines and the grass grows, there shall be friendship between us." But in the peace treaty he negotiated with the Creeks, Jackson confiscated 23 million acres of land in Alabama and Georgia—some of which belonged to the Cherokees.

In 1816, the Cherokees' principal chief, Pathkiller, sent a delegation to Washington to reclaim that land. The delegates, who included Ross and Ridge, made quite an impression while mingling with the city's elite. Ridge sang a Cherokee song so raunchy his interpreter declined to translate it. ("It's just like a white man's song," Ridge joked in his limited English, "all about love and whiskey.") Even so, a reporter from one newspaper, the *National Intelligencer*, wrote that "their appearance and deportment are such to entitle them to respect and attention."

Because of his fluency in English, Ross became one of the Cherokees' lead negotiators, and he proved more than a match for Secretary of War William Crawford. "It is foreign to the Cherokee principle to feign friendship where it does not exist," Ross said, implying a contrast with Washington bureaucrats. "You have told us that your Government is determined to do justice to our nation and will never use oppressive means to make us act contrary to our welfare and free will." The treaties the Cherokees had signed generally required them to give up large tracts of land but guaranteed their rights to whatever remained. Now they wanted those rights enforced.

After more than a month of back-and-forth debate, Crawford finally relented: the United States would restore the bulk of the land the Cherokees claimed. In return, the Cherokees agreed to sell a small tract in South Carolina for $5,000 (the 2011 equivalent of $78,800) to the state government.

In a move intended to prevent local chiefs from accepting bribes to sell off Cherokee land, the Cherokee council in 1817 established a national committee to handle all tribal business. When Ross arrived at the council meeting as a spectator, Ridge led him into a private conference and told him that he would be one of 13 members of the committee. Ross was only 26—a young man in a community where leadership traditionally came with age. Just a month later, he would have to confront Andrew Jackson directly.

Jackson had been serving as a federal Indian commissioner when he launched his first effort to remove the Cherokees en masse. In 1817, he appeared with two other agents at the Cherokees' council in Calhoun, just northeast of what is now Cleveland, Tennessee, to inform the tribe that if it refused to move west, it would have to submit to white men's laws, no matter what any treaties might say. The chiefs dismissed the agents without hesitation. "Brothers, we wish to remain on our land, and hold it fast," their signed statement said. "We appeal to our father the president of the United States to do us justice. We look to him for protection in the hour of distress."

Through threats and bribery Jackson eventually persuaded a few thousand Cherokees to leave Tennessee; Ross became the spokesman of those who remained—some 16,000 resolved to hold their ground. After years of trading land for peace, the council in 1822 passed a resolution vowing never to cede a single acre more. "If we had but one square mile left they would not be satisfied unless they could get it," Ross wrote to Secretary of War John C. Calhoun that October, referring to state Indian commissioners who regularly tried to buy out the tribe.

"But we hope that the United States will never forget her obligation to our nation."

In 1823, Georgia officials, recognizing Ross' growing power, dispatched a Creek chief to personally offer him $2,000 (about $42,300 today) to persuade the Cherokees to move. Ross asked for the offer in writing—then took it to Ridge. Together they exposed the bribery attempt in front of the tribal council and sent the emissary packing.

At the same time, what historians would call the Cherokee Renaissance was bringing the tribe more fully into the 19th century. Sequoyah, a mixed-blood Cherokee, distilled the Cherokee oral language into a set of 86 symbols; soon, the tribe enjoyed a higher rate of literacy than the settlers who called them savages. They started a newspaper, the *Cherokee Phoenix*. In 1825—after new president John Quincy Adams promised to honor the federal government's obligations to Indians—the Cherokees began their largest public works project, building a council house, courthouse and public square in northwestern Georgia, near present-day Calhoun. They named it New Echota, in honor of a village lost to settlers years earlier.

Ridge could not hide his pride. "It's like Baltimore," he told a visiting missionary, comparing it to the largest city he'd ever seen.

In 1827, the Cherokees adopted a written constitution that defined a government with executive, legislative and judicial branches. That same year, they acquired new leadership: Path-killer died, and Charles Hicks, his assistant and logical successor, followed him two weeks later. The council appointed an interim chief, but Ross and Ridge were making the decisions—when to hold council, how to handle law enforcement, whether to allow roads to be built through tribal land. The two men so relied on each other that locals called the three-mile trail between their homes the Ross Ridge Road.

If Ross aspired to be principal chief, he never spoke of it. But Ridge promoted his protégé's candidacy without naming him, dictating an essay to the *Cherokee Phoenix* that described removal as the tribe's most pressing issue and warning against electing leaders who could be manipulated by white men. Until then, every principal chief had been nearly full-blooded Cherokee. When the council voted in the fall of 1828, Ross—who was only 38—was elected principal chief by a vote of 34 to 6. The council named Ridge his counselor.

A month later, Andrew Jackson was elected president of the United States. He would test the Cherokees' leadership soon enough, but even before Jackson was inaugurated, Georgia presented a more immediate threat, passing laws that annexed Cherokee land and extended state laws to that territory. Within two years, the state would require any whites living among the Indians—such as missionaries—to sign an oath of allegiance to the state or get out.

Ross spent much of those two years in Washington, trying to overturn the new laws. Jackson's secretary of war, John Eaton, told Ross the tribe's troubles had been self-inflicted: by adopting a constitution, it had insulted Georgia's sovereignty. As the months passed and Georgia's deadline loomed, some 500 Cherokees abandoned their homes and headed west to join earlier emigrants. Major Ridge grew alarmed: the fewer Cherokees who remained, the easier they would be to displace. He set out on a speaking tour intended to calm tribe members inclined to flee. He told large crowds that they had been targeted not because they were weak, but because they were strong and had "unexpectedly become civilized.

"It is too much for us now to be honest, and virtuous, and industrious," he noted sarcastically, "because then are we capable of aspiring to the rank of Christians and Politicians, which renders our attachment to the soil more strong."

When Ross returned from Washington, he joined Ridge's campaign, rousing crowds with his defiant oratory He told a missionary friend that his "hopes of success were never greater."

But more trouble was on the way: gold had been discovered on tribal land in Georgia, drawing a new wave of settlers, and President Jackson was not about to stop them. In February 1830, the tribe exercised its legal right to evict squatters; Ridge, then 60, led a two-day raid in which Cherokees burned settlers' houses and outbuildings. After Georgia authorities sent a posse after the Cherokees, gunfire rang out through northern Georgia.

The timing could hardly have been worse: at that very moment, Congress was hotly debating the Indian removal bill, a measure Jackson had introduced to establish an "ample district" west of the Mississippi to which the Indians of the South could move. On one hand, he had said in his inaugural address, Indian emigration "should be voluntary, for it would be as cruel as unjust to compel the aborigines to abandon the graves of their fathers and seek a home in a distant land." On the other, he made it clear that Indians could not live as independent peoples within the United States: "surrounded by the whites with their arts of civilization" they would be doomed "to weakness and decay." They had either to submit to state laws or go.

Congress passed the removal bill that May, and by September Jackson had begun negotiating with the Chickasaws, the Choctaws and the remaining Creeks to move west. Within four years they would be under land cession treaties or on the move. Some Seminoles also left in the early 1830s, and others fought the Army in Florida for several years. But Ross refused even to meet with Jackson. Instead, he turned to the U.S. Supreme Court, asking the justices to invalidate Georgia's removal law.

As the court's spring session opened in March 1831, Georgia officials roamed the Capitol to rally states' rights advocates to the idea of stripping the justices of their power to review the acts of state governments. The justices—in an act that historians would say reflected their worry over the talk coming out of Congress—ruled that they lacked jurisdiction over the Cherokees' claims against Georgia. Chief Justice John Marshall offered their only hope when he wrote that "the Indians are acknowledged to have an unquestionable . . . right to the lands they occupy."

Ross used that opinion to bring another suit, this time challenging the arrests of white missionaries who had refused to swear allegiance to Georgia. Now faced with a case involving U.S. citizens, the court was forced to act. On March 3, 1832, the justices declared the arrests unconstitutional and said Georgia could not extend its laws to Cherokee land. They also ruled that the federal government, by treaty, had the authority to protect Indian tribes from state intrusions. Taking aim at removal, Marshall wrote, "Protection does not imply the destruction of the protected."

Ross wrote to some Cherokee delegates in Washington, "[T]here are great rejoicings throughout the [Cherokee] nation."

But Jackson declared the ruling "stillborn."

A month later, Major Ridge's son John and two other Cherokees were in Washington, trying to determine whether the federal government would enforce the court's decision. Jackson met with them only to send them home to tell their people "that their only hope of relief was in abandoning their country and removing to the West."

The Cherokees' "only hope of relief," Jackson said, "was in abandoning their country and removing to the West."

Jackson's resolve unnerved the younger Ridge. Gradually, he realized that court victory or not, his people were losing ground. But he could not relay that message to the tribe for fear of being branded a traitor, or killed. He was even hesitant to confide in his father, believing Major Ridge would be ashamed of him.

But the son underestimated his father. Major Ridge judged his people's prospects by their suffering, and he knew the situation was far worse than anyone had dared to admit. Forbidden to meet by Georgia law, the Cherokees had abandoned New Echota in 1831. Settlers were confiscating their homesteads and livestock. By sharing his thoughts on Jackson, John Ridge helped his father come to the conclusion that the tribe had to at least consider going west.

But Major Ridge kept his feelings private, believing he needed to buy time to persuade his people to think about uprooting. At the same time, he began to wonder how Ross could remain so strident in his resistance. Couldn't he see that his strategy was bearing no fruit?

Ross met twice with Jackson at the White House, to no avail. When Jackson offered $3 million to move the Cherokees west, arguing that Georgia would not give up its claims to Cherokee land, Ross suggested he use the money to buy off the Georgia settlers.

By spring 1833, the Cherokees were split between a National Party, opposed to removal, and a Treaty Party, in favor of it. As factional violence flared, some of the most influential Cherokees signed a letter to Ross saying their ongoing "course of policy" would "not result in the restoration of those rights" that had been taken from them. In signing the letter, Ridge acknowledged that he had softened on removal. In a closed meeting, the chiefs gave Ross until fall to resolve the impasse with the government before they made the letter public.

Under so much pressure—from the state of Georgia, the federal government and a stream of settlers—the tribe began to disintegrate. Some Cherokees—including Ross' brother Andrew—set out for Washington to broker their own deals. John Ridge quietly continued to recruit members to the Treaty Party and make overtures to Jackson. When Ross learned of these efforts, he tried to pre-empt them, proposing to cede Cherokee land in Georgia and to have Cherokees in other states become U.S. citizens.

By then, the rift between Ross and Major Ridge was widening: when Ridge heard of the chief's offer, he saw it not just as a bargaining ploy but as an abuse of power. Without the blessing of the other chiefs, Ridge said, Ross had no more power to make a treaty than his traitorous brother.

The majority of the tribe members remained opposed to removal, but the Ridges began advocating the idea more openly—and when they broached it at a council meeting in Red Clay, Tennessee, in August 1834, one Cherokee spoke of shooting them. Father and son slipped away unharmed, but by the end of the summer the Cherokees were trading rumors—false—that Ross and Major Ridge had each hired someone to kill the other.

In September 1834, Ridge visited Ross at his home to put the rumors to rest. They tried to talk as they once had, but the only thing they could agree on was that all talk of murder had to stop. Ridge believed Ross' intransigence was leading the Cherokees to destruction. Ross thought his oldest friend had become soft, unduly influenced by his son.

By January 1835, the council had sent Ross back to Washington with instructions to again seek federal protection, and the Treaty Party had sent John Ridge to broker a deal. Afraid of being outflanked by the Treaty Party, Ross told Jackson the Cherokees would leave their land for $20 million. He was stalling; he knew the federal government would never pay that much. When Jackson rejected him, Ross proposed that the Senate come up with an offer. When the Senate named its price as $5 million, Ross said he would take the offer to the council but wouldn't be bound by that figure. By then Jackson had lost his patience. In late 1835, he dispatched a commissioner to Georgia to seal an agreement with the Treaty Party leaders.

They met in New Echota, the deserted Cherokee capital. The terms were simple: the Cherokees would receive $5 million for all their land east of the Mississippi. The government would help them move and promise never to take their new land or incorporate it into the United States. The Cherokees would have two years to leave.

It was Major Ridge who outlined the final argument to those present. "They are strong and we are weak," he said. "We are few, they are many. . . . We can never forget these homes, I know, but an unbending, iron necessity tells us we must leave them. I would willingly die to preserve them, but any forcible effort to keep them will cost us our lands, our lives and the lives of our children. There is but one path to safety, one road to future existence as a Nation."

On December 29, a small group of Cherokees gathered at the home of Ridge's nephew Elias Boudinot to sign the Treaty of New Echota. After Ridge made his mark, he paused and said, "I have signed my death warrant."

John Ross tried to overturn the treaty for two years but failed. In May 1838, U.S. troops herded more than 16,000 Cherokees into holding camps to await removal to present-day Oklahoma. Indians who tried to flee were shot, while those who waited in the camps suffered from malnutrition, dysentery and even sexual assault by the troops guarding them. Within a month, the first Cherokees were moved out in detachments of around a thousand, with the first groups leaving in the summer heat and a severe drought. So many died that the Army delayed further removal until the fall, which meant the Cherokees would be on the trail in winter. At least a quarter of them—4,000—would perish during the relocation.

Ridge headed west ahead of his tribesmen and survived the journey, but on the morning of June 22, 1839, separate groups of vengeful Cherokees murdered him, John Ridge and Boudinot. Ross, appalled, publicly mourned the deaths. "Once I saved Major Ridge at Red Clay, and would have done so again had I known of the plot," he told friends.

John Ross served as principal chief for 27 more years. He oversaw the construction of schools and a courthouse for the new capital, and spent years petitioning the federal government to pay the $5 million it owed his people. (It wasn't fully paid until 1852.) Even as his health failed, Ross would not quit. In 1866, he was in Washington to sign yet another treaty-one that would extend Cherokee citizenship to freed Cherokee slaves—when he died on August 1, two months shy of his 76th birthday More than three decades later, the federal government appropriated Indian property in the West and forced the tribes to accept land reservations. Today, many of the country's 300,000 Cherokees still live in Oklahoma.

Critical Thinking

1. Analyze the attempts by leaders of the Cherokee Nation to retain their homelands and independence.

2. How did Andrew Jackson respond to their appeals?

From *Smithsonian*, March 2011, pp. 51–60. Copyright © 2011 by Brian Hicks. Reprinted by permission of the author.

Polk's Peace

By warmaking and shrewd negotiating, the 11th president expanded U.S. territory by a third.

ROBERT W. MERRY

ON FEBRUARY 28, 1848, President James K. Polk received a visit from Ambrose Sevier of Arkansas, chairman of the Senate Foreign Relations Committee, bearing bad news. His committee had just voted to recommend that the full Senate reject a peace treaty that had been painstakingly negotiated between the United States and Mexico.

The news struck Polk hard. Senate ratification would bring an end to a war that had dragged on for two years, cost the country nearly 14,000 lives, generated much venomous recrimination, and sapped Polk's own political standing and that of his Democratic Party. Rejection would mean more bloodshed in Mexico and more bitterness at home, not to mention the dreaded possibility that the United States would have to end the war by conquering more territory and subduing even more Mexican citizens.

Polk was particularly stung when he heard that the committee wanted him to send a proper delegation to Mexico to negotiate a treaty much like the one now before the Senate. The terms of the treaty weren't the problem; it was that it had been negotiated by Nicholas Trist after he had been dismissed from his diplomatic post by Polk.

Polk had felt the same way when he first learned how Trist had defied his recall and seized what he considered a rare and perishable opportunity to deal with the peace faction, which had seized control of Mexico's reeling government. If bellicose anti-American factions took over, Trist surmised, the chance for peace would be lost.

Polk curbed his anger when he saw that Trist's treaty conformed to presidential instructions. Besides, the president foresaw disaster looming if this opportunity evaporated. As he told his cabinet, the United States would never obtain better terms. If these terms were now rejected by the United States and hostilities resumed, the antiwar House would probably shut off authorization for troops and money. He might have to withdraw U.S. forces simply for their own protection, and the vast conquered territory—California and a huge swath of southwestern land—could be gone forever. In short, said the president, to reject the treaty could render it impossible "for my administration to be sustained." So he had sent it to the Senate, only to hear now that Foreign Relations Committee members were toying with blocking this fragile opportunity for peace.

There was no doubt in anyone's mind that the war with Mexico was Polk's war, which he had engineered following the U.S. annexation of Texas. Texas—and Polk—deemed that its territory extended to the Rio Grande, while Mexico held that the proper boundary was the Nueces River, some 200 miles to the east. Polk had sent an army to the east bank of the Rio Grande, which had promptly come under attack by Mexican troops, just as Polk had anticipated. And so he got his war.

Militarily, it had yielded a stunning record of U.S. triumph. Polk's generals never lost a battle, conquering vast provinces that, if retained, would render the United States one of the largest nations of the globe. An expeditionary force landed at Veracruz and marched all the way to Mexico City, where it raised the American flag atop fortresses and palaces that embodied centuries of Hispanic power.

Thus, Polk had captured just about everything he had wanted when he set in motion the events leading to war. But now he wanted a cessation of the domestic animosities engendered by the war. He wanted peace and a chance to position the Democrats to keep the White House in 1848.

On the day that Sevier visited the White House, his committee decided to send the treaty to the full Senate without recommendation, whereupon that august body went into executive session. Word leaked out over the next several days. "The result is extremely doubtful," wrote the president in his diary.

Polk figured that a dozen Democrats might vote against the treaty, largely because they wanted more territory. Given such resistance in the president's own party, it would take only seven or eight anti-Polk Whigs to kill the treaty.

On March 1 Polk's doubts turned to despair. The president spoke with at least five Senate Democrats, all of whom expected the treaty to go down. The next day brought a snowstorm—and happier news. The Whigs moved a bevy of amendments—all tabled or killed. Democrats Sam Houston of Texas and Jefferson Davis of Mississippi offered amendments demanding more territory, but Davis's amendment received only 10 votes, while Houston's never got to a tally. The tide was turning.

Finally, on March 10, the Senate ratified the treaty 38 to 14. Polk had had his war, and now he had his peace.

Victory and settlement culminated the presidential objectives of James Polk, by choice a one-term executive. Texas's territorial claim had been enforced to the last yard. The Oregon Territory had been brought into the Union, largely through Polk's tough and deft bargaining with the British. Now, with the peace treaty ratified, the United States acquired what became present-day California, New Mexico, Arizona, Utah, Nevada, and considerable fragments of other western states besides. Taken together, Polk's moves had expanded U.S. territory by a third and carried the nation to the Pacific on a front corresponding to its eastern coast.

But Polk paid a huge price for his success, politically and physically. His health had deteriorated throughout his presidency, and within four months of relinquishing power he died quietly in his sleep at age 53.

Critical Thinking

1. Analyze President Polk's policies that precipitated the war with Mexico.

2. Why did it prove so difficult for his administration to end the fighting?

ROBERT W. MERRY, author of *A Country of Vast Designs: James K. Polk, the Mexican War and the Conquest of the American Continent, Century* (Simon & Schuster 2009), recently retired as president and publisher of Congressional Quarterly, Inc.

From *American Heritage,* Winter 2010, pp. 48–49. Copyright © 2010 by American Heritage Publishing Co. Reprinted by permission.

UNIT 4

The Civil War and Reconstruction

Unit Selections

Learning Outcomes

After reading this Unit, you will be able to:

- The question as to what to do about slavery was both moral and economic. Analyze the debate over emancipation that took place on the eve of the Civil War.

- The Civil War began as a struggle over national unity, but became a conflict over the institution of slavery. What were the obstacles to issuing an emancipation proclamation earlier than Lincoln did? Why did emancipation precipitate a "constitutional dilemma"?

- Analyses of emancipation usually focus on white leaders such as Lincoln. What role did blacks play? How could one author refer to this as "the greatest slave rebellion in modern history"?

- Discuss the United States government's policies toward American Indians during the nineteenth century. What role did the buffalo play in the cultures of Plains Indians? Why did Indians resist moving to reservations?

- Analyze Abraham Lincoln's performance as commander in chief of U.S. armed forces. What qualities did he possess that enabled him to successfully lead such an enormous military undertaking even though he lacked experience and schooling?

- The last article in this volume analyzes the Civil War, emancipation, and reconstruction "on the world stage." What is meant by this phrase? Why were so many people around the globe interested in what happened in the United States during these years?

Student Website

www.mhhe.com/cls

Internet References

The American Civil War
http://sunsite.utk.edu/civil-war/warweb.html

Anacostia Museum/Smithsonian Institution
www.si.edu/archives/historic/anacost.htm

Abraham Lincoln Online
www.netins.net/showcase/creative/lincoln.html

Gilder Lehrman Institute of American History
www.digitalhistory.uh.edu/index.cfm?

Secession Era Editorials Project
http://history.furman.edu/~benson/docs/dsmenu.htm

Sectionalism plagued the United States from its inception. The Constitutional proviso that slaves would count as three-fifths of a person for representational purposes, for instance, or that treaties had to be passed by two-thirds majorities grew out of sectional compromises. Manufacturing and commercial interests were strong in the North. Such interests generally supported high tariffs to protect industries, and the construction of turnpikes, canals, and railroads to expand domestic markets. The South, largely rural and agricultural, strongly opposed such measures. Southerners believed that tariffs cost them money to line the pockets of Northern manufacturers, and had little interest in what were known as "internal improvements." Such differences were relatively easy to resolve because there were no moral issues involved, and matters such as tariffs aroused few emotions in the public.

The question of slavery added a different dimension. Part of the quarrel involved economic considerations. Northerners feared that the spread of slavery would discriminate against "free" farming in the west. Southerners just as adamantly believed that the institution should be allowed to exist wherever it proved feasible. Disputes in 1820 and again in 1850 resulted in compromises that papered over these differences, but they satisfied no one. As time wore on, more and more Northerners came to regard slavery as sinful, an abomination that must be stamped out. Southerners, on the other hand, grew more receptive to the idea that slavery actually was beneficial to both blacks and whites and was condoned by the Bible. Now cast in moral terms, the issue could not be resolved in the fashion of tariff disputes by splitting differences.

Four articles in this unit deal with the increasingly emotional atmosphere during the run up to the Civil War. "The Emancipation Question" shows that well before the Civil War began, influential magazines and newspapers in the North already were advocating emancipation. "Free at Last" describes how the Underground Railroad functioned as an escape route for runaway slaves. White Southerners detested and feared its existence for two reasons beyond the sheer number of escapees, which some scholars estimate to be around 150,000. First, it revealed the fallacy of Southern arguments that slavery was a benevolent institution and that slaves were a happy, contented lot. Second, it seemed clear that, whatever politicians might say, large numbers of Northerners were willing to break the law in order to undermine the "peculiar institution." "Abolitionist John Doy" and "John Brown's Raid on Harpers Ferry" provide two examples of the abolitionists' willingness to defy the law. Brown's raid in particular touched off an explosion of feverish charges and countercharges by both sides. The tendency in the North to treat Brown as a martyr confirmed Southern suspicions that abolitionists meant to destroy slavery by violence if necessary.

Moderates in the two national parties, the Whigs and Democrats, tried to keep the slavery question from tearing the country in two. Though suffering some defections, the Democrats managed to stay together until the elections of 1860. The Whigs, however, fell apart during the 1850s. The emergence of the Republican Party, with its strength almost exclusively based in

the North, signaled the beginning of the end. Southerners came to regard the Republicans as the party of abolitionism. Abraham Lincoln, Republican presidential candidate in 1860, tried to assure Southerners that although he opposed the spread of slavery he had no intentions of seeking to abolish the institution where it already existed. He was not widely believed in the South. Republican victory in 1860 seemed to them, or at least to the hotheads among them, to threaten not just slavery but the entire Southern way of life. One by one Southern states began seceding, and Lincoln's unwillingness to let them destroy the union led to the Civil War. "There Goes the South" describes this process.

In his inaugural address, Lincoln had promised to "hold, occupy, and possess" all government property, even if located within the Confederacy (which he never recognized as legitimate). Fort Sumter, in Charleston Harbor, presented a hard choice. To evacuate the post would appear to constitute a retreat before Confederate belligerency, to reinforce it not only would be difficult but would appear as an aggressive act. Lincoln cleverly escaped this dilemma by announcing that he would send only provisions, not troops, to Sumter. If the Southerners bombarded the fort, they would bear the onus of firing the first shots. They did.

The Civil War began as s struggle over national union, but ultimately became a conflict over the continued existence of slavery. "Lincoln and the Constitutional Dilemma of Emancipation" analyzes the many obstacles that prevented Abraham Lincoln from issuing the preliminary Emancipation Proclamation before he did. Among the most important factors in Lincoln's mind was the Constitution's protection of property rights. Although he knew he would be criticized by some for not going far enough, he also knew he would be condemned for having exceeded his executive powers. Author Edna Greene Medford argues that Lincoln satisfied himself that he was acting within his Constitutional powers. "Lincoln and Douglass" analyzes the relationship between the president and Frederick Douglass, a vocal Black leader who not only wanted an end to slavery but sought to achieve full equality for African-Americans.

Many narratives of the path to Emancipation skimp on the role African-Americans themselves played. "Steven Hahn Sings the Slaves Triumphant" emphasizes that they were not merely passive victims of slavery, but rather played a key role in destroying that institution. "A Slave's Audacious Bid for Freedom" tells the story of Wallace Turnage, one of many slaves who risked their lives to escape their miserable conditions.

By April 1865, Southern forces were depleted and exhausted after four years of costly fighting. General Robert E. Lee realized that the Confederacy no longer could continue to sustain a conventional war. Some of his subordinates urged that he disband the army and have his troops regroup as guerilla bands. Such a course would have prolonged the fighting for the foreseeable future and would have fanned the flames of hatred on both sides. "A Graceful Exit" discusses Lee's wise decision to ignore this advice and to surrender his forces at Appomattox Courthouse.

A struggle took place after the war ended over how the South would be reintegrated into the Union. The most important issue was what status Blacks would have in the postwar society. Moderates such as Lincoln wished to make Reconstruction as painless as possible even though this meant continued white domination of Southern states. Radical Republicans sought to grant freed people the full rights of citizenship, and were willing to use force to attain this goal. Southern whites resisted "Radical Reconstruction" any way they could, and ultimately prevailed when Northern will eroded. "The American Civil War, Emancipation, and Reconstruction on the World Stage" analyzes the events of these years and concludes that they "embodied struggles that would confront people on every continent."

White encroachment on Indian lands continued up to and after the Civil War. Railroads constructed after the conflict ended speeded this process. "How the West Was Lost" describes the westward expansion that disrupted and demoralized Indian tribal culture. One of the worst catastrophes for the Plains Indians was the destruction of the once huge buffalo herds that provided them with everything from food and clothing to weapons. The Indians fought back from time to time but confronted overwhelming odds. In the end most tribes were forced onto reservations where they became little more than wards of the state. To its great discredit the United States made and broke countless treaties with the Indians over the years.

Two articles in this unit fall outside the scope of the Civil War or the Westward movement. "Drake's Rock Oil" tells how "Colonel" E. L. Drake and his crew succeeded in drawing what was then called "rock oil" from the ground. This was a landmark event that would have worldwide consequences. Without Drake's achievement, author Daniel Yergin writes, the birth of the oil industry "might have been postponed another 10, 20, or 30 years." "It Was We, the People; Not We, the White Males" reprints suffragist Susan B. Anthony's passionate speech urging that both women and African-Americans be granted their full Constitutional rights.

Drake's Rock Oil

No one knew that oil could come from the ground until a bankrupt group of speculators hit pay dirt in northwestern Pennsylvania.

DANIEL YERGIN

By August 1859, "Colonel" E. L. Drake and his small crew were disheartened. Few if any of the locals believed that oil—liquid called rock oil—could come out of the ground. In fact, they thought Drake was crazy. A small group of Connecticut investors had set Drake up in the small lumber town of Titusville in northwestern Pennsylvania to try this "lunatic" scheme. The work was slow, difficult, and continually dogged by disappointment and the specter of failure. After a year, the venture had run out of money, and New Haven banker James Townsend had been paying expenses out of his pocket.

At the end of his resources, Townsend reluctantly sent Drake a money order as a final remittance and instructed him to pay his bills, close up the operation, and return to New Haven. Fortunately, mail delivery to the backwoods of northwest Pennsylvania was slow, and Drake had not yet received the letter when, on Sunday, August 28, William "Uncle Billy" Smith, Drake's driller, coming out to peer into the well, saw a dark fluid floating on top of the water. On Monday, when Drake arrived, he found Uncle Billy and his boys standing guard over tubs, washbasins, and barrels that were filled with oil. Drake attached a hand pump and began to do exactly what the scoffers had denied was possible—pump up the liquid. That same day he received Townsend's order to close up shop.

This event launched the American oil industry, a business that would transform the world. Had the elements not come together, and had the protagonists not possessed more willpower than reason, the birth of the industry might have been postponed another 10, 20, or 30 years.

Up until that time, Americans had lit their homes with lamps fueled primarily by whale oil. The world was running short of this commodity, and prices had reached the astronomical level of $2.50 a gallon. Finding a substitute would make a man rich.

An entrepreneur named George Bissell virtually stumbled upon the idea of drilling for "rock oil" and using it as a domestic lighting fluid. A graduate of Dartmouth College, Bissell had pursued a disparate range of jobs, from superintendent of schools in New Orleans to journalism. On his way back to the Northeast he had passed through rural, isolated northwest Pennsylvania—the back of beyond—and had come across something of the tiny rock oil industry. People gathered small volumes either by skimming it off creeks in Titusville's "Oil Valley," or wringing it out of rags soaked in seeps, and sold it for patent medicine. Visiting back at Dartmouth, Bissell saw a sample sent to a professor there, who said it might make a good lighting fluid. Bissell had one other flash of inspiration, supposedly from seeing the label of a patent medicine bottle in a pharmacy window, which showed a rig drilling for water. Could one drill for rock oil?

He connected with James Townsend, and they set about raising money. Townsend's talk about drilling for oil in western Pennsylvania did not exactly garner a positive response. The banker recalled people saying, "Oh Townsend, oil coming out of the ground, pumping oil out of the earth as you pump water? Nonsense! You're crazy."

Bissell and Townsend enlisted the aid of a Yale chemistry professor named Benjamin Silliman Jr., who wrote a report claiming that their company had "in their possession a raw material from which . . . they may manufacture very valuable products." With that endorsement, Bissell and Townsend were able to raise the money they needed.

But who would carry out their mission? Townsend lived in the same New Haven hotel as Edwin Drake, a retired railroad conductor and jack-of-all-trades. His most obvious qualifications were that he was available, he appeared to be tenacious in character, and, as a retired conductor, he could travel for free by rail. Dispatching Drake to Pennsylvania, the New Haven investors gave him what turned out to be a valuable send-off. Concerned about the frontier conditions and the need to impress the "backwoodsmen," Townsend sent ahead several letters addressed to "Colonel" E. L. Drake. Thus was "Colonel" Drake commissioned out of thin air, though a colonel he certainly was not.

Drake's tenaciousness paid off. After the discovery of oil, farmers along Oil Creek rushed into Titusville shouting, "The Yankee has struck oil." The news spread like wildfire and started a mad rush to acquire sites and start drilling. The population of tiny Titusville multiplied overnight, and land prices shot up.

The news of the oil strike spread like wildfire and started a mad rush to acquire sites and start drilling.

Other wells were drilled in the neighborhood, and more rock oil became available. Supply far outran demand, and the price plummeted. With the advent of drilling, there was no shortage of rock oil. The only shortage now was of whiskey barrels, into which the oil was poured. Soon the barrels cost almost twice as much as the oil they carried. (The wooden barrels may be long gone today, but not the measurement; this is why oil is still reckoned in "barrels" today.) Pennsylvania became the source from which oil promoters and drillers spread out across the country, to Kansas, Oklahoma, Texas, California, and onward around the world.

But not until the beginning of the 20th century, just as electricity began to displace kerosene for lighting, did the new invention of the automobile create the modern market for transportation fuels. Petroleum went on to become a huge industry, at the crossroads of the global economy and global politics.

Today oil supplies 40 percent of the world's total energy and, as a transportation fuel, truly makes the world go round. But for its first 40 years, the oil industry primarily served lamps. John D. Rockefeller of the Standard Oil Trust became the richest man in the United States as an illumination merchant.

"Colonel" Drake did not do so well. He became an oil trader but lost all his money and finally had to appeal to the state of Pennsylvania for a modest pension. He made a good case. "If I had not done it," he said of his oil well, "it would not have been done to this day."

Critical Thinking

1. How was "rock oil" obtained? What was used for lighting purposes previously?
2. How did the growing use of the automobile affect the consumption of oil?

DANIEL YERGIN recently released a new edition (Free Press 2009) of his 1992 Pulitzer-Prize-winning book, *The Prize: The Epic Quest for Oil, Money, and Power* (Simon & Schuster 1991). He is currently chairman of IHS Cambridge Energy Research Associates.

The Emancipation Question

A lively dialogue over the economics of slavery played out in newspapers and magazines on the eve of the Civil War.

Tom Huntington

One hundred fifty years ago on a "frigid and repulsive" January day in New York, 30-year-old William G. Sewell departed on a steamer for Barbados, the first stop on a tour of the Caribbean island colonies of the British West Indies. Doctors had recommended that the *New York Times* editor travel south because of tuberculosis. While recuperating, he would file a series of articles on a topic that would prove of enormous interest to Americans: how had the colony's islands been affected by the abolition of slavery 25 years earlier? The British West Indies had suffered its fair share of economic difficulties, and argument ensued over whether abolition had helped or harmed. The relevance to America's situation was obvious: the United States held 4 million people in bondage, and the debate over the peculiar institution's future threatened to tear the nation apart.

Sewell, a native of British Quebec, must have encountered the antislavery sentiments of his homeland, and perhaps shared them. But, as a former attorney, he used logic rather than emotion for his arguments. In an article published on April 20, 1859, he claimed that he would address fiduciary, not moral, issues. "I consider the question to be a commercial one—to be judged favorably or unfavorably by commercial rules," he wrote. He had "no sympathy with the argument of the Abolitionists, that the question of emancipation is one in which the black race are to be only considered, or that 'depreciation of property is as nothing compared with a depreciation of morality.'"

The British Empire had outlawed slavery in 1834 and phased it out over the next four years in a surprisingly peaceful transition. "Let us look at the facts," wrote Frenchman Alexis de Tocqueville in 1843: "the abolition of slavery in the nineteen English colonies has thus far not given rise to a *single* insurrection; it has not cost the life of a single man, and yet in the English colonies there are twelve times as many blacks as there are whites." However, the production of sugar, one of the staple crops of the West Indies, had fallen off since emancipation, and advocates on both sides of the debate argued over whether the end of slavery had caused the decline.

The *Times* started publishing Sewell's examination of these issues in March and continued them through the spring, summer,

and fall as he reported from Barbados, St. Vincent, Grenada, Jamaica, Trinidad, and other islands. (In 1861 Sewell published an expanded version as a book titled *The Ordeal of Free Labor in the British West Indies.*)

In Barbados Sewell acknowledged that sugar exports had declined, but he reported that exports had been decreasing even under slavery, with many plantations being sold for debt or abandoned. As Sewell asserted, "[N]o Barbadian planter would hesitate in 1859 to select free labor in preference to slave labor, as in his belief the more economical system of the two."

Nor did Sewell notice that the island's black population was suffering from a surfeit of freedom. "The masses are certainly no worse than they were under Slavery; while those who had the intelligence, industry and energy to rise, *have* risen to positions of competence, independence and wealth, which they never could have enjoyed under any other than a free system," he wrote. "Poor whites," however, suffered the most under the new conditions. "Incapable themselves of undergoing the hardships of field labor beneath a tropical sun, they employed, before emancipation, one or two slaves, upon whose services they lived. Deprived of this species of maintenance and having no resources of their own, they became such a burden to the community, that the Government has been called upon to adopt some measures for their relief."

> "Whether the whites and blacks can live together on terms of equality . . . is a problem yet unsolved," wrote a *Harper's Weekly* editor on July 16, 1859, in response to a series of pro-emancipation dispatches written for the *New York Times* by correspondent William G. Sewell from the British West Indies, where slavery had been illegal since 1834.

Sewell noted changes that emancipation had brought to the islands, including the arrival of indentured servants from Asia: "coolies" intended to replace the black laborers freed by emancipation. "The law provides for their free return after they have completed the term of industrial residence for which they were indentured," wrote Sewell, who approved of the practice.

In another article Sewell quoted a letter he had received from the British governor of the West Indies. The total cost of producing a hogshead of sugar with slaves, the governor wrote, had been more than 10 pounds. With free labor, the cost dropped to less than four. "There is very little doubt—and it cannot be intelligently questioned—that Barbados, under the *régime* of Slavery, never approached her present prosperous condition; and, in comparing the present with the past, whether that comparison be made in her commercial, mechanical, agricultural, industrial or educational status, I can come to no other conclusion than that the island offers a striking example of the superior economy of the free system," Sewell concluded. His verdict: while racial tensions were high on some of the islands, and Jamaica in particular was suffering from an economic decline, emancipation was not responsible for their struggles.

The popular *Harper's Weekly* jumped into the fray on September 3 with an editorial expressing uncertainty and anxiety over the issues Sewell had raised in his articles, including a somewhat panicky account of racial unrest in Barbados that the *Times* had published on June 29. "This is the destiny of the British West Indies," the editorial ran. "This is the result of emancipation. Improverishment and decay were the first fruits; extermination of the whites will be the ripe harvest."

Papers in the South nurtured little sentiment for emancipation. In July the editor of the *Register* in Mobile even advocated the repeal of federal laws passed in 1808 that ended the African slave trade. Proslavery sentiment was a regular feature in *DeBow's Review,* an agricultural journal published in New Orleans. In June 1859 the journal ran an article by noted Virginia agriculturist Edmund Ruffin about the effects on Southern farmers of the high prices for black slaves. Every step made to end slavery in Virginia, Ruffin declared, would "be more and more calamitous to the economical, social, and political interests of this commonwealth; and the complete consummation will be one of the greatest evils to the whole of the Southern States." Ruffin believed that slavery was "one of our chief blessings, and that its removal, by any means whatever, would be an unmixed evil and a curse to the whole community."

The views in *DeBow's* stood in marked contrast to what appeared in the *New York Times,* but both publications agreed on one thing: slaves were expensive. On August 26 the *Times* listed the results of a slave auction that had taken place in Bowling Green, Missouri. "The prices were good," an editorial writer reported. "A man verging upon three score brought about $800; a girl of six upwards of $500, and a girl of thirteen nearly $1,200.

"Such statements grate harshly on Northern ears, as well they may," the editorialist continued.

"An auction sale of human beings is a specially hideous spectacle when witnessed in a country which boasts of its freedom and civilization." The writer acknowledged that such sales had once taken place in New York City. "Slavery must fall in the South as it has fallen in the North; but what state of society shall succeed Slavery in the South is a grave question, not to be determined by the rash and angry agitations of partisan politics."

When war finally came, Edmund Ruffin helped usher it in. The agriculturist and Confederate "fire-eater" traveled to Charleston, South Carolina, as hostilities appeared imminent. On April 12, 1861, when Confederate cannon took aim at the Union stronghold of Fort Sumter out in the harbor, a Southern artillery battery gave Ruffin the honor of firing one of the first shots of the Civil War.

Sewell died of his illness the following year. Ruffin survived the war, but on June 17, 1865, after hearing news of the Confederate defeat, he penned a note in which he lambasted "the perfidious, malignant and vile Yankee race," and then killed himself with a pistol shot to the head.

Abolitionist John Doy

Tempers flare and violence reigns in the pre-Civil War battleground of Kansas.

TOM HUNTINGTON

On January 25, 1859, a small wagon expedition of three whites and 13 blacks stole away from Lawrence, Kansas, on the first leg of a journey that would take the African Americans to the free state of Iowa, far from Kansas and the ever-present threat of kidnapping by slave traders. For the three white abolitionists it was a protest against those who would deny their deepest beliefs about freedom and human rights.

The wagons splashed across the Kansas River and left Lawrence behind. Twelve miles outside town, after the party had descended a small hill, about 20 armed and mounted men emerged from behind a bluff. Guns leveled, they forced the wagons to a stop and accused the white men of stealing slaves. The expedition's white leader, John Doy, jumped from his horse and confronted a man he recognized. "Where's your process?" Doy demanded. The man shoved his gun barrel into Doy's head. "Here it is," he growled.

Ever since the passage of the Kansas-Nebraska Act in 1854, the Kansas territory had been thrust into the front lines of the increasingly rancorous national debate over slavery. The act nullified the Missouri Compromise, which had forbidden the expansion of slavery north of the 36°30 N line of latitude, and legislated that settlers could determine by popular vote whether or not to allow slavery in their territories. The stakes were high, and passions became inflamed. "The fate of the South is to be decided in Kansas," declared South Carolina Rep. Preston Brooks in March 1856. Four months later Brooks bludgeoned abolitionist Sen. Charles Sumner senseless with a cane on the floor of the Senate after the latter had delivered a speech entitled, "The Crime against Kansas."

Activists on both sides converged on Kansas, each intending to help tip the scales for or against slavery. "Border ruffians," who crossed over from slave-owning Missouri, began battling with abolitionist "free soilers." The violence gave the territory a new name: "Bleeding Kansas."

John Doy, a physician from Rochester, New York, heeded the call from abolitionist societies and moved to Kansas in July 1854. A full-bearded and serious-looking man, Doy helped found the town of Lawrence and built a house on its outskirts, where his wife and nine children joined him. As a bastion of free-soil sympathies, Lawrence became a target of proslavers, who sacked it on May 21, 1856. In retaliation, the abolitionist firebrand John Brown and his men murdered five slave owners near Pottawatomie Creek. Three months later Doy fought alongside Brown in a pitched battle at Osawatomie, 60 miles southeast of Lawrence.

Kansas became increasingly dangerous for African Americans, so on January 18, 1859, a group of Lawrence's citizens raised money to help blacks move to safety. Brown offered to take one group north to Canada and did so without incident. Doy also volunteered to help by taking another group about 60 miles northwest to the town of Holton, the first step on the road to Iowa. His passage proved less fortunate.

Among the African Americans on Doy's expedition were Wilson Hayes and Charles Smith, cooks at a Lawrence hotel. Doy knew that both of them were free men, although they had no papers. All the others had their "free papers," including William Riley, who had been kidnapped once before from Lawrence but had managed to escape.

Free or not, all 16 members of the party now found themselves in the hands of angry men bent on delivering them to slave-owning Missouri. The ambushers forced their captives on an overnight journey to Rialto Ferry, where they were put aboard a steamboat for passage across the Missouri River. On the opposite shore, an awaiting mob paraded Doy on horseback through town, beating and cursing him. One enraged man grabbed Doy by the beard and smashed his head repeatedly against a wall of the building where the prisoners were to spend the night.

The next morning John and his 25-year-old son Charles were pushed through the mob to the courthouse. The justice of the peace, who had "a face and eyes that looked as if all the milk of human kindness he ever possessed had long since soured," Doy later remembered, sent the third white man back to Kansas but ordered the Doys locked up in Platte City and put on trial for abducting slaves.

After another rough welcome in Platte City, the two Doys were thrown into a windowless cell, "an iron box, exactly eight feet square . . . and about seven feet high, furnished with a mattress on an iron bedstead, and with a horse rug and an old piece of cotton carpeting for a coverlid." The situation proved even worse for the African Americans. Hays, Smith, and Riley landed in the Platte City jail. Doy watched through the door grate as slave trader Jake Hurd brutally whipped Hays and Smith in a futile attempt to gain a confession that they were escaped slaves, then dragged them away. Riley managed to loosen the bars from his cell window and escaped back to Kansas—only to be later kidnapped once more as he was making his way to Nebraska.

Doy's counsel successfully petitioned to have the trial moved to the slightly less hostile town of St. Joseph, and the Doys bid farewell to their miserable Platte City cell on March 24. "Pale from confinement and want of light, cadaverous, emaciated, covered with vermin—for notwithstanding the clean clothes we had had the advantage of since my wife's arrival, we had not been able to free ourselves of them—with my joints swollen, my ankles, especially, so painful that I could hardly bear my weight upon them, I was weakened both in body and mind," Doy wrote.

The jail in St. Joseph was "a paradise after the cell at Platte City," and the jailer, named Brown, "proved to be a very humane man." The jury at the first trial in St. Joseph deadlocked, so the judge set Charles free and scheduled a second trial for the elder Doy on June 20. The second jury found him guilty and sentenced him to five years' hard labor. While Doy's counsel filed an appeal to the state supreme court, prosecutors planned a dozen more indictments against him on charges of stealing other slaves in the ill-fated expedition. He faced up to 65 years in prison.

But help was on its way. On the evening of July 23 a young man visited him in the jailhouse and slipped him a note reading "Be ready at midnight."

That night a storm hit St. Joseph. Amid its fury a man knocked on the jailhouse door and shouted to Brown the jailer that he had a horse thief he wanted locked up. Somewhat reluctantly, Brown went downstairs and opened the door. Two men held the alleged criminal, his hands bound. The jailer led them upstairs and opened the door to the cell. Suddenly the horse thief whipped off his bindings and one of his "captors" jammed a revolver against Brown's chest. "If you resist or try to give an alarm, you're a dead man," he warned. "We've come to take Dr. Doy home to Kansas, and we mean to do it; so you'd best be quiet."

Doy emerged from the cell, shook the jailer's hand, and left with his rescuers. He was so weak that two men needed to support him through the storm and down to the river, where boats were waiting. "By dint of hard pulling for the current of the Missouri is very strong there, we soon landed on the Kansas bank, which I had often gazed at longingly from the window of my cell," Doy wrote. His rescuers bundled their charge into a covered wagon for the 90-mile journey back to Lawrence, where Doy was "restored to my home, to my family and friends, and to the soil I love so well."

His ordeal was over, but the country's was just beginning. In October 1859 Doy's friend and fellow abolitionist John Brown led a raid on Harpers Ferry Virginia. Civil War erupted a year and a half later.

From *American Heritage*, April 17, 2009. Copyright © 2009 by American Heritage Publishing Co. Reprinted by permission.

John Brown's Raid on Harpers Ferry

RICHARD CAVENDISH

A virtual civil war over slavery in Kansas in the 1850s attracted the attention of John Brown, a devout Calvinist in his mid-fifties, who regarded slavery as an abominable sin against God and a breach of the principles of the Declaration of Independence. Five of his sons had moved to Kansas and in 1855 he joined them with a supply of rifles and swords. For several years after that he led a band of anti-slavery fighters in guerrilla warfare against pro-slavery activists.

Brown's plans changed over time. At one stage he hoped to create a new state for blacks, safe from attack in the Appalachian Mountains, to which all the slaves in the South would flock. Later he decided on an armed insurrection, which masses of blacks in both the South and the North would eagerly join. He would lead them to the mountains from which they would make raids into Virginia, Tennessee and Alabama. Black uprisings would then spread spontaneously thoughout the South until slavery was no more. To get the weapons he needed, he decided to seize the United States armoury at Harpers Ferry in Virginia (now in West Virginia), on the Potomac and Shenandoah rivers within 60 miles of Washington DC, where there were thousands of rifles and muskets in store.

Brown assembled a small force of 16 whites and five blacks at a farmhouse outside Harpers Ferry. Leaving three of them behind as a temporary rearguard, he and his men cut the telegraph wires east and west of the town and stormed the armoury. It was a rainy Sunday night, there were few people about and only a single watchman in the armoury, who was easily overcome. Brown and his men took some townspeople prisoners as hostages and also some local slave-owners, forcibly liberating their slaves and arming them with pikes; to the dismay of many of the slaves, who feared the consequences. The raiders also stopped a Baltimore and Ohio Railroad train passing through, but then allowed it to go on its way, carrying word of what was happening. The news spread round the countryside at lightning speed and the

reaction was swift and ferocious. By Monday morning armed militiamen, townspeople and local farmers were keeping up a hail of fire on Brown and his men, who holed up with some of their prisoners in a fire-engine house. The militia seized the bridges over the two rivers, cutting off any retreat, and the hoped-for influx of blacks eager to join Brown and his men completely failed to materialize.

Hoping to negotiate, Brown sent his son Watson and another man out under a white flag, but they were both promptly shot, Watson being mortally wounded. One of the prisoners in the engine house said afterwards that 'Brown commanded his men with the utmost composure, encouraging them to sell their lives as dearly as they could.' The mayor of Harpers Ferry, Fontaine Beckham, was killed by a bullet from the engine house, which only increased the vengeful fury of the crowd, a good few of whom were by now drunk. Another of Brown's sons, Oliver, was mortally wounded by a bullet from outside. In agony, he begged his father to finish him off, but Brown said, 'If you must die, die like a man.'

During Monday night a company of United States Marines arrived at Harpers Ferry, under the command of a certain Colonel Robert E. Lee, the future Confederate general. His aide-de-camp was another celebrated Confederate figure of the future, Lieutenant J.E.B. Stuart. On Tuesday morning Lee sent Stuart to the engine house under a flag of truce to offer to spare the lives of Brown and his men if they surrendered. Brown refused and the Marines immediately attacked the door of the engine house with sledgehammers and an improvised battering ram and burst in, firing as they entered. Brown was wounded and knocked unconscious, others of the defenders were shot or bayoneted and it was all over in a matter of minutes. To protect him from lynching, Brown was hurried to Charlestown, where at the end of the month he was tried for treason against the state of Virginia, conspiracy with slaves, and murder. His defenders stressed the history of mental instability on his mother's side of his family, hoping to get his sentence commuted for insanity, but Brown himself spurned any such talk. Lying on a cot in the courtroom, 'composed and heroic' as his biographer Stephen B. Oates described him, he was duly sentenced to death. He was hanged on December 2nd, behaving calmly and bravely throughout.

One of the witnesses to the execution, oddly enough, was John Wilkes Booth, the future assassin of Abraham Lincoln. Lincoln himself thought Brown 'a misguided fanatic,' but his death gave him immortality as an abolitionist martyr, whose 'soul is marching on.'

Critical Thinking

1. What effect did John Brown think his raid would have on Southern slaves?
2. Why did the raid stir up such emotions in both the North and South?

Free at Last

**A new museum celebrates the Underground Railroad.
The secret network of people who bravely led slaves
to liberty before the Civil War.**

FERGUS M. BORDEWICH

The phone rang one drizzly morning in Carl Westmoreland's office overlooking the gray ribbon of the Ohio River and downtown Cincinnati. It was February 1998. Westmoreland, a descendant of slaves, scholar of African-American history and former community organizer, had recently joined the staff of the National Underground Railroad Freedom Center. Then still in the planning stages, the center, which opened this past August in Cincinnati, is the nation's first institution dedicated to the clandestine pre-Civil War network that helped tens of thousands of fugitive slaves gain their freedom.

The caller, who identified himself as Raymond Evers, claimed that a 19th-century "slave jail" was located on his property in northern Kentucky; he wanted someone to come out to look at it. As word of the center had gotten around, Westmoreland had begun to receive a lot of calls like this one, from individuals who said their house contained secret hiding places or who reported mysterious tunnels on their property. He had investigated many of these sites. Virtually none turned out to have any connection with the Underground Railroad.

"I'll call you back tomorrow," Westmoreland said.

The next day, his phone rang again. It was Evers. "So when are you coming out?" he asked. Westmoreland sighed. "I'm on my way," he said.

An hour later, Westmoreland, a wiry man then in his early 60s, was slogging across a sodden alfalfa pasture in Mason County, Kentucky, eight miles south of the Ohio River, accompanied by Evers, 67, a retired businessman. The two made their way to a dilapidated tobacco barn at the top of a low hill.

"Where is it?" Westmoreland asked.

"Just open the door!" Evers replied.

In the darkened interior, Westmoreland made out a smaller structure built of rough-hewn logs and fitted with barred windows. Fastened to a joist inside the log hut were iron rings: fetters to which manacled slaves had once been chained. "I felt the way I did when I went to Auschwitz," Westmoreland later recalled. "I felt the power of the place—it was dark, ominous. When I saw the rings, I thought, it's like a slave-ship hold."

At first, Westmoreland had difficulty tracking down the history of the structure, where tobacco, corn and farm machinery had been stored for decades. But eventually Westmoreland located a Mason County resident who had heard from his father, who had heard from his grandfather, what had gone on in the little enclosure. "They chained 'em up over there, and sold 'em off like cattle," the Mason County man told Westmoreland.

At Westmoreland's urging, the Freedom Center accepted Evers' offer to donate the 32- by 27-foot structure. It was dismantled and transported to Cincinnati; the total cost for archaeological excavation and preservation was $2 million. When the Freedom Center opened its doors on August 23, the stark symbol of brutality was the first thing that visitors encountered in the lofty atrium facing the Ohio River. Says Westmoreland: "This institution represents the first time that there has been an honest effort to honor and preserve our collective memory, not in a basement or a slum somewhere, but at the front door of a major metropolitan community."

By its own definition a "museum of conscience," the 158,000-square-foot copper-roofed structure hopes to engage visitors in a visceral way. "This is not a slavery museum," says executive director Spencer Crew, who moved to Cincinnati from Washington, D.C., where he was director of the Smithsonian Institution's National

Museum of American History. "Rather, it is a place to engage people on the subject of slavery and race without finger-pointing. Yes, the center shows that slavery was terrible. But it also shows that there were people who stood up against it."

Visitors will find, in addition to the slave jail, artifacts including abolitionists' diaries, wanted posters, ads for runaways, documents granting individual slaves their freedom and newspapers such as William Lloyd Garrison's militant *Liberator,* the first in the United States to call for immediate abolition. And they will encounter one of the most powerful symbols of slavery: shackles. "Shackles exert an almost mystical fascination," says Rita C. Organ, the center's director of exhibits and collections. "There were even small-sized shackles for children. By looking at them, you get a feeling of what our ancestors must have felt—suddenly you begin to imagine what it was like being huddled in a coffle of chained slaves on the march."

Additional galleries relate stories of the central figures in the Underground Railroad. Some, like Frederick Douglass and Harriet Tubman, are renowned. Many others, such as John P. Parker, a former slave who became a key activist in the Ohio underground, and his collaborator, abolitionist John Rankin, are little known.

Other galleries document the experiences of present-day Americans, people like Laquetta Shepard, a 24-year-old black West Virginia woman who in 2002 walked into the middle of a Ku Klux Klan rally and shamed the crowd into dispersing, and Syed Ali, a Middle Eastern gas station owner in New York City who prevented members of a radical Islamic group from setting fire to a neighborhood synagogue in 2003. Says Crew, "Ideally, we would like to create modern-day equivalents of the Underground Railroad conductors, who have the internal fortitude to buck society's norms and to stand up for the things they really believe in."

The center's concept grew out of a tumultuous period in the mid-1990s when Cincinnati was reeling from confrontations between the police and the African-American community and when Marge Schott, then the owner of the Cincinnati Reds, made comments widely regarded as racist. At a 1994 meeting of the Cincinnati chapter of the National Conference of Christians and Jews, its then-director, Robert "Chip" Harrod, proposed the idea of a museum devoted to the Underground Railroad. Since then, the center has raised some $60 million from private donations and another $50 million from public sources, including the Department of Education.

The term underground railroad is said to derive from the story of a frustrated slave hunter who, having failed to apprehend a runaway, exclaimed, "He must have gone off on an underground road!" In an age when smoke-belching locomotives and shining steel rails were novelties, activists from New York to Illinois, many of whom had never seen an actual railroad, readily adopted its terminology, describing guides as "conductors," safe houses as "stations," horse-drawn wagons as "cars," and fugitives as "passengers."

Says Ira Berlin, author of *Many Thousands Gone: The First Two Centuries of Slavery in North America:* "The Underground Railroad played a critical role, by making the nature of slavery clear to Northerners who had been indifferent to it, by showing that slaves who were running away were neither happy nor well-treated, as apologists for slavery claimed. And morally, it demonstrated the enormous resiliency of the human spirit in the collaboration of blacks and whites to help people gain their freedom."

Thanks to the clandestine network, as many as 150,000 slaves may have found their way to safe havens in the North and Canada. "We don't know the total number and we will probably never know," says James O. Horton, a professor of American studies and history at George Washington University in Washington, D.C. "Part of the reason is that the underground was so successful: it kept its secrets well."

By the 1850s, activists from Delaware to Kansas had joined the underground to help fugitives elude capture. Wrote abolitionist Gerrit Smith in 1836: "If there be human enactments against our opening our door to our colored brother. . . . We must obey God."

As the nation's second great civil disobedience movement—the first being the actions, including the Boston Tea Party, leading to the American Revolution—the Underground Railroad engaged thousands of citizens in the subversion of federal law. The movement provoked fear and anger in the South and prompted the enactment of draconian legislation, including the 1850 Fugitive Slave Law, which required Northerners to cooperate in the capture of escaped slaves. And at a time when proslavery advocates insisted that blacks were better off in bondage because they lacked the intelligence or ability to take care of themselves, it also gave many African-Americans experience in political organizing and resistance.

"The Underground Railroad symbolized the intensifying struggle over slavery," says Berlin. "It was the result of the ratcheting up of the earlier antislavery movement, which in the years after the American Revolution, had begun to call for compensated emancipation and gradualist solutions to slavery." In the North, it brought African-Americans, often for the first time, into white communities where they could be seen as real people, with real families and real feelings. Ultimately, Berlin says, "the Underground Railroad forced whites to confront the reality of race in American society and to begin to wrestle with the reality in which black people lived all the time. It was a transforming experience."

For blacks and whites alike the stakes were high. Underground agents faced a constant threat of punitive litigation, violent reprisal and possible death. "White participants in the underground found in themselves a depth of humanity that they hadn't realized they had," says Horton. "And for many of them, humanity won out over legality." As New York philanthropist Gerrit Smith, one of the most important financiers of the Underground Railroad, put it in 1836, "If there be human enactments against our entertaining the stricken stranger—against our opening our door to our poor, guiltless, and unaccused colored brother pursued by bloodthirsty kidnappers—we must, nevertheless, say with the apostle: 'We must obey God rather than man.'"

From the earliest years of American bondage—the Spanish held slaves in Florida in the late 1500s; Africans were sold to colonists at Jamestown in 1619—slaves had fled their masters. But until British Canada and some Northern states—including Pennsylvania and Massachusetts—began abolishing slavery at the end of the 18th century, there were no permanent havens for fugitives. A handful of slaves found sanctuary among several Native American tribes deep in the swamps and forests of Florida. The first coordinated Underground Railroad activity can be traced to the early 19th century, perhaps when free blacks and white Quakers began to provide refuge for runaways in and around Philadelphia, or perhaps when activists organized in Ohio.

The process accelerated throughout the 1830s. "The whole country was like a huge pot in a furious state of boiling over," recalled Addison Coffin in 1897. Coffin served as an underground conductor in North Carolina and Indiana. "It was almost universal for ministers of the gospel to run into the subject in all their sermons; neighbors would stop and argue pro and con across the fence; people traveling along the road would stop and argue the point." Although abolitionists initially faced the contempt of a society that largely took the existence of slavery for granted, the underground would eventually count among its members Rutherford B. Hayes, the future president, who as a young lawyer in the 1850s defended fugitive slaves; William Seward, the future governor of New York and secretary of state, who provided financial support to Harriet Tubman and other underground activists; and Allan Pinkerton, founder of the Pinkerton Detective Agency, who in 1859 helped John Brown lead a band of fugitive slaves out of Chicago and on to Detroit, bound for Canada. By the 1850s, the underground ranged from the northern borders of states including Maryland, Virginia and Kentucky to Canada and numbered thousands among its ranks from Delaware to Kansas.

But its center was the Ohio River Valley, where scores of river crossings served as gateways from slave states to free and where, once across the Ohio, fugitives could hope to be passed from farm to farm all the way to the Great Lakes in a matter of days.

In practice, the underground functioned with a minimum of central direction and a maximum of grass-roots involvement, particularly among family members and church congregations. "The method of operating was not uniform but adapted to the requirements of each case," Isaac Beck, a veteran of Underground Railroad activity in southern Ohio, would recall in 1892. "There was no regular organization, no constitution, no officers, no laws or agreement or rule except the 'Golden Rule,' and every man did what seemed right in his own eyes." Travel was by foot, horseback or wagon. One stationmaster, Levi Coffin, an Indiana Quaker and Addison's uncle, kept a team of horses harnessed and a wagon ready to go at his farm in Newport (now Fountain City), Indiana. When additional teams were needed, Coffin wrote in his memoir, posthumously published in 1877, "the people at the livery stable seemed to understand what the teams were wanted for, and they asked no questions."

On occasion, fugitives might be transported in hearses or false-bottomed wagons, men might be disguised as women, women as men, blacks powdered white with talc. The volume of underground traffic varied widely. Levi Coffin estimated that during his lifetime he assisted 3,300 fugitives—some 100 or so annually—while others, who lived along more lightly traveled routes, took in perhaps two or three a month, or only a handful over several years.

The underground clarified the nature of slavery (fugitives brought ashore in Philadelphia in 1856) to Northerners. As the railroad accelera ted, "the whole country," wrote conductor Addison Coffin in 1897, "was like a huge pot in a state of boiling over."

One of the most active underground centers—and the subject of a 15-minute docudrama, *Brothers of the Borderland,* produced for the Freedom Center and introduced by Oprah Winfrey—was Ripley, Ohio, about 50 miles east of

Cincinnati. Today, Ripley is a sleepy village of two- and three-story 19th-century houses nestled at the foot of low bluffs, facing south toward the Ohio River and the cornfields of Kentucky beyond. But in the decades preceding the Civil War, it was one of the busiest ports between Pittsburgh and Cincinnati, its economy fueled by river traffic, shipbuilding and pork butchering. To slave owners, it was known as "a black, dirty Abolition hole"—and with good reason. Since the 1820s, a network of radical white Presbyterians, led by the Rev. John Rankin, a flinty Tennessean who had moved north to escape the atmosphere of slavery, collaborated with local blacks on both sides of the river in one of the most successful underground operations.

The Rankins' simple brick farmhouse still stands on a hilltop. It was visible for miles along the river and well into Kentucky. Arnold Gragston, who as a slave in Kentucky ferried scores of fugitives across the then 500- to 1,500-foot-wide Ohio River, later recalled that Rankin had a "lighthouse in his yard, about thirty feet high."

Recently, local preservationist Betty Campbell led the way into the austere parlor of the Rankin house, now a museum open to the public. She pointed out the fireplace where hundreds of runaways warmed themselves on winter nights, as well as the upstairs crawl space where, on occasion, they hid. Because the Rankins lived so close to the river and within easy reach of slave hunters, they generally sheltered fugitives only briefly before leading them on horseback along an overgrown streambed through a forest to a neighboring farmhouse a few miles north.

"The river divided the two worlds by law, the North and the South, but the cultures were porous," Campbell said, gazing across the river's gray trough toward the bluffs of Kentucky, a landscape not much altered since the mid-19th century. "There were antislavery men in Kentucky, and also proslavery men here in Ohio, where a lot of people had Southern origins and took slavery for granted. Frequently, trusted slaves were sent from Kentucky to the market at Ripley."

For families like the Rankins, the clandestine work became a full-time vocation. Jean Rankin, John's wife, was responsible for seeing that a fire was burning in the hearth and food kept on the table. At least one of the couple's nine sons remained on call, prepared to saddle up and hasten his charges to the next way station. "It was the custom with us not to talk among ourselves about the fugitives lest inadvertently a clue should be obtained of our modus operandi," the Rankins' eldest son, Adam, wrote years later in an unpublished memoir. "'Another runaway went through at night' was all that would be said."

One Rankin collaborator, Methodist minister John B. Mahan, was arrested at his home and taken back to Kentucky, where after 16 months in jail he was made to pay a ruinous fine that impoverished his family and likely contributed to his early death. In the summer of 1841, Kentucky slaveholders assaulted the Rankins' hilltop stronghold. They were repulsed only after a gun battle that left one of the attackers dead. Not even the Rankins would cross the river into Kentucky, where the penalty for "slave stealing" was up to 21 years' imprisonment. One Ripley man who did so repeatedly was John P. Parker, a former slave who had bought his freedom in Mobile, Alabama; by day, he operated an iron foundry. By night, he ferried slaves from Kentucky plantations across the river to Ohio. Although no photograph of Parker has survived, his saga has been preserved in a series of interviews recorded in the 1880s and published in 1996 as *His Promised Land: The Autobiography of John P. Parker.*

On one occasion, Parker learned that a party of fugitives, stranded after the capture of their leader, was hiding about 20 miles south of the river. "Being new and zealous in this work, I volunteered to go to the rescue," Parker recalled. Armed with a pair of pistols and a knife, and guided by another slave, Parker reached the runaways at about dawn. He found them hidden in deep woods, paralyzed with fear and "so badly demoralized that some of them wanted to give themselves up rather than face the unknown." Parker led the ten men and women for miles through dense thickets.

As many as 150,000 slaves may have gained freedom. "We will probably never know [the total]," says historian James O. Horton. "Part of the reason is that the underground was so successful: it kept its secrets well."

With slave hunters closing in, one of the fugitives insisted on setting off in search of water. He had gone only a short way before he came hurtling through the brush, pursued by two white men. Parker turned to the slaves still in hiding. "Drawing my pistol," he recalled, "I quietly told them that I would shoot the first one that dared make a noise, which had a quieting effect." Through thickets, Parker saw the captured slave being led away, his arms tied behind his back. The group proceeded to the river, where a patroller spotted them.

Though the lights of Ripley were visible across the water, "they might as well have been [on] the moon so far as being a relief to me," Parker recalled. Bloodhounds baying in their ears, the runaways located a rowboat quickly enough, but it had room for only eight people. Two would have to be left behind. When the wife of one of the men picked to stay behind began to wail, Parker would recall, "I witnessed an example of heroism that made me proud of my race." One of the men in the boat gave up his seat to the woman's husband. As Parker rowed toward Ohio and freedom, he saw slave hunters converge on the spot where the two men had been left behind. "I knew," he wrote later, "the poor fellow had been captured in sight of the promised land."

Parker carried a $2,500 price on his head. More than once, his house was searched and he was assaulted in the streets of Ripley. Yet he estimated that he managed to help some 440 fugitives to freedom. In 2002, Parker's house on the Ripley waterfront—restored by a local citizens' group headed by Campbell—opened to the public.

On a clear day last spring, Carl Westmoreland returned to the Evers farm. Since his first visit, he had learned that the slave jail had been built in the 1830s by a prosperous slave trader, John Anderson, who used it to hold slaves en route by flatboat to the huge slave market at Natchez, Mississippi, where auctions were held several times a year. Anderson's manor house is gone now, as are the cabins of the slaves who served in his household, tended his land and probably even operated the jail itself.

"The jail is a perfect symbol of forgetting," Westmoreland said at the time, not far from the slave trader's overgrown grave. "For their own reasons, whites and blacks both tried to forget about that jail, just as the rest of America tried to forget about slavery. But that building has already begun to teach, by causing people to go back and look at the local historical record. It's doing its job." Anderson died in 1834 at the age of 42. Westmoreland continued: "They say that he tripped over a grapevine and fell onto the sharp stump of a cornstalk, which penetrated his eye and entered his brain. He was chasing a runaway slave."

Critical Thinking

1. What did the existence of the "Underground Railroad" say about Southern claims that slaves were happy and contented?

2. What was the Fugitive Slave Law? What was it supposed to accomplish?

FERGUS M. BORDEWICH *is the author of Bound for Canaan: The Underground Railroad and the War for the Soul of America,* published by Amistad/HarperCollins.

There Goes the South

President-elect Abraham Lincoln remained strangely silent as threats of secession became a reality during the long winter before his inauguration.

H. W. BRANDS

On the eve of his victory in the 1860 presidential election, Abraham Lincoln surprised a well-wisher by declaring, "For personal considerations, I would rather have a full term in the Senate—a place in which I would feel more consciously able to discharge the duties required and where there was more chance to make a reputation and less danger of losing it—than four years of the presidency."

Lincoln's expression of 11th-hour doubt was not merely the disclaimer of a self-deprecating politician. The nearer he got to fulfilling his ambition of becoming president, the more he realized how daunting the job would be. He did his best to maintain a cheerful front as he monitored the final election returns at the Springfield, Ill., telegraph office on November 6. But his private secretary John Nicolay watched "the appalling shadow of his mighty task and responsibility" pass over him as he donned his overcoat around 1:30 A.M. and headed home in a melancholy mood. "It seemed as if he suddenly bore the whole world upon his shoulders, and could not shake it off."

Lincoln faced the unnerving prospect that by the time he took his oath of office on March 4—four months after the election—the Union would be in ruins. Southern radicals were already clamoring for secession. Meanwhile, even though Lincoln lacked the constitutional authority to act as president, people in both the North and the South looked to him for leadership as the nation plunged into a period of dangerous uncertainty.

Years later, Lincoln's first vice president, Hannibal Hamlin, chided eulogists for "constructing a Lincoln who was as great the day he left Springfield as when he made his earthly exit four years later." As president-elect, Lincoln was uncertain about whether the secession movement represented the bluster of a minority or a groundswell of popular Southern sentiment. Nor could he confidently predict whether Northerners would insist on holding the Union together or bid good riddance to the slave states. Moreover, he struggled at first with his own natural tendency to let pressing questions simmer until solutions bubbled to the surface. Should he try to reach some accommodation with Southern moderates in hopes of averting war? Or would that merely encourage the radical secessionists, who would interpret any accommodation as weakness and grow more convinced the North would never fight?

Only at his inauguration did he muster the will to attack the secessionists head on. By then it was too late to save the Union peacefully.

During the long winter interlude before he took office, Lincoln initially did nothing, hoping the crisis would pass. But when his inaction proved counterproductive and the secessionist momentum intensified, he felt obliged to alter course. Still, he moved quietly and indirectly, fearing that his words and deeds might provoke Southern moderates into joining the secessionists. Only at his inauguration did he muster the will to speak boldly and attack the secessionists head on.

By then it was too late to save the Union peacefully.

Lincoln had sought the presidency by means that invited confusion. He won the Republican nomination largely on the strength of his House Divided speech of 1858, in which he declared that America could not continue half slave and half free. But in the general election the Republicans promised to leave slavery alone in the states where it existed, and Lincoln embraced that promise without ever overtly disavowing the uncompromising message of the House Divided address.

In the mid-19th century presidential candidates didn't campaign for themselves, nor was it thought seemly for presidents-elect to speak on the record. But given the turmoil surrounding his election, many people thought Lincoln must explain his position on the unfolding crisis. A pointed appeal came from George Prentice, the editor of the *Louisville Journal*. Prentice was a discouraged Southern Unionist who urged Lincoln to make a public statement that would "take from the disunionists every excuse or pretext for treason."

Rebel Administration. Jefferson Davis (left) and Alexander Stephens were sworn in as president and vice president of the new Confederacy a month before Lincoln's inauguration. Stephens was on friendly terms with Lincoln and initially argued against secession.

"If what I have already said has failed to convince you, no repetition of it would convince you," Lincoln replied. His answer was a dodge; he wouldn't speak because he didn't want to commit himself before he had to.

The rumblings of secession increased, however, and Lincoln realized he had to give some sign of his thinking. Lyman Trumbull was a senator from Illinois who had been elected as a Democrat but subsequently converted to Republicanism. He and Lincoln were known to be close, and his words were often taken as coming from Lincoln. Two weeks after the election Lincoln wrote a brief passage for Trumbull to insert in a speech at Chicago. "I have labored in and for the Republican organization," Trumbull said, for himself and Lincoln, "with entire confidence that whenever it shall be in power, each and all of the states will be left in complete control of their own affairs respectively, and at as perfect liberty to choose, and employ, their own means of protecting property, and preserving peace and order within their respective limits, as they have ever been under any administration."

Lincoln's proxy statement failed dismally. It lacked the authority that words spoken by Lincoln himself would have carried, and its second-hand character suggested a timidity that augured ill for Lincoln's administration or his cause. Southern secessionists concluded that a man without the courage to speak

in his own voice would be a president without the nerve to challenge their separatist designs. Northern radicals complained that the Trumbull statement was a retreat from the moral clarity of the House Divided speech.

The criticism reinforced Lincoln's caution. "This is just what I expected, and just what would happen with any declaration I could make," he told a friend. "These political fiends are not half sick enough yet. 'Party malice' and not 'public good' possesses them entirely. 'They seek a sign, and no sign shall be given them.'"

Lincoln's diffidence encouraged others to take the stage. The secessionists called conventions and drafted resolutions to implement their separatist aims. Northern Unionists and Southern moderates weighed a constitutional amendment guaranteeing the future of slavery in the states where it already existed. Lame duck president James Buchanan sent an envoy, Duff Green, to test Lincoln's thinking on such an amendment.

"I do not desire any amendment," Lincoln told Green. An amendment, he reasoned, would be difficult to pass and nearly impossible to repeal. He blanched at the idea of grafting slavery so egregiously onto America's fundamental law. But he wouldn't rule it out entirely, if only because amending the Constitution was the prerogative of Congress and the states, not the president.

More promising, to Lincoln's view, was the approach of Alexander Stephens, a Georgia moderate Lincoln had known since the 1840s, when they served in the House of Representatives together. As Georgians debated their response to Lincoln's election, Stephens gave a widely noted speech opposing rash action. "I do not anticipate that Mr. Lincoln will do anything to jeopardize our safety or security," he said. "He can do nothing unless he is backed by power in Congress. The House of Representatives is largely in the majority against him. In the Senate he will also be powerless."

Lincoln read newspaper summaries of Stephens' remarks, and he wrote Stephens asking if he had prepared them for publication. Stephens replied that he had not, but that the news reports fairly characterized what he had said. He went on to offer Lincoln encouragement in his efforts to hold the nation together. "The Country is certainly in great peril and no man ever had heavier or greater responsibilities resting upon him than you have in this present momentous crisis," he said.

Lincoln appreciated the gesture, and he tried, through Stephens, to allay the concerns of Southern moderates. "Do the people in the South really entertain fears that a Republican administration would, directly or indirectly, interfere with their slaves?" he asked Stephens. "If they do, I wish to assure you, as once a friend and still, I hope, not an enemy, that there is no cause for such fears. The South would be in no more danger in this respect than it was in the days of Washington."

You think slavery is right and ought to be extended, while we think it is wrong and ought to be restricted. That I suppose is the rub.

Yet Lincoln conceded to Stephens that the issue ran deeper than political assurances. Southerners and Northerners had irreconcilable views on the morality of slavery. "You think slavery is right and ought to be extended, while we think it is wrong and ought to be restricted. That I suppose is the rub."

That was the rub, and it chafed the more as Lincoln's inauguration neared. A desperate Congress convened committees to find an arrangement to hold the Union together. Proposals included one to resurrect a popular sovereignty scheme advanced by Lincoln's old nemesis Stephen Douglas, by which residents of frontier territories would vote to permit or ban slavery. Lincoln still declined to issue a public statement, but he wrote Republican members of Congress to stiffen their resolve against any retreat on slavery in the territories. "Entertain no proposition for a compromise in regard to extension of slavery," he urged William Kellogg, a Republican representative from Illinois. "The instant you do, they have us

under again; all our labor is lost. . . . The tug has to come and better now than later." Lincoln told Elihu Washburne, another Illinois Republican: "Hold firm, as with a chain of steel."

Lincoln perceived Southerners' aggressiveness on the slave issue as inevitable. Their current demands were but the start. "If we surrender, it is the end of us, and of the government," he asserted privately. "They will repeat the experiment upon us ad libitum." The sole way out of the present impasse, Lincoln said, was by a route neither Northerners nor Southerners would accept: "a prohibition against acquiring any more territory." It was a great irony of American history that this very solution—which Lincoln and nearly every contemporary rejected as unworkable—had already been effected, in political practice if not in political theory. The continental expansion that was causing all the trouble had ended in 1848. The only substantial piece of North America to be added to the United States after 1860 was Alaska, which was unsuited to a large population of any sort, slave or otherwise.

As the winter dragged on, Lincoln realized he had underestimated the South. Those who spoke of secession were not bluffing. He decided he must state his position—albeit still not quite for public consumption. Thurlow Weed, the New York Republican boss whose support had been central to Lincoln's election, had convened Northern governors to prepare a riposte to the South. "I am unwilling to see a united South and a divided North," Weed wrote Lincoln. "Thus united, your administration will have its foundation upon a rock." What could Lincoln tell the governors, even in private, about his intentions?

Lincoln's response echoed what he had told other Republicans: He was "inflexible on the territorial question"—no slavery outside the Southern states. He added: "My opinion is that no state can, in any way lawfully, get out of the Union, without the consent of the others; and that it is the duty of the President, and other government functionaries, to run the machine as it is."

But the machine was already breaking up. South Carolina, amid great fanfare, had passed an ordinance of secession on December 20, and in the succeeding weeks several other states prepared to follow suit and leave the Union.

On February 11, Lincoln left Springfield for Washington. The psychological strain of the long, hard winter showed in his face and bearing; an acquaintance remarked that his body "heaved with emotion and he could scarcely command his feelings." Lincoln's voice broke as he told his Springfield neighbors, "I now leave, not knowing when, or whether ever, I may return."

The strain intensified as he headed east. The newspapers en route reported on the provisional Congress of the Confederate States of America, meeting in Montgomery, Ala. Seven states—South Carolina, Mississippi, Florida, Alabama, Georgia, Louisiana and Texas—sent delegates, although the Texans had to await the ratification of secession by the people of the Lone Star State. Lincoln read of the election of Jefferson Davis to be president of the Confederacy, and days later of Davis' inauguration with Alexander Stephens as his vice president. He also read that the Southern states were seizing the federal forts on their soil.

The progress of a president-elect en route to his inauguration was a once-in-a-lifetime event for many of the towns through which Lincoln's train passed, and at every stop people gathered and insisted that he speak. He was too good a politician not to oblige. "If the United States should merely hold and retake its own forts and other property, and collect the duties on foreign importations, or even withhold the mails from places where they were habitually violated, would any or all these things be 'invasion' or 'coercion'?" he asked an audience at Indianapolis. Then he waffled: "I am not asserting anything. I am merely asking questions."

At Philadelphia he learned that Allan Pinkerton, a detective hired by the railroad company to preempt sabotage, had heard rumors of an assassination plot in Baltimore, where secessionist sympathies ran strong. Lincoln at first resisted altering his schedule, but when additional evidence suggested real danger, he was persuaded. He disguised himself as an invalid and slipped through Baltimore in the dead of night.

He soon regretted that decision. Southern newspapers ridiculed his lack of courage; even Republican papers feared he had diminished himself on the verge of his inauguration.

Inauguration Day. With the unfinished Capitol as a backdrop, Lincoln finally addressed the nation's uncertain future.

All of Washington was on edge as Lincoln prepared to take his oath of office on March 4. General Winfield Scott, the army commander, stationed infantry, cavalry and artillery troops conspicuously about the capital, and special squadrons of policemen lined Pennsylvania Avenue. The great majority of the visitors who crowded the streets were from the Northern states—"judging from the lack of long-haired men in the crowd," an eyewitness observed. When the members of the House of Representatives were summoned to join the inaugural procession to the east side of the Capitol, their jostling for position escalated to curses, threats and near-fisticuffs. Chief Justice Roger B. Taney, whose decision in the *Dred Scott* case had elicited Lincoln's House Divided prophecy, visibly trembled as he stood near Lincoln on the rostrum.

Lincoln felt the tension as he looked out on the crowd. And he couldn't help reflecting that his caution had done nothing to ease the nation's crisis, which grew more acute by the day. Inaction had simply encouraged others to seize the initiative.

But now it was his turn—finally. He commenced by reiterating what he had been conveying in private: that slavery in the South was secure. "I have no purpose, directly or indirectly, to interfere with the institution of slavery in the States where it exists. I believe I have no lawful right to do so, and I have no inclination to do so."

Sadly, he continued, Southern radicals were not so tolerant. "A disruption of the Federal Union, heretofore only menaced, is now formidably attempted."

No disruption would be allowed. An unexpected steel entered Lincoln's voice—a tone few had anticipated and none in public heard. "The Union of these States is perpetual," he said. Secessionists would search in vain for constitutional authorization for their plan. "No government proper ever had a provision in its organic law for its own termination." If, as the secessionists contended, the Union was a union of states rather than of peoples, this afforded no easier exit, for, having been created by all the states, the Union required the consent of all the states to be destroyed. "No State, upon its own mere motion, can lawfully get out of the Union. . . . The Union is unbroken."

The Union of these States is perpetual. No State, upon its own mere motion, can lawfully get out of the Union. . . . The Union is unbroken.

And Lincoln vowed it would remain unbroken. "To the extent of my ability I shall take care, as the Constitution itself expressly enjoins upon me, that the laws of the Union be faithfully executed in all of the States."

The secessionists blamed Lincoln personally for endangering the peace of the Union; they had it just backward, he said. "In your hands, my dissatisfied fellow-countrymen, and not in mine, is the momentous issue of civil war. The Government will not assail you. You can have no conflict without being yourselves the aggressors. You have no oath registered in Heaven to destroy the Government, while I shall have the most solemn one to 'preserve, protect, and defend it.'"

These were fighting words. The secessionists had doubted Lincoln's resolve; his long silence had corroborated their doubts, to the point of encouraging their secession. But they could doubt him no longer. To speak of civil war was to make it possible.

Lincoln had never fought a civil war; none of his contemporaries had. He had only the vaguest notion of what it would mean or how it would be done. Yet if the secessionists persisted in their destructive ways, they would provoke a civil war.

He let his words hang in the March air above the Capitol grounds. Applause had interrupted him earlier; now the thousands were silent as they pondered his promise, and his threat. He gave both a moment to sink in.

Then he concluded more hopefully: "We are not enemies, but friends. We must not be enemies. Though passion may have strained, it must not break our bonds of affection. The mystic chords of memory, stretching from every battlefield and patriot grave to every living heart and hearthstone all over this broad land, will yet swell the chorus of the Union, when again touched, as surely they will be, by the better angels of our nature."

H. W. Brands is a history professor at the University of Texas and the author of 16 books. His latest is *Traitor to His Class,* a biography of Franklin Roosevelt.

Lincoln and the Constitutional Dilemma of Emancipation

EDNA GREENE MEDFORD

> The President shall be Commander in Chief of the Army and Navy of the United States, and of the Militia of the several States, when called into the actual Service of the United States.
>
> —U. S. Constitution, Article II, Section 2

On the afternoon of January 1, 1863, following nearly two years of bloody civil war, Abraham Lincoln set in motion events that would reconnect the detached cord of Union and that would begin to reconcile the nation's practices to its avowed democratic principles. Interpreting Article II, Section 2 of the Constitution broadly, the president used his war powers to proclaim freedom for those enslaved laborers caught in the dehumanizing grip of one of the Confederacy's most sacrosanct institutions. His bold move challenged prevailing notions of presidential prerogative and triggered criticism from his supporters as well as his opponents. While many abolitionists bemoaned the limited scope of the president's actions, alleging that he freed those persons over whom he had no control, while exempting from his edict those under Union authority, his more conservative critics charged that he had exceeded the powers the Constitution invested in the executive.

Lincoln anticipated the criticism. He knew that most abolitionists would be satisfied with nothing less than universal emancipation and that, contrarily, pro-South forces would find in his actions reason to brand him a betrayer of American liberties. Given that slavery evoked such polarization in the North, he realized that whatever action he took on the institution posed considerable danger to the goal of the war—preservation of the Union.

Although influenced by the practical considerations of containing the rebellion—that is, not losing any more slaveholding states to the Confederacy—Lincoln's greatest challenge regarding emancipation was to achieve it without violating constitutional guarantees. He understood slavery to be the cause of the war but he believed that the Constitution denied the president any easy solution for its eradication. Whatever his personal views on slavery (and there is incontrovertible evidence that he hated the institution on moral grounds as well as practical reasons), law and custom had deemed enslaved people property.[1] Because the Constitution protected property rights, Lincoln felt compelled to operate within those constraints. As war propelled him inexorably toward emancipation, he sought authority to do so within the framework that the Constitution provided.

The Civil War began as a struggle over national union, one half of the American people believed it indissoluble and fought to preserve it, while the other half wished to withdraw from it and secure their own identity. Northern attempts at appeasement and diplomacy having failed, war became the only recourse for a president convinced that secession was unconstitutional. Hence, in his first official act after hostilities commenced, Lincoln called up the state militias "to maintain the honor, the integrity, and the existence" of the nation.[2] The decision had not been an easy one. When he spoke before Congress in special session on July 4, 1861, he explained that.

"It was with the deepest regret that the Executive found the duty of employing the war-power, in defense of the government, forced upon him. He could but perform this duty, or surrender the existence of the government."[3]

Defense of the government ultimately led Lincoln to strike at the heart of the South's reason for challenging national union. It would prove even harder than prosecuting the war itself, because the Constitution—compromise document that it was—reflected the ambivalence of the framers over the issue of slavery. Lincoln had acknowledged "not grudgingly, but fully, and fairly," the constitutional rights of the slaveholder, but the treatment of slavery in the Constitution suggested to him that the framers had deliberately paved the way for the institution's eventual extinction.[4] The founding fathers and the earliest Congress were hostile to slavery; they tolerated it "only by necessity," he argued. The framers even excluded the words "slave" and "slavery" from the Constitution and chose instead to refer to those held in bondage as "persons" from whom "service or labor may be due." This was a deliberate attempt, thought Lincoln, to keep the idea of "property in man" out of this democratic document.[5] The founding fathers hid it away "just as an afflicted man hides away . . . a cancer, which he does not cut out at once, lest he bleed to death."[6] Hence, the Supreme Court's ruling in *Scott v. Sandford,* which declared that slaveholders could not be prohibited from taking their chattel wherever they wished, was "based upon a mistaken statement of fact . . . that the right of property in a slave is distinctly and expressly affirmed in the Constitution." That document was "literally silent" about any right of slaveholders to take their human property into the territories.[7]

Lincoln had always believed that Congress could prevent slavery from spreading into the territories, over which it had jurisdiction. But the government, he believed, did not have the constitutional authority to touch the institution where it had already been established. Indeed, the 1860 Republican platform on which he was elected to the presidency declared:

> That the maintenance inviolate of the rights of the States, and especially the light of each State to order and control its own domestic institutions according to its own judgment exclusively, is essential to that balance of power on which the perfection and endurance of our political fabric depend.[8]

Lincoln did not stand down from this position when in the weeks following his election several southern states seceded and formed the Confederate States of America. Far from seizing upon this as an opportunity to move against slavery, the newly elected president attempted to reassure the secessionists and their non-seceding slaveholding brothers that he had "no purpose, directly or indirectly, to interfere with the institution of slavery in the States where it exists. I believe I have no lawful right to do so, and I have no inclination to do so." Lincoln promised that "all the protection which, consistently with the Constitution and the laws, can be given, will be cheerfully given to all the States when lawfully demanded as cheerfully to one section, as to another."[9] It was a position he held throughout the war.

In promising to uphold the laws, Lincoln was speaking primarily about enforcement of the Fugitive Slave Act, passed in 1850 as one of the compromises after the war with Mexico resulted in the ceding of millions of acres to the United States. The Missouri Compromise had maintained a balance of free and slave states since 1820, but this new acquisition threatened to give advantage to one section over the other. In an effort to stay the rising crisis, Congress had proposed a series of measures that would appease each region. The Fugitive Slave Act aimed to assure southerners that the northern people would be equally obligated to protect the rights of the slaveholder. The law imposed fines on anyone who refused to assist in the apprehending of a fugitive or who facilitated any effort to prevent recovery. This attempt by Congress to resolve the conflict may have pleased the South, but it evoked anger and frustration among northerners who had no desire to become slave catchers.[10]

After the secessionist attack on Fort Sumter ignited armed conflict, Lincoln's declaration of noninterference met with increased criticism within the Union and initiated direct challenge to the administrations position. Undeterred by the president's pledge, enslaved African Americans had themselves seized the opportunity to obtain their freedom by flight. As Union troops advanced on the Confederacy, fugitives from slavery met them and offered loyalty, labor, and information in exchange for asylum. Even in the ostensibly loyal border states, black men and women sought to secure freedom as the chaos of war blurred distinctions between rebel and Unionist slaveholders.[11]

Without specific guidelines for dealing with fugitives, Union Commanders in the field implemented their own solutions. Some of them saw the advantage to sheltering runaways and chose to employ them in erecting defense against southern forces or utilized them in a variety of noncombatant occupations. General Benjamin Butler's declaration that these fugitives were contraband of war encouraged other commanders to embrace the designation.[12] But for every General Butler there was a Henry Halleck who barred fugitive slaves from the camps under his command. In the first months of the war, the Lincoln administration chose not to make any additional public pronouncements on the issue of fugitives, but the president, eager to keep the conflict contained and of short duration, privately queried the general-in-chief, Winfield Scott, if it "would be well to allow owners to bring back [slaves] which have crossed the Potomac" with Union troops.[13] As a consequence, runaways were banned from the Union camps of the Department of Washington and were prohibited from following soldiers on the move.[14]

Congress's attempt to turn the South's "peculiar institution" to the North's advantage and the emancipating actions of commanders in the field left Lincoln less than enthusiastic and, in some instances, downright perturbed. In August 1861, Congress had passed the First Confiscation Act, which provided for seizure of any property (including enslaved persons) that had been used to wage war against the government. The act did not address the status of the confiscated slaves once the war was over. Yet, concerned that such action would strengthen the resolve of the rebels and would likely be overturned by constitutional challenge, Lincoln reluctantly signed the measure and made little effort to enforce it.[15]

General John C. Frémont's proclamation of August 30 gave Lincoln even greater concern. As commander of the Department of the West, Frémont declared martial law in Missouri and issued a proclamation stipulating that "the property, real and personal, of all persons in the state of Missouri who shall take up arms against the United States . . . is declared to be confiscated and their slaves are hereby declared freemen."[16] Frémont's proclamation differed from the First Confiscation Act in that property could be seized without having been employed against the Union. Moreover, the human property thus confiscated was declared free. Citing concern that the decree might "alarm our southern Union friends, and turn them against us—perhaps ruin our rather fair prospect for Kentucky," Lincoln asked, and later commanded, the unyielding Frémont to place his proclamation in conformity with Congress's confiscation measure.[17]

In a letter written in late September to friend Orville H. Browning, fellow Republican and U.S. senator from Illinois, Lincoln reiterated these political concerns, especially the importance of securing the loyalty of Kentucky. But it was the constitutional question that was paramount. Lincoln argued that the general's proclamation, specifically the part which stipulated the liberation of the slaves, was "purely political, and not within the range of military law, or necessity." He challenged the notion that:

"If a commanding General finds a necessity to seize the farm of a private owner, for a pasture, an encampment, or a fortification, he has the right to do so . . . as long as the necessity lasts. . . . But to say the farm no longer belong to the owner, or his heirs forever, and this as well when the farm is not needed for military purposes as when it is, is purely political, without the savor of military law about it."[18]

Lincoln believed that this applied to slaves as well. Human property could be confiscated, "But when the need is past, it is not for [the confiscator] to fix their permanent future condition. That must be settled according to laws made by law-makers, and not by military proclamations. . . . Can it be pretended that it is any longer the government of the U.S. . . . wherein a General, or a President, may make permanent rules of property by proclamation?"[19]

When eight months later, General David Hunter, commander of the Department of the South, declared martial law and freed the slaves within the three states under his jurisdiction, an exasperated Lincoln rescinded the order, declaring that as president he would "reserve to myself" the question of whether or not as commander in chief he had authority to emancipate the slaves.[20]

Contrary to his response to the emancipating actions of commanders in the field, Lincoln did not challenge Congress's authority to free enslaved people in the District of Columbia when on April 11, 1862, that body approved a measure to emancipate "persons held to service or labor" in the city. As a federal enclave, Washington was under the jurisdiction of Congress, and hence, it had the constitutional authority to end slavery there. The city had been steadily moving toward eradication of the institution for some time, and so fewer than 3,200 African Americans out of a total black population of 11,000 were affected directly.[21] Nevertheless, many white Washingtonians challenged Congress's actions because they thought the maximum amount of three hundred dollars per slave was inadequate compensation and because they imagined that a free city would quickly become overrun with fugitives from slavery in Maryland and Virginia.[22]

But acknowledgment of constitutional authority did not suggest that the District Emancipation Bill was to Lincoln's liking. Weeks before, he had proposed a plan for gradual, compensated emancipation, implemented by the border states. In this way, constitutional constraints would be recognized while emancipation would sever the bond between the slaveholding Union states and their sisters in rebellion.[23] But none of those states had exhibited much interest. Hence, when Congress stepped in to implement emancipation for the District of Columbia, Lincoln was somewhat ambivalent. While the measure was making its way through Congress, he expressed his uneasiness "as to the time and manner of doing it." He preferred the initiative to come from one of the border states, but if this could not be achieved quickly, he hoped that the bill would stipulate an emancipation that was gradual, provided compensation to the owners, and was voted on by the people of the District.[24]

When Lincoln signed the District Emancipation Bill after delaying for five days, he sent a message to Congress that officially voiced his concerns. The president reminded them that he had "ever desired to see the national capital freed from the institution in some satisfactory way."[25] But he proposed an "amendatory or supplemental act" that would guarantee sufficient time for which to file claims for compensation. Moreover, he hinted at "matters within and about this act, which might have taken a course or shape, more satisfactory to my jud[g]ment."[26] Presumably, he was disturbed that emancipation had been carried out absent any opportunity for District residents to shape it as they did not have a vote.

One last action on the part of Congress would address the issue of emancipation of enslaved people before Lincoln issued his preliminary proclamation in September 1862. In July, Congress had passed the Second Confiscation Act. The measure, intended "to suppress Insurrection, to punish Treason and Rebellion, to seize and confiscate the Property of Rebels," provided for the freeing of all slaves of persons who were "adjudged guilty" of committing treason against the United States.[27] Again, certain features of the bill disturbed Lincoln, and again he responded by submitting written objections to Congress. While expressing his pleasure that loyal Unionist slaveholders were not touched by the measure and that persons charged with treason would enjoy "regular trials, in duly constituted courts," the president found it 'startling' that Congress could free a slave who resided in a state unless "it were said the ownership of the slave had first been transferred to the nation, and that congress had then liberated him." But what troubled Lincoln most about the Second Confiscation Act was the idea that forfeiture of title to the slave extended beyond the life of the rebel owner. The act, Lincoln believed, violated Article III, Section 3 of the Constitution that stipulated: "The Congress shall have Power to declare the Punishment of Treason, but no Attainder of Treason shall work Corruption of Blood, or Forfeiture except during the Life of the Person attainted."[28] The enforcement of the Second Confiscation Act would do just that by denying the property rights of the heirs of the person committing treason. Lincoln's objections led Congress to pass a joint resolution that disallowed any "punishment or proceedings under the act that would lead to forfeiture beyond the offender's natural life."[29]

The president's concerns regarding the Second Confiscation Act were no trivial matter. He was only two months away from issuing his Preliminary Emancipation Proclamation, which would announce his intention to make "forever free" those slaves in states and parts thereof still in rebellion by January 1, 1863. While the Constitution did not expressly give the president the authority to free slaves, Lincoln claimed such authority through the war powers. "The Constitution invests its Commander-in-Chief with the law of war, in time of war," he declared. "By the law of war, property, both of enemies and friends, may be taken" or destroyed if doing so hurts the enemy and helps the cause.[30] Hence, Lincoln claimed the right to issue the proclamation as a "fit and necessary war measurer."[31] By claiming military necessity, he sidestepped the constitutional concerns that had attended Congress's effort to legislate freedom under the clause regulating punishment for treason.

Despite objections to the proclamation, Lincoln declined to rescind the decree. "The promise [of freedom] being made, must be kept," he declared.[32] But his resoluteness masked the fear that his decree would face legal challenge. Moreover, he recognized that while freeing enslaved people in the Confederacy, slavery as an institution had not been abolished. Hence, during the summer of 1864, he joined Congress in pressing for the passage of a constitutional amendment banning slavery. When in February 1865, Congress passed the Thirteenth Amendment and submitted it to the states for ratification, Lincoln declared it "a King's cure for all the evils."[33] Interestingly, shortly thereafter, he drafted a recommendation to Congress that proposed that compensation payments be made to all the slaveholding states—including those currently in the Confederacy—provided the states were not in rebellion by April. The recommendation was never delivered to Congress because the president's cabinet unanimously rejected it.[34]

As he moved toward emancipation, Lincoln looked to the Constitution for guidance, ever careful to conform to what he believed were the guarantees of that document. Since enslaved people were deemed property, he felt it imperative to address the legality of efforts to liberate them from the perspective of the constitutional rights of the slaveholder. Although he acknowledged the humanity (albeit inferior to whites, in his estimation) of black men and women, issues of emancipation within the context of constitutional constraints precluded any humanitarian sentiment as a part of "official duty." "What I do about slavery, and the colored race, I do because I believe it helps to save the Union," he had declared. "[A]nd what I forbear, I forbear because I do not believe it would help to save the Union."[35] Despite the limitations it placed on presidential emancipation, the Constitution had given him the authority to save the Union and begin the destruction of slavery throughout the nation.

Notes

1. In his speech on the Kansas-Nebraska Act at Peoria, Illinois, on October 16, 1854, Lincoln had declared: "I hate [slavery] because of the monstrous injustice . . . I hate it because it deprives our republican example of its just influence in the world—enables the enemies of free institutions . . . to taunt us as hypocrites." See "Speech at Peoria," in *The Collected Works of Abraham Lincoln* (hereinafter cited as *Collected Works*), 8 vols., ed. Roy P. Basler (New Brunswick, NJ: Rutgers University Press, 1953), 2:255.

2. "By the President of the United States a Proclamation, April 15, 1861," *Collected Works,* 4:331–32.

3. "Message to Congress in Special Session, July 4, 1861," in *Collected Works,* 4:421.

4. Speech at Peoria, October 16, 1854, *Collected Works,* 2:256.

5. Address at Cooper Institute, February 27, 1860, *Collected Works,* 3:545.

6. Speech at Peoria, October 16, 1854, *Collected Works,* 2:274.

7. Address at Cooper Institute, February 27, 1860, *Collected Works,* 3:543–44.

8. Quoted in First Inaugural Address, 1861, *Collected Works,* 4:263.

9. Ibid.

10. For discussion of the Fugitive Slave Act and the Compromise of 1850, see Stanley W. Campbell, *The Slave Catchers: The Enforcement of the Fugitive Slave Law, 1850–1860* (Chapel Hill, NC: University of North Carolina Press, 1968).

11. See Harold Holzer, Edna Greene Medford, and Frank Williams, *The Emancipation Proclamation: Three Views* (Baton Rouge: Louisiana State University Press, 2006), 6–9.

12. Three fugitives from a rebel master sought asylum at Fortress Monroe (Virginia) in late May 1861, claiming that they were about to be taken out of Virginia and employed against the Union. As commander of the fort, Butler declared the men "contraband of war" and set them to labor for the Union. "Benj. F. Butler to Lieut. Gen. Winfield Scott. May 24, 1861," *The War of the Rebellion: A Compilation of the Official Records of the Union and Confederate Armies* (hereinafter *O.R.*), 128 vols. (Washington: Government Printing Office, 1880–1901), ser. 2, 1:752.

13. Lieutenant Colonel Schuyler Hamilton to Brigadier General Irwin McDowell, Washington, July 16, 1861, *O.R.,* ser. 2, 1:760.

14. General Orders, No. 33, July 17, 1861, Headquarters Department of Washington, in *O.R.,* ser. 2, 1:760.

15. See Allen C. Guelzo, *Lincoln's Emancipation Proclamation: The End of Slavery in America* (New York: Simon and Schuster, 2004), 45.

16. Proclamation of John C. Frémont, August 30, 1861, *O.R.,* ser. 1, 3:467.

17. To John C. Frémont, September 2, 1861, *Collected Works,* 4:506.

18. To Orville H. Browning, September 22, 1861, *Collected Works,* 4:531.

19. Ibid.

20. "Revocation of the Hunter Proclamation," *Collected Works,* 5:222.

21. Constance McLaughlin Green, *The Secret City: A History of Race Relations in the Nation's Capital* (Princeton: Princeton University Press, 1967), 33. In 1860, the total population of the District (including Washington and Georgetown) was just over 75,000.

22. Ibid., 59–60.

23. Message to Congress, March 6, 1862, *Collected Works,* 5:145.

24. Letter to Horace Greeley, March 24, 1862, *Collected Works,* 5:169.

25. Message to Congress, April 16, 1862, *Collected Works,* 5:192.

26. Ibid.

27. See Holzer, Medford and Williams, *The Emancipation Proclamation: Three Views,* 137–40.

28. To the Senate and House of Representatives, July 17, 1862, *Collected Works,* 5:329.

29. Ibid.

30. To Hon. James C. Conkling, August 26, 1863, *Collected Works,* 6:408.

31. The Final Emancipation Proclamation, *Collected Works,* 6:29. See also Daniel Farber, *Lincoln's Constitution* (Chicago: University of Chicago Press. 2003), 152–57.

32. To Hon. James C. Conkling, August 26, 1863, *Collected Works,* 6:409.

33. "Response to a Serenade," February 1, 1865, *Collected Works,* 8:255.

34. "Message to the Senate and House of Representatives," February 5, 1865, *Collected Works,* 8:261.

35. Letter to Horace Greeley, August 22, 1862, *Collected Works,* 5:388–89.

EDNA GREENE MEDFORD is Associate Professor and Director of Graduate Studies in the Department of History at Howard University. Specializing in nineteenth-century African American history, she also teaches both graduate and undergraduate courses in Civil War and Reconstruction, Colonial America, the Jacksonian Era, and Comparative Slavery. She has published more than a dozen articles and book chapters on African Americans, especially during the era of the Civil War. Her publications include the coauthored work, *The Emancipation Proclamation: Three Views,* Baton Rouge: Louisiana State University Press, 2006.

Critical Thinking

1. On what Constitutional Grounds did Lincoln justify the Emancipation Proclamation?

2. Which slaves did the proclamation actually free?

Lincoln and Douglass

PAUL KENDRICK AND STEPHEN KENDRICK

At dusk [on a day] in early April 1866, a large crowd filed into Representatives Hall of the imposing Illinois Capitol in Springfield. Just 11 months earlier, President Lincoln's rapidly blackening body had lain here in state as thousands of townspeople had filed past to say goodbye.

Now many of the same people gathered to hear a lecture entitled "The Assassination and Its Consequences," delivered by the country's foremost abolitionist, Frederick Douglass. For several months the powerful black orator had given the same speech across the nation, but this venue, more than any other, lent extraordinary gravity to his words. In the great room Lincoln had accepted the 1858 Republican Senate nomination and delivered his controversial "House Divided" speech. Though the obscure Illinois lawyer would lose that contest to his longtime rival Stephen A. Douglas, he found himself unexpectedly propelled to the presidency. Lincoln had also argued in front of the Illinois Supreme Court more than 200 times in this building.

Standing on the podium, Douglass immediately commanded attention with his splendid mane of graying hair swept back from his broad forehead, his blazing brown eyes, deep regal voice, and overwhelming physical presence. "Prior to the Civil War," he began, "there was apparently no danger menacing our country, but a few farseeing men foresaw the calamities that have come upon us, and their warnings were treated as idle talk . . . The few listen and the many pass on, unheeding the precipice over which they are being hurled."

The slave child Frederick Bailey, born in 1818, had gradually transformed himself into the master orator Frederick Douglass, internationally known by the 1840s through the force of his eloquence fused to a compelling dignity. Only fellow abolitionist Wendell Phillips equaled him as a speaker. No one on the national stage could match the powerful, redemptive quality of his life story, which was compelling for more than his daring escape from slavery on Maryland's Eastern Shore. With dogged perseverance, he had toured for years from town to town, often at the risk of his life, to evoke the horrors of human bondage. He had written a best-selling personal testimony about his struggle for freedom, edited the nation's most notable black newspaper, and finally, through his forceful recruitment of black soldiers, he had become the principal voice of his people.

The intent of Douglass' talk in Springfield was not to dwell on that past, but to confront the new realities facing a victorious North and a nation without Lincoln. "The danger impending over us is the cold, cruel wanton surrender and betrayal of our friends and allies," cried Douglass. There were the thousands of slaves who had streamed into Union lines as "contraband." Many other black men and women had supported the war effort by picking crops, feeding the troops, and providing valuable information. Most of all, Douglass pointed to the contribution of the 180,000 black soldiers who were finally granted the right to carry a musket. One Union soldier in ten had been black. Lincoln had rightly noted that it had been this tenth that provided the margin for Union victory.

Though he did not admit it that night, Douglass had spent the last four years engaged in a long and public contest with a president who was not only slow to emancipate slaves and reluctant to put black soldiers into combat, but had made no firm commitment to give the vote to the black man, except perhaps for "those who had served in battle or of exceptional intelligence." This night Douglass set aside all their struggles.

When it counted, Lincoln had effectively collaborated with Douglass's decades-long pursuit of the total and irrevocable destruction of slavery. That an outspoken black abolitionist and a cautious prairie lawyer would ever meet, much less profoundly influence one another and form a partnership, is astounding. It was largely the brute extremities of war that had drawn them together in what Douglass in 1862 called "characters of blood and fire." Even with their deep disagreements, they had forged a strong bond of mutual understanding and respect. As a result, Douglass' personal mission to liberate black Americans became inescapably bound up in Lincoln's life—and death.

The president had made clear for three years that saving the Union was his overarching goal, and from the first shot at Fort Sumter on, Douglass had been equally clear that this was not enough. The hope of reunion with the South, he argued, was doomed unless the higher mission of eradicating slavery was brought to the fore. "What business, then, have we to be pouring out our treasure and shedding our best blood like water for that worn-out, dead and buried Union, which had already become a calamity and a curse?" This direct challenge to Lincoln was only part of a larger story of the dispute between these formidable men over the meaning of the war and, thus, the truth of America.

The epic emancipation of four million slaves remains one of the greatest stories in world history, a truth largely unrecognized by Americans because we have failed to register the essential role of African Americans in the Civil War, and because of the muted, almost amnesiac manner in which the story has been told of the failure of Reconstruction. In this story, Douglass is a national hero, an indomitable fighter who faced down nearly impossible odds. Writing three autobiographies set him up well to step into an ennobling heroic part, for he understood that his life had always been the story of his people advancing to redemption. He knew that his personal odyssey from oppressed insignificance to world standing vindicated the struggle of black people and challenged a nation that refused to offer manhood, equality, and even the right to vote to so many of their fellows.

The first conversation between Douglass and Lincoln on August 10, 1863, remains one of the pivotal moments in American history: when a former slave could enter the office of the president to discuss significant issues and festering problems and, more remarkable still, when the president could seem to enjoy Douglass' opinions and views, no matter how contrary to his own. And Douglass freely recalled, "Lincoln is the first white man I ever spent an hour with who did not remind me I was a Negro."

Yet these admirable sentiments do not come close to encompassing the true nature of their conflict, as when after the new president's first inauguration Douglass contemptuously noted, "What an excellent slave hound he is." Or as he wrote in 1862, "Mr. Lincoln assumes the language and arguments of an itinerant Colonization lecturer, showing all the inconsistencies, his pride of race and blood, his contempt for Negroes and his canting hypocrisy." Douglass wrote in a letter to the editor Theodore Tilton, just after his second White House meeting in 1864, that "when there was any shadow of a hope that a man of a more decided anti-slavery conviction and policy could be elected, I was not for Mr. Lincoln."

Lincoln possessed an ability to absorb criticism and rise above political abuse that beggars imagination today. Douglass himself certainly came to understand that this measured politician had indeed been the essential man in this national crisis, perhaps the only leader who could have both preserved the Union and won emancipation. Douglass saw Lincoln in all his imperfections and perceived his "slowness" in responding to the black cry for freedom, yet stated in the dedication of the Freedmen's Memorial monument to Lincoln in 1876 that blacks were correct to love him: "We came to the conclusion that the hour and the man of our redemption had somehow met in the person of Abraham Lincoln." Lincoln bonded to one of his severest critics because he sensed that they shared common ground, as was evident in the Gettysburg Address, where for all time he calmly and simply evoked the vision of America's "new birth of freedom."

Lincoln and Douglass alike understood that the fate of this special destiny was irrevocably bound to the "peculiar institution." The war was nothing less than an agonizing rebirth that would either ratify or nullify this destiny. Neither victory for the North nor the abolition of slavery was ever foreordained. Any compromise before the guns of Fort Sumter would have left those four million slaves under the burden and the lash. If the First Battle of Bull Run had gone the North's way, then the general vision of a quick resolution of the war would have left slavery in place.

If McClellan had possessed the courage to drive home the Peninsula Campaign in 1862 or risked his men to destroy Gen.

Robert E. Lee's forces at Antietam, the South might have collapsed before Lincoln signed the Emancipation Proclamation on September 22, 1862. Then McClellan, a man who had publicly expressed his desire that slavery continue undisturbed, would have wielded great power.

If Lee had not possessed the headstrong will to order Pickett's charge but instead had maneuvered his army toward Harrisburg and Philadelphia, then Europe might well have decisively moved into the conflict and stymied any further prosecution of the war by the Lincoln administration. Had Atlanta not fallen when it did, Lincoln would likely have lost the 1864 election to McClellan, effectively leaving slavery alive.

Douglass understood how close his cause came to failure. Abolitionism was largely upheld by people for whom slavery was an abstraction. The price of saving the Union seemed at several points to be nothing short of the sacrifice of his people. Above all, he understood that Lincoln was fighting a different war than he was. There were many plausible paths to victory for Lincoln that could have meant disaster for Douglass' mission.

Douglass viewed the war not just through the lens of Union army victories in battle, but through the emerging sense of Lincoln and the Union that the Confederacy and the "peculiar institution" of slavery must be fully defeated at one and the same time. This realization dawned slowly among Northerners and, even by the last year of the war, was never assured. Douglass emerged as a figure second only to Lincoln because he spoke the truth, spoke it to powerful figures who did not wish to hear it, accurately predicted the path the war would take, and offered everything he had, including the lives of his children, to gain freedom for others.

Lincoln's mission was to save the Union, while Douglass' mission was different and two-pronged: emancipation through this conflict, and then established equality. The latter quest speaks with particular power and relevance over the years. At the heart of Douglass' message was the belief that the nation must confront the interconnectedness of black and white. Many, including Lincoln, had tried to evade this reality. Douglass understood that the Union itself would not survive without the monumental contributions of African Americans, though their rightful place would not be secured until white Americans respected their rights and allowed them their due share of opportunities within the country as a whole. Douglass prophesied that for the nation to be redeemed, we would need each other, then and now. Lincoln needed black soldiers to win his war; Douglass needed Lincoln to win his people's freedom; and they needed each other to move the nation forward. Their relationship, their struggle, tells us much about ourselves as a people and why the failure to fully achieve Douglass' vision of equality means that our Civil War is not yet over.

Critical Thinking

1. Who was Frederick Douglass? Who were his constituents?
2. Analyze his differences with Lincoln over what rights African Americans should enjoy.

From *American Heritage*, Winter 2009, pp. 36–39. Copyright © 2009 by American Heritage Publishing Co. Reprinted by permission

Steven Hahn Sings the Slaves Triumphant

The Pulitzer Prize–winning historian recasts the Civil War as a black revolt that forged African-American activism.

GENE SANTORO

Steven Hahn contends that blacks played a more active role in bringing an end to slavery than historians generally recognize. Indeed, in his latest book, *The Political Worlds of Slavery and Freedom,* he characterizes the Civil War as "the greatest slave rebellion in modern history." He argues that some Northern black communities may have functioned like Haitian or Brazilian "maroons"—independent sites peopled and governed by runaway slaves that were vital to sustaining black political and military struggles for emancipation.

Why Do You Call the Civil War a Slave Rebellion?

It's true that there was no big bloody uprising, like in Haiti. But the Confederates had no confusion about what the slaves were doing—fleeing north, refusing to work, demanding wages and so on. It was rebellious behavior, and they wanted government intervention to put it down. In *Black Reconstruction,* W.E.B. Du Bois writes about the "general strike" among slaves. You don't have to be a Marxist like him to see that he was really saying slaves were important political actors in the Civil War.

What about the Abolitionist Movement?

The public still has this idea that, with the exception of Harriet Tubman, white people are rescuing black people. But historians have learned that the abolitionist movement was made chiefly of people of African descent. In the 1830s and 1840s in the Northern states, blacks had access to a public sphere of politics, and held conventions to press against discrimination and for political rights, which carried through the Civil War. They're the ones who subscribed to abolitionist newspapers. They set up

and staffed the Underground Railroad. They knew where to go in order to be hidden and protected, or get employment.

The abolitionist movement was chiefly people of African descent.

What Made You Think Runaway Slaves Had a Key Role in All This?

In other slave societies, maroons, or runaway slave communities, establish independence, support revolts and become important politically. In the United States, it appeared that outside of Spanish Florida, the lower Mississippi and a few swamps, not much was going on that way. But then I started thinking about slavery and emancipation as a long national experience, not a sectional one, and I started to speculate.

How?

There were still slaves in the North at the time of the Civil War, even though they lived in states where theoretically slavery wasn't legal. Free blacks' status in the North could be contested; they could be kidnapped. Most people in the North, including Lincoln, supported the Fugitive Slave Law. So slavery was effectively legal everywhere. Then how do you think about the communities of African Americans in the Northern states? Historians write as if Northern and Southern blacks had little to do with each other, yet we know by the end of the antebellum period a lot of African Americans in the North were born in the

South. What if some of these communities were like maroons? The people in them were fugitives from slavery who had to arm and defend themselves against paramilitary invasions, just as maroon communities elsewhere did.

For Example?

In Lancaster County, Pa., in 1851, there was a shootout between around 100 blacks and a Maryland slaveowner who was looking for four runaway slaves with his son and friends and a U.S. marshal. This is the kind of situation where the maroon analogy makes sense. Here are black people across the Mason-Dixon line in Pennsylvania, collected among themselves out in a rural area. Many of them are fugitives from slavery. They are armed. They have networks of communication designed to alert them to trouble. The slaveowners get deputized by the federal government.

How Did Slaves Push Emancipation?

When the war starts, the federal government doesn't really have a policy about slavery. Lincoln goes out of his way to assure Southern slaveholders that he will not tamper with, as he puts it, a "domestic institution." He tells Southerners that as the Union Army is marching through, if they need help putting down slave rebellions, the army will do that. Now, part of the reason is that he knows Northern sentiment is divided and he doesn't want to be distracted from saving the Union. But slaves have their own ideas about what's going on, and they act by running away to Union camps. They have local intelligence: Where's the Union Army? What's going on? Initially, the Union side doesn't want them and sends them back, so it's a risky undertaking.

What Changes the Situation?

Fairly early on, the Union side learns that the Confederacy is using slave labor to build fortifications. So the logic becomes, if we send them back, they'll be used against us. All of a sudden they're declared contraband of war, which still acknowledges they're property. But little by little, as the Union Army moves into the deeper South, slaves come in the hundreds and thousands. As the war drags on, they realize that black labor and, eventually, 200,000 black Union soldiers, will be important in saving the Union. So slavery becomes destabilized by what the slaves did.

How Does This Shape the Emancipation Proclamation?

Most people think it just establishes the idea of freedom and frees slaves in areas where the Union Army isn't. But they forget about the provision allowing blacks to enlist. This is a huge and amazing move, very different from the preliminary proclamation Lincoln issued in September 1862. Because of African-American participation in the war, they were in a position to make claims afterward about citizenship and equality.

How Did All This Change America?

The Civil War completed the Revolutionary period's nation-building process. Look at the world of the 1850s. The sovereignty of the federal government was in dispute and local sovereignties were emphasized. There was a nativist movement looking to deprive growing numbers of immigrants of any political rights. Then look at the country in the late 1860s and 1870s, where you have the Reconstruction amendments, when the idea of national citizenship for the first time comes into being, when you begin a massive process of enfranchisement after a decade and a half of disfranchisement, including women's suffrage. Obviously this process was painfully slow, and met with serious pushbacks all along the way. But if the war had ended in an armistice instead of unconditional surrender, none of this would have happened for much longer. Slavery might have continued deep into the 20th century.

How Does Barack Obama Fit into This Picture?

Obama is clearly part of a new segment of African descent in the United States. As immigration laws changed in the 1960s and 1970s, more people from Africa and the Caribbean came here, some with a good deal of education and resources. He's also the product of the civil rights movement and affirmative action, which really contributed to the growth of a black middle class. That segment of the black population is much more integrated with other groups. So his election is a tribute to what the struggle for civil rights accomplished, but it could also reemphasize class distinctions. He is going to run into problems with African Americans who expect a lot of things from him, which as president of the entire country, he won't be able to deliver.

A Slave's Audacious Bid for Freedom

David W. Blight

Mobile, Alabama, August 1864

One hot summer day in wartime Mobile, a city garrisoned by 10,000 Confederate troops, 17-year-old Wallace Turnage was driving his owner's carriage along Dauphin Street in the crowded business district when a worn harness broke, flipping the vehicle on its side. Thrown to the ground, Turnage narrowly avoided the crushing wheels of a passing streetcar. The stunned teenager shook himself off, then set off for the house of his owner, the rich merchant Collier Minge. Turnage was no stranger to hardship: he had already been sold three times, losing contact with his family. Ugly scars on his torso bore witness to many severe beatings and even torture. Yet his life was about to get even worse before it got better.

Born in Green County near Snow Hill, North Carolina, Turnage, the son of a 15-year-old slave woman named Courtney and an 18-year-old white man, Sylvester Brown Turnage, was thus one of the nearly quarter million slave children of mixed race in the 1850s, many the products of forced sexual unions. In the spring of 1860, Turnage's indebted owner had sold the 13-year-old for $950 to Hector Davis, a slave trader in Richmond, Virginia, leaving the boy to survive as best he could, orphaned in a dangerous and tyrannical world. One of Richmond's richest dealers in human property, Davis owned a three-story slave jail and auction house. By one estimate, slave traders in Richmond during the late 1850s netted $4 million per year (approximately $70 million in 2008 dollars). Davis often sold nearly $15,000 worth of slaves per week.

For the next several months, Turnage prepared his fellows in the "dressing room" for the auction floor. One day he himself was told to climb up on the block and sold to an Alabama planter, James Chalmers, for $1,000. Three days later he found himself on a large cotton plantation near Pickensville, Alabama, close to the Mississippi line.

It was mid-1860, a pivotal election year during which the American union was dissolving under slavery's westward expansion. Now a field slave, the young man had to adapt to another alien environment, falling prey to fear,

violence, and loneliness. After several whippings, he ran away for the first of five times.

In the aftermath of the Civil War, Turnage wrote an extraordinary narrative, only recently discovered, of his path to freedom. In beautiful, if untutored and unedited prose, Turnage described a runaway's horrific struggle for survival. His fight with the slave system was one desperate collision after another, amidst the double savagery of slavery and war. Each of the first four times that he broke for liberty, he crossed the Mississippi line and headed north along the Mobile and Ohio Railroad, yearning, as he wrote, "to get home," which for him must have vaguely meant North Carolina. Each escape had been prompted by a violent encounter with an overseer. On one occasion, when the overseer approached him with a cowhide whip ready, Turnage stood his ground, "spoke very saucy," and fought long and hard, his foe nearly biting off his ear. For this resistance he was pushed facedown on the ground, his hands tied to a tree, and given 95 lashes.

During one bid for freedom, he traveled some 80 miles across the war-ravaged country, hiding among fencerows and gullies. Taken in by other slaves, betrayed by one couple, chased and mauled by bloodhounds, he struggled to outlast winter cold, starvation, and Confederate patrols. One sadistic slave-catcher, who held him in a cabin until his owner arrived, pistol-whipped and stabbed him, then pitched him into a burning fireplace in a drunken rage. Locked in neck chains and, at times, wrist chains attached to other fugitives, Turnage learned the logic of terror but also somehow summoned the strength never to surrender to his own dehumanization.

For all the miseries and dislocation of war, Turnage remained far too valuable for Chalmers to let escape. But after the fourth runaway in early 1863, the cotton planter sold him at the slave jail in Mobile, where he fetched the robust price of $2,000. Turnage labored in Mobile as a jack-of-all-trades house slave for the Minge family over the next 15 months until that August day in 1864 when the carriage flipped.

When Turnage arrived at the Minge house with news of the ruined carriage, his mistress excoriated him. He "got angry and spoke very short with her," and then fled "down into the city of Mobile," where for a week he "wandered from one house to another where I had friends." Hiding in haylofts and sheds, Turnage was discovered one day in a stable by a "rebel policeman" who pressed a cocked pistol to his breast. Dragged by the neck to the "whipping house," Turnage was soon confronted by his master, who ordered him stripped, strung up by his wrists on the wall, subjected to 30 savage lashes with a device "three leathers thick," and then told to walk home. On the way back, he took a different turn and simply walked out of Mobile, striding at dusk through a huge Confederate encampment, undoubtedly mistaken for a black camp hand.

For the next three weeks, Turnage traversed the snake- and alligator-infested swamps of the Foul River estuary, moving 25 laborious miles along the western shore of Mobile Bay, where on August 5, Adm. David Farragut's fleet won the largest naval battle of the Civil War. Turnage remembered seeing warships in the distance and hearing guns. In fear and desperate hunger, he crossed the Dog and Deer rivers, then somehow swam the fearsome Foul River, where he was "troubled all day with snakes." Today this extensive, beautiful wetland offers a gentle yet forbidding waterscape; alligators crawl in their wallows, laughing gulls squawk everywhere as delta grass—"broom sage" to Turnage—sways waist-high in the summer breeze.

After reaching Cedar Point, the southern tip of the mainland, he could make out the stars and stripes flying above a Union-occupied island fort. He made a "hiding place in the ditch" to protect himself from the swamp water and ducked Confederate patrols, growing "so impatient seeing the free country in view and I still in the slave country." The sun may have been blinding and his body all but spent, but Turnage's choices were clear: "It was death to go back and it was death to stay there and freedom was before me; it could only be death to go forward if I was caught and freedom if I escaped." This timeless expression of the human will to choose freedom at whatever risk manifests itself in most slave narratives.

Turnage was a desperate hero. After praying especially hard one night, he discovered that the tide had swept in an old rowboat, as if "held by an invisible hand." Grabbing a "piece of board," he began to row the rickety craft into the waves of Mobile Bay. A "squall" bore down on him, "the water like a hill coming with a white cap on it." Just as the heavy seas struck his boat, he heard "the crash of oars and behold there was eight Yankees in a boat." Turnage jumped into the Union craft just as his own vessel capsized. For a few long moments the oarsmen "were struck with silence" as they contemplated the gaunt young man crouched in front of them. Looking back to the shore, he could see two Confederate soldiers glaring after him. As the liberators' boat bounced on the waves, he inhaled his first breaths of freedom.

The Yankees took him to the sand island fort, wrapped him in a blanket, fed him, and gave him a tent to sleep in for the night—likely the first acts of kindness he had ever experienced from white people. The next day they took him in a skiff to Fort Gaines on Dauphine Island, the long sandbar at the mouth of Mobile Bay. In that fortress, whose cannon-crowned brick walls stand intact to this day, Turnage was interviewed by Gen. Gordon Granger, commander of all Union forces in the Mobile region, who was eager for intelligence about the city, which he hoped soon to capture. Granger offered Turnage the choice of enlisting in a newly raised black regiment as a soldier or becoming a servant to a white officer. Turnage opted for the job of mess cook for one Capt. Junius Turner of a Maryland regiment, whom he accompanied to the end of the war, marching into Mobile with the Union army in April 1865.

Sometime shortly after the war he traveled to North Carolina and retrieved his mother and four half-siblings. He moved to New York City, struggled to make a living as a common laborer, and managed to keep his family together until he died in 1916. He was married three times, losing his first two wives at a young age, and fathered seven children, only three of whom survived infancy under the grueling hardships of the black urban poor.

His memoir's final paragraph is a stunning, prayerful statement about the meaning of freedom.

Sometime in the 1880s, gripped by the dogged desire to be remembered, Turnage put down his narrative, which comes to an abrupt end after his dramatic escape at sea and liberation. But the final paragraph is a stunning, prayerful articulation of natural rights and the meaning of freedom: "I had made my escape with safety after such a long struggle and had obtained that freedom which I desired so long. I now dreaded the gun and handcuffs and pistols no more. Nor the blowing of horns and the running of hounds; nor the threats of death from the rebels' authority. I could now speak my opinion to men of all grades and colors, and no one to question my right to speak." As one of the "many thousands gone" prophesied in the old slave spiritual, Wallace Turnage crafted his own emancipation hymn.

From *American Heritage*, Fall 2008. Copyright © 2008 by American Heritage Publishing Co. Reprinted by permission.

A Graceful Exit

In one momentous decision, Robert E. Lee spared the United States years of divisive violence.

JAY WINIK

As April 1865 neared, an exhausted Abraham Lincoln met with his two top generals, Ulysses S. Grant and William Tecumseh Sherman, to discuss the end of the Civil War, which finally seemed to be within reach. Nevertheless, the president—"having seen enough of the horrors of war"—remained deeply conflicted. To be sure, the endless sound of muddy boots tramping across City Point, Virginia, and the heavy ruts left by cannon wheels marked Grant's preparations for a final all-out push to ensnare the Army of Northern Virginia. Yet Lincoln could not shake off his deep-seated fears that Robert E. Lee would somehow escape Grant's clutches or, worse still, that his worn but still formidable forces would melt into the western mountains to continue the war indefinitely as marauding guerrilla bands. Nor was this idle speculation. Lee himself had once boasted that if he could get his army into the Blue Ridge Mountains, he could continue the war for another "20 years."

Grant himself shared Lincoln's foreboding, later confessing, "I was afraid every morning that I would awake from my sleep to hear that Lee had gone . . . and the war was prolonged." At one point during their final meeting at City Point, a morose Lincoln pleaded, "My God! Can't you spare more effusions of blood? We have had so much of it." Indeed, what most haunted him now was the belief that the war might end only after some final mass slaughter, or that it would dwindle into a long twilight of barbarism or mindless retaliation, as had happened in so many other civil wars, thus unleashing an endless cycle of more bloodshed and national division. To reunite the country, Lincoln believed the conflict's close must be marked by something profoundly different: a spirit of reconciliation.

But after four years of bloodletting, could it? Distressingly, on the fateful morning of April 9, 1865, the decision ironically seemed to be more in Lee's hands than in Lincoln's. When the first glimmer of sun broke around 5 A.M., Lee's vaunted army was at last surrounded, and the aging general now faced a decision that would forever shape the nation's history.

With gunfire still rattling in the distance, Lee convened a council of war. The talk turned to surrender, whereupon one of Lee's top aides protested that "a little more blood more or less now makes no difference." Instead he suggested that the Confederates play the trump card that Lincoln most dreaded and dissolve into the hills as guerrillas. As Lee carefully listened, he knew that this option was not lightly to be ignored. Just days earlier, the fleeing Confederate president, Jefferson Davis, had issued his own call for guerrilla struggle. And hundreds of Lee's men had already vanished into the countryside on their own initiative, anticipating precisely that.

Could Lee have done it? Here, surely, was temptation. No less than for Davis, the momentous step of surrender was anathema to him. Moreover, the South's long mountain ranges, endless swamps, and dark forests were well suited for a protracted partisan conflict. Its fighters, such as the cunning John Mosby and the hard-bitten cavalryman Nathan Bedford Forrest, not to mention young Confederates such as Jesse James, had already made life a festering hell for the Union forces with lightning hit-and-run raids. If Lee had resorted to guerrilla war, he arguably could have launched one of the most effective partisan movements in all history.

If he had resorted to guerrilla war, Lee arguably could have launched one of the most effective partisan movements in all history.

In fact, in Missouri a full-scale guerrilla war characterized by ruthless reprisals and random terror was already under way with such ferocity that the entire state had been dragged into a whirlpool of vengeance. As jurist and political philosopher Francis Lieber ominously told Lincoln, "Where these guerrillas flourish, [they create] a slaughter field."

In hindsight, we can see that in a countrywide guerrilla war, the nation would quickly have become mired in a nightmarish conflict without fronts, without boundaries between combatant and civilian, and without end. It could well have brought about the Vietnamization of America or, even more distressingly, its Iraqization, disfiguring this country for decades, if not for all time.

But after careful deliberation, Lee rejected the option of protracted anarchy and mayhem, insisting that "we would bring on a state of affairs that would take the country years to recover from." By this one momentous decision, he spared the United States generations of divisive violence, as well as the sepsis of malice and outrage that would have invariably delayed any true national reconciliation.

But if this were perhaps Lee's finest day, so too it was Grant's. At the surrender at Appomattox Courthouse, Grant, heeding Lincoln's injunction for a tender peace now that the war was close at hand, treated Lee's defeated army with extraordinary generosity, not as hated foes but as brothers to be embraced. The most poignant moment of this most poignant of days came after the instruments of surrender were signed, and an emotion-choked Lee mounted his horse Traveler and let out a long, deep sigh. In a brilliant masterstroke, Grant walked out onto the porch of the Wilmer McLean house and, in front of all his officers and men, silently raised his hat to the man who just that morning had been his ardent adversary, saluting him as an honored comrade—a gesture quickly echoed by innumerable other Union officers.

This one small act would loom large in the months to come, rippling out into every corner of the South and setting a tone for the healing that was so critical if the country were "to bind up" its wounds, as Lincoln so eloquently put it. And lest anyone mistake the importance of reconciliation for both sides, Lee would later remark: "I surrendered as much to Lincoln's goodness as I did to Grant's armies."

Critical Thinking

1. What course of action did some of General Robert E. Lee's subordinates advocate?

2. How might such a course have affected the outcome of the Civil War?

JAY WINIK, the author of *April 1865* (HarperCollins 2001) and *The Great Upheaval* (Harper 2007), serves on the governing board of the National Endowment for the Humanities.

How the West Was Lost

CHRIS SMALLBONE

At the beginning of the nineteenth century the United States neither owned, valued nor even knew much about the Great Plains. This vast tract of grassland which runs across the centre of the continent was described as the 'Great American Desert', but by the end of the century the United States had taken it over completely. As the 'new Americans' (many of them black) pushed the frontier to the west, they established their culture at the expense of that of the indigenous peoples, then known to the incomers as 'Indians'.

The great natural resource of the Plains was the buffalo, which migrated in vast herds. The peoples of the Great Plains hunted and ate the buffalo, made tepees from their hides and utilized most other parts to make tools, utensils and weaponry. Some of them, for example the Mandan and Pawnee, lived in semi-permanent villages; others, like the Lakota and Cheyenne, lived a nomadic life. When necessary, as in life or death situations of war or in securing food in the hunt or moving camp they could be very organized and disciplined, but normally life was very loosely structured. Different peoples or nations were distinguished by language or dialect and in variations of customs and beliefs. But all depended upon nature for survival and had a spiritual approach to it.

Before the arrival of the new Americans the native groups were often in conflict with neighbouring peoples for resources such as horses and land. The latter resulted in some movement in their patterns of settlement. Thus, the Cheyenne and Arapaho had divided into northern and southern groups in the 1820s. Some Cheyenne and Arapaho moved south, following reports of large numbers of wild horses and vast buffalo herds in the land south of the Platte River, while others remained north of the Platte near the Black Hills where they effectively became a separate group, closely allied with the Lakota. Other peoples, such as the Pawnee, Crow and Arikara (or Rees), had become enemies of the Lakota when supplanted by them earlier in the century. The northern Cheyenne and Arapaho were an exception, most other peoples in the northern Plains were enemies of the Lakota. Indeed the name for them adopted by the new Americans, Sioux, was the Ojibwe word for enemy. In the mid-eighteenth century the Lakota had moved gradually westwards from what was to be Minnesota, defeating other peoples as they went and pushing them into new hunting grounds.

In 1840, when the Oregon Trail from Independence, Missouri to the Pacific was first used, the frontier of the United States was roughly at the line of the Mississippi-Missouri, only about one third of the way across the continent. Just two generations later, by 1890, the indigenous peoples had been supplanted and the western frontier no longer existed. Apart from one or two later additions, today's map of the United States was firmly in place.

To understand how this took place one needs to step outside the strict chronology of the events. The new Americans split the Plains environment and those who depended upon it into two. This began in the 1840s with the overland trails to Oregon and California, initiating the age of the Wagon Train, and was cemented by the completion of the transcontinental and Kansas Pacific Railroads in the late 1860s. A series of treaties were signed, confining the native Americans to ever-smaller areas, and every opportunity was taken for incursion into these areas by prospectors, hunters, and settlers, supported by soldiers.

Even before the trails were opened, trading posts were established at key communications points, such as at the confluence of the North Platte and Laramie rivers in Wyoming, where fur traders Robert Campbell and William Sublette built Fort William in 1834. In 1849 it was bought by the United States military to protect and supply emigrants travelling the Oregon Trail and renamed Fort Laramie. In the early 1840s relationships between the travellers and the native Americans on the trail had been good, but as the decade wore on relations became more tense, especially as numbers of the emigrants escalated with the California Gold Rush in 1849. Numbers of those seeking a quick fortune far exceeded those steadier individuals who wished to raise crops in the western coastlands of Oregon and California. As these numbers increased so did incidents between the two cultures. The settlement of the Plains did not become a problem for the native Americans until later, especially in the post-Civil War expansionist mood, when the 'sodbusters' were spurred on by the offer of free land through the Homestead Act of 1862. In the late 1840s the concern for the native Americans was that traffic down the Oregon Trail was keeping the buffalo from their traditional habitat in this area. As the numbers of incidents increased the government sought to alleviate the problem by attempting to keep the native Americans away from the trail. In doing so they used a method already used to legitimize riding roughshod over the eastern native Americans: the Treaty.

The various treaties between the United States and the indigenous peoples of the west were of as little value as they had been in the east. In 1851 the United States Indian agent Thomas

Fitzpatrick invited all of the peoples of the Plains to a meeting in the vicinity of Fort Laramie. It was attended by members of the Lakota (Sioux), Cheyenne, Arapaho, Shoshone, Assiniboine, Crow, Mandan, Hidatsa, and Arikara nations. All these peoples still ranged widely across the central Plains, whereas the Comanche and the Kiowa, who did not attend the Fort Laramie meeting, were far in the south, in the vicinity of the Santa Fe Trail, and a separate treaty was signed at Fort Atkinson with them two years later.

By the 1851 Treaty of Fort Laramie, the government bound 'themselves to protect the aforesaid Indian nations against the commission of all depredations by the people of the said United States' and promised annuity goods for fifty years (later amended by the Senate to fifteen years). The native American chiefs guaranteed safe passage for settlers along the Platte River, and accepted responsibility for the behaviour of their followers in specified territories and recognized 'the right of the United States government to establish roads, military and other posts'. However, military posts already existed on the Oregon Trail: Fort Kearny had already been established in Nebraska as a stopping-off point and garrison in 1848, Fort Bridger in Wyoming as a fur-trading post in 1843, as well as Fort Laramie itself. Nor was the United States army a disciplined force: as emigrant William Kelley commented on the troops at Fort Kearny:

> A most unsoldierly looking lot they were: unshaven, unshorn, with patched uniforms and a lounging gait. The privates being more particular in their inquiries after whiskey, for which they offered one dollar the half-pint; but we had none to sell them even at that tempting price.

It is not surprising that conflicts arose with native Americans.

Also, noble words meant little when the arbiters of 'justice' attempted to mete it out in a summary manner. Only three years after the treaty, Lieutenant Grattan attempted to bully Conquering Bear's Lakota into giving up a visitor who was accused of helping himself to a lame cow. His troops were annihilated, which led to retaliatory action by the Army, when any available native Americans were punished, regardless of whether they had been involved in the original action. This approach reflected the Army's attitude generally, as indeed had Grattan's action in the first place.

However little value could be placed on the promises in the treaties, their terms stand as clear indicators of the new Americans perceptions of how to deal with what they called the 'Indian Problem', at any one point. The Treaty of 1851 was an attempt to protect travellers on the Oregon Trail, which had become of high importance as a result of the discovery of gold in California in 1848. However, the commitment to protecting 'Indian nations' from 'depredations' by United States citizens was of far lower priority to the new Americans and was never properly enforced.

Similarly in a treaty signed in 1861 at Fort Lyon in the southern Plains, the Cheyenne promised to remain in the vicinity of the Arkansas River and not to interfere with the gold-miners along the Smoky Hill Trail from Kansas City to Denver attracted to the area from 1858 onwards. Yet only three years later, in November 1864, an estimated 200 peaceful men, women and children of the Southern Cheyenne and Arapaho were massacred by the Third Colorado Regiment of volunteers and regular troops at Sand Creek. The leader of the outrage, John Chivington, fed the bloodlust of his troops, and was fond of the chilling phrase which rationalized the killing of infants: 'Nits make Lice'.

The idea of limiting to set areas peoples accustomed to a free-ranging existence following their source of life—the buffalo herds—was as unrealistic as it was racist. The concept of the native Americans' land being restricted to a reservation dated from the earliest treaties, and was consolidated in the 'removal' of eastern peoples into Indian Territory (later Oklahoma) in the 1830s under the direction of President Andrew Jackson. The National Park concept is generally credited to artist George Catlin, known for his paintings of native Americans. In 1832 he advocated that the wilderness might be preserved, 'by some great protecting policy of government . . . in a magnificent park . . . A nation's Park, containing man and beast, in all the wild and freshness of their nature's beauty!' In 1864, Congress donated Yosemite Valley to California for preservation as a state park. The second great Park, Yellowstone, was founded in 1872, during the presidency of Ulysses S. Grant, who developed an 'Indian Peace Policy' at this time which aimed to 'civilize' them. By 1876 this policy had increased the number of houses sevenfold, the acres under cultivation sixfold, the ownership of livestock by fifteen times, and tripled the number of teachers and schools. The concept of the reservation was surely similar to that of National Parks and as such was recognition that the new Americans saw the native Americans as no more or less significant than the flora and fauna.

The native Americans unleashed a robust raiding campaign in response to the massacre at Sand Creek which interfered with the United States government's wish to expand and consolidate economically after of the Civil War (1862–65). The Union-Pacific and Kansas-Pacific railroads were built across the Plains in the 1860s. To confine the Southern Cheyenne and Arapaho and to protect the settlers, travellers, railroad workers and miners, the United States government perceived the need for another treaty later in the decade and despatched a 'Peace Commission'. This resulted in the treaty of Medicine Lodge Creek, signed in 1867 between the United States Army and 5,000 Southern Cheyenne, Arapaho, Comanche, Kiowa and Kiowa-Apache. Under its terms the indigenous peoples gave up their claims to 90 million acres in return for reservations in central Indian Territory (Oklahoma). Yet just four years later, after a method of tanning the buffalo hides to produce a good-quality leather was developed, the buffalo-hunters moved in. They annihilated the buffalo, in a wasteful and devastating manner, in a few short years. In 1872-73 three million buffalo perished and by 1874 the hunters had moved so far south that the Treaty of Medicine Lodge Creek was a dead letter. All the land given to the Cheyenne and Arapaho had been stripped of the buffalo on which they depended. This was recognized by General Philip Sheridan when he said of the buffalo hunters:

> These men have done (more) in the last two years, and will do more in the next year to settle the vexed Indian question, than the entire regular army has done in the last thirty years.

The sorry remnants of the Southern Cheyenne and Arapaho united with the Comanche and Kiowa, and fought back in a last-ditch attempt at resistance: the Red River War (1874-75). Now without the animal that had long been their prime source of existence, they were harried and starved into submission. They were encircled in the Texas Panhandle by five columns of troops, who came at the native Americans from all directions, keeping them on the move, giving them no rest. The troops burned and destroyed whatever possessions they left behind, including tepees and winter food stores, as they hastily withdrew their families to safety. A small group of a few dozen warriors still roaming free despite constant harassment came into Forts Sill and Reno in Oklahoma in 1875, where they were humiliated, and seventy-one men and one woman, many indiscriminately chosen, were transported to prison in Miami, Fort Marion.

As the land available to the native Americans shrank, some chiefs refused to accept this and fought back against the Army. This allowed the new Americans to claim that the native American leaders could not control their followers and any agreements were therefore broken. This development supported the new American claim to Manifest Destiny whereby they justified their behaviour as the act of 'taming' a savage wilderness. Later commentators refined this argument to suggest that the native Americans had no cultural tradition of commitment to a permanent system of leadership and government.

It was undoubtedly true that the indigenous peoples functioned with loose social structures based on respect being given to an individual based on their qualities rather than on the office they hold, with no lasting obligation to follow their leaders' directives. However, the new Americans did not show themselves to be any more committed to acting upon agreements or attempting to enforce the rule of law. For as long as the land was seen as a useless desert, the new Americans were content to leave it to the native Americans. However, as soon as something of value was discovered—usually precious metals but, also the buffalo once the market had been established for their hides—the new Americans themselves violated the treaties with impunity. Thus when buffalo-hunters went to Fort Dodge in 1872 to ask if they could hunt south of the Cimarron, thereby violating the Treaty of Medicine Lodge Creek, Colonel Irving Dodge had replied,

Boys, if I were a buffalo hunter, I would hunt where the buffalo are.

While in the southern Plains the native Americans were driven south, confined to ever-smaller areas and ultimately defeated, those in the north were more successful at repelling the invaders in the short term. The Lakota were themselves usurpers, for they had moved into the northern Plains in the late eighteenth century from the north and displaced peoples such as the Crow, Pawnee and Arikara, who remained so hostile to them that they proved willing to ally with the Army against the Lakota. As in the south, miners moved into the area, despite the Treaty of 1851 and this resulted in armed conflict. When gold was discovered in Virginia City, Montana, in 1862, Forts Phil Kearney and C.F. Smith were built to protect miners using the Bozeman Trail taking them north from the Oregon Trail. Helped by Crazy Horse, the Lakota chief Red Cloud led his Lakota and Northern Cheyenne warriors in a war in the Powder Valley of Wyoming in 1866-68 which culminated in these forts being evacuated and burned. A second Treaty of Fort Laramie (1868) followed, very much on terms dictated by the native Americans which reaffirmed the principles set out in the earlier treaty of 1851. It granted the Lakota a large area in Dakota including the Black Hills, important for hunting, a source of lodge poles and an area sacred to them: the United States army withdrew from the forts they had built and they were burned by the exuberant Lakota and northern Cheyenne.

Yet the advantage was to be short-lived; once again the discovery of gold by an expedition led by George Armstrong Custer in 1874, was to result in the rules being rewritten. Attempts to hoodwink the native Americans into selling the Black Hills in 1875 met with a rebuff: commissioners were told by Red Cloud that the asking price was $600,000,000, a figure so far in excess of the Commissioners' valuation that it rendered negotiation futile. Tactics rehearsed in the southern Plains were now re-enacted in the north. Lakota and Northern Cheyenne were given notice to 'come in' to Fort Robinson in Nebraska: those not doing so would be deemed 'hostile'. Three encircling columns under Generals Gibbon, Crook and Terry were assembled to harry and destroy. However, the Lakota chose to fight. This surprised the arrogant Custer who commanded Terry's troops but who underestimated his foe and chose to ride the glory trail in defiance of all logic. In the south the tactics of relentless pursuit had worked, not because of fatalities experienced by the native Americans, but because when their homes were attacked the priority of the warriors was to get their families to safety. Their abandoned possessions could then be commandeered or destroyed. The choice of Custer fitted with the expectation that the Lakota and northern Cheyenne would try to escape as had happened in the south. In September 1867 he had been court-martialled for deserting his command, ordering deserters to be shot, damaging army horses, failing to pursue Indians attacking his escort and not recovering bodies of soldiers killed by Indians; but it was his reckless direct approach appealed to his superiors.

However the Lakota and their allies proved more than a match for their enemies. At the battle against General Crook at the Rosebud River in June 1876, it was only a rearguard action fought by a Crow contingent supporting the Army which enabled General Crook to withdraw, and ten days later Custer's force was wiped out at the Little Big Horn by Lakota and Northern Cheyenne warriors.

When the news of Custer's defeat hit the newsstands in the east, the country was in the midst of centenary celebrations. A shocked nation recoiled; public opinion hardened and resources were found to put more troops in the field. The victors of the Little Big Horn were driven north into Canada.

While in most cases incursions onto land 'granted' to the native Americans in both areas was linked in both northern and southern Plains to the discovery of gold, the eventual supplanting of groups in the south was not. Here it was as a result of the native Americans fighting back after their source of life, the buffalo, had been decimated on the very land that had been promised to them less than a decade previously. The defeat in the south came at the end of a long line of losses that followed each discovery by the new Americans that the land of the Great Plains was not as useless as they had first thought. The native Americans were driven south by the slaughter of the buffalo. The buffalo had been wiped out by 1878 in the south, and two years later the hunters moved in on the northern herd, protected by the post-Little Big Horn United States military campaign against the victors. By 1884 few buffalo remained, and in 1885 they were virtually extinct. On the northern Plains, although the Lakota and their allies achieved some military successes, they were ultimately to suffer the same fate: the loss of land promised to them. They were driven further away from the heart of the Great Plains. The Oregon Trail and the railroad which carried travellers, information and goods to link east and west of the nation, was also the dividing line between north and south for the vast buffalo herd and the native Americans who relied on them.

The result for all native Americans of Plains was the same: confinement on reservations. A law was passed in 1871 which formally ended the practice of treaties which had considered the native Americans to be separate nations from the United States. Native American culture was undermined by the practice of removing young children from their families to be 'educated' in residential schools where they were beaten if they spoke their native tongue. Finally in 1887 a law was passed under which the president of the United States was given the power to divide up the reservations, which resulted in another boom-time for the land speculators. Gold, the bison and protecting travellers provided short term reasons for conflict, but ultimately in the clash of cultures, as Red Cloud, Oglala Lakota, observed:

> The white man made us many promises, more than I can ever remember, but they never kept but one; they promised to take our land and they took it.

Critical Thinking

1. Discuss the importance of the buffalo to some Indian cultures.
2. How did the near-extinction of these animals affect such cultures?

This article first appeared in *History Today,* April 2006, pp. 42–49. Copyright © 2006 by History Today, Ltd. Reprinted by permission.

'It Was We, the People; Not We, the White Males'

A suffragist's bold argument that women deserve to be citizens.

On November 1, 1872, Susan B. Anthony entered a barbershop in Rochester, N.Y., that doubled as a voter registration office and insisted she had as much right to vote as any man. Startled officials allowed her to register after she threatened to sue them. Four days later she cast a ballot for Ulysses S. Grant for president. She was arrested and charged with voting illegally. Before the case went to trial in June 1873, she gave the speech below in 29 nearby towns. A federal judge was unmoved and ordered the jury to find her guilty.

SUSAN B. ANTHONY

Not Until When?

Years in which Major Nations Gave Women Equal Voting Rights:

New Zealand	**1893**
Finland	**1906**
Norway	**1913**
Canada	**1918**
Germany	**1918**
United States	**1920**
United Kingdom	**1928**
France	**1944**
Japan (with limitations)	**1945**
China	**1947**
Mexico	**1953**
Switzerland	**1971**

Friends and fellow citizens:

I stand before you tonight under indictment for the alleged crime of having voted at the last presidential election, without having a lawful right to vote. It shall be my work this evening to prove to you that in thus voting, I not only committed no crime, but, instead, simply exercised my citizen's rights, guaranteed to me and all United States citizens by the National Constitution, beyond the power of any state to deny.

The preamble of the Federal Constitution says: "We, the people of the United States, in order to form a more perfect union, establish justice, insure domestic tranquillity, provide for the common defense, promote the general welfare, and secure the blessings of liberty to ourselves and our posterity, do ordain and establish this Constitution for the United States of America." It was we, the people; not we the white male citizens; nor yet we, the male citizens; but we, the whole people, who formed the Union. And we formed it, not to give the blessings of liberty, but to secure them; not to the half of ourselves and the half of our posterity, but to the whole people—women as well as men. And it is a downright mockery to talk to women of their enjoyment of the blessings of liberty while they are denied the use of the only means of securing them provided by this democratic-republican government—the ballot.

For any state to make sex a qualification that must ever result in the disfranchisement of one entire half of the people, is to pass a bill of attainder, or, an ex post facto law, and is therefore a violation of the supreme law of the land. By it the blessings of liberty are forever withheld from women and their female posterity.

To them this government has no just powers derived from the consent of the governed. To them this government is not a democracy. It is not a republic. It is an odious aristocracy; a hateful oligarchy of sex; the most hateful aristocracy ever established on the face of the globe; an oligarchy of wealth, where the rich govern the poor. An oligarchy of learning, where the educated govern the ignorant, or even an oligarchy of race, where the Saxon rules the African, might be endured; but this oligarchy of sex, which makes father, brothers, husband, sons, the oligarchs over the mother and sisters, the wife and daughters, of every household—which ordains all men sovereigns, all women subjects, carries dissension, discord, and rebellion into every home of the nation.

Webster, Worcester, and Bouvier all define a citizen to be a person in the United States, entitled to vote and hold office.

The only question left to be settled now is: Are women persons? And I hardly believe any of our opponents will have the hardihood to say they are not. Being persons, then, women are citizens; and no state has a right to make any law, or to enforce any old law, that shall abridge their privileges or immunities. Hence, every discrimination against women in the constitutions and laws of the several states is today null and void, precisely as is every one against Negroes.

Critical Thinking

1. Analyze Susan B. Anthony's arguments for the rights of women.

2. How might a white male at the time responded to her?

From *American History,* October 2010.

The American Civil War, Emancipation, and Reconstruction on the World Stage

EDWARD L. AYERS

Americans demanded the world's attention during their Civil War and Reconstruction. Newspapers around the globe reported the latest news from the United States as one vast battle followed another, as the largest system of slavery in the world crashed into pieces, as American democracy expanded to include people who had been enslaved only a few years before.[1]

Both the North and the South appealed to the global audience. Abraham Lincoln argued that his nation's Civil War "embraces more than the fate of these United States. It presents to the whole family of man, the question, whether a constitutional republic, or a democracy . . . can, or cannot, maintain its territorial integrity." The struggle. Lincoln said, was for "a vast future," a struggle to give all men "a fair chance in the race of life."[2] Confederates claimed that they were also fighting for a cause of world-wide significance: self-determination. Playing down the centrality of slavery to their new nation, white Southerners built their case for independence on the right of free citizens to determine their political future.[3]

People in other nations could see that the massive struggle in the United States embodied conflicts that had been appearing in different forms throughout the world. Defining nationhood, deciding the future of slavery, reinventing warfare for an industrial age, reconstructing a former slave society—all these played out in the American Civil War.

By no means a major power, the United States was nevertheless woven into the life of the world. The young nation touched, directly and indirectly, India and Egypt, Hawaii and Japan, Russia and Canada, Mexico and Cuba, the Caribbean and Brazil, Britain and France. The country was still very much an experiment in 1860, a representative government stretched over an enormous space, held together by law rather than by memory, religion, or monarch. The American Civil War, played out on the brightly lit stage of a new country, would be a drama of world history. How that experiment fared in its great crisis—regardless of what happened—would eventually matter to people everywhere.

More obviously than most nations, the United States was the product of global history. Created from European ideas, involvement in Atlantic trade, African slavery, conquest of land from American Indians and European powers, and massive migration from Europe, the United States took shape as the world watched. Long before the Civil War, the United States embodied the possibilities and contradictions of modern western history.

Slavery was the first, most powerful, and most widespread kind of globalization in the first three centuries after Columbus. While colonies came and went, while economies boomed and crashed, slavery relentlessly grew—and nowhere more than in the United States. By the middle of the nineteenth century, the slave South had assumed a central role on the world stage. Cotton emerged as the great global commodity, driving factories in the most advanced economies of the world. The slaves of the South were worth more than all the railroads and factories of the North and South combined; slavery was good business and shrewd investment.

While most other slave societies in the hemisphere gradually moved toward freedom, the American South moved toward the permanence of slavery. Southerners and their Northern allies, eager to expand, led the United States in a war to seize large parts of Mexico and looked hungrily upon the Caribbean and Central America. Of all the slave powers—including the giants of Brazil and Cuba, which continued to import slaves legally long after the United States—only the South and its Confederacy fought a war to maintain bondage.[4]

Ideas of justice circulated in global intercourse just as commodities did and those ideas made the American South increasingly anomalous as a modern society built on slavery. Demands for universal freedom came into conflict with ancient traditions of subordination. European nations, frightened by revolt in Haiti and elsewhere and confident of their empires' ability to prosper without slavery, dismantled slavery in their colonies in the western hemisphere while Russia dismantled serfdom.

Black and white abolitionists in the American North, though a tiny despised minority, worked with British allies to fight the acceptance of slavery in the United States. A vision of the South as backward, cruel, and power-hungry gained credence in many places in the North and took political force in the Republican party. The global economy of commodities and ideology, demanding cotton while attacking slavery, put enormous and contradictory strains on the young American nation.[5]

Meanwhile, a new urge to define national identity flowed through the western world in the first half of the nineteenth century. That determination took quite different forms. While some people still spoke of the universal dreams of the French and American Revolutions, of inalienable attributes of humankind, others spoke of historical grievance, ethnic unity, and economic self-interest. Many longed for new nations built around bonds of heritage, imagined and real.[6]

White Southerners, while building their case for secession with the language of constitutions and rights, presented themselves as a people profoundly different from white Northerners. They sought sanction for secession in the recent histories of Italy, Poland, Mexico, and Greece, where rebels rose up against central powers to declare their suppressed nationhood, where native elites led a "natural, necessary protest and revolt" against a "crushing, killing union with another nationality and form of society".[7]

As the South threatened to secede, the Republicans, a regional party themselves, emphasized the importance of Union for its own sake, the necessity of maintaining the integrity of a nation created by legal compact. It fell to the United States, the Republicans said, to show that large democracies could survive internal struggles and play a role in world affairs alongside monarchies and aristocracies.[8]

Once it became clear that war would come, the North and the South seized upon the latest war-making strategies and technologies. From the outset, both sides innovated at a rapid pace and imported ideas from abroad. Railroads and telegraphs extended supply lines, sped troop reinforcements, and permitted the mobilization of vast armies. Observers from Europe and other nations watched carefully to see how the Americans would use these new possibilities. The results were mixed. Ironclad ships, hurriedly constructed, made a difference in some Southern ports and rivers, but were not seaworthy enough to play the role some had envisioned for them. Submarines and balloons proved disappointments, unable to deliver significant advantages. Military leaders, rather than being subordinated by anonymous machinery, as some expected, actually became more important than before, their decisions amplified by the size of their armies and the speed of communication and transport.[9]

The scale and drama of the Civil War that ravaged America for four years, across an area larger than the European continent, fascinated and appalled a jaded world. A proportion of the population equal to five million people today died and the South suffered casualties at a rate equal to those who would be decimated in Europe's mechanized wars of the twentieth century.

The size, innovation, and destructiveness of the American Civil War have led some, looking back, to describe it as the first total war, the first truly modern war. Despite new technologies and strategies, however, much of the Civil War remained old-fashioned. The armies in the American Civil War still moved vast distances on foot or with animals. The food soldiers ate and the medical care they received showed little advance over previous generations of armies. The military history of the Civil War grew incrementally from world history and offered incremental changes to what would follow. Although, late in the war, continuous campaigning and extensive earthen entrenchments foreshadowed World War I, Europeans did not grasp the deadly lesson of the American Civil War: combining the tactics of Napoleon with rapid-fire weapons and trenches would culminate in horrors unanticipated at Shiloh and Antietam.[10]

Diplomacy proved challenging for all sides in the American crisis. The fragile balance of power on the Continent and in the empires centered there limited the range of movement of even the most powerful nations. The Confederacy's diplomatic strategy depended on gaining recognition from Great Britain and France, using cotton as a sort of blackmail, but European manufacturers had stockpiled large supplies of cotton in anticipation of the American war. British cartoonists, sympathetic to the Confederacy, ridiculed Abraham Lincoln at every opportunity, portraying him as an inept bumpkin—until his assassination, when Lincoln suddenly became sainted. Overall, the North benefited from the inaction of the British and the French, who could have changed the outcome and consequences of the war by their involvement.[11]

Inside the United States, the change unleashed by the war was as profound as it was unexpected. Even those who hated slavery had not believed in 1861 that generations of captivity could be ended overnight and former slaves and former slaveholders left to live together. The role of slavery in sustaining the Confederacy through humbling victories over the Union created the conditions in which Abraham Lincoln felt driven and empowered to issue the Emancipation Proclamation. The Union, briefly and precariously balanced between despair and hope, between defeat and victory, was willing in 1862 to accept that bold decision as a strategy of war and to enlist volunteers from among black Americans.[12]

The nearly 200,000 African Americans who came into the war as soldiers and sailors for the Union transformed the struggle. The addition of those men, greater in number than all the forces at Gettysburg, allowed the Union to build its advantage in manpower without pushing reluctant Northern whites into the draft. The enlistment of African Americans in the struggle for their own freedom ennobled the Union cause and promised to set a new global standard for the empowerment of formerly enslaved people. The world paid admiring attention to the brave and disciplined black troops in blue uniforms.[13]

The destruction of American slavery, a growing system of bondage of nearly four million people in one of the world's most powerful economies and most dynamic nation-states, was a consequence of world importance. Nowhere else besides Haiti did slavery end so suddenly, so completely, and with so little compensation for former slaveholders.[14] Had the United States failed to end slavery in the 1860s the world would have felt the difference. An independent Confederate States of America would certainly have put its enslaved population to effective use in coal mines, steel mills, and railroad building, since industrial slavery had been employed before secession and became more common during wartime. Though such a Confederacy might have found itself stigmatized, its survival would have meant the evolution of slavery into a new world of industrialization. The triumph of a major autonomous state built around slavery would have set a devastating example for the rest of the world, an encouragement to forces of reaction. It would have marked the repudiation of much that was liberating in Western thought and practice over the preceding two hundred years.[15]

Driven by the exigencies of war, Northern ideals of color-blind freedom and justice, so often latent and suppressed, suddenly if briefly bloomed in the mid-1860s. The Radical Republicans sought to create a black male American freedom based on the same basis as white male American freedom: property, citizenship, dignity, and equality before the law. They launched a bold Reconstruction to make those ideals a reality, their effort far surpassing those of emancipation anywhere else in the world. The white South resisted with vicious vehemence, however, and the Republicans, always ambivalent about black autonomy and eager to maintain their partisan power, lost heart after a decade of bitter, violent, and costly struggle in Reconstruction. Northern Democrats, opposing Reconstruction from the outset, hastened and celebrated its passing.[16]

If former slaves had been permitted to sustain the enduring political power they tried to build, if they had gone before juries and judges with a chance of fair treatment, if they had been granted homesteads to serve as a first step toward economic freedom, then Reconstruction could be hailed as a turning point in world history equal to any revolution. Those things did not happen, however. The white South claimed the mantle of victim, of a people forced to endure an unjust and unnatural subordination. They won international sympathy for generations to follow in films such as *Birth of a Nation* (1915) and *Gone With the Wind* (1939), which viewed events through the eyes of sympathetic white Southerners. Reconstruction came to be seen around the world not as the culmination of freedom but as a mistake, a story of the dangers of unrealistic expectations and failed social engineering. Though former slaves in the American South quietly made more progress in landholding and general prosperity than former slaves elsewhere, the public failures of Reconstruction obscured the progress black Southerners wrenched from the postwar decades.[17]

When the South lost its global monopoly of cotton production during the Civil War, governments, agents, and merchants around the world responded quickly to take the South's place and to build an efficient global machinery to supply an ever-growing demand in the world market. As a result, generations of black and white sharecroppers would compete with Indian, Brazilian, and Egyptian counterparts in a glutted market in which hard work often brought impoverishment. The South adapted its economy after the war as well. By the 1880s, the South's rates of urban growth, manufacturing, and population movement kept pace with the North—a remarkable shift for only twenty years after losing slavery and the Civil War—but black Southerners were excluded from much of the new prosperity.[18]

As the Civil War generation aged, younger men looked with longing on possible territorial acquisitions in their own hemisphere and farther afield. They talked openly of proving themselves, as their fathers and grandfathers had, on the battlefield. Some welcomed the fight against the Spanish and the Filipinos in 1898 as a test of American manhood and nationalism. The generation that came of age in 1900 built monuments to the heroes of the Civil War but seldom paused to listen to their stories of war's horror and costs.

The destruction of slavery, a major moral accomplishment of the United States Army, of Abraham Lincoln, and of the enslaved people themselves, would be overshadowed by the injustice and poverty that followed in the rapidly changing South, a mockery of American claims of moral leadership in the world. Black Southerners would struggle, largely on their own, for the next one hundred years. Their status, bound in an ever-tightening segregation, would stand as a rebuke to the United States in world opinion. The postwar South and its new system of segregation, in fact, became an explicit model for South Africa. That country created apartheid as it, like the American South, developed a more urban and industrial economy based on racial subordination.

Americans read about foreign affairs on the same pages that carried news of Reconstruction in the South. Even as the Southern states struggled to write new constitutions, Secretary of State William Henry Seward purchased Alaska in 1867 as a step toward the possible purchase of British Columbia. President Grant considered annexation of Santo Domingo, partly as a base for black Southern emigration; he won the support of black abolitionist Frederick Douglass, who wanted to help the Santo Domingans, but was opposed by Radical Republican Senator Charles Sumner.

Americans paid close attention to Hawaii in these same years. Mark Twain visited the islands in 1866, and Samuel Armstrong—the white founder of Hampton Institute, where Booker T. Washington was educated—argued that Hawaiians and former slaves in the South needed similar discipline to become industrious. At the same time, Seward signed a treaty with China to help supply laborers to the American West, a treaty that laid the foundation for a large migration in the next few decades. In 1871, American forces intervened militarily in Korea, killing 250 Korean soldiers. The leaders of the Americans admitted they knew little about their opponents, but brought the same assumptions about race to the conflict that they brought to their dealings with all non-Europeans everywhere, Koreans—like Hawaiians, Chinese, American Indians, and African Americans—needed to be disciplined, taught, and controlled.

No master plan guided Americans in their dealings with other peoples. In all of these places, the interests of American businessmen, the distortions of racial ideology, and hopes for partisan political advantage at home jostled with one another. As a result, the consequences of these involvements were often unclear and sometimes took generations to play out. Nevertheless, they remind us that Americans paid close attention to what was happening elsewhere, whether in the Franco-Prussian War (1870–1871), where the evolution of warfare continued to become more mechanized and lethal, or the Paris Commune (1871), where some thought they saw the result of unbridled democracy in chaos and violence—and wondered if Reconstruction did not represent a similar path.

Some people around the world were surprised that the United States did not use its enormous armies after the Civil War to seize Mexico from the French, Canada from the English, or Cuba from the Spanish. Conflict among the great powers on the European Continent certainly opened an opportunity and the United States had expanded relentlessly and opportunistically throughout its history. Few Americans, though, had the stomach for new adventures in the wake of the Civil War. The fighting against the American Indians on the Plains proved warfare enough for most white Americans in the 1870s and 1880s.[19]

The United States focused its postwar energies instead on commerce. Consolidated under Northern control, the nation's economy proved more formidable than ever before. The United States, its economic might growing with each passing year, its railroad network and financial systems consolidated, its cities and towns booming, its population surging westward, its mines turning out massive amounts of coal and precious minerals, its farms remarkably productive, and its corporations adopting new means of expansion and administration, became a force throughout the world. American engineers oversaw projects in Asia, Africa, and Latin America. American investors bought stock in railroads, factories, and mines around the globe. American companies came to dominate the economies of nations in Latin America.[20]

Americans became famous as rich, energetic, and somewhat reckless players amid the complexity of the world. As the Civil War generation aged, younger men looked with longing on possible territorial acquisitions in their own hemisphere and farther afield. They talked openly of proving themselves, as their fathers and grandfathers had, on the battlefield. Some welcomed the fight against the Spanish and the Filipinos in 1898 as a test of American manhood and nationalism. The generation that came of age in 1900 built monuments to the heroes of the Civil War but seldom paused to listen to their stories of war's horror and costs.

The American Civil War has carried a different meaning for every generation of Americans. In the 1920s and 1930s leading historians in a largely isolationist United States considered the Civil War a terrible mistake, the product of a "blundering generation." After the triumph of World War II

and in the glow of the Cold War's end, leading historians interpreted the Civil War as a chapter in the relentless destruction of slavery and the spread of democracy by the forces of modernization over the forces of reaction. Recently, living through more confusing times, some historians have begun to question straightforward stories of the war, emphasizing its contradictory meanings, unfulfilled promises, and unintended outcomes.[21]

The story of the American Civil War changes as world history lurches in unanticipated directions and as people ask different questions of the past. Things that once seemed settled now seem less so. The massive ranks, fortified trenches, heavy machinery, and broadened targets of the American Civil War once seemed to mark a step toward the culmination of "total" war. But the wars of the twenty-first century, often fought without formal battles, are proving relentless and boundless, "total" in ways the disciplined armies of the Union and Confederacy never imagined.[22] Nations continue to come apart over ancient grievances and modern geopolitics, the example of the United States notwithstanding. Coerced labor did not end in the nineteenth century, but instead has mutated and adapted to changes in the global economy. "A fair chance in the race of life" has yet to arrive for much of the world.

The great American trial of war, emancipation, and reconstruction mattered to the world. It embodied struggles that would confront people on every continent and it accelerated the emergence of a new global power. The American crisis, it was true, might have altered the course of world history more dramatically, in ways both worse and better, than what actually transpired. The war could have brought forth a powerful and independent Confederacy based on slavery or it could have established with its Reconstruction a new global standard of justice for people who had been enslaved. As it was, the events of the 1860s and 1870s in the United States proved both powerful and contradictory in their meaning for world history.

Notes

1. For other portrayals of the Civil War in international context, see David M. Potter, "Civil War," in C. Vann Woodward, ed., *The Comparative Approach to American History* (New York: Basic Books, 1968), pp. 135–451; Carl N. Degler, *One Among Many: The Civil War in Comparative Perspective*, 29th Annual Robert Fortenbaugh Memorial Lecture (Gettysburg, PA: Gettysburg College, 1990); Robert E. May, ed., *The Union, the Confederacy, and the Atlantic Rim* (West Lafayette, IN; Purdue University Press, 1995); Peter Kolchin, *A Sphinx on the American Land: The Nineteenth-Century South in Comparative Perspective* (Baton Rouge: Louisiana State University Press, 2003). My view of the workings of world history has been influenced by C. A. Bayly, *The Birth of the Modern World, 1780–1914: Global Connections and Comparisons* (Malden, MA: Blackwell, 2004). Bayly emphasizes that "in the nineteenth century, nation-states and contending territorial empires took on sharper lineaments and became more antagonistic to each other at the very same time as the similarities, connections, and linkages between them proliferated" (p. 2). By showing the "complex

interaction between political organization, political ideas, and economic activity," Bayly avoids the teleological models of modernization, nationalism, and liberalism that have dominated our understanding of the American Civil War.

2. Lincoln quoted in James M. McPherson, *Abraham Lincoln and the Second American Revolution,* reprint (New York: Oxford University Press: 1992, 1991), p. 28.

3. The seminal work is Drew Gilpin Faust, *The Creation of Confederate Nationalism: Ideology and Identity in the Civil War South* (Baton Rouge: Louisiana State University Press, 1988). For an excellent synthesis of the large literature on this topic, see Anne S. Rubin, *A Shattered Nation: The Rise and Fall of the Confederacy, 1861–1868* (Chapel Hill: University of North Carolina Press, 2005).

4. For a useful overview, see Robert W. Fogel, *Without Consent or Contract: The Rise and Fall of American Slavery* (New York: W. W. Norton, 1989).

5. David Brion Davis, *Slavery and Human Progress* (New York: Oxford University Press, 1984); Davis, *The Problem of Slavery in the Age of Revolution, 1770–1823* (Ithaca, NY: Cornell University Press, 1975), and Davis, *Inhuman Bondage: The Rise and Fall of Slavery in the New World* (Oxford University Press, 2006).

6. For helpful overviews of the global situation, see Steven Hahn, "Class and State in Postemancipation Societies: Southern Planters in Comparative Perspective," *American Historical Review* 95 (February 1990): 75–98 and Hahn, *A Nation Under Our Feet: Black Political Struggles in the Rural South From Slavery to the Great Migration* (Cambridge, MA: Belknap Press of Harvard University Press, 2003).

7. Quoted in Faust, *Creation of Confederate Nationalism,* p. 13.

8. There is a large literature on this subject, not surprisingly. A useful recent treatment is Susan-Mary Grant, *North Over South: Northern Nationalism and American Identity in the Antebellum Era* (Lawrence: University of Kansas Press, 2000). Peter Kolchin also offers penetrating comments on nationalism in *A Sphinx on the American Land,* 89–92.

9. Brian Holden Reid, *The American Civil War and the Wars of the Industrial Revolution* (London: Cassell, 1999), 211–13; John E. Clark Jr., *Railroads in the Civil War: The Impact of Management on Victory and Defeat* (Baton Rouge: Louisiana State University Press, 2001); Robert G. Angevine, *The Railroad and the State: War, Politics, and Technology in Nineteenth-Century America* (Stanford, CA: Stanford University Press, 2004).

10. For a range of interesting essays on this subject, see Stig Forster and Jorg Nagler, eds., *On the Road to Total War: The American Civil War and the German Wars of Unification, 1861–1871* (Washington, DC: The German Historical Institute, 1997).

11. See D. P. Crook, *The North, the South, and the Powers, 1861–1865* (New York: Wiley, 1974); R. J. M. Blackett, *Divided Hearts: Britain and the American Civil War* (Baton Rouge: Louisiana State University Press, 2001); James M. McPherson, *Crossroads of Freedom: Antietam* (Oxford: Oxford University Press, 2002); May, ed., *The Union, the Confederacy, and the Atlantic Rim;* and Charles M. Hubbard, *The Burden of Confederate Diplomacy* (Knoxville: University of Tennessee Press, 1998).

12. See Allen C. Guelzo, *Lincoln's Emancipation Proclamation: The End of Slavery in America* (New York: Simon and Schuster. 2004).

13. See Joseph T. Glatthaar, *Forged in Battle: The Civil War Alliance of Black Soldiers and White Officers* (New York: Free Press, 1990).

14. See Leon Litwack, *Been in the Storm So Long: The Aftermath of Slavery,* 1st Vintage ed. (New York: Vintage, 1980, 1979) and the major documentary collection edited by Ira Berlin, Leslie S. Rowland, and their colleagues, sampled in *Free At Last: A Documentary History of Slavery, Freedom, and the Civil War* (New York: The New Press, 1992).

15. See Davis, *Slavery and Human Progress,* for a sweeping perspective on this issue.

16. The classic history is Eric Foner, *Reconstruction: America's Unfinished Revolution, 1863–1877* (New York: Harper and Row, 1988). I have offered some thoughts on Reconstruction's legacy in "Exporting Reconstruction" in *What Caused the Civil War? Reflections on the South and Southern History* (New York: W. W. Norton, 2005).

17. On the legacy of Reconstruction, see David W. Blight, *Race and Reunion The Civil War in American Memory* (Cambridge, MA: Belknap Press of Harvard University Press, 2001).

18. For a fascinating essay on the South's loss of the cotton monopoly, see Sven Beckert, "Emancipation and Empire: Reconstructing the Worldwide Web of Cotton Production in the Age of the American Civil War," *American Historical Review* 109 (December 2004): 1405–38. On South Africa: John W. Cell, *The Highest Stage of White Supremacy: The Origins of Segregation in South Africa and the American South* (Cambridge: Cambridge University Press, 1982) and George M. Fredrickson, *White Supremacy: A Comparative Study in American and South African History* (New York: Oxford University Press, 1981).

19. See the discussion in the essays by Robert E. May and James M. McPherson in May, ed., *The Union, the Confederacy, and the Atlantic Rim.*

20. For the larger context, see Eric J. Hobsbawm, *The Age of Empire, 1875–1914* (New York: Pantheon, 1987) and Bayly, *Birth of the Modern World.*

21. I have described this literature and offered some thoughts on it in the essay "Worrying About the Civil War" in my *What Caused the Civil War?*

22. Reid, *American Civil War,* p. 213.

Bibliography

Surprisingly, no one book covers the themes of this essay. To understand this era of American history in global context, we need to piece together accounts from a variety of books and articles. For recent overviews of different components of these years, see Jay Sexton, "Towards a Synthesis of Foreign Relations in the Civil War Era. 1848–1877," *American Nineteenth-Century History* 5 (Fall 2004): 50–75, and Amy Kaplan, *The Anarchy of Empire in the Making of U. S. Culture* (Cambridge, MA; Harvard University Press, 2002).

Robert F. May, in the introduction to the book he edited, *The Union, the Confederacy, and the Atlantic Rim* (West Lafayette, IN: Purdue University Press, 1995), provides a useful summary of the larger context of the war. Though it is older, the perspective of D. P. Crook, *The North, the South, and the Powers, 1861–1865* (New York: Wiley, 1974) brings a welcome worldliness to the discussion. On the crucial debate in Britain, see Howard Jones, *Union in Peril: The Crisis Over British Intervention in the Civil War* (Chapel Hill: University of North Carolina Press, 1992) and R. J. M. Blackett, *Divided Hearts: Britain and the American Civil War* (Baton Rouge: Louisiana State University Press, 2001).

James M. McPherson offers characteristically insightful, and hopeful, analysis in several places. Perhaps the single best focused portrayal of the interplay between events in the United States and in the Atlantic World is in his *Crossroads of Freedom: Antietam* (Oxford: Oxford University Press, 2002). McPherson's essay, " 'The Whole Family of Man': Lincoln and the Last Best Hope Abroad," in May, ed., *The Union, the Confederacy, and the Atlantic Rim,* makes the fullest case for the larger significance of the war in encouraging liberal movements and belief around the world.

Peter Kolchin's *A Sphinx on the American Land: The Nineteenth-Century South in Comparative Perspective* (Baton Rouge: Louisiana State University Press, 2003), offers an elegant and up-to-date survey that puts the conflict in the larger context of emancipation movements. A useful overview appears in Steven Hahn, "Class and State in Postemancipation Societies: Southern Planters in Comparative Perspective," *American Historical Review* 95 (February 1990): 75–98.

Another pioneering work is Drew Gilpin Faust, *The Creation of Confederate Nationalism: Ideology and Identity in the Civil War South* (Baton Rouge: Louisiana State University Press, 1988). Faust changed historians' perspective on nationalism in the South, which had been considered largely fraudulent before her account. Building on Faust are two recent books that offer fresh interpretations: Anne S. Rubin, *A Shattered Nation: The Rise and Fall of the Confederacy, 1861–1868* (Chapel Hill: University of North Carolina Press, 2005) and Susan-Mary Crant, *North Over South: Northern Nationalism and American Identity in the Antebellum Era* (Lawrence: University of Kansas Press, 2000).

On the much-debated issue of the relative modernity and totality of the Civil War, see Stig Förster and Jörg Nagler, eds., *On the Road to Total War: The American Civil War and the German Wars of Unification, 1861–1871* (Washington, DC: The German Historical Institute, 1997); the essays by Stanley L. Engerman and J. Matthew Gallman, Farl J. Hess, Michael Fellman,

and Richard Current are especially helpful. Brian Holden Reid, in *The American Civil War and the Wars of the Industrial Revolution* (London: Cassell, 1999), offers a concise but insightful portrayal of the war in larger military context.

For a powerful representation of the role of slavery in this history, David Brion Davis's works are all helpful. His most recent account synthesizes a vast literature in an accessible way: *Inhuman Bondage: The Rise and Fall of Slavery in the New World* (Oxford University Press, 2006).

Excellent examples of what might be thought of as the new global history appear in Sven Beckert, "Emancipation and Empire: Reconstructing the Worldwide Web of Cotton Production in the Age of the American Civil War," *American Historical Review* 109 (December 2004): 1405–38 and Gordon H. Chang, "Whose 'Barbarism'? whose 'Treachery'? Race and Civilization in the Unknown United States-Korea War of 1871," *Journal of American History* 89 (March 2003): 1331–65.

Critical Thinking

1. Analyze the statement: "Had the United States failed to end slavery in the 1860s the world would have felt the difference."

2. Discuss how Radical Reconstruction, which began with such high hopes, ended in failure.

EDWARD L. AYERS is Dean of the College of Art and Sciences at the University of Virginia, where he is also the Hugh P. Kelly Professor of History. He has published extensively on nineteenth-century Southern history, his most recent publication being *In the Presence of Mine Enemies: War in the Heart of America, 1859–1863* (2003), which received the Bancroft Prize. An earlier book, *The Promise of the New South* (1992), was a finalist for both the Pulitzer Prize and the National Book Award. In addition, Ayers has created and directs a prize-winning Internet archive, "Valley of the Shadow: Two Communities in the American Civil War," containing original sources related to two towns at either end of the Shenandoah Valley, one in Virginia and the other in Pennsylvania.

Test-Your-Knowledge Form

We encourage you to photocopy and use this page as a tool to assess how the articles in *Annual Editions* expand on the information in your textbook. By reflecting on the articles you will gain enhanced text information. You can also access this useful form on a product's book support website at www.mhhe.com/cls.

NAME: DATE:

_____

TITLE AND NUMBER OF ARTICLE:

_____

BRIEFLY STATE THE MAIN IDEA OF THIS ARTICLE:

_____

LIST THREE IMPORTANT FACTS THAT THE AUTHOR USES TO SUPPORT THE MAIN IDEA:

_____

WHAT INFORMATION OR IDEAS DISCUSSED IN THIS ARTICLE ARE ALSO DISCUSSED IN YOUR TEXTBOOK OR OTHER READINGS THAT YOU HAVE DONE? LIST THE TEXTBOOK CHAPTERS AND PAGE NUMBERS:

_____

LIST ANY EXAMPLES OF BIAS OR FAULTY REASONING THAT YOU FOUND IN THE ARTICLE:

_____

LIST ANY NEW TERMS/CONCEPTS THAT WERE DISCUSSED IN THE ARTICLE, AND WRITE A SHORT DEFINITION: